A Bibliography of
ROBERT BURNS

A Bibliography of
ROBERT BURNS

J. W. EGERER

OLIVER & BOYD

EDINBURGH AND LONDON

1964

OLIVER AND BOYD LTD

Tweeddale Court
Edinburgh 1

39A Welbeck Street
London W 1

First Published 1964

Printed in Great Britain
at the Press of the Publishers

FOR
HARRIET GREENE MILLIKEN

PREFACE

THE arrangement of this bibliography is chronological from 1786 to the present. If there is more than one edition listed in any single year (and that is the rule rather than the exception), the arrangement of the material in that year is alphabetical according to the place of publication ; when there is more than one edition in one place during a single year, the arrangement is further subdivided alphabetically according to title (*i.e.,* " *Complete Poems* " precedes " *Poems* "). And finally, should there be identical titles, published in identical places, in an identical year, the arrangement is alphabetical according to the name of the publisher (*i.e.,* " *Poems* . . . London : Jones, 1823* " precedes " *Poems* . . . London : Smith, 1823* ").

I have tried to include all of the appearances of Burns's poetical and prose works in all media, except anthologies and reprints of poems or prose works in periodicals, between 1786 and 1802. After 1802, I have included, with a very few exceptions—for example, §337 (1831 Frome), a reprinting of " The Cotter's Saturday Night," frankly as social propaganda— only " formal " editions, that is to say editions which claim to be complete and bear such titles as *The Letters of Robert Burns, The Poems of Robert Burns*, etc. There are complete descriptions of the material included in 1786-1802, and check-listings (*i.e.,* author, title, imprint) after 1802. There is one exception in this latter category, *The Reliques of Robert Burns* . . . London : 1808 (§ 112), a book important enough and rare enough to merit a full description.

If there has been any special endeavour on my part it is to emphasise the first appearances in print of Burns's writings. These occur not only in " formal " editions but in newspapers, magazines, chapbooks, biographies, books of criticism, and auction catalogues. Except for first appearances in periodicals and catalogues, the first printings are all noted in pp. 1-291.

Although I have seen and handled most of the material listed in the bibliography, it has been impossible to find everything ; therefore I have had to fall back on quoting from such standard reference books as *The Memorial Catalogue of the Burns Exhibition*, Glasgow 1898, and the bibliographical studies available. Such quoted material is placed between *guillemets* («« »»), an indication that I have *not* handled the material myself. And here a word of warning : some of the earlier "-bibliographers " had rather vivid imaginations, and their dating of an item or even their listing an item does not necessarily mean that the date is correct or that the item exists. The *Memorial Catalogue* is surely an exception to this somewhat acid remark in so far as it describes an actual exhibition.

This bibliography aims at completeness. That it is not complete I am quite sure, but I am equally sure that I have included all the editions of any importance, along with a great many editions of very little importance except that they act as a census. If nothing else, these editions prove Burns's fantastic popularity during the nineteenth century (was he, during this period, more popular than Shakespeare ?) But what happened to this popularity after 1900 ? Surely there are more editions than I have noted during our own century, and I can say in the same breath that I must undoubtedly have missed a few things in the nineteenth century. The only sure fact about a bibliography is that it is never finished.

★   ★   ★

And now for the pleasant task of thanking the many people whose help has been invaluable.

First, surely, is Mr C. W. Black, the City Librarian of Glasgow, who read every line of the galleys against the books in the Burns Collection of the Mitchell Library, the largest collection of its kind in the world. His efforts on my behalf were so far above and beyond the call of duty that my most heartfelt thanks are indeed feeble. Next, I must thank a man who, were he still alive, would, because of his monumental modesty, never have allowed his name to appear here, Mr A. M. Donaldson of Vancouver, B.C., who also read about a third of the galleys before his death.

I can say without hesitation that, during the time I was gathering material for this book, I received the most cordial welcome and unlimited help from all the librarians whom I met, but especially let me thank the following : Dr William Beattie of the National Library of Scotland ; Mrs M. G. Brown, County Librarian of Kirkcudbright ; Mrs Nancie Campbell, the Carnegie Library, Dunfermline (who also furnished me with the most prodigal hospitality) ; Dr J. C. Corson of the University

Library, Edinburgh ; Miss Catherine L. Dickson, Edinburgh Public Library ; Mr J. W. Forsyth, the Public Library, Ayr ; Mr John Gordan, the Berg Collection, New York Public Library ; Mr Arthur Hudd, the British Museum ; Mr Alexander Laing, the Baker Library, Hanover, N.H. ; Miss Marion P. Linton, the National Library of Scotland ; the late Mr Thomas McMynn, the Burns Cottage Museum, Alloway ; Mr J. R. Seaton, the National Library of Scotland ; and Mrs Elizabeth Sherrard, Keeper of Rare Books, the Baker Library, Hanover, N.H. Finally, the Arts and Science Research Fund of New York University kindly gave me five hundred dollars for typing and photostats.

For invaluable advice and direction, may I thank Mr Joseph Toy Curtiss, Mr C. Beecher Hogan, Mr Edward Lazare, and Mr F. A. Pottle.

Let me also give brief and inadequate notice to those poor, harassed souls who helped me read proof: Mrs Lincoln Ellsworth, M. Xavier Fourcade, Mr M. D. Horowitz, and Mr H. S. L. Wiener.

And, penultimately, with a small but fervent paragraph entirely to herself, let me thank my able typist, Mrs Joseph Gross.

Lastly, my deepest gratitude to Mr R. L. C. Lorimer, of Oliver and Boyd Ltd, who saw the book through the press.

J. W. EGERER

New York City
Feast of the Conversion of St. Paul
1964

CONTENTS

ABBREVIATIONS

Libraries

B.C. = Burns Cottage Museum, Alloway.

B.M. = British Museum.

D.C. = Burns Collection, Baker Library, Dartmouth College, Hanover, N.H.

E.U.L. = Edinburgh University Library.

Horn. = Hornel Collection, Kirkcudbright.

Lin. = Gibson Burns Collection, Linenhall Library, Belfast.

Mitch. = Burns Collection, Mitchell Library, Glasgow.

Mur. = Murison Burns Collection, Public Library, Dunfermline.

N.L.S. = National Library of Scotland.

N.Y.P. = New York Public Library.

S.R. = Burns Collection, Library of the Scottish Rite Cathedral, Washington, D.C.

Tink. = Collection of Chauncey Brewster Tinker, Yale University, New Haven, Conn.

Wid. = Widener Memorial Library, Harvard University, Cambridge, Mass.

Yale = Sterling Memorial Library, Yale University, New Haven, Conn.

Authorities

Angus = W. CRAIBE ANGUS, *The Printed Works of Robert Burns*, Glasgow 1899.

Bib. B. = [JAMES M'KIE.] *Bibliotheca Burnsiana*, Kilmarnock 1866.

Burman = C. CLARK BURMAN, *An Account of the Art of Typography*, Alnwick 1896.

B. Chr. = *Annual Burns Chronicle and Club Directory* (since 1953, *The Robert Burns Chronicle*), Kilmarnock 1892.

Camb. Bib. = *The Cambridge Bibliography of English Literature*, ed. F. W. BATESON, 3 vols. and supplement, Cambridge 1940.

Chambers = *The Life and Work of Robert Burns*, ed. ROBERT CHAMBERS, 4 vols., Edinburgh and London 1891.

Gebbie   =   *The Complete Works of Robert Burns*, 6 vols., Philadelphia
                GEBBIE and Co. 1886.
Gibson   =   [Gibson, J.]   *The Bibliography of Robert Burns*, Kilmar-
                nock 1881.
H. & H.   =   *The Poetry of Robert Burns*, edd. W. E. HENLEY and T. F.
                HENDERSON, 4 vols., Edinburgh 1896.
Letters   =   *The Letters of Robert Burns*, ed. J. DE LANCEY FERGUSON,
                2 vols., Oxford 1931.
M.C.   =   *Memorial Catalogue of the Burns Exhibition*, Glasgow 1898.
Sneddon   =   *Catalogue of the M'Kie Burnsiana Library* . . . compiled by
                DAVID SNEDDON, Kilmarnock 1909.
Snyder   =   F. B. SNYDER, *The Life of Robert Burns*, New York 1932.

DATED EDITIONS

1. 1786 Kilmarnock

POEMS, | CHIEFLY IN THE | SCOTTISH DIALECT, | by | ROBERT BURNS. | [*ornamented rule*] | The Simple Bard, unbroke by rules of Art, | He pours the wild effusions of the heart : | And if inspir'd, 'tis Nature's pow'rs inspire ; | Her's all the melting thrill, and her's the kindling fire. | Anonymous. | [*ornamented rule*] | Kilmarnock : | Printed by John Wilson. | [*double rule*] | M, DCC, LXXXVI.

[*border, consisting of a double border of printers' devices : outside, double rules interspersed with ornaments at corners* (4) *and in the centres of the lines* (4) ; *inside, running ornamented rule touching ornaments at four corners*]

Format. 8vo, in half-sheets. 22·7 × 14·9 cm., untrimmed, in original blue paper wrappers.

Signatures. a4 ; A-Ff4. Except leaves [a, A2, F2, M2, T2, Ff2], which are unsigned, the first two leaves of each half-sheet are signed.

Contents. Pp. viii+[9]-240 : [i], Title-page ; [ii], Registration ; iii-vi, Preface ; vii-viii, Table of Contents ; [9]-240, Text and Glossary.

Original Material :[1]

Preface	*p.* iii
The Twa Dogs, a Tale	[9]
Scotch Drink	22
The Author's Earnest Cry and Prayer, to the Right Honorable and Honorable, the Scotch Representatives in the House of Commons	29
The Holy Fair	40
Address to the Deil	55
The Death and Dying Words of Poor Mailie, the Author's only Pet Yowe, An Unco Mournfu' Tale	62
Poor Mailie's Elegy	66

[1] *I.e.* poems, etc., by Burns, not previously published in any book.

Comment. Issued in blue paper wrappers. Endpapers (2). In many copies examined, the figure on p. 200 is imperfect ; in some, badly mangled. The finest two copies I have seen are in the Burns Cottage Museum, Alloway, and the Berg Collection in the New York Public Library. They are in the original wrappers, untrimmed. Most copies have been heavily trimmed and many rebound. Paper watermarked with fleuron, three leaves (the central leaf in the general shape of a beetroot, the two flanking leaves as in the classic fleur-de-lis), and a stem, like the handle of a sceptre. Countermarked with a monogram (?) containing a block " B " and a swash " B."

It was probably during Feb. or Mar. 1786 that Burns decided on his own, or was persuaded by his friends, to gather his manuscripts for publication. Proposals were sent out, and when enough people had subscribed,[2] the manuscripts were given to John Wilson, printer in Kilmarnock.

These proposals are first mentioned in a letter to Robert Aiken, dated 3 April 1786, in which Burns writes : " My Proposals for publishing I am just going to send to the Press."[3] On 15 April he writes to Gavin Hamilton : " My Proposals came to hand last night, and I know you would wish to have it in your power to do me a service as early as anybody, so I inclose you half a sheet of them."[4] Many of the poet's friends were pressed into service and responded with proper enthusiasm.[5]

Between mid-April and mid-June, Burns was much too busy composing, proof-correcting, and fleeing the wrath of Jean Armour's father to write many letters, but on 12 June he wrote to David Brice : " You will have heard that I am going to commence Poet in print ; and tomorrow, my works go to the press. —I expect it will be a Volume of about two hundred pages. —It is just the last foolish action I intend to do ; and then turn a wise man as fast as possible."[6]

Snyder gives no authority for his statement that the actual work of printing was begun on 13 July.[7] The letter, dated 17 July, in which Burns tells Brice that he has " been so throng printing my Poems," tells us that the poems were in the press by that date. Though we do not know how much Burns actually supervised the printing himself, he probably had very little time to spend in the shop of John Wilson. Armour was, more than ever, dogging his footsteps. " Would you believe it ? "

---

[2] 350 subscriptions were needed : cp. letter to Moore, in *Letters*, 1.115.
[3] *Letters*, 1.24. One of these proposals is reproduced in Snyder, p. 150, and in *M.C.*, in facsimile, opp. p. 252. [4] *Letters*, 1.24.
[5] Snyder, p. 151. [6] *Letters*, 1.31. [7] Snyder, p. 151.

he writes to Richmond on 30 July 1786, "Armour has got a warrant to throw me in jail till I find security for an enormous sum.—This they keep an entire secret, but I got it by a channel they little dream of ; and I am wandering from one friend's house to another, and like a true son of the Gospel have nowhere to lay my head."[8]

The first sentence of this letter—" My hour is now come "—has been construed by most biographers to mean that the book of poems appeared on the following day—in other words on 31 July. However, the volume may quite possibly have appeared earlier, for in his autobiographical letter to Dr John Moore the poet says : " So soon as I was master of nine guineas, the price of wafting me to the torrid zone, I bespoke a passage in the very first ship that was to sail . . ."[9] And in the same letter to Richmond, mentioned above, he writes : " I have orders within three weeks at farthest to repair aboard the Nancy, Capn Smith, from Clyde, to Jamaica, and to call at Antigua."[10] It is clear from these two letters that the " nine guineas " were already in his hand by 30 July, which means that a sufficient number of volumes had been sold to give him this sum, over and above what he owed the printer. However, he did not pay Wilson until Oct. 1786. On 9 July, Burns had written to Richmond : " My book will be ready in a fortnight."[11] If the " fortnight " may be taken literally, it would seem to mean that the book was out by 23 July, or (if we accept the statement that the nine guineas had been paid him by 30 July) perhaps even earlier. Though the evidence is too sketchy for us to determine the exact date, the poems were certainly released during the last ten or twelve days of July 1786.

Reviews

Edinburgh Magazine, or Literary Miscellany, Edinburgh, IV (Oct. 1786), 284-8 ; probably by its editor, J. Sibbald.

The Lounger, Edinburgh, No. 97 (Dec. 1786), 385-8 ; by Henry Mackenzie, the " Man of Feeling."

The Monthly Review, . . . London, LXXV (Dec. 1786), 439-48 ; by James Anderson, " a student of agriculture " (1739-1808).

The English Review, London, IX (Feb. 1787), 89-93 ; probably by Dr John Moore.

The Critical Review, London, First Series, LXIII (May 1787), 387-8.

The New Annual Register for 1786, London, VII (1787), [279-80].

---

[8] *Letters*, 1.35.
[9] *Letters*, 1.115 : 612 copies were printed.
[10] *Letters*, 1.35.
[11] *Letters*, 1.33.

2. 1787 Edinburgh

POEMS, | CHIEFLY IN THE | SCOTTISH DIALECT. | [*rule*] | By | ROBERT BURNS. | [*rule*] | [*diamond rule*] | Edinburgh : | Printed for the Author, | and sold by William Creech | [*broken rule*] | M, DCC, LXXXVII.

Half-title

[*bar with flowers*] | POEMS, | CHIEFLY | SCOTTISH. | [*bar with flowers*].

Format. 8vo, in half-sheets. 22·3 × 14·3 cm., untrimmed, original boards.

Signatures. a-f4 ; A-Yy4. The first leaf of each half-sheet is signed.

Contents. Pp. xlviii + [9]-368 : [i], Half-title ; [ii], blank ; [iii], Title-page ; [iv], Registration ; [v]-viii, Dedication to the Noblemen and Gentlemen of the Caledonian Hunt ; ix-xlvi, Subscribers' Names, with addenda ; xlvii-xlviii, Table of Contents ; [9]-368, Text and Glossary.

Original Material :

Death and Doctor Hornbook. A True Story	*p.* 55
The Brigs of Ayr. A Poem	66
The Ordination	84
The Calf	92
Address to the Unco Guid, or the Rigidly Righteous	143
Tam Samson's Elegy	148
A Winter Night	199
Stanzas on the Same Occasion [" Why am I loth to leave this earthly scene ? . . ."]	234
Verses left at a Reverend Friend's House [" O thou dread Pow'r . . ."]	237
The First Psalm	239
A Prayer	241
The first six Verses of the Ninetieth Psalm	243
To Miss L—— [*i.e.* " Susie " Logan]	251
To a Haggis	261
Address to Edinburgh	274
John Barleycorn. A Ballad	306
A Fragment [" When Guilford good . . ."]	311
Song [" Behind yon hills where Stinchar flows . . ."]	322
Green Grow the Rashes. A Fragment	325
Song [" Again rejoicing Nature sees . . ."]	327
Song [" The gloomy night is gath'ring fast . . ."]	330
Song [" No Churchman am I . . ."]	336

Comment. Issued in French gray paper boards, with frontispiece (portrait of R. B. engraved, after Alexander Nasmyth, by Beugo). On p. xxxvii, " Roxburgh " is misprinted " Boxburgh," and in some copies the page-number on p. 232 is misprinted " 332." This edition is actually, at least in part, two editions : on p. 263, in the " Address to a Haggis," st. viii, l. 3, the word " skinking," in some copies, is misprinted " stinking." This is one of about three hundred variations which distinguish these two " editions," which have thus come to be called the " stinking " and " skinking." Burns himself explains these variations in the postscript appended to a letter to Mrs Dunlop dated 22 Mar. 1787 : " I have to-day corrected the last proof sheets of my poems, and have now only the Glossary and subscribers names to print. . . . Printing this last is much against my will, but some of my friends whom I do not chuse to thwart will have it so. . . . I have both a second and a third Edition going on as the second was begun with too small a number of copies. . . . The whole I have printed is three thousand." [12]

All the variations occur in the gatherings A-Ii and Ll-Mm.[13] Apparently it was not till the printer had set and printed all sheets up to and including Mm that it was realised that there was a shortage of copies, for from there to the end (Nn-Yy) everything is identical in the two " editions." It is obvious that the List of Subscribers was not printed until the very end, along with gatherings a-f (Title-page, Dedication, etc.). Does this mean, then, that gathering Kk (identical in both editions, and sandwiched in between gatherings that show variations) was forgotten by both printer and type-setter, and that exactly the same set-up was used for both editions ? I am inclined to believe that this is perhaps the correct explanation. That the " skinking " edition was the first printed has been deduced from the fact that it shows closer agreement with § 1 (1786 Kilmarnock).[14] Mr I. R. Grant tells me that according to his calculations the total printed was 2,894. Copies of either (*a*) the " skinking " or (*b*) the " stinking " edition in original boards are very rare.

Burns was already in Edinburgh on 29 Nov. 1786, when he wrote to Mr George Reid, Barquharie, apologising for having lent Reid's " pownie " to John Samson instead of " returning him by the Carrier." [15] He had come to the capital with one purpose in mind—to publish a second edition. Wilson had

[12] *Letters*, 1.82.
[13] Cp. J. B. Murdoch, " The Second Edition of Burns," in *B.Chr.*, IV (1895), 107-20.
[14] Cp. *The Nation*, XCI (1911), 211-12 ; and *The Library Chronical*, XIV (1947), 1.3-14.   [15] *Letters*, 1.53.

refused to print another volume unless he received payment
of £27, which seemed to Burns as large a sum as the " British
national debt." [16] But if there still was money to be made,
Burns was not going to miss the chance of making it. On or
about 27 September, he wrote to Richmond, the man he was
going to stay with in Edinburgh : " I am going perhaps to
try a second edition of my book————If I do, it will detain me
a little longer in the country ; if not, I shall be gone as soon as
harvest is over." [17] On 15 November he wrote to Mrs Dunlop
of Dunlop : " I am thinking to go to Edinburgh in a week or
two at farthest, to throw off a second Impression of my book." [18]
There is no mention of Jamaica in this letter, and by this time
Burns may have abandoned any ideas of leaving Scotland.
Robert Aiken, Ayr, had apparently made some attempt to
find, in Edinburgh, a publisher willing to assume the responsibility of a second edition. When it became clear that this
attempt had not succeeded, Burns decided to take matters into
his own hands, and in a letter to John Ballantine, Ayr, dated
20 November, he writes : " I hear of no returns from Edinburgh
to Mr Aiken respecting my second edition business, so I am
thinking to set out the beginning of next week for the City
myself." [19]

The poet's friend, Dr John Mackenzie, Mauchline, who
was also a friend of Sir John Whitefoord of Blairquhan, had
advised Burns to avail himself, on reaching the city, of Sir John's
interest in his poetry. Consequently it was to the Laird of
Blairquhan that Burns turned first, and in a letter to him,
written c. 1 December, he writes : " I have, Sir, in one or two
instances, been patronized by those of your character in life,
. . . but you are the first gentleman in the country whose
benevolence and goodness of heart has interested himself for
me, unsolicited and unknown." [20]

Whitefoord was certainly the right sort of person to introduce
Burns to Edinburgh society. He was a country gentleman,
born in 1734 and had lived in Ayrshire until 1786 when, because
of a bank failure in Ayr, he was forced to sell all his estates and
move to the capital.[21] He was a great friend of the Earl of
Glencairn, and it was to Sir John that Burns sent the " Lament
for James, Earl of Glencairn," [22] when that nobleman died in

[16] *Letters*, 1.46.   [17] *Letters*, 1.44.   [18] *Letters*, 1.50.
[19] *Letters*, 1.53.   [20] *Letters*, 1.54.
[21] G. E. Cockaygne, *Complete Baronetage*, Exeter 1900-1906, IV.400-1.
[22] H. & H., 1.278 (433).

1791. How many of the prominent Edinburgh people Burns met at Whitefoord House in the Canongate it is impossible to say, but Sir John, " a remarkably smart, active little man," with affable manners and the " address . . . of a gentleman," [23] must have attracted the best element in town.

On 7 December, just a week later, Burns was able to write to Gavin Hamilton :

> For my own affairs, I am in a fair way of becoming as eminent as Thomas a Kempis or John Bunyan ; and you may expect henceforth to see my birthday inserted among the wonderful events, in the Poor Robin's and Aberdeen Almanacks, along with the black Monday, & the battle of Bothwel bridge.—My Lord Glencairn & the Dean of Faculty, Mr H. Erskine, have taken me under their wing ; . . . Through my Lord's influence it is inserted in the records of the Caledonian Hunt, that they universally, one & all, subscribe for the 2^d Edition. My subscription bills come out tomorrow, and you shall have some of them next Post. [24]

In other words, not more than a week's time had passed before Burns had met a great many influential people in Edinburgh and was well on his way to fulfilling the purpose which had brought him to the city, the printing of his book. Six days later, on 13 December, he wrote his friend John Ballantine :

> I have found a worthy, warm friend in Mr Dalrymple of Orangefield who introduced me to lord Glencairn, . . . By his interest it is passed in the Caledonian Hunt, & entered in their books, that they are all to take each a Copy of the second Edition, . . . I have been introduced to a good many of the noblesse, but my avowed Patrons & Patronesses are, the Duchess of Gordon— the Countess of Glencairn, with my lord & lady Betty— the Dean of Faculty [25]—Sir John Whiteford.—I have likewise warm friends among the Literati, Professors Stewart, Blair, Greenfield, and Mr McKenzie the Man of feeling. . . . I am nearly agreed with Creech to print my book ; and, I suppose, I will begin on monday.[26]

[23] John Kay, *A Series of Original Portraits* . . ., Edinburgh 1842, 2 vols., II (PT. I), 59-60.
[24] *Letters*, I.55-6.
[25] The Hon. Henry Erskine (see *Letters*, II.350).
[26] *Letters*, I.56-7.

The publication of the Edinburgh edition was finally announced in an advertisement that appeared in the *Edinburgh Advertiser* on 17 Apr. 1787 :[27]

> This day is published, Price Five Shillings, by . . . William Creech, Handsomely bound in one vol. 8vo, and embellished with the Head of the Author, elegantly engraved by Beugo, Poems, Chiefly in the Scottish Dialect, by Robert Burns. N.B.—as this book is published for the sole benefit of the Author, it is requested that subscribers will send for their copies, and none will be delivered without money.

Gibson says that the edition was published on 21 April,[28] but in a letter to John Ballantine dated 18 April Burns says : " I have taken the liberty to send a hundred copies of my book to your care."[29] There can be little doubt that, as stated in the above advertisement, the edition was published on 17 April.

As Snyder points out, Creech was not technically the publisher of the Edinburgh edition. Smellie, the printer, and Scott, the binder, looked to Burns for their money.[30] Creech, therefore, did not assume any financial responsibility, and only lent his name to the venture. The first annoucement, however, read :

> *In the Press, and speedily will be published*, by William Creech, Elegantly printed in one volume 8vo, price 5s in boards, a Second Edition of Burns's Poems, with corrections and large Additions. This book is printed by subscription for the sole benefit of the author—as several private subscription papers are in circulation, it is requested that, when filled up, they may be transmitted to Mr. Creech.[31]

On the other hand, the title-page of the edition reads, " Printed for the author, and sold by William Creech." There may, therefore, have been some change in the original agreement. But whatever the arrangement was, Burns chose the best man in Edinburgh to bring out his book.

Creech was born in 1745 and educated at the University of Edinburgh. He had originally intended to be a doctor but instead became apprentice to Alexander Kincaid, bookseller

---

[27] In *M.C.*, 40, this date is given as 7 Apr. 1787, in the *Edinburgh Evening Courant*.
[28] Gibson, p. 5.   [29] *Letters*, 1.84.   [30] Snyder, 222.
[31] *The Edinburgh Advertiser*, 26 Dec. 1786.

and printer, who was then in partnership with John Bell. In 1766, Creech journeyed to London to enlarge his experience, and spent most of the following year in Paris and Holland. He returned early in 1768 but did not stay long. He is said to have made an extensive tour on the Continent, during the years 1770-1, with Lord Kilmaurs, ultimately the thirteenth Earl of Glencairn, and he seems to have remained a friend of the Cunningham family, for it was through the fourteenth Earl that Burns first met Creech, and it was probably the Earl who persuaded Creech to foster the publication. In 1773, when Kincaid withdrew from business, Creech became sole owner and remained so for above forty years. His shop was situated at the top of the High Street, and, long before Burns first set foot in it, the circulating library that Allan Ramsay ran on the premises had already made it famous. Once he was established as a bookseller, Creech turned to publishing and became the original publisher for such men as Dr Blair, Dr Beattie, Dr George Campbell, Dr Cullen, Dr Gregory, Henry Mackenzie, Adam Ferguson, Dugald Stewart, and many others. He published also the *Mirror* and the *Lounger*. His civic activities were many and varied. He founded the Speculative Society (1764),[32] and helped to found the Society of Booksellers of Edinburgh and Leith. He was a town councillor, and also for two years (1811-13) Lord Provost of Edinburgh. He took an active part in the formation of the Edinburgh Chamber of Commerce.[33]

3. 1787 Belfast

POEMS, | CHIEFLY IN THE | SCOTTISH DIALECT. | [*rule*] | By ROBERT BURNS. | [*rule*] | [*diamond rule*] | Belfast : | Printed and sold by James Magee, | No. 9 Bridge-Street. | [*rule*] | M, DCC, LXXXVII.

Format.   12mo.   15·7×9·5 cm., trimmed and bound in full calf.

Signatures.   A6 ; B-L12 ; M-O6. The first five leaves of each sheet, and the first three of each half-sheet, are signed.

Contents.   Pp. xii+274 : [i], Title-page ; [ii], blank ; [iii]-vi, Dedication to the Caledonian Hunt ; vii-x, Extract from *The Lounger*, No. 97 ; [xi-xii], Table of Contents ; [1]-274, Text and Glossary ; one blank leaf.

   [32] Cp. *The History of the Speculative Society, 1764-1904*, Edinburgh 1905, pp. 2 ff.
   [33] H. R. Plomer, *A Dictionary of the Printers and Booksellers . . . from 1726 to 1775*, Oxford . . . Bibliographical Society 1932, pp. 296-7.

Comment. Issued in French gray paper boards, with frontispiece (portrait of R.B. engraved by P. Halpin). I is unsigned, and p. [106] is misnumbered " 16."

The *Belfast News-letter* for Tuesday 25 Sep. 1787 contains the following advertisement :

> Burns, (the Ayrshire Ploughman's) Poems. This day is published, and Sold by James Magee, Belfast, and by the Booksellers in Town and Country, price 2s. 8½d. in boards, 3s. 3d. bound. A neat Edition of those celebrated Poems, printed from the last Edinburgh Copy, revised by the Author, (and which sold at 6s. 6d. in boards) with a copious *Glossary* not in some of the former editions, and embellished with an engraving of the head of the Author, which is esteemed a striking likeness.— September 24, 1787.

Thus it seems certain that this pirated edition was published on 24 Sep. 1787, and I have accordingly placed it before § 5 (1787 London), which was advertised in May 1787, but probably not published till November, or early December, 1787.[34]

James Magee is said to have been one of the most prominent Belfast publishers of the day,[35] but little is known about him. He was born in 1739 and died in 1789. Though his shop was at 9 Bridge Street, he also gave the location of his place of business as " Near the Four Corners," and " At the Crown and Bible " ;[36] but both were in Bridge Street, and Professor Pottle has suggested that both these names refer to the same premises.

Magee's edition of Burns's *Poems* was also issued in Dublin under the imprint of William Gilbert : see below § 4 (1787 Dublin).

4. 1787 Dublin

POEMS, | CHIEFLY IN THE | SCOTTISH DIALECT. | [*rule*] | By ROBERT BURNS. | [*rule*] | [*diamond rule*] | Dublin : | Printed for William Gilbert, | Great-George's-Street. | [*rule*] | M, DCC, LXXXVII.

Comment. Otherwise the same as § 3 (1787 Belfast).

---

[34] See below, pp. 12-17.
[35] G. Benn, *A History of the Town of Belfast*, London 1877, p. 429.
[36] Plomer, *Dictionary of the Printers and Booksellers . . . from 1726 to 1775*, p. 394.

This edition was advertised for sale in Finn's *Leinster Journal* on 29 Sep. 1787. This is why I have placed it, with § 3 (1787 Belfast), before § 5 (1787 London).

Gilbert, a bookseller, seems to have had some connexion with Magee (perhaps in a business partnership like that which existed between Creech in Edinburgh and Strahan and Cadell in London). Though the *Dublin Directory* gives his address as 26 South Great George's Street,[37] his shop was probably situated at No. 46. The dates of his birth and death are unknown, but as early as 1773 he appeared as one of the signers of the " petition to the House of Commons respecting paper."[38]

5. 1787 London

POEMS, | CHIEFLY IN THE | SCOTTISH DIALECT. | By | ROBERT BURNS. | [*diamond rule*] | The third Edition. | [*diamond rule*] | London : | Printed for A. Strahan ; T. Cadell in the | Strand ; and W. Creech, Edinburgh. | MDCCLXXXVII.

Half-title

POEMS, | CHIEFLY | SCOTTISH.

Format. 8vo. 23 × 14·6 cm., untrimmed, in original boards.

Signatures. A8 ; a-b ; B-Z8 ; A-a4. The first four leaves of each sheet are signed ; the first two of the half sheet.

Contents. Pp. xlviii+[13]-372 : [i], Half-title ; [ii], Registration ; [iii], Title-page ; [iv], blank ; [v]-viii, Dedication to the Caledonian Hunt ; ix-x, Table of Contents ; xi-xlviii, Subscribers' Names ; [13]-372, Text and Glossary.

Comment. Set from the " stinking " edition (cp. § 2, 1787 Edinburgh), and issued in French gray paper boards, with frontispiece (portrait of R.B., engraved, after Nasmyth, by L. Beugo). Rarely found in very good condition. The best copy I have seen is in N.L.S. ; the D.C. copy, in original boards, untrimmed, is also in fine condition, except that it lacks a frontispiece.

Burns printed about 3,000 copies of § 2 (1787 Edinburgh),[39] of which nearly 2,900 were subscribed for by 1,300 subscribers,

---

[37] " Wilson's Dublin Directory " (contained in *The Treble Almanack for the Year MDCCXCV*), Dublin [1795], p. 50.
[38] Plomer, *Dictionary of the Printers and Booksellers . . . from 1726 to 1775*, p. 386.
[39] *Letters*, 1.82.

leaving just over 100 to be distributed through other channels. One of the subscribers was Creech, who subscribed for 500. In default of other evidence, it might, at first sight, seem reasonable to assume that Creech sold most of his 500 in Edinburgh, or in Scotland. As will presently be shown, this assumption would not, however, be justified.

Strahan and Cadell, Creech's London agents, inserted the following notice in *The London Chronicle* on 3 May 1787 and again on 8 May :

> In a few days will be published in one Volume Octavo, Price 6s., in boards, Poems chiefly in the Scottish Dialect. By Robert Burns. Printed for A. Strahan and T. Cadell, in the Strand ; and W. Creech in Edinburgh. By whom, in a few days will be published, The Lounger ; in 3 vols. 12 mo. by the Authors of the Mirror. Of whom also may be had, New Editions of
> 1. The Mirror, a periodical Paper published at Edinburgh, 3 vols. 9s.
> 2. The Man of Feeling, 3s.
> 3. Man of the World, 2 vols. 6s.
> 4. Julia Roubigne, 2 vols. 6s.

The "few days" stretched on to a few months, and when this London edition was published is difficult to determine. However, on 5 July 1787, this announcement appeared in the same newspaper :

> This day was published, Price 6s. in boards, Elegantly printed in one volume Octavo, And illustrated with a head of the author, The *second edition* of *Poems* in the Scottish Dialect by Robert Burns. *Printed in Edinburgh* For an account of Robert Burns, the Ayrshire Ploughman, and of the Poems, vide Lounger, No. 97, Vol. iii.
> 1. The Lounger
> 2. The Mirror
> 3. The Man of Feeling.

The italics in the above quotation are my own. They are meant to emphasise the fact that this book was the Edinburgh *not* the London edition. This means that the London edition was not published by this date, 5 July. Creech, apparently, was having trouble disposing of his lot of 500 copies, so he shipped some of them to his London agents, a not unusual thing for him to do, as can be seen by consulting the advertisement above which appeared in *The London Chronicle* for 3 May 1787. In this advertisement are such items as *The Lounger* and *The Mirror*, which were *published in Edinburgh*.

This opinion is further supported by the following announcement which appeared in *The St. James's Chronicle* on 24 and 26 July 1787 :

> In a few days will be published, Price 6s. in Boards. Elegantly printed in one Volume, Octavo, Illustrated with the Head of the Author The *Second Edition*[40] of Poems. Chiefly in the Scottish Dialect. By Robert Burns. Printed for A. Strahan ; T. Cadell, in the Strand ; and W. Creech, in Edinburgh. N.B. For an account of Robert Burns, and of the Poems, vide Lounger, No. 97, Vol. iii.
>
> Of the above Bookseller may be had,
>
> 1. The Lounger, By the authour of the Mirror, 3 Vols. 9s. sewed.
> 2. The Mirror. A periodical Paper published at Edinburgh, 3 Vols. 6th Edition, 7s. 6d. sewed.
> 3. The Man of Feeling, 3s.

This was printed three weeks after the announcement of the " publication " of the " second edition . . . Printed in Edinburgh," which means that the London edition was not out by 26 July. Therefore, when a week later one finds this advertisement

> This day was published, Elegantly printed in Three Volumes, 12mo. Price 9s. sewed, A New Edition, being the Third of the Lounger. By the Authors of the Mirror. Printed for A. Strahan ; T. Cadell, in the Strand ; and W. Creech, at Edinburgh.
>
> Of whom may be had the New Editions of
>
> 1. The Mirror . . .
> 2. The Man of Feeling . . .
> 3. Man of the World . . .
> 4. Julia de Roubigne . . .
> 5. Poems chiefly in the Scottish Dialect, by Robert Burns, the Ayrshire Ploughman (for an account of whom, and his writings, vide Lounger, Number 97) 8vo 7s.[40]

[40] My italics.

—it must refer to the Edinburgh edition and not to the long-awaited London edition, if only for the reason that the London edition, announced to sell for six shillings, did sell for that price when it was finally issued. This change in price is to be especially noted, for it undoubtedly means that the copies of the Edinburgh edition which Creech had sent from that city were now selling so well that Strahan and Cadell had decided to take advantage of the situation and raise the price on the remaining volumes.

Furthermore, reviews of the Edinburgh edition had appeared in London magazines as late as August issues (really as late as September because these magazines did not appear until the month following the date which was announced on them). London reviewers would probably not continue to write accounts of books published in other places if they had already appeared in London.

The advertisement (see above) which was printed in *The London Chronicle* on 4 Aug. 1787 was reprinted, verbatim, in *The St. James's Chronicle* on 29 September and 2 October, except for the fact that the fifth item, the Burns's *Poems*, was missing. Strahan and Cadell had, apparently, disposed of the Edinburgh edition by those dates, and could no longer advertise it for sale. The way was now clear for the publication of the London edition.

The next dates on which the *Poems* are advertised are 6 and 8 Nov. 1787, in *The St. James's Chronicle*, as the fifth item in an advertisement which is identical with that printed in *The London Chronicle* for 4 August : they were advertised to sell for seven shillings.

Two theories : either (i) that this is the Edinburgh edition, of which a few copies were overlooked, or (ii) that it was, finally, the London edition which the booksellers hoped to dispose of for one shilling more than the original price set on it. I am tempted to believe the latter for the following reasons.

It would appear that the Edinburgh edition, shipped to London by Creech, sold so well that the London agents raised the price (this was early in August). This edition was completely sold out, as there is no mention of any Burns titles for sale for a period of three months (August through October), although such publications as the *Man of Feeling* and *The Lounger* continued to be advertised. When the London edition was ready, early in November, its London publishers, Strahan and Cadell, decided to keep the price up to *seven shillings* instead of the original price

of six shillings which they had advertised the preceding May.
In other words, although a London edition was contemplated as
early as 3 May, Strahan and Cadell, informed by Creech that
the Edinburgh edition was not selling very well, decided to
delay publication.   When, however, they saw that the books
which Creech had shipped to them did sell well in London, they
not only recommenced their printing activities on a London
edition, but raised the price on the copies of the Edinburgh
edition which were in their hands.[41]   For these reasons I am
convinced that the first London edition of Burns's poems appeared
in November 1787.

Another reason to give credence to this conclusion is the fact
that a review appeared in the *Monthly Review* in December 1787.[42]
Since this magazine had been most prompt in printing a review
of the Kilmarnock edition, one is inclined to believe that this
promptness was reflected to an even greater extent when con-
sidering a book published in London.   This is a review of the
London and not the Edinburgh edition.   The heading of the
article reads as follows :

> *Poems*, chiefly in the Scottish Dialect.   By Robert Burns.
> *Second Edition.*[43]   8vo.   6s.   Creech, Edinburgh ;   Cadell,
> London.   1787.

Because the above has " Cadell, London," there is no doubt
of the fact that the review was written of the English edition.
The Edinburgh edition has only Creech's name on its title-page,
whereas the London edition has Cadell's, along with, of course,
Strahan's.   There are, however, two statements in the above
advertisement which are not applicable to the London edition.

---

[41] For a different interpretation, see Anna M. Painter, " American Editions
of the *Poems* of Burns before 1800," in *The Library*, 4th ser., XII (1932), 438,
439 n.   Miss Painter reprints an advertisement used by the N.Y. publishers of
Burns's *Poems*, which reads in part : " The Demand for these Poems was so great,
that the whole of the first Edition (only published last May) were sold in a few
weeks, and the second edition is already printed in London, price *Six Shillings*,
sterling, in boards."   From this Miss Painter concludes that the London
edition was published some time in June :   but, in view of the advertisement in
The St. James's Chronicle for 24 Jul. 1787, the London edition cannot have been
published before 1 Aug. 1787, and my explanation of the advertisement
reprinted by Miss Painter would be that the person who brought the news to
America had seen one of the earlier advertisements and notices in the London
press, and had, reasonably but wrongly, concluded that the London edition
was already on the verge of publication.

[42] *The Monthly Review*, London, LXXVII (Dec. 1787), 491.

[43] My italics.

In the first place, it is called " Second Edition," and, furthermore, the sale price is given as six shillings. The London edition has, on the title-page, " Third Edition," not " Second " ; and, as has been shown above, it was last advertised, on 6 November, to sell for *seven* shillings. It is possible that R. Griffiths, the publisher of the *Monthly Review*, or his literary critic, had forgotten that such an edition as the Kilmarnock had ever existed, a statement which seems utterly fantastic in view of the fact that the writer of the review referred back to the previous article on the Kilmarnock edition. On the other hand, he may have been ignorant of the existence of the Edinburgh (the second edition), and, when he read " Third Edition " on the title-page of the London edition, took it for a mistake. What is perhaps even more plausible is that he did not look at this section of the title-page at all, and, of course, some one else set up the heading of the article. Two suppositions may explain the change in price from seven shillings back to six.[44] The change may have been made by Strahan and Cadell to conform with their original plan of selling the edition for the lower price, or they may have had to effect the change in order to dispose of the edition which was then on their hands. The other possibility is that the typesetter who set up the advertisement which appeared in *The St. James's Chronicle*, 6 November, made an error. But these contradictions are slight in view of the preponderance of evidence on the other side. I am, therefore, convinced that the London edition was published some time during November of the year 1787, and any reference to a Burns edition before that time was to the first Edinburgh, § 2 (1787), or the Kilmarnock, § 1 (1786).

6. [1787] London

A | TOUR, | in 1787, | from | London, | to the | Western High-lands | of | Scotland. | Including Excursions to the Lakes of | Westmorland and Cumberland, | with | minute Descriptions of the principal Seats, | Castles, Ruins, &c. throughout the Tour. | [*diamond rule*] | London : | printed for L. Davis, Holborn ; Messrs. Robson | and Clark, New Bond Street ; W. Lowndes, | Fleet-Street ; H. Gardner, Strand ; and J. Wal- | ker, Paternoster-Row.

[44] It has been suggested to me by a publisher that only the Edinburgh edition sold for seven shillings—the public paid for the carriage between that city and London.

Format. 12mo. 19×11.3 cm., untrimmed, in original paper boards, rebacked.

Signatures. a6; A-M12; N6; O2. With the exception of [E6, I6], the whole sheets are signed on the first six leaves ; the half-sheets on the first three.

Contents. Pp. [one blank leaf+]x+304 : [I], Title-page ; [II], blank; [III]-IX, Preface ; [x], blank ; [1]-303, Text ; [304], Errata.

Original Material :
    " Admiring nature in her wildest Grace "   *p.* 167

The author was Stebbing Shaw (1762-1802)

7. [1787]

THE | CALF ; | The Unco Calf's Answer ; | Virtue — to a Mountain Bard ; | and | The De'il's Answer | To his vera worthy frien' | ROBERT BURNS. | [*rule*] | Printed in the present year.

Format. 8vo, in one half-sheet. 15·7×8·2 cm., trimmed.

This is probably the first chapbook issue of any of Burns's poems. According to Henley and Henderson, " it [*i.e.* " The Calf "] was printed in 1787 (presumably before its appearance in the Edinburgh edition) with some other verses, in a tract called *The Calf.*"⁴⁵ But a note on p. 2 of the chapbook states : " The following Poem was presented to us some time ago for publication, but at the same time judging it too personal, an acknowledge-ment was made to our correspondent ; but as it now appears in print under Mr. Burns' poems, we take the liberty to insert it, with *The Calf's Answer,* which we have just received, addressed to Mr. Robert Burns.—Glasgow Advertiser." This proves beyond doubt that the poem was first published in § 2 (1787 Edinburgh). The poem appears on pp. [2]-3.

8. 1787-1803 Edinburgh ⁴⁶

a. VOL. I [1787]

THE | SCOTS MUSICAL MUSEUM. | Humbly dedicated to the—— | Catch Club | instituted at Edinᵣ. June 1771. | By | JAMES JOHNSON. | Vol. I. Price 6/ | [*vignette : shepherd and shepherdess seated on the bank of a river*] | Edinburgh. Sold and Subscriptions taken in, by & for the | Publisher. N. Stewart,

---

⁴⁵ H. & H., 1.401.   ⁴⁶ Cp. also Appendix I.

R. Bremner, Corri & Sutherland— | R. Ross Edin^r; & all the
Music Sellers in London—[*engraved throughout*]

Format. 12mo, in half-sheets. 21·4×13·5 cm., slightly trimmed, in
original marbled boards.

Signatures. None ; engraved throughout.

Contents. Pp. vi+102. [i], Title-page ; [ii], blank ; iii, Preface ;
iv-vi, Index ; 1-101, Text ; [102], blank. Some copies have, at
the end of this volume, an index which includes authors' names.

Original Material :
    57. [*number of song as it appears in the MUSEUM*]. Here awa',
        there awa'. [only the last 4 ll. : cp. *Letters*, 1.93]   *p.* 58
    78. Young Peggy   79
    99. Bonie Dundee   100

Comment. Issued in May 1787, [Preface dated May 27] probably in
paper wrappers, although I have never seen a copy in this condition.
According to Gibson's notes in the Linenhall Library, Belfast,[47]
the above is definitely the first state in which the title-page was
issued. Gibson bases his conclusion on the fact that, in this volume,
the names of the authors of the songs do not appear in the index,
whereas in later issues these names were added. This, however,
is no proof, for the above title-page could have been on any issue
of the *Musical Museum*. The reasons why I am convinced that this
is the first issue of the title-page is that in other copies that I have
examined, the point between the word " Publisher " and the name
" N. Stewart " has been changed into a dash, and that the
vignette on the above title-page is contained within a perfectly
plain frame. Johnson elaborated on this frame in later issues,
and changed the design and imprint of the title-page as time went
on. The text of the various volumes was preserved on pewter
plates so that, although different title-pages may appear on the
same volume, the rest of the book remained unchanged.

b. VOL. II [1788]

THE | SCOTS MUSICAL MUSEUM. | Humbly dedicated
to the | Catch Club | instituted at Edin^r June 1771. | By |
JAMES JOHNSON | Vol. II Price 6/ | [*vignette : shepherd and
shepherdess seated on the bank of a river*] | Edin^r Printed and sold
by James Johnson, Engraver, Bells Wynd :——Sold also | by
N. Stewart, R. Bremner, Corri & Sutherland, R. Ross, C.
Elliot, W. Creech, J. Sibbald, | Edin^r A. McGowan, & W.

---

[47] This is a series of handwritten notes by the late Andrew Gibson, who
donated his extensive Burns collection to the Linenhall Library in Belfast.

C

Gould, Glasgow. Boyd, Dumfries ; More, Dundee ; Sherriffs, |
Aberdeen ; Morison & Son, Perth ; Fisher & Atkinson, New-
castle ; Massey, Manches- | -ter ; C. Elliot, T. Kay, & Co.
N° 332, Strand, Longman & Broadrip, N° 26, Cheapside,
London. [engraved throughout]

Format. 12mo, in half-sheets. 21·5 × 12·8 cm., trimmed, in original
marbled boards.

Signatures. None ; engraved throughout.

Contents. Pp. VI+102-208 : [I], Title-page ; [II], blank ; III, Preface ;
IV-VI, Index ; 102-208, Text ; [209], blank.

Original Material :

Comment. Probably issued in the same manner as Vol I. Though the Preface is dated 1 Mar. 1788, the book was actually published on 14 Feb. 1788.[48] The title-page transcribed above is probably the first state, although I am certainly not dogmatic about it.

c. Vol. III [1790]

THE | SCOTS MUSICAL MUSEUM. | Humbly dedicated to the | Catch Club. | Instituted at Edin.r June 1771. | By | JAMES JOHNSON | Vol. III Price 6/ | [*vignette : shepherd and shepherdess seated on the bank of a river*] | Printed & sold by James Johnson Music seller Edinburgh, | and to be had at Mr. T. Preston No. 97 Strand London. [*engraved throughout*]

Format. 12mo, in half-sheets. 20·9×14 cm., trimmed and rebound.

Signatures. None ; engraved throughout.

Contents. Pp. vi+209-310 : [i], Title-page ; [ii], blank ; iii, Preface ; iv-vi, Index ; 209-310, Text.

Original Material :

207.	Tibbie Dunbar	*p.* 216
209.	My Harry was a Gallant gay	218
212.	The Taylor fell thro' the bed	221
213.	Ay waukin, O	222
215.	Beware O bonie Ann	224
218.	Laddie lie near me	226
220.	The Gardener wi' his Paidle	229
223.	On a bank of Flowers	232
224.	The day returns	233
225.	My love she's but a Lassie yet	234
229.	Jamie come try me	238
231.	My bony Mary	240
232.	The lazy mist	241
233.	The Captain's Lady	242
235.	I Love my Jean	244
239.	Carle, an' the king come	248
249.	Whistle o'er the lave o't	258
255.	O, were I on Parnassus Hill	264
257.	The Captive Ribband	266
258.	There's a youth in this City	266
259.	My heart's in the Highlands	268
260.	John Anderson my Jo	269
263.	Awa whigs awa	272
264.	Ca' the ewes to the knowes	273

[48] *Letters*, I.188.

Comment. Probably issued in the same manner as the preceding volumes. The Preface is dated 2 Feb 1790. Later issues of Vols. I and II also had the same title-page as above. I am calling it the first state because it is in its simplest form, not by any means a conclusive opinion.

d. VOL. IV [1792]

* [*The title-page is the same as the title-page of Vol. III, except that " III " is altered to " IV " or " IIII."*]

Format. 12mo in half-sheets. 21·6 × 13·2 cm., trimmed and rebound.

Signatures. None ; engraved throughout.

Contents. Pp. vi+311-414 : [i], Title-page ; [ii], blank ; iii, Preface ; iv-vi, Index ; 311-413, Text ; [414], blank.

Original Material :

Comment. Probably issued in the same manner as the preceding volumes. The Preface is dated 12 Aug. 1792.

e. VOL. V. [1796]

THE | SCOTS MUSICAL MUSEUM. | Humbly dedicated to the | Catch Club. | Instituted at Edin͚. June 1771. | By | JAMES JOHNSON | Vol. V | Price 6/ | [*vignette : shepherd and shepherdess seated on the bank of a river*] | Edin͚. printed & sold by Johnson &

Co, Music Sellers Head of | Lady Stair's Close, Lawn Market ; where may be had a Variety of | Music, & Musical Instruments, Instruments lent out, tun'd & repair'd. [*engraved throughout*]

Format. 12mo, in half-sheets. 22·5 × 13·5 cm., slightly trimmed, in original marbled boards.

Signatures. None ; engraved throughout.

Contents. Pp. VI+414-516 : [I], Title-page ; [II], blank ; III-IV, Preface ; IV-VI, Index ; 414-516, Text.

Original Material :

[49] In *Letters*, II.322-3, this letter is described as having first appeared in §112 (London 1808 = Cromek).

Comment. Probably issued in the same manner as the preceding volumes. Later issues of any of the volumes preceding this could have title-page as above.

f. Vol. VI [1803]

THE SCOTS | MUSICAL MUSEUM | in six Volumes. | Consisting of six hundred Scots Songs | with proper Bases for the | piano forte &c. | Humbly dedicated | to the Society | of | Antiquaries of Scotland | by JAMES JOHNSON | In this Publication the original Simplicity of our | ancient national Airs is retained unincumbered | with useless Accompaniments & Graces depriving the | Hearers of the sweet Simplicity of their native Melodies. | Volume [*blank*] Pr. 7ˢ | Butterworth *scripsit.* | Printed & sold by James Johnson Music Seller Edinburgh to be had at | T. Preston Nº 97 Strand London, McFadyen Glasgow, & at all the principal | Music Sellers. [*engraved throughout*]

Format. 12mo, in half-sheets ; 22·5 × 13·5 cm., slightly trimmed, in original marble boards.

Signatures. None ; engraved throughout.

Contents. Pp. VI+517-620 : [I], Title-page ; [II], blank ; III, Preface ; IV-VI, Index ; 517-620, Text.

Original Material :

[50] *Letters,* I.138-9.

Comment. The above title-page was issued with the five preceding
volumes as well as with Vol. VI. That is the reason why the
volume number was left blank on the title-page and, usually,
inserted by hand. The whole was issued as a set in 1803 and re-
issued in 1839 (§ 417A] and in 1853 (§ 567A).

During the last eight years of his life, Burns directed most of his
talents to the writing of songs. Though there are a few songs
in § 1 (1786 Kilmarnock) and § 2 (1787 Edinburgh), it may
be doubted whether Burns ever thought very seriously of devoting
himself to Scottish song literature ; and, but for James Johnson,
Burns's songs, " which we reckon by far the best that Britain has
yet produced,"[51] might have died still-born.

According to Grove,[52] James Johnson (b. [?] 1750, d. 11 Feb.
1811), the son of Charles Johnson, was a famous Edinburgh
music-engraver. For nearly forty years he held the bulk of
the Scottish trade, and from 1772 to about 1790 practically every
piece of music issued in Scotland was engraved by him. He
was probably apprenticed to James Reed, an early Edinburgh
music-engraver. In 1788, Johnson (who had lived previously in
Bell's Wynd) opened a music shop in the Lawnmarket,[53] where
he remained until his death.

The Scots Musical Museum seems to have been his great life
work, and it was through this publication that he became
connected with Burns. He was a member of the Crochallan
Fencibles, an Edinburgh convivial club, and it was probably
through this group that he first met the poet. Burns and Johnson

---

[51] T. Carlyle, " Burns," in *Critical & Miscellaneous Essays*, 6 Vols., London,
1869, II.34.
[52] Cp. *Grove's Dictionary of Music and Musicians*, 5th edn., London, 1954,
IV. 647.
[53] It must in fact have been later than 1788 that Johnson moved to the
Lawnmarket, for Burns addressed a letter to him at Bell's Wynd on 19 Jun.
1789, for which see *Letters*, 1.340.

became fast friends from the beginning, and on [4 May 1787] Burns wrote him : " Had my acquaintance w^t you been a little older, I would have asked the favor of your correspondence ; as I have met w^t few people whose company & conversation gave me so much pleasure——"[54] This friendship continued throughout the rest of the poet's life, and a few weeks before his death he wrote to Johnson : " You are a good worthy, honest fellow, & have a good right to live in this world."[55] According to Snyder, whose account of the poetical work that Burns did for Johnson is very thorough, Burns seems virtually to have been the editor of the *Museum* almost from the beginning until his death in 1796.[56] It is quite possible that he wrote the prefaces for Vols. II-IV, and on 15 Nov. 1788 he wrote to Johnson : " I am preparing a flaming Preface for your third Volume.[57] Of course this does not provide evidence that Burns wrote the prefaces for Vols. II and IV, nor does it even amount to proof that the preface that actually appeared in Vol. III was the " flaming Preface " that Burns promised to contribute, for Johnson might well have inserted one of his own composition. In default of any direct evidence, we cannot be sure that Burns wrote any of these prefaces, but the internal evidence cannot be said to point to any other author.

Though Johnson may, perhaps, have intended to issue a volume a year, he did not do so. For whereas Vol. I (which contained only two of Burns's songs and part of a third) appeared in May 1787, and Vol. II in 1788, Vol. III did not come out till 1790, Vol. IV did not follow till two years later, Vol. V was not published till 1796, some time after the poet's death, and the last volume was not finally issued till 1803. " Burns's connection with the *Museum*," says Snyder, " is not hard to summarize. Virtually all the poetry that he wrote between the spring of 1787 and the autumn of 1792 went into it. All told, he sent Johnson over two hundred songs, set to the tune which he himself considered most appropriate. Many of these songs were absolutely and entirely his own creation ; others were adaptations of old and ineffective lyrics ; still others were mosaics of fragments lifted from many different sources. But in virtually every case the text furnished Johnson was Burns's ; even his most obvious borrowings were re-shaped by his genius, and, as Henley and Henderson put it, ' stamped with his image and lettered with his superscription.' "[58]

[54] *Letters*, 1.89.   [55] *Letters*, ii.322.   [56] Snyder, 258-62.
[57] *Letters*, 1.275.   [58] Snyder, p. 262.

9. 1788 Paisley

ANIMADVERSIONS | on some | Poets and Poetasters | of the present Age | especially R——t B——s, and J——n L——k. | With a Contrast of some of the for- | mer Age. | By JAMES MAXWELL, | Poet in Paisley. | [*diamond rule*] | Paisley : | Printed by J. Neilson, and sold by the Author. | M, DCC, LXXXVIII.

Format. 8vo, in half-sheets. 17 × 10·2 cm., trimmed and bound.

Signatures. [A]-C4. The first leaf of each gathering is signed.

Contents. Pp. 24 : [1], Title-page ; [2], blank ; [3]-24, Text.

Original Material. Pp. 4-8 are devoted to a poem called : " On the Ayrshire Ploughman Poet, or Poetaster, R.B." At the end of this diatribe, on p. 8, appears " Another specimen of the same Author, said to have been written on a Window in Stirling." This is the first appearance of the lines beginning : " Here Stewarts once in triumph reign'd . . ."

Comment. Issued stabbed. Extremely rare. I have seen but one copy.

10. 1788 Philadelphia

POEMS, | CHIEFLY IN THE | SCOTTISH DIALECT. | By | ROBERT BURNS. | [*diamond rule*] | Philadelphia : | Printed for, and sold by Peter Stewart and | George Hyde, the West Side of Second-Street, | the ninth Door above Chesnut-Street. | M, DCC, LXXXVIII.

Format. 12mo, in half-sheets. 16 × 8·7 cm., trimmed, in contemporary calf.

Signatures. A4 ; B-Bb6 ; Cc4. A is one-half of an octavo with vertical chain lines ; Cc is the same but with horizontal chain lines. The first and third leaves are signed, for example, B and B2 ; the second leaf is unsigned. The gathering Cc is signed on the first and second leaves, *i.e.*, in perfectly normal order.

Contents. Pp. viii+[9]-304 : [i], Title-page ; [ii], blank ; [iii]-vi, Dedication to the Caledonian Hunt ; [vii]-viii, Table of Contents ; [9]-304, Text and Glossary.

Comment. Issued in paper boards (?). In the Huntington Library copy the page-number on p. 21 is printed upside down. This irregularity does not occur in any other copy I have examined. Follows § 2 (1787 Edinburgh, " Stinking " Edition). Very rare ; I have never seen a copy in original boards.

The honour of publishing the first American edition of Burns's poems goes to Peter Stewart and George Hyde of Philadelphia. They did not issue any proposals for printing. Instead they determined to release an edition of the *Poems* and let them sell themselves on their own merit : resorting to a form of advertising, common enough in the eighteenth century, they reprinted many of the forthcoming poems in *The Pennsylvania Packet*, from 24 Jul. 1787 to 14 Jun. 1788.[59] The Philadelphia edition actually appeared on 7 Jul. 1788.[60]

11. 1788 New York

POEMS, | CHIEFLY IN THE | SCOTTISH DIALECT. | By ROBERT BURNS. | To which are added, | SCOTS POEMS, | selected from the works of | ROBERT FERGUSON. | [*diamond rule*] | New-York : | Printed by J. and A. M'Lean, Franklin's Head, | No. 41, Hanover-Square. | M, DCC, LXXXVIII.

Format. 8vo, in half-sheets. 20·8 × 13·2 cm., untrimmed, in original boards.

Signatures. [A]-Mm4 ; Nn2 ; Oo-Qq4. The first two leaves of each half-sheet are signed.

Contents. Pp. viii+[9]-306 : [i], Title-page ; [ii], blank ; [iii]-v, Dedication to the Caledonian Hunt ; [vi], blank ; [vii]-viii, Table of Contents ; [9]-306, Text and Glossary ; one leaf.

Comment. Issued in blue paper boards (portrait of R.B., engraved by Scot, Philadelphia, tipped-in in D.C. copy).

Miss Painter believes that the publication of § 10 (1788 Philadelphia) on 7 Jul. 1788 gave an impetus to this N.Y. edition, which appeared *c*. 17 Dec. 1788. Its publishers, J. and A. Maclean, were natives of Glasgow who had come to America in 1783.[61]

See also below, § 46 (1799 New York).

[59] See Anna M. Painter, " American Editions of Burns before 1800," an unpublished dissertation in the Sterling Library, Yale University. Miss Painter records only 24 reprints of the poems ; she overlooked the reprinting of " O thou dread pow'r," which appeared in *The Pennsylvania Packet* on 24 May 1788.

[60] *The Pennsylvania Packet*, 7 Jul. 1788.

[61] Anna M. Painter, " American Editions of the *Poems* of Burns before 1800," in *The Library*, 4th Ser., XII (1932), 441-2.

12. 1789 Belfast

POEMS, | CHIEFLY IN THE | SCOTTISH DIALECT. | [*diamond rule*] | By ROBERT BURNS. | [*diamond rule*] | Belfast : | Printed and sold by James Magee, | No. 9, Bridge-Street. | [*diamond rule*] | M, DCC, LXXXIX.

Format. 12mo, 16·2 × 8·7 cm., trimmed and bound in contemporary calf.

Signatures. A6 ; B-L12 ; MO6. The whole sheets are signed on the first, second, and fifth leaves ; the half-sheets on the first, second, and third leaves.

Contents. Pp. xii × 274 : [i], Title-page ; [ii], blank ; [iii]-vi, Dedication to the Caledonian Hunt ; vii-x, Extract from *The Lounger*, No. 97 ; (xi-xii], Table of Contents ; [1]-274, Text and Glossary ; one blank leaf.

Comment. Page-by-page reprint of § 3 (1787 Belfast), with frontispiece (portrait of R.B., engraved by Halpin).

13. 1789 Dublin

POEMS, | CHIEFLY IN THE | SCOTTISH DIALECT. | [*diamond rule*] | By ROBERT BURNS. | [*diamond rule*] | Dublin : | Printed for William Gilbert, | Great George's-Street. | M, DCC, LXXXIX

Comment. Otherwise the same as § 12 (1789 Belfast), with frontispiece (portrait of R.B., engraved by P. Halpin).

14. 1789 Kilmarnock

POEMS, | by | DAVID SILLAR, | [*ornamented rule*] | Nor will the best some hints refuse: | The narrow soul, that least brings forth, | To an advice the rarest bows; | Which the extensive mind allows, | Being conscious of it's genuine worth, | Fears no eclipse; nor with dark pride declines, | A ray from light, that far inferior shines. | Ramsay. | [*ornamented rule*] | Kilmarnock : | Printed by John Wilson. | [*double rule*] | M, DCC, LXXXIX. [*border:* same as §1 (*Kilmarnock, 1786*)]

Format. 8vo, in half-sheets. 21·4 × 14·1 cm., trimmed, in original blue
paper boards.

Signatures. A-Hh4. The first two leaves of each half-sheet are signed.

Contents. Pp. viii + [9]-[248] : [i], Title-page ; [ii], Registration ;
[iii]-iv, Dedication to Hugh Montgomery, Esq., of Skelmorlie ;
[v]-vi, Preface ; [vii]-viii, Table of Contents ; [9]-247, Text and
Glossary ; [248], blank.

Original Material :
   To the Author [" Auld nibor, I'm three times, doubly, o'er   *p.* [9]
   your debtor."]

David Sillar (1760-1830) was one of Burns's close friends, and
Burns helped him to get subscribers for his book.[62] We do not
know when Burns sent the above poem to him.

15. [?1789. Dumfries]

THE AYRSHIRE GARLAND. | An excellent new Song. Tune.
The Vicar and Moses.

Format. Single sheet, 25·9 × 20·2 cm., untrimmed.

Original Material. The Ayrshire Garland.

" The Ayrshire Garland " is the first version of " The Kirk's
Alarm " and contains only these thirteen stanzas:
   i. " Orthodox, Orthodox . . ."   vii. " Simper James . . ."
   ii. " Doctor Mac . . ."   viii. " Sing't Sawney . . ."
   iii. " Town of Ayr . . ."   ix. " Daddie Auld . . ."
   iv. " D'rymple mild . . ."   x. " Pauky Clark . . ."
   v. " Calvin's Sons . . ."   xi. " Jamie Goose . . ."
   vi. " Rumble John . . ."   xii. " Poet Willie . . ."
                   xiii. " Barr Steenie . . ."

This is probably the first of Burns's poems to appear in a
broadside. On 17 Jul. 1789, Burns writes to Mrs. Dunlop:

   You will be well acquainted with the persecutions that
   my worthy friend, D^r M^cgill, is undergoing among your
   Divines.—Several of these reverend lads, his opponents,
   have come thro' my hands before; but I have some
   thoughts of serving them up again in a different dish.—
   I have just sketched the following ballad [*The Kirk's*

Alarm], & as usual I send the first rough-draught to
you.—I do not wish to be known in it, tho' I know, if
ever it appear, I shall be suspected.—If I finish it, I am
thinking to throw off two or three dozen copies at a Press
in Dumfries, & send them, as from Edin^r to some Ayrshire folks on both sides of the question. . . . This is all the
length I have gone.—Whether I proceed any further is
uncertain.—[63]

16. 1789

THE | PRAYER | OF | HOLY WILLIE, | a canting, hypo-
critical, Kirk Elder. | With Quotations from the *Presbyterian
Eloquence.* | [*rule*] | An *Ignis Fatuus* that bewitches, | And leads
men into pools and ditches: | This light inspires, and plays
upon | The nose of saint, like bagpipe drone, | As if hypocrisy
and nonsense | Had got th'advowson of his conscience; | As if
religion were intended | For nothing else but to be mended: |
Still so perverse and opposite, | As if he worshipp'd God for
spite. | Hudibras. | [*broken rule*] | Printed in the Year M DCC
LXXXIX.

Format. 8vo, half-sheet ; 17·9 × 10·2 cm.

Contents. Pp. 8 : [1] Title-page. [2], " To the Reader " ; [3]-8, Text.

Original Material. Holy Willie's Prayer.

17. 1790 Belfast

POEMS, | CHIEFLY IN THE | SCOTTISH DIALECT. |
[*diamond rule*] | By ROBERT BURNS. | [*diamond rule*] | Belfast:
| Printed and sold by William Magee, | No. 9 Bridge-Street. |
[*rule*] | M, DCC, XC.

Format. 12mo. 16·1 × 9·5 cm., trimmed and bound in contemporary
    calf.

Signatures. A6 ; B-L12 ; M-O6. The first five leaves of each sheet,
    and the first three of the half-sheets, are signed : signatures are
    omitted on leaves [C4 ; D3,4 ; E3,4 ; G3,4 ; H3,4 ; I3,4,5 ;
    K3,4 ; L3,4].

[63] *Letters*, 1.345-6.

Contents. Pp. xii+274 : [i], Title-page ; [ii], blank ; [iii]-vi, Dedication to the Caledonian Hunt ; vii-x, Extract from *The Lounger*, No. 97 ; [xi-xii], Table of Contents ; [1]-274, Text and Glossary ; 1 blank leaf.

Comment. Issued in boards, with frontispiece (portrait of R.B. by P. Halpin) ; a page-by-page reprint of § 12 (1789 Belfast).

18. 1790 Dublin

POEMS, | CHIEFLY IN THE | SCOTTISH DIALECT. | [*rule*] | By ROBERT BURNS. | [*diamond rule*] | Dublin: | Printed for William Gilbert, | Great George's-street. | M, DCC, XC.

Comment. Otherwise the same as §17 (1790 Belfast).

19. 1790 Edinburgh

Robert Chambers' Bibliography to his *Life and Works of Robert Burns.* Edinburgh: 1851, contains the following entry:

Poems, etc., Edinburgh. W. Creech [July] 1790.[64]

Now, *The Edinburgh Evening Courant* for 22 Jul. 1790 contains the following advertisement:

Poems, by Robert Burns, 1 vol. 8vo., the 3rd edition, with a head of the Author, price 6s in boards.

And in a letter, written in [Oct. ? 1791], Burns himself wrote to Peter Hill:

He [Creech] wrote me a fine, fair letter, telling me that he was going to print a third Edition; & as he had a brother's care of my fame, he wished to add every new thing I have written since, & I should be amply rewarded with—a copy or two to present to my friends!— He has sent me a copy of the last Ed[n] to correct, &c.— but I have as yet taken no notice of it; & I hear he has published without me.[65]

It was perhaps from these data that Chambers concluded that Creech brought out a new Edinburgh edition in 1790. I doubt that Chambers had ever seen an actual copy, for, so far as I know,

---

[64] IV.312.   [65] *Letters*, II.95.

no one else ever has, and none now seems to exist. In the face of this, it is hard to believe that such an edition was ever issued.

What then is the explanation of the advertisement in *The Edinburgh Evening Courant* for 22 Jul. 1790? As we have already seen,[66] copies of § 5 (1787 London), the "Third Edition," were still being sold in 1790. In the advertisement of 22 Jul. 1790, the edition offered for sale in Edinburgh is specifically described as "the 3rd edition." § 5 (1787 London) was re-issued in 1790 with the 1787 title-page, and bound in at the back of this re-issue is an extra gathering, a publisher's catalogue, with the following heading:

> The following valuable books are printed for A. Strahan and T. Cadell, in the Strand. 1790.

Hence there can be little doubt that the copies which Creech was offering for sale were copies of § 5 (1787 London) that still remained unsold, and that Strahan and Cadell had shipped to him for disposal in Edinburgh, at 6s. By Oct. 1791 Burns probably was no longer in close touch with Creech, and on hearing rumours of a new Edinburgh edition being sold he might understandably have jumped angrily to the conclusion that Creech had by-passed him. (It might be pointed out here that Creech had every right in the world to bring out a new edition, since he had purchased the copyright.)

On the whole, this seems a simpler explanation of the facts as known to us than that all copies of an edition which only Chambers had seen have since vanished.

20. 1790 [? Paisley]

POEMS | AND | SONGS, | By ALEXANDER TAIT. | [*diamond rule*] | Printed | for, and sold by the author only. | M DCC XC.

Format. 8vo, in half-sheets ; 16 × 9·7 cm., trimmed and bound.

Signatures. A-Pp4. The first leaf of each half-sheet is signed.

Contents. Pp. vi + [7]-304 : [i], Title-page ; [ii], List of Errata ; [iii]-vi, Table of Contents ; [7]-304, Text.

Original Material :
The Kirk's Alarm (two new stanzas]   *p.* 170

Comment. Issued stabbed ; probably printed by John Neilson, Paisley.[67]

---

[66] Above, p. 33.   [67] Cp. *The New Paisley Repository*, 19 Feb. 1853.

The version of the " The Kirk's Alarm " printed here follows the same order as that in § 15 (1789), *The Ayrshire Garland*, as far as the end of st. ix ("Daddie Auld . . ."). It then omits st. x ("Pawky Clark . . ."), with the result that sts. xi ("Jamie Goose . . ."), xii (" Poet Willie . . ."), and xiii (" Barr Steenie . . .") become sts. x, xi, and xii, respectively. The original material (" Cessnock Side . . ." and " Davie Douf . . .") make fourteen stanzas altogether.

Tait's volume includes three scurrilous poems about Burns, viz., " B–rns in his Infancy," " B–rns in Lochly," and " B–rns's Hen." In spite of the tone of these poems, Tait may, at one time, have been on good terms with Burns, otherwise he could scarcely have printed two additional stanzas in this version of " The Kirk's Alarm."

21. 1791 London

THE| ANTIQUITIES | OF | SCOTLAND | By FRANCIS GROSE Esq.ʳ F.A.Sˢ | of London and Perth. | The Second Volume. | [*engraving of ruined castle beside mountain torrent*] | Pub. April 11, 1791, by S. Hooper. | London, Printed for S. Hooper, N.º 212, High Holborn. | MDCCXCI. [*engraved throughout*]

Variant :
    " Pub. . . . Hooper." Omitted in some copies.

Format. 4to, in half-sheets ; 34·9 × 23·7 cm., untrimmed, bound.

Signatures. a2 ; [b] ; Yy-Zz2 ; 3A2 ; 2B2 ; Cc-Iii2 ; Kkk1.

Contents. Pp. [171]-308+iv : [171]-308, Text and Addenda ; [i]-iv, County Index.

Original Material :
    Tam o' Shanter   *p.* 199

Comment. Issued in boards (?). Vol. I, published in 1789, contains pp. xxiv+170+4 (numbered 173*-6*). Though supposedly continuous with Vol. I, the page-numbering of Vol. II shows, as can be seen, a slight technical irregularity.

Captain Francis Grose began his studies of ruined Scottish ecclesiastical structures in 1787. Burns had met him by 17 Jul. 1789,[68] and the two men at once took a liking to each other. Grose became much interested in the folklore of Ayrshire,

[68] *Letters*, 1.346.

which the poet had at his fingertips, and persuaded Burns to write a poem about one of the historical monuments in that county (Alloway Kirk) after Burns had persuaded him to include that monument in the forthcoming second volume of the *Antiquities*. Early in 1791, Burns accordingly sent Grose a copy of " Tam o' Shanter." It was published in the *Edinburgh Herald* for 18 Mar. 1791, and in the *Edinburgh Magazine* for Mar. 1791. When finally published in the *Antiquities*, it was printed in small type and double columns, as a footnote, on pp. 199-201.[69]

22. [?1791. ?Dumfries]

THE WHISTLE, | a | Poem, | by | ROBERT BURNS, | the Ayrshire Poet. | [*rule*] | I sing of a Whistle, a Whistle of worth, | I sing of a Whistle, the pride of the North, | Was brought to the court of our good Scottish King, | And long with this Whistle all Scotland shall ring. | [*double rule*]

Format.   8vo, half-sheet ;   14·8 × 8·9 cm., slightly trimmed, bound.

Contents.   Pp. 8 : [1], Title-page ; [2], Advertisement ; [3]-8, Text.

Original Material.   The Whistle.[70]

Comment.   Pp. 4 and 8 only are numbered.

Burns had composed the poem, or at least part of it, by 16 Oct. 1789.[71] The pamphlet itself was probably printed in Sep.-Oct. 1791, and it is probably to this he refers when he writes Robert Cleghorn [Oct. 1791]: " I enclose you a proof-sheet, one out of a dozen I got from the Publisher, to give among my friends. —It is a poem of mine which perhaps you have seen from our friends Dunbar or Cunningham, who got M.S.S. copies of it.—"[72]

23. 1792 Edinburgh

THE | STATISTICAL ACCOUNT | OF | SCOTLAND. | Drawn up from the Communications | of the | Ministers | of the | different Parishes. | [*rule*] | By SIR JOHN SINCLAIR, Bart. | [*rule*] | Volume Third. | " *Ad consilium de republica dandum,*

---

[69] Grose sent Burns a dozen copies of the proof sheets : Cp. *Letters*, II.57.
[70] Originally (?) published in *The London Star*, 2 Nov. 1791.
[71] *Letters*, I.362-3.   [72] *Letters*, II.93.

caput est nosse rempublicam." | Cicero, de Orat. lib. ii. | [*diamond rule*] | Edinburgh: | printed and sold by William Creech; | and also by J. Donaldson, A. Guthrie, and Jo. and Ja. | Fairbairn, Edinburgh; T. Cadell, J. Debrett, and J. | Sewel, London; Dunlop and Wilson, Glasgow; | Angus and Son, Aberdeen. | [*broken rule*] | M, DCC,XCII.

Half-Title

THE | STATISTICAL ACCOUNT | OF | SCOTLAND

Format. 8vo, in half-sheets ; 21·7 × 12·5 cm., trimmed.

Signatures. [a]-b4 ; A-Zz4 ; 3A-4H4 (-4H3,4). Apart from [a], which is unsigned, the first leaf of each half-sheet is signed.

Contents. Pp. xvi+612 : [i], Half-title ; [ii], blank ; [iii], Title-page ; [iv], blank ; [v]-vii, Table of Contents ; [viii], blank ; [ix]-xi, Advertisement ; xii-xvi, Address to the Reader ; [1]-594, Text ; [595]-612, Appendix.

Original Material :
Letter to Sir John Sinclair   *p.* 598

Comment. Issued in gray paper boards.

This vast, fascinating, and important work was issued in twenty-one volumes between 1791 and 1799.

24. 1792 London

ESSAYS | on the | Lives and Writings | of | Fletcher of Saltoun | and the | Poet Thomson: | Biographical, critical, and political. | With some Pieces of Thomson's never before published. | [*diamond rule*] | By D. S. EARL OF BUCHAN. | [*double rule*] | London: | Printed for J. Debrett, | opposite Burlington-House, Piccadilly. | [*rule*] | MDCCXCII.

Half-Title

ESSAYS | on the | Lives and Writings | of | Fletcher of Saltoun | and the | Poet Thomson.

Format. 8vo, 22·4 × 13·3 cm., untrimmed, in original boards.

Signatures. [A4] ; B-X8. Apart from [A], which is unsigned, the first four leaves of each sheet are signed.

Contents. Pp. viii+xl+280 : [i], Half-title ; [ii], blank ; [iii], Title-page ; [iv], blank ; [v]-viii, Table of Contents ; [i]-xxxix, Intro-duction ; [Xl], blank ; [1], Fly-title ; [2], blank ; 3-280, Text.

Original Material :

Address to the Shade of Thomson (with letter) [73]   *p.* 244

Comments. Issued in gray paper boards, with frontispiece (portrait of Fletcher of Saltoun by Anna Forbes).

In 1791, the Earl of Buchan decided to honour the poet Thomson's memory with a ceremony at Ednam Hall, Roxburghshire, and invited Burns to take part in the celebration, which was to take place on 22 September, Thomson's birthday, and was to take the form of crowning a bust of James Thomson with a wreath of bays. Burns declined, but sent Lord Buchan a copy of his "Address to the Shade of Thomson." The "Address" appeared in the *Edinburgh Advertiser* on 13 Sep. 1791, and in several other periodical publications. In Lord Buchan's *Essays*, it appears under the heading:

> Mr. Burns, the Airshire Bard's Apology for not attending the Anniversary Meeting: and the Address to the Shade of Thomson.

25. 1793 Edinburgh

a. Vol. I

POEMS, | CHIEFLY IN THE | SCOTTISH DIALECT. | By | ROBERT BURNS. | [*double rule*] | In two Volumes. | [*double rule*] | The second Edition considerably enlarged. | [*double rule*] | Vol. I. | [*diamond rule*] | Edinburgh: | Printed for T. Cadell, London, and William | Creech, Edinburgh. | [*broken rule*] | M,DCC,XCIII.

Half-title

[*double rule*] | POEMS, | CHIEFLY | SCOTTISH. | [*double rule*]

Format. 12mo ; 20·4×12·7 cm., untrimmed, in original boards.

Signatures. π6 ; A-K12. The first six leaves of each sheet are signed.

Contents. Pp. xii+238 : [1], Half-title ; [ii], blank ; [iii], Title-page ; [iv], Registration ; [v]-viii, Dedication to the Caledonian Hunt ; [ix]-xi, Table of Contents ; [xii], blank ; [1]-237, Text ; [238] ; one blank leaf.

[73] *Letters,* II.85-6.

b. VOL. II

Format. As Vol. I.

Signatures. π2 ; A-L12 ; M10.

Contents. Pp. [iv]+284 : [i], Half-title ; [ii], blank ; [iii], Title-page ; [iv], Registration ; [1]-283, Text and Glossary ; [284], blank.

[74] Originally published in *The Weekly Miscellany*, Glasgow, for 30 Nov. 1791.

[75] Originally published in *Stuart's Star* (London) for 7 May 1789, and in other periodicals.

[76] Originally published in *The Edinburgh Magazine*, XII (Aug. 1790), 143-4.

[77] Originally published in *The Gazeteer and New Daily Advertiser* (London) for 30th Sep. 1790.

[78] Originally published in *The Edinburgh Evening Courant* for 11 Aug. 1789, and in other periodicals. (H.H., 1.446, have 27 Aug.)

[79] Originally published in *Stuart's Star* (London) for 18 Apr. 1789.

[80] Originally published in *The Edinburgh Magazine*, X (Nov. 1789), 357-8.

[81] Originally published in *The Edinburgh Courant* for 6 Sep. 1787.

On the Birth of a Posthumous Child, born in peculiar
  circumstances of Family-Distress   *p.* 243
The Whistle [cp. also § 22]   245

Comment. Vol. I has frontispiece (portrait of R.B., after Nasmyth,
engraved by I. Beugo). Issued in boards. The N.L.S. copy has
corrections in Burns's hand.

Creech probably made a handsome profit on § 2 (1787 Edinburgh), which had now apparently been sold out for at least
two years.[82] Burns had written, since then, a good many new
poems; the knowledge that he had done so was bound to whet
the curiosity of the public that had lionised him five years before;
and in these circumstances Creech may well have reckoned
that a new edition would have good prospects.

In Mar. or Apr. 1792, Creech seems to have written to Burns
asking him what new poems he could provide for a new edition,
and how much he wanted for them (Creech, of course, had
bought the copyright of all the poems in § 2 [1787 Edinburgh]);
and Burns replied:

> I suppose, at a gross guess that I could add of new
> materials to your two volumes, about fifty pages.—I
> would also correct & retrench a good deal.—These
> said fifty pages you know are as much mine as the
> thumb-stall I have just now drawn on my finger which
> I unfortunately gashed in mending my pen. A few
> Books which I very much want, are all the recompence I
> crave, together with as many copies of this new edition of
> my own works as Friendship or Gratitude shall prompt
> me to *present.*[83]

The edition was advertised in the *Edinburgh Courant* for 16 Feb.
1793.[84] Almost two weeks later Burns wrote to Creech:

> I understand that my Book is published.—I beg that
> you will, *as soon as possible,* send me twenty copies of it.—
> As I mean to present them among a few Great Folks
> whom I respect, & a few Little Folks whom I love,
> these twenty will not interfere with your sale.—If you
> have not twenty copies ready, send me any number you
> can.—It will confer a particular obligation to let me
> have them by first Carrier.[85]

[82] Otherwise he would not still have been selling copies of § 5 (1787 London)
— as apparently he was — in Edinburgh in 1791. Cp. above, p. 33.
[83] *Letters,* II.114.   [84] Snyder, 409.   [85] *Letters,* II.151-2.

These letters show what sort of relationship existed between Burns and Creech at this period. The parsimonious publisher had been very slow about giving Burns any money for the first edition, and had not offered him anything for a second: but in answer to Creech's query about how much he might want, Burns asked only for a few books and a few copies of the new edition. And when the edition has finally been published, Creech does not even inform Burns of it, Burns writes that he *understands* his book is published, and *begs* the publisher for some more copies !

26. 1793 Belfast

a. VOL. I

POEMS, | CHIEFLY IN THE | SCOTTISH DIALECT. | By | ROBERT BURNS. | [*diamond rule*] | In two Volumes. | [*diamond rule*] | Vol. I. | [*diamond rule*] | Belfast: | Printed by William Magee, Bridge-Street. | [*diamond rule*] | M,DCC,XCIII.

Format. 12mo ; 16·8 × 10·2 cm., trimmed and bound in contemporary calf, two volumes in one.

Signatures. A6 ; B-L12 ; M-O6. Except leaves [C4] and [F4], which are unsigned, the whole sheets are signed on the first five leaves ; the half-sheets on the first three.

Contents. Pp. xii+274 : [i], Title-page ; [ii], blank, [iii]-vi, Dedication to the Caledonian Hunt ; vii-x, Extract from *The Lounger*, No. 97 ; [xi-xii], Table of Contents ; [1]-274, Text and Glossary ; one blank leaf.

b. VOL. II

Half-title

[*double rule*] | POEMS, | CHIEFLY | SCOTTISH | [*double rule*]

Signatures. A-D12. The first five leaves of each sheet are signed.

Contents. Pp. 96 : [1], Half-title ; [2], blank ; [3], Title-page (as Vol. I, except vol. no., but not printed from the same set-up) ; [4], blank ; [5]-94, Text ; 95-6, Table of Contents.

Original Material :
Delia   *p.* 89
Epigram on Francis Grose [" The Devil once heard . . ."]   94

Comment. Issued in blue boards. Vol. I has frontispiece (portrait of R.B. by P. Halpin).

This edition was announced for publication on 29 Jun. 1793,[86] and was sold for 1s 1d. It contains all the poems printed in § 25 (1793 Edinburgh), with slight rearrangement of material. Vol. I is a page-by-page reprint of § 17 (1790 Belfast), and contains the Glossary; Vol. II contains all the new material that first appeared in § 25 (1793 Edinburgh). Hence it seems probable that it was originally intended to be only a one-volume edition (otherwise the Glossary would hardly have been inserted at the end of Vol. I); that Vol. I had already been set when Magee received a copy of § 25 (1793 Edinburgh) ; and that he had then set and printed Vol. II, containing all the new material on § 25 (1793 Edinburgh). This material does not bulk very large, and Vol. II of Magee's edition also contains some additional poems by other authors.

According to Henley and Henderson, who see no justification for regarding it as a production of Burns's, " Delia " was first published in § 69 (1802 Glasgow).[87] Henley and Henderson also say that the " Epigram on Francis Grose " was first published in *The Scots Magazine* in June 1797.[88] The version which appears in Henley and Henderson differs greatly from that given by Magee, which reads as follows:

> The Devil once heard that Old Grose was a-dying,
> And whip ! on the wings of the wind he came flying;
> But when he beheld honest Francis a-moaning,
> And mark'd each bed-post with its burthen a-groaning;
> Confounded he roar'd, ' I shall leave him, by G—,
> ' Ere carry to H-ll such a damnable load.'

Vol. II of Magee's 1793 edition also contains: p. 90, " A Rosebud by my early Walk," which he seems to have lifted from § 8*b* (1788 Edinburgh=Johnson, Vol. II), p. 197; p. 91, " Musing on the roaring Ocean," also from Johnson, II.91; " Willie brewed a Peck of Mault," from § 8*c* (1790 Edinburgh=Johnson, Vol. III), p. 301 ; and p. 93, " The blue ey'd Lassie," from § 8*c* (1790 Edinburgh=Johnson, Vol. III), p. 304.

There was no Dublin edition in 1793, but in several copies I have seen, a copy of Vol. II of this Belfast edition of 1793 is bound up with a copy of § 18 (1790 Dublin). The simplest explanation would seem to be that Gilbert, the Dublin bookseller, had been less successful in selling § 18 (1790 Dublin) than

---

[86] *Belfast News Letter* for that date.   [87] H. & H., IV.107.
[88] H. & H., II.437.

Magee in selling § 17 (1790 Belfast), and that Magee shipped some copies of Vol. II of this 1793 Belfast edition to Dublin, where they were bound up with copies of § 18 (1790 Dublin) that remained on hand.

27. [1793-4] Edinburgh

A SELECTION OF | SCOTS SONGS| Harmonized improved | with simple and | adapted Graces | Most respectfully dedicated to the | Right honourable | Lady Katherine Douglas | by | PETER URBANI | Professor of Music | Book. 2.^{d} Pr. 12/ | Entered at Stationers Hall. | Printed for the Author and sold at his House | Foot of Carrubers Close and at the Music Shops | Edin.^{r} McGouan Glasgow Longman and | Broadrip London Mrs Rhimes and | Mr. Lee Dublin. | J. Johnson Sculp.^{t} Edin.^{r} [*engraved throughout*]

Format. Folio.

Signatures. None ; engraved throughout.

Contents. Pp. [vi]+50 : [i], Title-page ; [ii], blank ; [iii], Advertisement ; [iv], Dedication to Lady Katherine Douglas ; [v-vi], List of subscribers' names ; 1-50, Text.

Original Material :
   O my Love's like a red, red Rose   *p.* 16

Comment. Issued stabbed. Entered at Stationers Hall on 19 Jun. 1794 but was published on 5 Apr. 1794.[89] This is the second volume of a series : the first was published on 28 Jan. 1793.[90]

According to a note contained in the Advertisement to this volume, " The words of the Red, Red Rose, were obligingly given to him [Urbani] by a celebrated Scot's poet who was so struck with them when sung by a country girl, that he wrote them down, and not being pleased with the air, begged the author to set them to Music, in the stile of the Scot's Tune."[91] Urbani published two more volumes ; one in 1798, which contained two songs by Burns, although these were not first appearances ; another in 1800, in which twenty-six of the twenty-eight

---

[89] *The Caledonian Mercury* for that date.
[90] *The Edinburgh Courant* for that date.
[91] For an account of how Urbani got the song and Burns's feeling towards Urbani — " Urbani has told a damned falsehood " — cp. *Letters,* II.262-3.

songs published were written by Burns, although none of them
is new. One spurious song, *Evan Banks*, " Slow spreads the
gloom . . .," appeared in this later volume.

28. 1793-1818 London[92]

a. [Vol. 1, Set 1, 1793]

A select Collection | [*diamond rule*] of [*diamond rule*] | ORIGINAL
SCOTISH AIRS | for the Voice. | To each of which are
added, | introductory & concluding Symphonies, & | Accompany-
ments for the Violin & Piano Forte. | By | Pleyel. | With select &
characteristic Verses by the most admired Scotish | Poets,
adapted to each Air; many of them entirely new. | Also | suitable
English Verses in Addition to such of the Songs as are written |
in the Scottish dialect. | Price 10.^{s} 6.^{d} Entered at Stationer's
Hall. Set [1] | [*diamond rule*] | London, printed and sold by
Preston & Son, | at their Wholesale Warehouses, N.º 97, Strand. |
For the Proprietor. [*engraved throughout*]

Format. Folio ; 38·7 × 28·1 cm., untrimmed, in original wrappers.

Signatures. None ; engraved and printed.

Contents. Pp. viii+25 : [i], Title-page ; [ii], blank ; iii-vi, Preface ;
[vii], Table of Contents ; [viii], blank ; 1 [*recto*], blank ; 1 [*verso*]-25
[*recto*], Text ; 25 [*verso*], blank.

Original Material :

Here awa, there awa	*p.* 2
Behind yon Hills	4
Braw Lads on Yarrow Braes	11
From thee, Eliza, I must go [Also in § 1]	15
There's auld Rob Morris	17
Oh, open the Door	21
When wild War's deadly Blast	22

Comment. Issued stabbed, in purple paper wrappers. There are 13
leaves of printed text and 13 leaves of engraved music, inserted
alternately so that the words and music of each song appear *en
regard*. The recto of the first leaf and the verso of the last are, of
course, blank. Double pagination, 1-25. The Preface is printed,
and bears date 1 May 1793. The t.p. of this and other sets of the
Scotish Airs was almost always signed by Thomson and the set
numbers were also inserted in his own hand.

[92] Cp. also Appendix II.

b. [Vol. I, SET 2, 1798]

A select Collection | [*diamond rule*] of [*diamond rule*] | ORIGINAL SCOTISH AIRS, | for the Voice. | To each of which are added | introductory & concluding Symphonies, & | Accompanyments for the Piano Forte & Violin. | By | Kozeluch. | With select & characteristic Verses by the most admired Scotish Poets, adapted | to each Air, the greater Number of these written for this Work by | BURNS. | Also suitable English Verses in Addition to most of the Songs | in the Scotish Dialect. | [*diamond rule*] | Price 10§ 6ᵈ Entered at Stationers Hall.   Set [2] | [*diamond rule*] | London, printed & sold by Preston, | at his Wholesale Warehouses, N⁰ 97 Strand. | Sold also by the Proprietor G. THOMSON Edinburgh. [*engraved throughout*]

Format and Signatures. As Set 1.

Contents. Pp. viii+26-50 : arranged as in Set. 1

Original Material :

O stay, sweet warbling Wood-lark, stay	*p.* 26
Here is the Glen, and here the Bower	27
The Day returns, my Bosom Burns	28
O were I on Parnassus Hill	29
How lang and dreary is the Night	31
Sweet fa's the Eve on Craigieburn	32
O saw ye bonie Lesley	33
O Love will venture in	36
Nae gentle Dames, tho' e'er so fair	37
O mirk, mirk, is the Midnight Hour	38
Where Cart rins rowing to the Sea	39
Turn again, thou fair Eliza	42
Ye Banks and Braes o' bonny Doon	43
Fate gave the Word, the Arrow sped	45
True hearted was he the sad Swain	46
Duncan Gray came here to Woo	48
Let not Woman e'er Complain	48
O Poortith cauld, and restless Love	49
The lazy Mist hangs	50

Comment. With Set 1, this makes up the first volume of Thomson's *Original Scotish Airs* as originally planned, but it was not published until after the poet's death.[93]   In the Preface, Thomson explains that publication was delayed by Pleyel's negligence, and that before he could continue the work he had to engage the services of another musician, Kozeluch.

[93] Preface dated August 1798.

c. [Vol. II, Set 3, 1799]

Title-page. Identical with t.p. of Set 2.

Format and Signatures. As Sets 1 and 2.

Contents. Pp. viii+51-75 : arranged as Sets 1 and 2.

Original Material :

John Anderson my Jo	*p.* 51
How cruel are the Parents	51
Last May a braw Wooer cam' down the lang Glen	52
In Summer when the Hay was mawn	54
O this is no my ain Lassie	56
Blythe hae I been on yon Hill	58
Thine am I, my faithful fair	59
Blythe was she	61
Husband, Husband, cease your Strife	62
Contented wi' little	65
My heart is a-breaking, dear Titty	66
O wat ye wha that lo'es me	67
Now rosy May comes in wi' Flowers	69
It was the charming Month of May	69
Canst thou leave me thus, my Katy	70
O meikle thinks my Love o' my Beauty	73
Robert Bruce's Address to his Army at Bannockburn [" Scots wha ha'e "]	74
Here's a Health to ane I lo'e dear	75

Comment. Set 3 was advertised for sale in *The Glasgow Courier* for Tuesday 3 Sep. 1799. It was probably published simultaneously with Set 4, together with which it makes up the second volume of Thomson's *Original Scotish Airs* as originally planned. In addition to the original items already noted, it also contains (p. 53) " O wat ye wha's in yon Town," a song that had previously been published in § 8*e* (1796 Edinburgh=Johnson) and in § 32*b* (1797 Glasgow=Brash and Reid, Vol. II), III.

d. [Vol. II,] Set 4, ? [1799]

A select Collection | [*diamond rule*] of [*diamond rule*] | ORIGINAL SCOTISH AIRS | for the Voice. | To each of which are added, | introductory & concluding Symphonies, & | Accompanyments for the Violin & Piano-Forte, | chiefly by | Kozeluch, | and partly by | Pleyel. | With select & characteristic Verses by the most admired Scotish | Poets, adapted to each Air, many of them entirely new by | BURNS. | Also English Verses, in Addition to such of the Songs as are written | in the Scotish Dialect. | [*diamond rule*] | Price 10! 6ᵈ Entered at Stationers Hall. 4th Set | [*diamond rule*] | London, printed & sold by Preston & Son, | at their Wholesale Warehouses, N.° 97, Strand. | Sold also by the Proprietor G. THOMSON, Edinburgh. [*engraved throughout*]

Format and Signatures. As Sets 1, 2 and 3.

Contents. Pp. viii+76-100 : arranged as Sets 1, 2 and 3.

Original Material :

Comment. The Preface to Set 4 is identical with the Preface to Set 3, which together make the second volume of Thomson's *Original Scotish Airs*. It was probably published simultaneously with Set 3.⁹⁴

In addition to the original items already noted, Set 4 contains : p. 85, " The Gloomy Night," originally published in § 2 (1787 Edinburgh) ; p. 89, " O my Love's like a Red, Red Rose," originally published in § 27 (1793 Edinburgh=Urbani ; p. 16 has a note about this song, " From an old Ms. in the editor's possession ") ; p. 93, " Now westlin winds, and Sportsmen's Guns," previously published as " Song, composed in August," in § 1 (1786 Kilmarnock).

e. [Vol. III, 1801]

FIFTY | SCOTTISH SONGS, | with | Symphonies & Accompaniments, | wholly by | Haydn. | [*double rule*] | Vol. III. | [*double*

⁹⁴ Cp. *The Glasgow Courier*, 3 Sep. 1799.

rule] | [*vignette*: *lyre, horn, book, and leaves*] | Edinburgh: | [*double rule*] | Printed for G. THOMSON, York-Place, | by J. Moir. [*ornament*] | 1802. [*second engraved title-page*]

Format. Folio.

Signatures. None ; engraved and printed.

Contents. Pp. viii+50 : [i], Title-page ; [ii], blank ; [iii], Table of Contents ; [iv], blank ; [v]-[viii], Preface ; [1 *recto*], blank ; 1 [*verso*]-50 [*recto*], Text ; [50] [*verso*], blank.

Comment. Most editors of Burns's works have called this publication Vol. III of Thomson's *Original Scotish Airs*, but I am not convinced that Thomson originally planned it as part of that work. First, it is entitled *Fifty Scottish Songs*. Secondly, it comprises 50 pp., and, unlike Sets 1-4 of the *Original Scotish Airs*, is not divided into two parts of 25 pp. each. Thirdly, instead of following on from the end of Set 4, and beginning from (inclusive) p. 101, the pagination runs from p. 1 to p. 50 ; while Vol. IV, Pt. 1, the next in the series, *does* run from, including, p. 101 to, including, p. 150. (It is interesting to note here that the t.p. of Vol. IV, Pt. 1, in D.C. is numbered, presumably in Thomson's hand, " 3.")

This volume contains a frontispiece (" The Soldier's Return," engraved by Joseph Thomson), and a Preface dated Dec. 1801. Though the copies in D.C., Lin. and N.L.S. are the only ones I have seen in this condition, the volume seems to have been issued with both an engraved and a printed title-page.

It contains several songs of which the words had already been printed in § 50 (1800 Liverpool=Currie), viz. : p. 2, " Where are the joys " ; p. 11, " Long, long the Night " (according to Thomson, the first stanza, however, is not by Burns) ; p. 15, " O bonie was yon rosy Briar " ; p. 16, O Logan sweetly dids't thou glide " ; p. 21, " Lassie wi' the lintwhite Locks."

f. VOL. IV [Pt. 1, 1803]

A | select Collection of | ORIGINAL SCOTTISH AIRS, | for the Voice | with introductory & concluding Symphonies | & Accompaniments for the | Piano Forte, Violin & Violoncello, | by | Haydn, | with | select & characteristic Verses both Scottish and English | adapted to the Airs, including upwards of | one hundred new Songs by | BURNS. | Price of each Volume, the Voice & Piano Forte, one Guinea. | The Violin & Viol? Parts separate 6. Sh. | [*vignette*: *The Genius of Caledonia decorating an Urn on which is a bas-relief of the head of Burns by P. Thomson after*

Stothard] | Now see where Caledonias Genius mourns | And plants the holly round the tomb of Burns | [*diamond rule*] | Volume [4] Ent^d at Stationers Hall. | London, printed & sold by T. Preston, 97, Strand. | Sold also by G. THOMSON the Editor & Proprietor Edinburgh. [*engraved throughout*]

Format. Folio ; 36·8×27·4 cm., trimmed, in original boards.

Signatures. A-N2, engraved and printed alternate leaves. Only the printed leaves are signed.

Contents. Pp. [iv]+101-50 : [i], Title-page ; [ii], blank ; [iii], Index to the Airs ; [iv], Index to the Poetry ; [101 *recto*], blank ; 101 [*verso*]-150 [*verso*], Text.

Comment. Issued in gray paper boards, with, between pp. [ii] and [iii], an engraving (" The Soldier's Return "). Though this follows immediately after Vol. III, the pages are numbered from (inclusive) p. 101 to (inclusive) p. 150. This pagination follows on from Set 4, and is continued in Vol. IV, Pt. 2. However, at this point Thomson seems to have changed his mind again (cp. Vol. III) and included Vol. III as part of the whole series in spite of the fact that it does not follow the pagination of the rest of the series. On p. 150 of Vol. IV appears the date 1803.

g. VOL. IV [Pt. 2, 1805]

Title-page. Identical with t.p. of Vol. IV, Pt. I, except for part-number.

Format. Folio ; 36·6×28·6 cm., trimmed, in original boards.

Signatures. None

Contents. Pp. [iv]+151-200+8 : [i], Title-page ; [ii], blank ; [iii-iv], Advertisement ; [151 *recto*], blank ; 151 [*verso*]-200 [*verso*], Text ; [1-2], Index to the Airs ; [3]-[7], Glossary of the Scottish Words ; [8], blank.

Comment. Issued in gray paper boards, with frontispiece (portrait of R.B., engraved by P. Thomson). On p. 200 appears the date 1805. This part part contains several songs of which the words had already appeared in § 50 (1800 Liverpool=Currie), viz. : p. 152, " There was a Lass, and she was fair " ; p. 154, " Behold the Hour " ; p. 156, " O Lassie, are thou sleeping yet " ; p. 156, " Forlorn my Love "; p. 157, " Sleep'st thou, or wak'st thou "; p. 160, " O Philly, happy be that day " ; p. 161, " How can my poor Heart be glad " ; p. 163, " The Honest Man, the best of Men " ; and p. 195, " When o'er the Hill the Eastern Star."

h. VOL. V [1818]

A select Collection of | ORIGINAL SCOTTISH AIRS | with introductory & concluding Symphonies | & accompaniments for the | Piano Forte, Violin & Violoncello | by | Haydn & Beethoven. | With select Verses adapted to the Airs, including upwards of | one hundred new Songs by | BURNS, | together with his celebrated Poem of | The Jolly Beggars | set to Music by | Henry R. Bishop. | Price of each Volume, the Voice & Piano Forte one Guinea.—The Violin & Viol.º parts separate 6 Sh. | [*vignette*: *a shepherd*] | My vows & sighs like silent air | Unheeded never move her ! | Vol. 5.   Ent.ᵈ at Stationers Hall. | London, printed & sold by Preston, 97, Strand, and by G. THOMSON the Editor and Proprietor Edinburgh.   [*engraved throughout*]

Format.   Folio ;   40 × 28·5 cm., trimmed, in original boards.

Signatures.   π2 ;   A-G2 ;   [H1] ;   [I-K2] ;   [L1].

Contents.   Pp. [ii] + 4 + 201-231 + 30 + [6] :   [i], Title-page ;   [ii], blank ; [1]-2, Advertisement ;   [3-4], Index ;   201 [double page]-30 [*recto*], Text of Songs ;   [231], blank ;   [1], Title-page ;   [2], Preface ;   [3]-30, Text and music of the Jolly Beggars ;   [1-5], Glossary ;   [6], blank.

Comment.   In 1803 Thomson began bringing out a new edition of the first four volumes of the *Original Scottish Airs* ; and having collected enough extra material, he added this fifth volume, uniform with the other four.   At the end of the Advertisement appears the date June 1818.

George Thomson (1757-1851) was the son of Robert Thomson, a schoolmaster at Limekilns, Fife.   His family eventually moved to Edinburgh, where he was apprenticed to the law.   Through the influence of John Home, the author of *Douglas*, he entered the Board of Trustees for the Encouragement of Manufactures in Scotland as a junior clerk, in 1780.   Soon afterwards, he became principal clerk, a position which he retained until 1839.   In 1781 he married the daughter of a Lieutenant Miller, of the 50th Regiment, by whom he had two sons and six daughters.[95] According to Grove,

> His place in musical history is that of the most enthusiastic, persevering and successful collector of the melodies of Scotland, Wales and Ireland, a work begun in his youth and continued for forty years or more.[96]

[95] *D.N.B.*, XIX.722.

[96] *Grove's Dictionary of Music and Musicians*, 3rd edn., v.322-4.

Though Thomson had seen Burns in Edinburgh during the winter of 1786-7, he never met him personally.[97] He first began corresponding with the poet in Sept. 1792, asking him for help with the great publishing venture he had begun. Thomson had planned to collect and edit all the Scottish songs he could find, but the task proved to be so great that he had to call on Burns for help in revising old songs and providing words for many of the tunes.[98] Burns's reputation as a writer and reviser of songs had already been made through Johnson's *Musical Museum*, and it was only natural that Thomson should turn to the foremost poet in Scotland for help with his venture. Although Burns was in need of money at this time, he absolutely refused to take anything for his labours, as he considered it beneath his dignity to accept any remuneration for what he considered to be a duty of love and patriotism.[99]

29. 1794 Edinburgh
a. VOL. I

POEMS, | CHIEFLY IN THE | SCOTTISH DIALECT. | By | ROBERT BURNS. | [*double rule*] | In two Volumes. | [*double rule*] | A new Edition, considerably enlarged. | [*double rule*] | Vol. I. | Edinburgh: | Printed for T. Cadell, London, and William | Creech, Edinburgh. | [*broken rule*] | M DCC XCIV.

Half-title

[*double rule*] | POEMS | CHIEFLY IN THE | SCOTTISH DIALECT. | [*double rule*]

Format. 12mo ; 18·7 × 11·7 cm., trimmed, in contemporary calf.
Signatures. π6 ; A-K12. The first six leaves of each sheet are signed.
Contents. Pp. xii+238 : [i], Half-title ; [ii], Registration ; [iii], Title-page ; [iv], blank ; [v]-viii, Dedication to the Caledonian Hunt ; [ix]-xi, Table of Contents ; [xii], blank ; [1]-237, Text ; [238], blank ; one blank leaf.

b. VOL. II
Format. As Vol. I.

Signatures. π2 ; A-L12 ; M10.

[97] Cp. J. Cuthbert Hadden, *George Thomson*, London, 1898, 135-6.
[98] Snyder, p. 411.   [99] *Letters*, II.123.

Contents. Pp. [iv]+284 : [i], Half-title ; [ii], blank ; [iii], Title-page ; [iv], Registration ; [1]-283, Text and Glossary ; [284], blank.

Comment. A reprint, but with additional errors, of § 23 (1793 Edinburgh). Issued in boards.

30. 1795

AN | ADDRESS | TO THE | DEIL. | By ROBERT BURNS. | With the | Answer. | By John Lauderdale, | Near Wigton. [*diamond rule*] | Printed in the Year 1795.

Format. 8vo, half-sheet ; 17·8 × 10·8 cm., trimmed, unbound.

Contents. Pp. 8 : [1], Title-page ; [2]-8, Text.

Comment. A chapbook. The " Address to the Deil " appears on pp. [2]-5, reprinted from § 1 (1786 Kilmarnock).

31. 1795-6

During the years 1795-6, Burns became involved in politics in and about Dumfries. Of the four political ballads that he wrote during this period three, perhaps four, were first published as broadsides, and are as follows:

a. " Wham will we send to London Town." There is a copy of this very rare broadside in B.M.

b. " Fy, let us a' to K[irkcudbright]." Copies in B.C., B.M., and E.U.L.

c. " Wha will buy my Troggin ? " Copies in the library at Abbotsford and in B.C.

d. " Twas in the Seventeen Hunder' Year." This makes its first appearance in any regular edition in § 365 (1834-36 Glasgow =Hogg and Motherwell), 1.312. I have not seen a copy of the original.

J. C. Ewing has reproduced *a*, *b*, and *c* in his *Bibliography of Robert Burns. 1759-1796.* Edinburgh (privately printed) 1909 [reproduced from the Edinburgh Bibliographical Society].

32. ?1795-8 Glasgow

a. VOL. I (1795[6])

POETRY: | ORIGINAL AND SELECTED. | [*ornament*] | " The Muse, by fate's eternal plan, design'd | " To light, exalt, and harmonize the mind ; | " To bid kind pity melt, just anger glow; | " To kindle joy, or prompt the sighs of wo; | " To shake with horror, rack with tender smart. | " And touch the finest strings that rend the heart." | Blacklock. | [*ornament*] | Glasgow: | Printed for and sold by | BRASH & REID.

Format. 8vo, in half-sheets ; 14·6×8·6 cm., trimmed and rebound.

Contents. Supplementary engraved title-page ; [1], Title-page ; [2] blank ; [3], Preface ; [4], blank ; [5]-8, Table of Contents ; twenty-four pamphlets of 8 pp. each.

Comment. This is the first volume of Brash and Reid's collected pamphlets. The pamphlets were issued, stabbed, in 8vo, half-sheets, consisting of four leaves, eight pages, each. When the first twenty-four of them had been issued, they were collected and bound up into one volume with the above title-page. The supplementary engraved title-page has a large illustration of the Muse of Poetry sitting beside a bust of Burns, engraved by R. Scott. The pamphlets probably began being published late in 1795 or early in 1796 for by 19 Jul. 1796, at latest,[1] the first twenty-four had been published, bound up together, and issued in this volume.

Only four of these twenty-four pamphlets contain poems by Burns, viz. :

III. Tam o' Shanter
IV. The Soldier's Return
XIII. John Anderson, my Jo
XXIII. Here awa', there awa', wandering Willie
Behind yon Hills where Lugar flows

b. VOL. II [1797]

POETRY; | ORIGINAL AND SELECTED. | [*ornament*] | The Poet's eye, in a fine frenzy rolling, | Doth glance from heaven to earth, from earth to heaven; | And as imagination bodies forth | The forms of things unknown, the Poet's pen | Turns them to shape, and gives to airy nothing | A local habitation, and a name. | Shakespeare. | [*ornament*] | Glasgow: Printed for and sold by BRASH & REID.

Format. 8vo, in half-sheets ; 14·3×8·6 cm., trimmed and rebound.

---

[1] Cp. *The Glasgow Courier*, 19 Jul. 1796. (But No. xxiv contains an account of the death and burial of Burns and he died on 21 Jul.!)

Contents. As Vol. I.

Comment. Vol. II contains twenty-four pamphlets, issued in the same way as those in Vol. I, and was advertised for sale in *The Glasgow Courier* for 4 Mar. 1797.

Six of these twenty-four pamphlets contain material by or relative to Burns, viz. :

    I. Monody on the Death of Robert Burns
   II. [An account of R.B.'s interment]
       Verses to Burns's Memory [3 poems]
       Epitaph for Robert Burns, written by himself [" Is there a whim-inspired fool . . . ? "]
       A Prayer in the Prospect of Death
  III. O wat ye wha's in yon Town
       Open the Door to me, Oh !
  IV. An Honest Man the Best o' Men [This is the song " Is there for honest poverty," with the first and second stanzas interposed. According to H. & H.,[2] it first appeared in §50 (1800 Liverpool=Currie), but it had previously been published in *The Glasgow Magazine* for Aug. 1795.]
   V. Hear ! Land o' Cakes
  VI. Braw Lads on Yarrow Braes
       From thee, Eliza, I must go

c. Vol III [?1798]

POETRY; | ORIGINAL AND SELECTED. | [*diamond rule*] | With wayworn feet a Pilgrim woe begone | Life's upward road I journied many a day, | And hymning many a sad yet soothing lay | Beguil'd my wandering with the charms of song. | Lonely my heart and rugged was my way, | Yet often pluck'd I as I pass'd along | The wild and simple flowers of Poesy. | —and scorn not thou | The humble offering— | Southey. [*diamond rule*] | Glasgow: | Printed for and sold by | BRASH & REID.

Format and *Contents.* As Vols. I and II.

Comment. Contains twenty-four pamphlets, issued in the same way as those in Vols I and II. The sixth of these pamphlets contains a poem entitled " Elegy on the Thirty-first of December," and the seventh a poem entitled " New Year's Day." Since Vol. II was published in Mar. 1797 and Vol. IV in Dec.1798, these titles presumably refer to 31 Dec. 1797 and 1 Jan. 1798, and Vol. III thus seems to have been issued in 1798.

[2] H. & H., III.489.

Four of the twenty-four pamphlets included in Vol. III contain material by or relating to Burns, viz. :

   v. Patie and Ralph : An Elegiac Pastoral on the Death of Robert Burns. By Robert Lochore, Author of Margaret and the Minister, a Morning Walk, &c.
   xii. The Lament of the lovely Lass of Inverness, for the bloody Battle of Drumossie Muir : a favourite Scots Song. By Robert Burns the Ayrshire Poet.
   xiii. Caledonia : a favourite Scots Song. According to H. & H.,[3] this first appeared in § 50 (1800 Liverpool = Currie).
   xiv. Colin : A Pastoral Elegy, to the Memory of Robert Burns the Ayrshire Poet.

d. Vol. IV [?1798]

POETRY; | ORIGINAL AND SELECTED. | [*ornamented rule*] | The Bard the Muse's laurel justly shares, | A Poet he, and touch'd with Heaven's own fire ; | Who with bold rage, or solemn pomp of sounds, | Inflames, exalts, and ravishes the soul : | Now tender, plaintive, sweet almost to pain, | In love dissolves you ; now in sprightly strains | Breathes a gay rapture thro' your thrilling breast ; | Or melts the heart with airs divinely sad ; | Or wakes to horror the tremendous strings. | Armstrong. | [*ornamented rule*] | Glasgow : | printed and sold by | Brash & Reid.

Format and Contents. As Vols. I, II, and III.

   Four of the twenty-four pamphlets included in Vol. IV contain material by Burns, viz. :

   vi. Tam Glen
      Gin a Body meet a Body
   xi. The Speech of King Robert the Bruce (" Scots wha hae . . .")
   xxii. " Now westlin winds and slaught'ring guns."
   xxiii. The Tooth-Ache
      " Ye banks and braes of Bonnie Doon."
Was probably published in Dec. 1798.

The Brash and Reid pamphlets are very scarce, but no Glasgow library is considered complete without a set of them. They were published for Brash and Reid, two Glasgow publishers; two of them bear the imprint of Chapman and Lang, printers, but the rest have no printer's imprint.

[3] H. & H., iv.94.

33. 1796 Glasgow

AN | UNCO MOURNFU | TALE. | [*diamond rule*] | To which is added, | The Antiquarian. | [*diamond rule*] | By | [*rule*] ROBERT BURNS. | [*diamond rule*] | Glasgow: | Printed for and sold by STEWART & MEIKLE, Booksellers, | Trongate. | 1796.

Format. 8vo, half-sheet ; 15·8 × 9·8 cm., trimmed.

Contents. Pp. 8 : [1], Title-page ; [2]-8, Text.

Original Material :

An unco Mournfu' Tale	*p.* [2]
The Antiquarian [" Hear Land o' Cakes . . ."][4]	6

Comment. Issued stabbed.

This is the first of the pamphlets, containing much important original work of Burns, which were printed for Stewart and Meikle. See also §§ 39-45.

Thomas Stewart was a nephew of Burns's friend John Richmond,[5] and it was from him that he obtained manuscript copies of the poems.

34. 1797 Edinburgh

a. Vol. I

POEMS, | CHIEFLY IN THE | SCOTTISH DIALECT. | By | ROBERT BURNS. | [*rule*] | In two Volumes. | [*rule*] | [*double rule*] | A new Edition, considerably enlarged. | [*double rule*] | Vol. I. | Edinburgh: | Printed for T. Cadell jun. and W. Davies, London; | and William Creech, Edinburgh. | [*broken rule*] | M DCC XCVII.

Half-title

[*double rule*] | POEMS | CHIEFLY IN THE | SCOTTISH DIALECT. | [*double rule*]

Format. 8vo ; 18·7 × 11·8 cm., trimmed, in contemporary calf.

Signatures. [a2] ; b4 ; A-P8. Except leaves [F4, I3, 4] which are unsigned, the first four leaves of each sheet are signed.

---

[4] Originally published in *The Edinburgh Evening Courant*, 27 Aug. 1789.
[5] H. & H., ii.306.

Contents. Pp. xii+238 : [i], Half-title ; [ii], Registration ; [iii], Title-page ; [iv], blank ; [v]-viii, Dedication to the Caledonian Hunt ; [ix]-xii, Table of Contents ; [1]-237, Text ; [238], blank ; one blank leaf.

b. VOL. II

Format. As Vol. I.

Signatures. π2 ; A-S8.

Contents. Pp. [iv]+288 : [i], Half-title ; [ii], Registration ; [iii], Title-page ; [iv], blank ; [1]-287, Text and Glossary ; [288], blank.

Comment. A reprint of § 29 (1794 Edinburgh). Issued in boards. Vol. I has frontispiece (portrait of R.B., after Nasmyth, engraved by Beugo). Vol. II has pp. [106] and [242] numbered respectively, 206 and 232.

35. 1798 Edinburgh

a. VOL. I

POEMS, | CHIEFLY IN THE | SCOTTISH DIALECT. | By | ROBERT BURNS. | [*rule*] | In two Volumes. | [*rule*] | [*double rule*] | A new Edition, considerably enlarged. | [*double rule*] | Vol. I | Edinburgh: | Printed for T. Cadell jun. and W. Davies, London; | and William Creech, Edinburgh. | [*broken rule*] | MDCCXCVIII.

Half-title

[*double rule*] | POEMS, | CHIEFLY IN THE | SCOTTISH DIALECT. | [*double rule*]

Format. 8vo ; 20·8 × 12·5 cm., trimmed, in contemporary calf.

Signatures. [a2] ; b4 ; A-P8. The first four leaves of each sheet are signed.

Contents. Pp. xii+238 : [i], Half-title ; [ii], Registration ; [iii], Title-page ; [iv], blank ; [v]-viii, Dedication to the Caledonian Hunt ; [ix]-xii, Table of Contents ; [1]-237, Text ; [238], blank ; one blank leaf.

b. VOL. II

Format. As Vol. I.

Signatures. π2 ; A-S8.

Contents.   Pp. [iv]+288 : [i], Half-title ; [ii], Registration ; [iii], Title-page ; [iv], blank ; [1]-287, Text and Glossary ; [288], blank.

Comment.   A page-by-page reprint of § 34 (1797 Edinburgh). Vol. I. has frontispiece (portrait of R.B., after Nasmyth, engraved by Beugo).

36. 1798 Philadelphia

POEMS, | CHIEFLY IN THE | SCOTTISH DIALECT. | By | ROBERT BURNS. | (From the latest European Edition) | [*diamond rule*] | Two Volumes in one. | [*diamond rule*] | Philadelphia: | Printed by Patterson & Cochran, | No. 148, South Fourth-Street. | 1798.

Format.   12mo, in half-sheets ;   16·7 × 10·2 cm., trimmed, in contemporary calf.

Signatures.   A4 ; B-Aa6 [including the signature " W "] ; Bb4.

Contents.   Pp. viii+[9]-304 :   [i], Title-page ;   [ii], blank ;   [iii]-v, Dedication to the Caledonian Hunt ;   vi-viii, Table of Contents ; [9]-302, Text and Glossary ;   one blank leaf.

Comment.   Reprint (?) of § 34 (1797 Edinburgh).

37. 1799 Edinburgh

ELEGY | ON | THE YEAR EIGHTY-EIGHT, | By ROBERT BURNS. | [*short broken line above short rule*] | Elegy | on Puddin' Lizzie | [*short broken line above short rule*] | Colin Clout | A Pastoral, | &c. &c. | [*double rule*] | " Love, that raises sic a clamour, | " Driving lads and lassies mad, | " Wae's my heart ! had coost his glamour, | " O'er poor Colin, Luckless lad ! " | [*double rule*] | Edinburgh: | Printed by David Willison, Craig's Close, | for GEORGE GRAY, Bookseller, No 3 | North Bridge Street. | 1799.

Format.   8vo ;   14·6 × 8·7 cm.

Contents.   Pp. 16.

Original Material :

Comment. One of the rarest of Burnsian bibliographical items. The above was collated from photostats sent me by Mr Davidson Cook. I have *not* seen a copy.

The " Elegy " and the lines " Written at Dalnacardoch " had previously appeared in *The Edinburgh Courant* for 10 Jan. 1790 and 2 Jul. 1792 respectively; and the lines " Written . . . at Carron " had previously appeared in *The Edinburgh Evening Courant* for 5 Oct. 1789. George Gray, the publisher of this tract, who ran a bookshop and circulating library at No. 3 North Bridge, Edinburgh,[6] appears to have re-discovered the above poems in the newspapers and published them.[7]

38. [1799] Glasgow

THE POLYHYMNIA——N? 18. | [*double rule*] | Containing | Eliza, | The Bonny Lass of Ballochmyle, | By ROBERT BURNS, | Song, | By a Lady, | and | The Bonny Lass of Cree. | [*ornament*] | While others mingle with the giddy crowd, | And prove the tools or shadows of the proud; | Be't mine, through lone romantic dells to stray | By winding streams, and muse the time away. | [*vignette of two doves on branches*] | Glasgow: | Printed for and sold by | John Murdoch, | Bookseller and Stationer, Trongate.

Format. 8vo, half-sheet ; 15·1 × 9·9 cm., trimmed.

Contents. Pp. 8 : [1], Title-page ; [2]-8, Text.

Original Material :
The Lass of Ballochmyle [but cp. also § 37 n. 7].   *p.* 5

Comment. Issued stabbed.

This pamphlet was gathered with nineteen others, bound up in one volume with the title-page:

> THE | POLYHYMNIA: | Being a | Collection | of | Poetry, original and selected. | [*diamond rule*] | By a | Society of Gentlemen. | [*diamond rule*] | With tales of Love to entertain the Fair, | To soften wrath, and smooth the brow of care, | To bid the generous tear of pity flow,

---

[6] *Edinburgh and Leith Directory*, Thomas Aitchison, [Edinburgh] 1800, p. 110.
[7] " Sonnets from *The Robbers*, by Alex Thomson, Esq. The Pretender's Soliloquy, Bruce's Address, and The Lass of Ballochmyle, by Burns. The Minstrel, &c. &c., &c. Edinburgh. George Gray. [F'cap 8vo.] 1799 No. II of Gray's ' Tracts.' " Angus, p. 115.

| And soothe the wretch till he forget his wo, | The task
is ours.— | [*vignette of two doves on branches*] | Glasgow: |
Printed for and sold by | John Murdoch, | Bookseller and
Stationer, Trongate. [*second engraved t.p.*]

and issued by 6 Jul. 1799, on which date it was advertised in
The Glasgow Courier.[8] This volume contains a preface in which
the editors promise that " Polyhymnia will be resumed next
winter." This means, presumably, that publication of the
earlier pamphlets in the series had been going on during the
winter 1798-9; and this particular one, No. 18, was probably
published some time during May or June 1799. Issued in
marbled wrappers with label on front wrapper.

39. [1799] Glasgow

THE | JOLLY BEGGARS: | a Cantata. | [*ornament*] | By |
ROBERT BURNS. | [*ornament*] | Here's to budgets, bags, and
wallets ! | Here's to all the wandering train ! | Here's our ragged
brats and callets ! | One and all cry out, Amen ! [*vignette: flowers,
Pan-pipes, horn and violin*] | Glasgow: | Printed for and sold by |
STEWART & MEIKLE.

Format. 8vo ; 15·9 × 8·6 cm., trimmed.

Contents. Pp. 16 : [1], Title-page ; [2], blank ; [3]-15, Text ; [16],
Advertisement.

Original Material :
The Jolly Beggars   *p.* [3]

Comment. Issue stabbed.

This was published on 13 Jul. 1799.[9] It is the first edition of *The
Jolly Beggars*, but it is not complete, inasmuch as the " Merry
Andrew " episode[10] is left out. It is also the second of the Stewart
and Meikle tracts, and the following advertisement appears at
the end of it:

> On Saturday next will be published, *The Kirk's Alarm*,
> A Letter to a Taylor, and some other poems, by Robert
> Burns. Stewart and Meikle intend publishing Original
> and Selected Poetical pieces of merit, at One Penny and
> Twopence each—Those already published are . . .

---

[8] Cp. *B. Chr.*, IX (1900) 125.   [9] Cp. *Glasgow Courier* for 11 Jul. 1799.
[10] H. & H., II.306-7. Cp. also John C. Weston, " The Text of Burns' ' The
Jolly Beggars '," in *Studies in Bibliography*, XIII (1960), 239-48.

Then follows a list of six, including:

2. An Unco Mournfu Tale—By Robert Burns, price 1d.

For *An unco mournfu' Tale*, the first of the Stewart and Meikle
tracts containing material by Burns, see above, § 33 (1796
Glasgow); and for *The Kirk's Alarm*, see next item.

40. [1799] Glasgow

THE | KIRK'S ALARM: | a Satire. | A Letter to a Taylor, | The
Deil's awa' wi' the Exciseman, | and An | unco mournfu' Tale |
&c. &c. | [*ornament*] | By ROBERT BURNS, | The Ayrshire
Poet. | [*diamond rule*] | Orthodox, orthodox, wha believe in John
Knox, | Let me sound an alarm to your conscience; | There's a
heretic blast has been blawn i' the wast, | That what is no
sense, must be nonsense. | [*vignette: horn, lyre and palm-leaf*] |
Glasgow: | Printed for and sold by | STEWART & MEIKLE.

Format. 8vo ; 15·9 × 9·9 cm., trimmed.

Contents. Pp. 16 : [1], Title-page ; [2]-15, Text ; [16], Advertisement.

Original Material :
     Robert Burns's Answer ["What ails ye now, ye lousy
       bitch . . ."]   *p.* 7
     Epitaph on John Dove ["Here lies Johnny Pidgeon . . ."]   10

Comment. Issued stabbed.

This is the third of the Stewart and Meikle tracts, and was
probably published on 20 Jul. 1799.[11] The advertisement on
p. [16] reads:

> And on Saturday next, will be published, Price Two-
> pence, Holy Willy's Prayer, A Letter to John Goudie,
> and some other small Pieces, by Robert Burns, never
> before published.

41. [1799] Glasgow

HOLY WILLIE'S PRAYER, | Letter to John Goudie, | Kil-
marnock, | and | Six favourite Songs, | viz. | Duncan Gray, | The
Lass that made the Bed to me, | A Man's a Man for a' that,
| Of a' the Airt's the Win' can blaw, | Now westlin Winds, | I

---

[11] Cp. notice at the end of *The Jolly Beggars*, § 39 [1799 Glasgow].

gaed a waefu' Gate Yestreen. | [*ornament*] | By ROBERT BURNS,
| the Ayrshire Poet. | [*vignette*: *a horn, lyre, and palm-leaf*] | Glasgow:
| Printed for and sold by | STEWART & MEIKLE.

Format. 8vo ; 15·9×9·9 cm., trimmed.

Contents. Pp. 16 : [1], Title-page ; [2]-16, Text.

Original Material :
    O Goudie Terror o' the Whigs   *p.* 6
    O thou whom Poetry abhors   8

Comment. Issue stabbed.

This is the fourth of the Stewart and Meikle pamphlets containing
material by Burns; it was probably published on 10 Aug. 1799.[12]
The following advertisement appears on p. 16 *ad fin.*:

> Of Stewart and Meikle may be had, The Jolly Beggars;
> or Tatterdemalions: a cantata. By Robert Burns, price
> 2d. The Kirk's Alarm, etc. . . . and on Saturday 17
> August will be published, The Dominie Deposed; with
> the sequel by William Forbes, A.M.

42. [1799] Glasgow

Extempore Verses | ON | DINING WITH LORD DAER, |
Accompanied with a Prose Letter to a Friend. | By ROBERT
BURNS, | The Ayrshire Poet. | [*ornament*] | And The | Dominie
depos'd; | or, | Some Reflections | on his | Intrigue with a Young
Lass. | By William Forbes, A.M. | late School-master at Peter-
coulter. | [*ornament*] | For had I right the gully guided, | An wi'
a wife mysel' provided, | To keep me frae that, wae betide it, |
That's kent to a', | I'd stay'd at hame, or near beside it; | Now
that's awa'. | [*vignette*: *horn, lyre, and palm-leaf*] | Glasgow: |
Printed for and sold by STEWART & MEIKLE.

Format. 8vo ; 15·9×9·9 cm., trimmed.

Contents. Pp. 16 ; [1], Title-page ; [2]-16, Text.

---

12 Cp. notice at the end of *The Kirk's Alarm*, § 40 (1799 Glasgow).

Original Material :
   On Dining with Lord Daer   *p.* [2]
   Letter [to Dr. John Mackenzie, Oct. 1786],[13] beginning
     "I never spent an afternoon among great folks . . ."   4
Comment. Issued stabbed.

This pamphlet, the fifth of the Stewart and Meikle tracts which contained material by Burns, was probably published on Sat. 17 Aug. 1799, the date already announced in the advertisement at the end of § 41 (1799 Glasgow).

43. [1799] Glasgow

THE | INVENTORY. | By ROBERT BURNS, | The Ayrshire Poet. | [*ornament*] | The | Dominie depos'd. | (Concluded) | Lines in the Palace of Scone, | The Comforts of Marriage, | and The | Plundered Lark, &c. | [*ornament*] | Thus, to his fatal cost, hath Cinna found, | That wedlock's holy joys are just a sound; | That peace will end, where happiness begins, | And wives are the grand scourge of human sins. | [*vignette*: *flowers, Pan-pipes, horn and violin*] | Glasgow, | Printed by Chapman and Lang, | for STEWART & MEIKLE.

Variant

. . . Lang, Trongate, | for . . .

Format. 8vo ; 15·9 × 9·9 cm., trimmed.

Contents. Pp. 16 : [1], Title-page ; [2]-16, Text.

Original Material :
   The Inventory   *p.* [2]

This pamphlet, the sixth of Stewart and Meikle's tracts which contained material by Burns, was probably published on 24 Aug. 1799, the date already announced in the advertisement at the end of § 41 (1799 Glasgow).

44. [1799] Glasgow

THE | HENPECK'D HUSBAND, | Address to his Illegitimate Child, | An Epigram, | and | On a Bank of Flowers. | [*diamond rule*] | By ROBERT BURNS, | The Ayrshire Poet. | [*ornament*] | To which are added, | Stanzas to the Memory of Burns, | The

[13] *Letters*, I.146. Ferguson says that this first appears in § 112 (1808 London= Cromek).

Wounded Hussar, | and | The Galley Slave, &c. &c. | [*vignette*: *flowers, Pan-pipes, horn, and violin*] | Glasgow, | Printed by Chapman & Lang, | for STEWART & MEIKLE.

Format. 8vo ; 15·9×9·9 cm., trimmed.

Contents. Pp. 16 : [1], Title-page ; 2-16, Text.

Original Material :
The Henpeck'd Husband	*p.* 2
Burns's Address to His Illegitimate Child	2
Highland Pride [first version]	4

Comment. Issued stabbed.

This pamphlet, the seventh of the Stewart and Meikle tracts which contained material by Burns, was probably published a week after § 43 [1799 Glasgow,] *i.e.* on 31 Aug. 1799.

45. [1799] Glasgow

THE | PASSAGE OF MOUNT ST. GOTHARD, | by the Duchess of Devonshire. | [*diamond rule*] | To which are added, | The Chevalier's Lament, | The Lass of Gowrie, | Song on Miss Peggy K——, | Shelah O'Neil, | Last May a Braw Wooer, | The Banks of the Devon. | Epitaph on a Wag, | by | Robert Burns, | The Ayrshire Poet. | and Corin's Professions, | by P. Pindar, Esq. | &c. &c. | [*vignette*: *flowers, Pan-pipes, violin and horn*] | Glasgow: | Printed by Chapman & Lang, | for STEWART & MEIKLE.

Format. 8vo ; 15·9×9·9 cm., trimmed.

Contents. Pp. 16 : [1], Title-page ; [2]-16, Text.

Original Material :
The Small Birds rejoice [which, according to H. & H., IV. 92, also appeared in § 37 (1799 Edinburgh)]	*p.* 7
Upon a Simmer Afternoon [not included in H. & H. and probably not by Burns]	8

Comment. Issued stabbed.

This pamphlet, the eighth of Stewart and Meikle's tracts which contained material by Burns, was probably published a week after § 44 ([1799] Glasgow), for on p. 16 it has the following advertisement:

Of Stewart and Meikle may be had, *The Henpecked Husband*, etc. by Robert Burns, price 2d.

The spurious poem " Shelah O'Neil " is herein first attributed to Burns. The pamphlet also contains: p. 9, " Young Peggy blooms," which had previously appeared in § 8a (1787 Edinburgh=Johnson, Vol. I), No. 78; p. 12, " Last May a braw Wooer," which also appeared in § 28c (Sep. 1799 London =Thomson, Set. 3), p. 52; and p. 14, " How pleasant the Banks," which had previously appeared in § 8b (1788 Edinburgh=Johnson, Vol. II, No. 157). The inclusion of so much borrowed material suggests that Stewart and Meikle had, at this time, run out of original items. The Stewart and Meikle tracts were issued, bound, in one volume in 1800, cp. below, § 49 (1800 Glasgow), and were still being re-issued separately and as a volume as late as 1801.

46. 1799 New York

POEMS, | CHIEFLY IN THE | SCOTTISH DIALECT. | [*double rule*] | By ROBERT BURNS. | [*double rule*] | To which are added, | Scots Poems, | selected from the Works of | Robert Ferguson. | [*double rule*] | New-York: | Printed and sold by John Tiebout, | No. 358 Pearl-Street. | [*double rule*] | 1799.

Comment. The rest of the book consists of the sheets of § 11 (1788 New York).

That § 11 (1788 New York) was considered a drug on the American market as early as 1791 is shown by an advertisement which appeared in the *New York Journal and Patriotic Register* for 3, 17, 21, and 28 Feb. and 3 Mar. 1791:

New American Books. *Just published and to be sold cheap* by Robert Hodge . . . Burn's Poems Chiefly in the Scottish dialect.

And Miss Painter notes that an edition which she identifies with § 11 (1788 New York) was advertised for sale at Salem, Mass., on 1 Apr. 1794.[14] It seems that in 1799, eleven years after the first

---

[14] " American Editions of the *Poems* of Burns before 1800," in *The Library*, 4th ser., XII (1932), 453.

New York edition was originally published, copies of it still
remained unsold, and that Tiebout, who had, apparently, bought
the sheets from the McLeans, tried to get rid of them by issuing
them with a new title-page.

47. 1800 Belfast

a. VOL. I

POEMS, | CHIEFLY IN THE | SCOTTISH DIALECT. |
[*double rule*] | By ROBERT BURNS. | [*double rule*] | In two
Volumes. | [*diamond rule*] | Vol. I. | [*double rule*] | Belfast: | Printed
by William Magee. | [*diamond rule*] | 1800

Format. 12mo ; 16·5 × 10·3 cm., trimmed, rebound.

Signatures. A6 ; A[*]-B[*]12 ; B12 ; C8 [-C8] ; D-K12 ; L-O6.
Except leaves [A*2], [A4, signed "A3 "], [B2] and [O3], which are
unsigned, or mis-signed, the whole sheets are signed on the first
five leaves ; the half-sheets on the first three.

Contents. Pp. xii+274 : [i], Title-page ; [ii], blank ; [iii]-vi, Dedica-
tion to the Caledonian Hunt ; vii-x, Extract from *The Lounger*,
No. 97 ; xi-xii, Table of Contents ; [1], " A Memoir . . . by R.
Heron ; " [2], blank ; [3]-274, Text and Glossary.

b. VOL. II

Half-title

[*double rule*] | POEMS, | CHIEFLY | SCOTTISH | [*double
rule*]

Signatures. A-D12. Except leaves [A1,2], [B4] and [B5, signed "B4"],
which are unsigned, or mis-signed, the first five leaves of each
sheet are signed.

Contents. Pp. 96 : [1], Half-title ; [2], blank ; [3], Title-page ; [4],
blank ; [5]-94, Text ; [95-96], Table of Contents to Vol. II.

A page-by-page reprint of § 26 (1793 Belfast) except for the
insertion of the Heron *Memoir* in Vol. I.

48. 1800 Edinburgh

a. VOL. I

POEMS, | CHIEFLY IN THE | SCOTTISH DIALECT. | By |
ROBERT BURNS. | [*rule*] | In two Volumes. | [*rule*] | [*double

rule] | A new Edition, considerably enlarged. | [*double rule*] | Vol. I. | Edinburgh: | Printed by Adam Neill and Co. | For T. Cadell jun. and W. Davies, London; | and W. Creech, Edinburgh. | [*broken double rule*] | 1800.

Variant

. . . Neill & Co. . . .

Half-title

[*double rule*] | POEMS, | CHIEFLY IN THE | SCOTTISH DIALECT. | [*double rule*]

Format. 8vo ; 18·4×11·7 cm., trimmed, in contemporary calf.

Signatures. a2 ; b4 ; A-P8. The first leaf of each half-sheet, and the first four leaves of the whole sheets, are signed.

Contents. Pp. xii+238 : [i], Half-title ; [ii], Registration ; [iii], Title-page ; [iv], blank ; [v]-viii, Dedication to the Caledonian Hunt ; [ix]-xii, Table of Contents ; [1]-237, Text ; [238], blank ; one blank leaf.

b. VOL. II

Format. As Vol. I.

Signatures. π2 ; A-S8.

Contents. Pp. [iv]+288 : [i], Half-title ; [ii], Registration ; [iii], Title-page ; [iv], blank ; 1-287, Text and Glossary ; [288], blank.

Comment. Probably issued in paper boards, cp. § 25, 29 and 34 (1793, 1794, and 1797 Edinburgh).

This is the last of the series of reprints from § 25 (1793 Edinburgh). Oddly enough, though § 25, 29 and 34 all read " skinking," this edition (II.64) reads "stinking."

49. [1800] Glasgow

THE | POETICAL MISCELLANY; | containing | posthumous | Poems, Songs, Epitaphs and Epigrams. | [*ornament*] | By | ROBERT BURNS, | The Ayrshire Poet. | [*diamond rule*] | And several other Poetical Pieces | original and selected. | [*vignette* : *flowers, Pan-pipes, violin, and horn*] | Glasgow, | Printed by Chapman and Lang, | For Stewart & Meikle. | [*ornament*] | 1800.

F

Variant

. . . Epigrams | [*diamond rule*] | By . . . Poet. | [*scrolled rule*] |
And . . . | For Thomas Stewart, | Bookseller and Stationer. |
1800.

Contents. [*recto*], Title-page ; [*verso*], " To the Public. ; " Table of
Contents, covering both sides of one leaf ; seven of the tracts already
published by Stewart and Meikle § 39-45 (1799 Glasgow).

Comment. Issued with frontispiece (engraving, by R. Scott, of satyr
and nymph crowning Burns with a wreath of bays) ; very rare.

This is the form in which §§ 39-45 (1799 Glasgow=Stewart
and Meikle Tracts) were gathered and reissued. It does not
agree with the collations of the original issues, and evidently
was reset and reprinted.

50. 1800 Liverpool
a. VOL. I

THE | WORKS | OF | ROBERT BURNS; | with | an Account
of his Life, | and | a Criticism on his Writings. | To which are
prefixed, | some Observations on the Character and Condition
| of | the Scottish Peasantry. | In four Volumes. | [*diamond rule*] |
Vol. I. | [*vignette: branches encircling Burns's seal*] | Liverpool,
| Printed by J. McCreery, Houghton-Street; | for T. Cadell, jun.
and W. Davies, Strand, London; | and W. Creech, Edinburgh. |
Sold also by Bell and Bradfute, P. Hill, and Manners and Miller,
Edinburgh; | Brash and Reid, and J. Murdoch, Glasgow; J.
Brown, Aberdeen; W. Boyd, | Dumfries; J. Morrison, Perth;
J. Forsyth, Ayr; and by Merritt and | Wright, W. Robinson,
W. Harding, and E. Rushton, Liverpool. | [*double rule*] | 1800.

Half-title

Vol. I. | THE | LIFE | OF | ROBERT BURNS; | with | a
Criticism on his Writings. | To which are prefixed, | some
Observations on | the Scottish Peasantry.

Format. 8vo ; 22·4 × 14·3 cm., untrimmed, in original boards.

Signatures. π2 ; a-b4 ; [A4] ; B-Aa8 ; Bb4 ; [Cc1].

Contents. Pp. xxviii+376+[2] : Title-page ; *verso,* blank ; [i], Half-title ; [ii], blank ; [iii]-xviii, List of Subscribers ; [xix]-xxiii, Dedication to Captain Graham ; [xxiv], Advertisement and List of Errata ; [xxv]-xxvi, Table of Contents ; [1]-31, Prefatory Remarks ; [32], blank ; [33]-336, Life of Burns ; 337, Prefatory note to a poem in memory of Burns ; [338], blank ; 339-44, Poem in memory of Burns * ; [345-76], Appendix ; [375] ''Postscript '' ; [376], blank ; one leaf of addenda.

Original Material :

Letter to Dr. John Moore, 2 Aug. 1787 [1.104]	*p.* 35
Letter to William Burnes, 27 Dec. 1781 [1.4]	101
Letter to Miss Alexander, 18 Nov. 1786 [1.50]	122
Streams that glide in Orient plain	185
Birthday Ode for 31st December 1787	188
In Wood and Wild	208
When [Morine] deceased	210
O once I loved a bonnie lassie	360
Extempore [" O why the deuce . . ."]	362
O leave novels, ye Mauchline belles	363

In his " Life of Burns " Currie quotes (pp. 157-61) from the *Second* [Edinburgh] *Commonplace Book,* and (pp. 163-6) from the *Border Tour.* He also includes Burns's letter to [Robert Ainslie] of 28 June 1787.[15]

Comment. Issued in French gray paper boards, with frontispiece (portrait of R. B., after Nasmyth, engraved by I. Neagle). Twenty large copies on Whatman paper.

b. VOL. II

Half-title

Vol. II. | General | Correspondence; | including | Pieces | of Miscellaneous | Poetry.

Format. As Vol. I.

Signatures. π2 ; a6 ; b4 ; B-Gg8 ; Hh4 ; Ii2.

Contents. Pp. xxviii+476 : [i], Title-page [as Vol. I, except vol. no. and vignette, which consists of a bunch of thistles encircled by a snake] ; [ii], blank ; [iii], Half-title ; [iv], blank ; [v]-x, Advertisement ; [xi]-xxvi, Index to the Letters ; [xxvii], Index to the Poetry ; [xxviii], Errata ; [1]-476, Text and Glossary.

---

15 *Letters,* 1.98.
* By William Roscoe.

Original Material :

Vol. II also contains the following letters :

[16] Refs. are to *Letters* ; dates as given (sometimes erroneously) by Currie.

Ref.	Addresee	Date	
183	Mrs Dunlop	12 Feb. 1788	*p.* 139
205	Mrs Dunlop	7 Mar.	140
213	Mr Cleghorn	31 Mar.	142
219	Mrs Dunlop	28 Apr.	147
220	Prof. D. Stewart	3 May	156
221	Mrs Dunlop	4 May	157
223	Mrs Dunlop	27 May	159
226	Mrs Dunlop	13 Jun.	162
II.62	Mr P. Hill	n.d.	165
I.240	Mrs Dunlop	2 Aug.	170
233	Mrs Dunlop	10 Aug.	174
244	Mrs Dunlop	16 Aug.	177
157	Graham of Fintry	n.d.	181
262	Mr P. Hill	1 Oct.	186
272	Mrs Dunlop	13 Nov.	191
269	[Editor of the *Edinburgh Evening Courant*]	8 Nov.	193
276	Mrs Dunlop	17 Dec.	198
II.84	A young Lady [Miss Deborah Duff Davies]	Dec. 1788	201
I.54	Sir John Whitefoord	1787	204
282	Mrs Dunlop	1 Jan. 1789	208
284	Dr Moore	4 Jan. 1789	211
298	Bishop Geddes	3 Feb.	215
311	Mrs Dunlop	4 Mar 1789	221
326	Rev. P. Carfrae	1789	225
316	Dr Moore	23 Mar.	228
318	Mr Hill	2 Apr.	231
329	Mrs Dunlop	4 Apr.	235
330	Mr Cunningham	4 May	238
338	Mr M'Auley	4 Jun	245
341	Mrs Dunlop	21 Jun.	247
357	[Peter Stuart]	n.d.	260
358	Mrs Dunlop	6 Sep.	263
369	R. Graham	9 Dec.	273
372	Mrs Dunlop	13 Dec.	276
II.1	Mr G. Burns	11 Jan. 1790	285
4	Mrs Dunlop	25 Jan. 1790	288
11	Mr Cunningham	13 Feb.	295
15	Mr Hill	2 Mar.[17]	300
18	Mrs Dunlop	10 Apr.	303
28	Dr Moore	14 Jul.	310
35	Mrs Dunlop	8 Aug.	313
I.243	Mr Cunningham	8 Aug. 1790	315
II.48	Mrs Dunlop	Nov. 1790	321

[17] Completed in § 783 (1877 Edinburgh=Scott Douglas).

Ref.	Addressee	Date	
54	Mr Cunningham	23 Jan. 1791	p. 324
51	Mr Hill	17 Jan.	327
69	A. F. Tytler	n.d.	334
55	Mrs Dunlop	7 Feb. 1790	336
72	Lady W. M. Constable	n.d.	339
25	Mrs Graham	n.d.	340
60	Rev. G. Baird	n.d.	345
57	Dr Moore	28 Feb. 1791	347
56	Rev. A. Alison	14 Feb.	355
64	Mr Cunningham	12 Mar.	357
68	Mrs Dunlop	11 Apr.	360
77	Mr Cunningham	11 Jun.	363
87	Lady E. Cunningham	n.d.	372
99	Mr Ainslie	n.d.	374
164	Miss Davies	n.d.	382
75	Mrs Dunlop	17 Dec. 1791	385
140	Mrs Dunlop	5 Jan. 1792	388
106	Mr Wm. Smellie	22 Jan. 1792	390
150	Mr W. Nicol	20 Feb. 1792	393
236	Mr Cunningham	3 Mar. 1792	396
115	Mrs Dunlop	22 Aug. 1792	399
118	Alex. Cunningham	10 Sep. 1792	403
125	Mrs Dunlop	24 Sep. 1792	410
128	Mrs Dunlop	n.d.	413
135	Mrs Dunlop	6 Dec. 1792	415
153	Miss B**** [Anna Benson]	21 Mar. 1793	420
35	Miss C.—— [Helen Craik]	Aug. 1793	422
222	John M'Murdo	Dec. 1793	425
133	Mrs R——[18] [Maria Riddell]	n.d.	427
131	A Lady	n.d.	429
299	Mr —— [John Syme]	1794	431
215	Mrs ——[19]	n.d.	433
216	Mrs ——[19]	n.d.	435
227	Mrs ——[19]	n.d.	437
163	Mrs ——[19]	n.d.	438
229	Mrs ——[19]	n.d.	439
299	John Syme	n.d.	441
242	Miss ——[20]	n.d.	443
234	Mr Cunningham	25 Feb. 1794	446
226	[Mrs Robert Riddell]	n.d.	450
223	Mrs Dunlop	15 Dec. 1795	453
280	Mrs Dunlop	20 Dec. 1795	459

[18] Ferguson thinks that Currie made a mistake and that the letter was addressed to Louisa Fontenelle.   [19] Mrs Walter Riddell.
[20] According to Ferguson, Letters, II.242, the addressee probably was Sophy or Elinor Riddell, sister of Walter Riddell.

Ref.	*Addressee*	*Date*	
289	Mrs —*	20 Jan. 1796	*p.* 463
315	Mrs Dunlop	31 Jan. 1796	464
323	Mrs R[iddell]	4 Jun.	466
325	Mr Cunningham	7 Jul.	467
329	Mrs Burns	n.d.	470
326	Mrs Dunlop	12 Jul.	471

c. VOL III

Half-title

Vol. III. | Poems, | formerly published, | with some Additions | to which is added, | a History of these Poems by | Gilbert Burns.

Format. As Vol. I.

Signatures. π2 ; A-Aa8 ; Bb-Cc4 ; A8 ; B4 ; C-D8.

Contents. Pp. [4]+xvi+384+56 : [1], Title-page [as Vol. I, except for vol. no. and vignette, which consists of a beehive surrounded by a plough, a wheatsheaf, a sickle, and a copy of the " Mountain Daisy," with a lark hovering above] ; [2], blank ; [3], Half-title ; [4], blank ; [i]-v, Dedication to the Caledonian Hunt ; [vi], blank ; [vii]-x, Table of Contents ; [xi]-xiv, Index ; [xv], Errata ; [xvi], blank ; [1]-384, Text ; [1]-22, Appendix ; [23]-55, Glossary; [56], blank ; one blank leaf.

Original Material :
Written in Friar's Carse	*p.* 300
On my Early Days [" I mind it weel in early date . . ." : not included in H.&H.]	377
Song [" In Mauchline there dwells six proper belles . . ."]	380
On the Death of Sir James Blair [" The Lamp of day . . ."]	381
Once fondly loved	384

Comment. The text, as far as p. 384 (except for the original material listed above) is a reprint of § 25 (1793 Edinburgh). The rest of the Volume contains " Poems not in the Second Edition," Appendixes, and a glossary.

d. VOL. IV

Half-title

Vol. IV. | Correspondence | with | Mr. George Thomson; | including Poetry, | hitherto unpublished or uncollected.

Format. As Vol. I.

Signatures. π2 ; a4 ; b8 ; B-Bb8 ; Cc4 ; Dd8 ; Ee4.

* Mrs Walter Riddell.

Contents. [4]+xxiv+416 : [1], Title-page [as Vol. I, except vol. no. and vignette, which consists of a pipe, a branch of Scots pine, a Scots bonnet, and a piece of tartan] ; [2], blank ; [3], Half-title ; [4], blank ; [i]-iii, Preface ; [iv], blank ; [v]-xiv, Index to the Letters ; [xv]-xxiii, Table of Contents ; [xxiv], Errata ; [1]-406, Text ; [407]-415, Glossary ; [416], blank.

Original Material. Vol. IV contains most of R.B.'s correspondence with Thomson, here published, though fragmentarily, for the first time :[21]

Ref.	Date	
122	16 Sep. 92	*p.* 3
126	n.d.	8
129	8 Nov. 92	13
132	14 Nov.	17
134	1 Dec.	23
135	4 Dec.	25
146	Jan. 93	29
148	26 Jan.	36
152	20 Mar.	41
155	Mar.	43
160[22]	n.d.	44
160[22]	n.d.	46
162[22]	n.d.	50
166	7 Apr.	55
160	Apr. 93	62
172	Apr.	66
179	Jun.	70
178	25 Jun.	73
*180[23]	2 Jul.	79
181	Jul.	82
*187	Aug.	86
188	Aug.	87
189	Aug.	92
*190	Aug. 93	94
191	Aug.	97
193	Aug.	101
*194	Aug.	103
194	Sep.	107
196	Sep.	110
198	Sep.	115
196	Sep.	125
206	Sep.	129

[21] Refs. to *Letters,* II ; dates as given (sometimes erroneously) by Currie.

[22] Given, in part, as three separate letters ; completed in § 783 (1877 Edinburgh=Scott Douglas) ; printed by Scott Douglas and in *Letters* as one letter.

[23] Those letters marked with an asterisk first appeared, according to Ferguson, in § 783 (1877 Edinburgh=Scott Douglas).

Ref.	Date	
207	Sep.	p. 134
*213	Oct.	138
*221	Dec.	145
*243	May 94	150
250	Jul.	152
254	30 Aug.	155
255	Sep. 94	159
256	Sep.	162
264	19 Oct 94	172
270	Nov. 94	187
275	19 Nov.	200
*279	Dec.	213
283	Jan. 95	215
287	Feb.	220
289	7 Feb.	223
293	May 95	226
296	n.d.	232
300	May	234
*306	n.d.	237
*302	n.d.	246
*303	n.d.	248
*317	Feb. 96	254
319	Apr.	258
320	n.d.	261
320	n.d.	263
328	12 Jul. 96	264

Vol. IV also contains the following poems, here published for the first time :

This was the first collected edition of Burns's work. Dr James
Currie, a Liverpool physician, was not fitted to edit it; the text
is most inaccurate, and although masses of manuscript material
appear to have been placed at his disposal, he deliberately
omitted many items that he considered unsuitable, or only
presented them in a fearfully mangled condition. He has
often therefore been accused of being too squeamish and of
paying too much regard to the feelings of the poet's family. It
should, however, be borne in mind that, as Henley and Henderson remark, the edition " was projected by the dead man's
friends—especially Cunningham and Syme—as a memorial to
his genius and *as an aid to the fund for his widow and children.*"[24]
As Dr R. D. Thornton has recently suggested,[24a] Currie's task was
primarily to raise money for Burns's dependents, and there were
many items that he could not have printed in their original
form, or even at all, without alienating the goodwill of many
influential readers, especially in Scotland. As a result he forfeited
the best opportunity that any editor has ever had to establish a
definitive text.

[24] H. & H., II.279. My italics.
[24a] In *James Currie: The Entire Stranger and Robert Burns*, Edinburgh, 1963.

51. [?1800]

MERRY | MUSES | OF | CALEDONIA; | A Collection of | favourite Scots Songs, | ancient and modern; | selected for the Use of the Crochallan Fencibles. | Say, Puritan, can it be wrong, | To dress plain truth in witty song? | What honest Nature says, we should do; | What every lady does,—or would do | [*double rule*]

Format. 12mo, in half-sheets.

Signatures. A-K6 ; L4. The first three leaves of each half-sheet are signed.

Contents. Pp. 128 : [1], Title-page ; [2], blank ; [3]-122, Text ; [123]-127, Index ; [128], blank.

Original Material :
The Fornicator [4 stanzas]   *p.* 3
I'll tell you a Tale of a Wife [8 stanzas ; see letter to Robert
    Maxwell of 20 Dec. 1789, in *Letters*, I.377]   23
When Maukin Bucks [see letter to Thomson (? Jan 1795) in
    Letters, II.283]   49
When Princes and Prelates [8 stanzas ; see letter to Thomson
    (? Jul. 1794) in *Letters*, II.250]   79
Act Sederunt of the Court of Session [see letter to Robert
    Cleghorn of 25 Oct. [? 1793], in *Letters*, II.212]   94
Come cow me Minnie [*ibid.*]   121

Comment. Probably issued in paper wrappers. The leaves of the unique copy (which belongs to the Earl of Rosebery) have been let in, leaf by leaf, to different paper. During this process, the whole book was heavily trimmed on all four sides, so that many page-numbers and many signatures have been obliterated ; even some of the text has been mutilated. Watermarks appear on certain leaves, as follows :
B3, C3—1799
D1, E3, F3, H1, I1, K3, L1—1800
Hence the conjectural dating of the edition.

Burns, at his death, possessed a considerable collection of bawdy verse in his own handwriting. It was apparently for his own use, and there is no evidence that he had ever intended to have it printed.

An untraceable tradition has it that the book was printed at Dumfries; but the Crochallan Fencibles were a well-known Edinburgh drinking-club, and this rarity was probably printed in the capital. Manuscripts that have turned up since 1800 afford some reason to believe that the text was not set from Burns's own holograph, but only from a copy of it.

Most of the material in the book is probably not by Burns, and in the foregoing list of original material I have only included such pieces as can definitely be assigned to him.

52. [1801 Alnwick]

This edition does not exist. Through a printing error it was listed in the catalogue of the Murison Collection (p. 22).

53. 1801 Berwick

a. Vol. I

POEMS, | CHIEFLY IN THE | SCOTTISH DIALECT. | In two volumes. | By ROBERT BURNS. | To which is prefixed the | Life of the Author. | [*double rule*] | The simple bard, unbroke by rules of art, | Pours forth the wild effusions of the heart; | And if inspir'd, its nature's powers inspire; | Her's all the melting thrill, her's all the kindling fire. | [*double rule*] | All the Poems and Songs that were in the Edition printed at Edin- | burgh in 1787, are in these two Volumes. | Vol. I. | [*ornamented rule*] | [*vignette*: *head of R.B.*] | [*ornamented rule*] | Berwick: | printed by H. Richard-son. | 1801.

Variants etc.

1. . . . H. Richardson, for J. Taylor, Bookseller. 1801.
2. Poems | chiefly in the Scottish Dialect | by | Robert Burns. | [*diamond rule*] | In two Volumes | A new edition, which includes all the | Poems and Songs | in that printed at Edin. in 1787 under the Author's own inspection: | Also | his Life & an Appendix, containing his other | select Pieces. | [*vignette*: *head of R.B.*] | [*double rule*] | Vol. I. | [*double rule*] | Berwick upon Tweed: | printed by H. Richardson, | for | J. White & C<u>o</u> Boston United States. America [*engraved throughout*]
3. [*Same as var. 2, above, except*] . . . H. Richardson, | sold by David Forbes, Edinr. | 1801. [*engraved throughout*]

Format. 12mo, in half-sheets. 17·7 × 10·2 cm., untrimmed, in original boards.

Signatures. a6 (+one leaf) ; B-U6.

Contents. Pp. 244 : [1], Title-page ; [2], blank ; [3-4], Table of Contents ; [5]-6, " The Life of Robert Burns " ; [7]-10, Preface to the Kilmarnock edition ; [11]-14, Dedication to the Caledonian Hunt ; [17]-243, Text ; [244], blank. (Order in B.M. and N.L.S. copies : Title-page [verso blank] ; " The Life of Robert Burns " ; Preface to the Kilmarnock edition ; Dedication to the Caledonian Hunt ; Table of Contents.)

Comment. Issued in French gray paper boards. Paper label on spine : " Burns' Poems Vol. I." A leaf, containing the Table of Contents, pp. [3-4], is pasted between a and a2, hence the extra leaf in the gathering " a ". In some copies this extra leaf has been omitted altogether ; in one copy I examined, the Tables of Contents for Vols I and II were printed on a single half-sheet and folded and bound in at the beginning of the text.

b. VOL. II

Signatures. A6 (+one leaf) ; B-Q6 ; R4 ; S-Y6.

Contents. Pp. [1-4]+[7]-262 : [1], Title-page (as Vol. I, except vol. no.); [2], blank ; [3-4], Table of Contents ; [7]-202, Text and Glossary ; [R4, blank] ; [203]-262, Appendix and Index to Appendix.

The most probable explanation of the variants on the original printed title-page and of those on the engraved title-page that has been substituted for it in some copies is that Richardson succeeded in making arrangements for part of the edition to be sold by J. Taylor before he had printed the whole of it, but that he did not reach agreement with David Forbes or with White and Co. until after it had all been printed, and that the engraved title-page, with the appropriate variant of the imprint, was then substituted for the original printed title-page.

54. 1801 Edinburgh

a. VOL. I

POEMS | by | ROBERT BURNS, | with his | Life and Character. | [*ornamented rule*] | In two Volumes. | [*double rule*] | Embellished with beautiful Engravings. | [*double rule*] | Volume I. | [*double rule*] | [*vignette: beehive, lark, plough, etc.*] | Edinburgh: [*double rule*] | Printed by Oliver & Co. | [*rule*] | 1801.

Half-title

Oliver's Edition. | [*double rule*] | POEMS | by | ROBERT BURNS. | [*double rule*]

Format. 12mo, in half-sheets.

Signatures. [a6]-c6 ; d4 ; A-B6 ; C4(-C4) ; D-P6.   14×8·4, trimmed, in contemporary calf.

Contents. Pp. xliv+[1]-30+37-180 (Pp. 31-36 were purposely omitted): [i], Half-title ; [ii], blank ; [iii], Title-page ; [iv], blank ; [v]-viii, Dedication to the Caledonian Hunt ; [ix]-xii, Table of Contents ; [xiii]-xliv, "A Concise Account of the Life and Character of the Author " ; [1]-30, Text, through Stanza 6 of " Death and Doctor Hornbook " ; 37-180, Text, beginning with Stanza 3 of " Death and Doctor Hornbook."

Comment. Issued in French gray paper boards, with frontispiece (portrait of R.B., after Nasmyth, engraved by R. Scott). The leaf 12 is unsigned. An engraving of the Holy Fair is inserted between C3 and D1 (pp. 30-31).

This is probably the first issue, in so far as the title-page has the simplest imprint (not, however, conclusive evidence). The first thirty pages (A-B6, C3) appear to have been printed in a shop other than Oliver's, for not only is the fount different, but so also is the setting. In view of the differences between Vol. I, pp. 1-30, and the rest of the volume, it seems probable that these pages were set by another printer who had projected an edition of Burns's poems but abandoned the project after he had set A-B6 and C3 ; that Oliver bought up the type already set ; and that he incorporated the sheets printed from it into his own edition. But since the D.C. copy is the only one that I have seen, this explanation is inevitably somewhat speculative.

b. VOL. II

Signatures. π2 ; A-U6 (-U6).

Contents. Pp. [iv]+238 : [i], Half-title ; [ii], blank ; [iii], Title-page (identical with Vol. I, except vol. no.) ; [iv], blank ; [1]-238, Text and Glossary ; one leaf.

Comment. t.p. of this Vol. : "... Co. Fountain Well, | High Street . . ."

This edition contains nearly all the original material contained in §§ 58 and 69 (1801 Glasgow=Duncan, and 1802 Glasgow =Stewart); but being in Edinburgh, and not, so far as we know, acquainted with Richmond or any member of Burns's family, Oliver was not likely to have access to unpublished MSS. See below, p. 87, for a discussion on the question between Duncan and Stewart.

55. 1801 Edinburgh

[*Title-page as in* § 54 (1801 *Edinburgh*), *except that the imprint reads*] . . . Oliver & Co. Fountain Well, High Street. [*rule*] 1801.

Variants

1. . . . Oliver & Co., High Street. Sold by J. & J. Scrymgeour, and Brash & Reid, Booksellers, Glasgow. [*rule*] 1801.
2. . . . Oliver & Co. Sold by A. Guthrie, T. Brown and A. Mackay, Booksellers. 1801.

Format. 12mo, in half-sheets. 12·2 × 8·7 cm., trimmed.

Signatures. a-c6 ; d4 ; A-P6. With the exception of [I2], the first three leaves of each half-sheet are signed.

Contents. Pp. xliv+180 : [i], Half-title (as in § 54) ; [ii], blank ; [iii], Title-page ; [iv], blank ; [v]-viii, Dedication to the Caledonian Hunt ; [ix]-xii, Table of Contents ; [xiii]-xliv, A Concise Account of the Life and Character of the Author ; 1-180, Text.

Comment. Issued in French gray paper boards, with frontispiece (portrait of R.B., after Nasmyth, engraved by R. Scott). Engraving, *The Holy Fair*, inserted between C3 and C4.

b. Vol. II

[*Title-page as in Vol. I, with the same variants, except in the case of var. 1, where instead of*] . . . Oliver & Co., High Street. Sold by J. & J. Scrymgeour . . . [*Vol. II reads*] . . . Oliver & Co. Fountain Well, High Street. Sold by J. & J. Scrymgeour . . .

Comment. The rest of the volume is the same as the first issue, § 54 (1801 Edinburgh), Vol. II.

56. 1801 Edinburgh

POEMS, | CHIEFLY IN THE | SCOTTISH DIALECT | by | ROBERT BURNS. | [*vignette: plough, thistle etc.*] | Vol. I. | [*diamond rule*] | Edinburgh | Printed & sold by James Robertson. 1801. [*engraved throughout*]

Format. 16mo, in half-sheets. 10·4×6·4 cm., trimmed, decorated edges, marbled boards, leather backed.

Signatures. a4 ; A-O8. With the exception of [A2, E3, O2], the first four leaves of each half-sheet are signed : but [E4, F2] are signed, respectively, G4, E2.

Contents. Pp. x+[11]-234 : [i], Title-page ; [ii], blank ; [iii],-vi, Dedication to the Caledonian Hunt ; [vii]-x, Table of Contents ; [11]-234, Text.

Comment. Issued with frontispiece (portrait of R.B., after Nasmyth, engraved by W. Archibald).

b. VOL. II

Signatures. 1 leaf ; A-L8 ; M4 ; a-b8. With the exception of [F3], the first four leaves of each half-sheet are signed.

Contents. Pp. [3]-185 : [i], Title-page (identical with Vol. I, except vol. no.) ; [ii], blank ; [3]-185, Text ; [186], blank ; [1]-32, Glossary.

This edition contains all the material which appeared in § 48 (1800 Edinburgh=Cadell and Davies) as well as some songs lifted from § 28 (1793-1818 London=Thomson). At the end of Vol. II there appear a biographical account, an account of Burns's interment, and some verses in his memory, all lifted from § 32 (? 1795-8 Glasgow=Brash and Reid).

Cadell and Davies *v.* Robertson is certainly the most important of the lawsuits which arose over the question of pirated Burns material during 1801 and 1802. Cadell and Davis applied by bill of suspension for an interdict in 1801. At the same time they raised an action againt Robertson,

> concluding not for *penalties*, but for *damages*, on account of the infringement on their property, by publishing these additional poems [*i.e.*, those added in § 25 (1793 Edinburgh)]. . . . The bill of suspension and interdict was passed, and conjoined with the action for damages. This action the Court of Session decided (16th May 1801) by recalling the interdict, sustaining the defenses against the action of damages, and assoilzieing the defender. . . . The pursuers complained . . . to the House of Lords . . . (16th July 1811) . . . It may now, therefore, be held as law in Scotland, as it has long been in England, that Authors and their assignees have a statutory right to their literary property for 14 or 28 years . . . though their works may not have been entered in Stationers Hall.[25]

---

[25] *Gentleman's Magazine*, LXXXII (Mar. 1812), 283-4.

57. 1801 Glasgow

POEMS | ASCRIBED TO | ROBERT BURNS, | the Ayrshire Bard, | not contained in any Edition of his Works | hitherto published. | [*scrolled rule*] | Glasgow, | Printed by Chapman & Lang, | for Thomas Stewart, Bookseller and Stationer. | [*scrolled rule*] | 1801.

Variant

... Stationer. [*omitting second scrolled rule and date*]

Format. 8mo, on half-sheets. 22·7 × 14·4 cm., untrimmed, in original boards.

Signatures. π4 ; A-M4 (−M4). The first two leaves of each half-sheet are signed.

Contents. Pp. [viii]+94 : [i], Title-page ; [ii], blank, [iii-v], Advertisement ; [vi], blank ; [vii-viii], Table of Contents ; [1]-[94], Text and additional Table of Contents.

Original Material :

The Inventory [completed from § 50 (1800 Liverpool= Currie)]	*p.* 46
Epigram [" Who'er he be . . ." second version]	53
On Miss Jean Scott [" Oh ! had each Scot of ancient times . . ."]	59
Lines [" He who of R-k-n sang . . ."]	60
Lines [" Kemble, thou cur'st my unbelief . . ."]	62
Epitaph on Holy Willie [" Here Holy Willie's sair worn clay . . ."]	68
Lines Written Extempore in a Lady's Pocketbook [" Grant me indulgent heaven . . ."]	74
Lines to Mr John Ranken [" Ae day as death . . ."]	81
Verses [" I am a Keeper of the law . . ."]	82
Letter to Mr Robert Muir [7 Mar. 1788 ; *Letters*, 1.207]	91

Comment. Issued in French gray as well as marbled boards. A square label, on the front cover, reads, " Price 2s. 6d. Poems, Songs, &c. ascribed to Robert Burns, The Ayrshire Bard, not contained in any edition of his works hitherto published." This announcement is surrounded by a wreath or a beaded frame. The book apparently was meant to have ended on K4 (p. 86), but two more

G

gatherings were added. The leaf G3 (pp. 53-54) is a cancel.[26] There were two issues of this edition, one advertised in *The Glasgow Courier* on 2 January 1801 ; the other, also advertised in the same newspaper, on 3 May 1801. Whether or not the earlier issue consisted of A-K4 only I cannot say, for all the copies I have examined were complete, as described above.[27] However, the earlier issue can be definitely recognised by the original leaf G3, which was not cancelled until the later issue. The footnote on p. 75 appears in a short and a long form : " The Printer of the Aberdeen Journal," and " The printer of the Aberdeen Journal, in whose house Mr. Skinner first saw Burns's Poems." It would seem logical to infer that the amplified form was the later printing, but both notes occur in copies with and without the cancelled leaf. The book was uniform in size with § 50 (1800 Liverpool = Currie), so that it could be bound in with any one of the volumes of that edition.

This volume was published by Thomas Stewart, after he had terminated his partnership with Meikle. Stewart, as we have seen, had access to a great deal of original Burns material through his nephew, John Richmond.

[26] G3 Cancelland (*recto*) : " Epigram. Burns being sent to the North Country on the Excise Business, where they are very averse to paying the Duties, and look on the Excisemen as a burden upon them, was, one day, invited to dine with some of the Distillers, where they took little notice of him, but were busy enquiring at one another how their Friends did ; without being observed, he took a diamond and wrote on a pane of glass as follows :
Highland pride, Highland scab, Highland hunger,
If God Almighty sent me here,
'Twas surely in his anger.
G3 Cancellans (*recto*) : " Epigram. Burns, accompanied by a friend, having gone to Inverary at a time when some company were there on a visit to his Grace the Duke of Argyll, finding himself and his companion entirely neglected by the Inn-keeper, whose whole attention seemed to be occupied with the visitors to his Grace, expressed his disapprobation of the incivility with which they were treated in the following lines :
Whoe'er he be that sojourns here,
I pity much his case,
Unless he come to wait upon
The Lord their God, his Grace.
There's naething here but Highland pride,
And Highland scab and hunger ;
If Providence has sent me here,
'Twas surely in an anger.
[27] But cp. *M.C.*, 279: " re-issue [of 278] (with additional poems and letter)" ; and J. C. Ewing, (*Glasgow Evening Times*, 22 Jan. 1902) : " The work was re-issued (for sale 4 May 1801) with eight pieces added since it was first published." The copy in the Hornel collection has only the first ten gatherings, but it has been very tightly rebound and there is no way of telling whether or not gatherings L and M had been removed before binding.

58. 1801 Glasgow

POEMS, | CHIEFLY IN THE | SCOTTISH DIALECT. | By | ROBERT BURNS. | [*double rule*] | A new Edition, considerably enlarged. | [*double rule*] | Glasgow: | Printed by Thomas Duncan, Saltmarket. | [*rule*] | 1801.

Format. 12mo, in half-sheets. 16·6×9·7 cm., trimmed and re-bound.

Signatures. A-Gg6. The first three leaves of each half-sheet are signed.

Contents. Pp. iv+[5]-[360] : [i], Title-page ; [ii], blank ; [iii]-iv, Dedication to the Caledonian Hunt ; [5]-226, Text and Glossary (on p. 226, " End of the Edinburgh Edition of 1800, which contains Eighteen Poems more than the edition of 1787 ") ; 227-250, Life and Character ; 251-353, Additional Poems ; [354], blank ; 355-359, Index ; [360], blank. The arrangement of the material, through p. 226, follows that of § 48 (1800 Edinburgh) except for " Anna, thy charms," and " O, open the door."[28]

Original Material :

The Jolly Beggars [complete, *i.e.* with the addition of the Merry Andrew episode]	*p.* 251
To James Tennant of Glenconner	262
Written on the Window of the Globe Tavern	272
For Mr Walter Riddel	274
Epitaph on Walter S—— [" Sic a reptile was Wat . . ."][29]	274
Lines under the picture of Miss Burns	274
A Grace [" Lord, we thank an' thee adore . . ."]	274
Written on a window at the King's Arms, Dumfries	276
On John Bushby	276
Epitaph on the Marquis	293
" From the white blossomed Sloe "[30]	293
On the Commemoration of Rodney's Victory[31]	296
Epitaph on D—C—[" Here lies in earth . . ."]	296
Scots Prologue for Mr. Sutherland	298

---

[28] The material on pp. 337-53 is not by Burns.

[29] H. & H., ii.455, say, mistakenly, that this first appeared in § 69 (1801 Glasgow=Stewart), but see further comment. Walter S.=Walter Riddell.

[30] Originally published in *The Edinburgh Advertiser*, 8 Aug. 1800.

[31] Originally published in *The Edinburgh Advertiser*, 19 Apr. 1793.

A Quatrain :   307

[" The King's most humble servant, I
Can scarcely spare a minute ;
But I'll be wi' you by an' bye,
Or else the deil's be in it."[32]]

Anna [" Yestreen I had a pint o' wine . . ."]   327
The Five Carlins   328

Comment. Issued, stabbed, in nine parts, probably in boards. Signatures
omitted on [D2] and [S3] ; [Aa3] is signed " Z3 " ; p. [156] is
numbered 165 ; p. [198] is unnumbered.

This edition is beset with problems, not the least important
being to answer the question: Did the original material first see
the light of day in this book, or did the new poems first appear
in § 54 (1801 Edinburgh=Oliver) or in § 69 (1802 Glasgow
=Stewart) ?

H. & H. do not commit themselves, since they use all three
indiscriminately as original sources; other commentators
maintain a discreet silence. J. C. Ewing (whose opinions I have
gleaned from conversations with him) was convinced that
Duncan had stolen the new material from Stewart. His reasoning
was as follows: Stewart began the publication of his edition,
§ 69, in parts on 27 July 1801 and finished issuing the parts
early in 1802. When the book was bound up and issued as a
volume, the title-page bore the date 1802. Stewart, John Richmond's nephew, had access to original manuscript material:
Duncan, so far as we know, did not. Duncan began issuing his
edition, also in parts, at about the same time as Stewart. The
method was simple; he merely copied the material from Stewart,
part by part, and when the edition was complete, presumably in
1802, issued the whole volume with the fraudulent date 1801 on
the title-page.

So far so good. But all the new material in Stewart also appears
in Duncan, and it may be objected that the arrangement of the
material in the two editions is entirely different. Duncan would
therefore have had to wait for the entire Stewart edition to be
published before he could begin his own effort. But, since the
first 226 pp. are merely a reprint of § 48 (1800 Edinburgh),

---

[32] H. & H. do not include this piece in their edition. J. G. Lockhart (*The
Life of Robert Burns*, Edinburgh 1828, p. 207) claims that it is genuine : " ' The
above answer to an invitation was written extempore on a leaf torn from his
[Burns's] Excise-book.'—Cromek's MSS."

he could have issued his parts as he chose and then added the new material at the end of the volume. (The new material does actually appear in the last three parts.) Why Duncan should have chosen to rearrange the material and deliberately put the date 1801 on a book that, under one of the foregoing circumstances, could not have been published before the second quarter of 1802, remains somewhat obscure.[33] So much for Duncan and Stewart.

The place that Oliver occupies in this publishing trinity can only be described as anonymous. Much, but not all, of the additional material appears in his publication—one notable exception is the Merry Andrew episode from *The Jolly Beggars*— and the biographical account is exactly the same as that in Duncan. It is almost certain that, being situated in Edinburgh, he had even less opportunity to use original manuscripts. My conclusion is that he stole indiscriminately: *The Jolly Beggars* from § 57, *Poems Ascribed to Robert Burns*, or from §§ 33, 39-45, the Stewart and Meikle pamphlets, and other poems from Duncan. But, if he stole, the question remains, why did he not steal everything?

It seems logical to infer that pride of place must be given to Duncan, in so far as he had the largest amount of new material, and was closer to the source of supply, *i.e.* Stewart. Can Stewart perhaps have turned over the new material to Duncan simply to see what would happen in a legal way? We know that when § 69, his own edition appeared, Stewart was very jumpy about it;[34] so is there any reason not to believe that in 1801, merely to see what happened, he might have sent up a trial-balloon? Duncan was an obscure printer of chapbooks, and (note well) his title-page does not contain the name of any publisher. His edition must have been a small one—to my knowledge there are only four copies still in existence—which tends to substantiate the idea of a trial-balloon. I am, therefore, willing to venture the opinion that the new poetry in Duncan first saw the light of day in that edition.

---

[33] The Paisley Edition of this year (§ 63) offers something else again. It contains material that is common to both Duncan and Stewart ; the date on the title-page would lead one to believe that there was some sort of plot to pre-date books that were published in 1802.

[34] Stewart was always aware that he might get into difficulties over new material ; his previous adventures in this field had been with chapbooks, a comparatively safe medium, and his publication in 1801 has the ambiguous title, *Poems ascribed to Robert Burns* (§ 57).

59. 1801 Glasgow

POEMS, | CHIEFLY IN THE | SCOTTISH DIALECT. | By | ROBERT BURNS. | [*scrolled rule*] | To which are added, | several other Pieces, | not contained in any former Edition | of his Poems. | [*ornamented rule*] | Glasgow, | Printed and sold by Chapman and Lang, | Booksellers and Stationers, Trongate. | [*ornamented rule*] | 1801.

Variants

1. . . . Chapman & Lang, for William M'Clellan, Bookseller and Stationer, Trongate. 1801.[35]

2. . . . Glasgow: Printed and sold by Chapman and Lang and Messrs Lackington, Allen & Co., London. 1801.

3. . . . Glasgow, Printed & sold by Chapman and Lang and Robert Ogle, London. 1801.

4. . . . Poems, | and a | Life of the Author. | [*ornamented rule*] | Glasgow, Printed and sold by Chapman and Lang, and Messrs Vernor & Hood, London. 1801.

Format. 12mo, in half-sheets. 17·4 × 10·6 cm., trimmed, in original (?) boards with leather back and corners.

Signatures. a6 ; [A]-Gg6. With the exception of [D2] and [U3], the first three leaves of each half-sheet are signed.

Contents. Pp. xii+360 : [i], Title-page ; [ii], blank ; [iii]-vii,. Life of Robert Burns ; [viii]-ix, Dedication to the Caledonian Hunt ; [x]-xii, Table of Contents ; [1]-360, Text.

Comment. Issued in marbled boards (?) with frontispiece (portrait of R.B., engraved by Mackenzie). An engraving of the Burns Cottage at Alloway, by R. Scott, is inserted between [a] and [a2].

60. 1801 London

ALONZO AND CORA, | with | other original Poems, | principally elegiac. | [*diamond rule*] | By ELIZABETH SCOT, | a Native of Edinburgh. | [*diamond rule*] | To which are added | Letters in Verse | by Blacklock and Burns. | [*double rule*] | London: | printed and published by Bunney and Gold, Shoe-Lane; |

---

[35] Chambers, IV.315, notes a " Glasgow : W. M'Millan [?]."

and may be had of | Rivington, St. Paul's Church-yard; Robinsons, Paternoster-Row; | Cadell and Davies, Strand; Egerton, Whitehall; and Faulder, | Bond-Street. Likewise of Crutwell, Bath; Tessyman, York; and | Creech, Edinburgh. | [*rule*] | 1801.

Half-title

[*double rule*] | ALONZO AND CORA | [*double rule*]

Format. 8vo, in half-sheets. 22·7×14·4 cm., untrimmed in original boards.

Signatures. [A2] ; a-b4 ; B-Y4. The first two leaves of each half-sheet are signed.

Contents. Pp. [xx]+168 : [i], Half-title ; [ii], blank ; [iii], Title-page ; [iv], blank ; [v], Dedication ; [vi], blank ; [vii-xiii], List of Subscribers ; [xiv], blank ; [xv-xvi], Table of Contents ; [xvii-xx], Preface ; [1]-168, Text.

Original Material :
        The Answer [" Guidwife : I mind it weel . . ."]   *p.* 158

Comment. Issued in French gray paper boards.

" The Answer," a poetical epistle, was addressed to Elizabeth Scott, a friend of the poet's. Currie printed the first forty-two lines in § 50 (1800 Liverpool), but Elizabeth Scott did not publish her book until 1801, and this was the first time that the poem appeared in its entirety.

61. 1801 London
a. Vol. I

THE | WORKS | OF | ROBERT BURNS; | with | an Account of his Life, | and | a Criticism on his Writings. | To which are prefixed, | some Observations on the Character and Condition | of | the Scottish Peasantry. | [*diamond rule*] | In four Volumes. | Vol. I. | [*diamond rule*] | The second Edition. | [*vignette: as in* § 50 *a.* (1800 *Liverpool=Currie, Vol. I*) | London: | printed for T. Cadell, Jun. and W. Davies, Strand; | and W. Creech, Edinburgh. | Sold also by Bell and Bradfute; P. Hill, and Manners and Miller, Edinburgh; | Brash & Reid, and Dunlop & Wilson, Glasgow; A. Brown, Aberdeen; W. Boyd, | Dumfries; J.

Morrison, Perth; J. Forsyth, Ayr; and by Merritt and | Wright, W. Robinson, W. Harding, and E. Rushton, Liverpool. | [*double rule*] | 1801. | Printed by R. Noble, in the Old Bailey.

Format. 8vo. 21·1 × 13 cm., trimmed, in contemporary calf.

Signatures. [a2] ; b4 ; B-Bb8 ; Cc4 (-CC4). The first two leaves of each sheet are signed.

Contents. Pp. [IV]+xxiv+390 : [I], Half-title ; [II], blank ; [III], Title-page ; [iv], blank ; [i]-v, Dedication ; [vi], Advertisement ; [vii]-viii, Table of Contents ; [1]-389, Text ; [390], blank.

The text of this volume is the same as that of the first edition § 50 (1800 Liverpool). However, there is no postscript, no list of subscribers, and the advertisement is different. Appendix III (pp. 377-89) is taken up with an introduction to the work and a long letter from Gilbert Burns to Dr Currie. Work had been started on this edition before the end of 1800.[36]

b. VOL. II

Format. As Vol. I.

Signatures. [a2] ; b4 ; c8 ; B-Gg8 ; Hh2.

Contents. Pp. [IV]+xxiv+468 : [I], Half-title ; [II], blank ; [III], Title-page ; [IV], blank ; [i]-v, Advertisement ; [vi], blank ; [vii]-xxiii, Table of Contents ; [xxiv], Index ; [1]-467, Text ; [468], blank.

Original Material :

VI	Proclamation to the Muses	*p.* 26
XXXVII	Letter to the Earl of Glencairn	116
	1 Feb. 1788 [*Letters*, 1.178]	
LXIV	Letter to Professor D. Stewart	198
	20 Jan. 1789 [*Letters*, 1.288]	
LXXX	Letter to Miss Williams	249
	Aug. [?] 1789 [*Letters*, 1.352]	
LXXXVII	Letter to Charles Sharpe	275
	22 Apr. 1791 [*Letters*, II.70]	275

the following letters, which appeared in § 50.*b*, are missing here:

I-IV To a female Friend, written about 1780.

XXXII From Mr John Hutchinson, 14 June 1787.

XI-XII From Sir John Whiteford.

XXXV From Mr W——, 13 September 1787.

XXXVI From Mr A—— M——.

[36] *B. Chr.*, VIII (1899), 35.

c. Vol. III

Format. As Vol. I.

Signatures. A-Ee8.

Contents. Pp. xvi+432 : [i], Title-page ; [ii], blank ; [iii], Half-title ; [iv], blank ; [v]-viii, Dedication to the Caledonian Hunt ; [ix]-xvi, Table of Contents ; [1]-431, Text, Appendix, and Glossary ; [432], blank.

Comment. This volume was printed by Luke Hansard, Great Turnstile, Lincoln's Inn Fields.

The volume is the same as § 50.*c*, save that the four poems which appeared between pp. 377 and 384 are omitted :

On my early days [" I mind it weel . . ."]
Song [" In Mauchline there dwells . . ."]
On the death of Sir James Hunter Blair
" Once fondly Lov'd . . ."

d. Vol. IV

Format. As Vol. I.

Signatures. A8 ; b4 ; B-Dd8.

Contents. Pp. xxiv+416 : [i], Title-page ; [ii], blank ; [iii], Half-title ; [iv], blank ; [v]-vii, Preface ; [viii], blank ; ix-xvi, Table of Contents ; xvii-xxiv, Indexes ; [1]-415, Text and Glossary ; [416] blank.

Comment. This volume was also printed by Luke Hansard. It is a page-by-page resetting of § 50.*d*.

62. 1801 Montrose

POEMS, | CHIEFLY IN THE | SCOTTISH DIALECT. | [*double rule*] | By | ROBERT BURNS. | [*double rule*] | A new Edition. | [*double rule*] | [*vignette*: *castle, river, etc.*] | Montrose: | Printed by Da. Buchanan; sold by him, and by | W. Mortimer, Aberdeen. | [*rule*] | 1801.

Format. 12mo, in half-sheets. 13·6×8·8 cm., trimmed, rebound.

Signatures. π8 ; A-R6 ; S4 (-S1) ; T-U6 ; [X4 (-X4)] -Cc6. The first three leaves of each half-sheet are signed.

Contents. Pp. xvi+298 : [i], Title-page ; [ii], blank ; [iii]-iv, Dedication to the Caledonian Hunt ; [v]-vi, Table of Contents ; [vii]-[ix] (the three pages numbered as follows : [vii], no number ; [viii], numbered vi ; [ix], numbered v), Preface to the Kilmarnock edition ; [x], blank ; [xi]-[xv] (the five pages numbered as follows : [xi], no number ; xii, numbered " viii " ; xiii, numbered " ix " ; xiv, numbered " x " ; xv, numbered " xi "), " Life of Robert Burns " ; [xvi], blank ; [1]-238, Text and Glossary ; one unnumbered leaf, recto and verso containing a table of contents for the Appendix ; [239]-297, Appendix ; [298], blank.

Comment. Woodcuts throughout.

63. 1801 (-1802) Paisley

a. Vol. I

POEMS, | CHIEFLY IN THE | SCOTTISH DIALECT. | [*diamond rule*] | By ROBERT BURNS, | [*diamond rule*] | Paisley: | printed by J. Neilson, | for R. Smith, Bookseller, near the Cross. | [*double rule*] | 1801. [*extra engraved title-page*]

Format. 12mo, in half-sheets. 12·9 × 8·2 cm., trimmed, in contemporary marbled boards, leather backed.

Signatures. A-S6. The first three leaves of each half-sheet are signed ; those of the gathering E are signed, E, F, and E3.

Contents. Pp. [2]+vi+[7]-216 : Title-page ; verso, blank ; [i-ii], Table of Contents ; [iii]-v, Dedication to the Caledonian Hunt ; [vi], blank ; [7]-214, Text ; [215-16], Table of Contents.

Comment. Issued in boards (?), with frontispiece (portrait of R.B., probably a crude copy—the head faces right—of portrait by Nasmyth, engraved by ? Deurie).

b. Vol. II

POEMS | CHIEFLY IN THE | SCOTTISH DIALECT. | [*rule*] | By ROBERT BURNS. | [*rule*] | [*diamond rule*] | Paisley: | printed by J. Neilson, | for R. Smith, Bookseller, near the Cross. | [*double rule*] | 1802. [*extra engraved title-page*]

Format. As Vol. I.

Signatures. A-S6. The first three leaves of gathering L are signed L, L3 (missing in some copies), L3.

Contents. Pp. 216 : [1], Title-page ; [2], blank ; [3]-23, Sketch of the Life and Character of Burns ; [24]-26, Table of Contents ; [27]-216, Text and Glossary.

Comment. Issued in boards (?). The colophon reads " Paisley, printed by J. Neilson, 1802."

The material in these two volumes seems to have been taken indiscriminately from § 69 (1802 Glasgow=Stewart) and/or § 58 (1801 Glasgow=Duncan). The arrangement of the poems follows Stewart, though not altogether, and some of the poems in Stewart are omitted. The biographical sketch is a peculiar mosaic of the biographical material in Stewart and Duncan, as well as material from other sources. More than half is taken from the article by Maria Riddell.[37] According to the Rev. James Thomson:[38]

> Disaster attended publication. In 1801 had come an end to the copyright of the 1787 edition, but not therewith, of course, that of the twenty new pieces in the edition of 1793. A number of publishing firms overlooked or disregarded this fact. The consequence was that the pirates (Smith among them) were pursued in the Court of Session, fined, and their editions " interdicted."

64. 1801 Philadelphia

a. Vol. I

THE | WORKS | OF | ROBERT BURNS; | with an Account of his Life, | and | a Criticism on his Writings. | To which are prefixed, | some Observations on the Character and Condition | of | the Scottish Peasantry. | In four Volumes. | [*diamond rule*] | Vol. I. | [*double rule*] | Philadelphia: | Printed by Budd and Bartram, | for Thomas Dobson, at the Stone House, | No. 41, South Second Street. | [*double rule*] | 1801.

Format. 12mo, in half-sheets. 17·7 × 10·8 cm., trimmed.

Signatures. [A]-Ii6 ; Kk2. With the exception of [S2] and [Gg2], the first and third leaves of each half-sheet are signed.

Contents. Pp. xii+376 : [i], Title-page ; [ii], blank ; [iii]-vii, Dedication to Capt. Moore ; [viii], Advertisement ; [ix]-x, Table of Contents ; [xi], " The Life of Robert Burns " ; [xii], blank ; [1]-344, Text ; [345]-376, Appendixes.

[37] Maria Riddell, *Biographical Sketch of Robert Burns*, London: 1796.
[38] *B. Chr.*, xxxii (1923), 20.

b. VOL. II

Signatures. A-Tt6.

Contents. Pp. xxviii+476.

c. VOL. III

Signatures. [A]-Pp6.

Contents. Pp. [4]+xiv+384+54.

d. VOL IV

Signatures. [A]-Oo6.

Contents. Pp. [2]+xxvi+416.

An almost verbatim and page-for-page reprint of § 50 (1800 Liverpool=Currie). The first American collected edition.

65. 1802 Dundee

POEMS | by | ROBERT BURNS, | with his | Life and Character. | [*diamond rule*] | Dundee: | printed by F. Ray, High-Street. | [*rule*] | 1802.

Half-title

[*double rule*] | POEMS | by | ROBERT BURNS. | [*double rule*]

Format. 12mo, in half-sheets.   13·9×8·4 cm., heavily trimmed and rebound.

Signatures. [a]-b6 ; A-T6. The first three leaves of each half-sheet are signed.

Contents. Pp. xxiv+228 : [i], Half-title ; [ii], blank ; [iii], Title-page ; [iv], blank ; [v]-vi, Table of Contents ; [vii]-x, Dedication to the Caledonian Hunt ; [xi]-xxiv, " The Life and Character of the Author " ; [1]-227, Text and Glossary ; [228], blank.

This is the first Dundee edition. It contains no material that does not appear in § 48 (1800 Edinburgh). The " Life and Character " were abridged from § 54 (1801 Edinburgh=Oliver).

66. 1802 Edinburgh

POEMS | by | ROBERT BURNS; | with his | Life and Character, | and a | complete Glossary. | [*double rule*] | Embellished with a Portrait of the Author. | [*double rule*] | [*vignette: pipe, pine-branch, tartan*] | Edinburgh: | [*double rule*] | Printed by Oliver & Co. Fountain Well, | High Street. | [*broken rule, but sometimes a solid rule*] | 1802.

Format 12mo. 13·1 × 7 cm., trimmed, in contemporary calf.

Signatures. One leaf ; π2 ; a12 ; A-B6 (in spite of the signatures, this is one gathering of twelve leaves) ; B-I12 ; Z12. With the exception of [H6], which is signed G6, the first six leaves of each sheet are signed. The last six leaves of A are signed " B1," " B3 " on the first and third leaves.

Contents. [VI]+xxiv+212+28 : [I], Title-page ; [II], blank ; [III-IV], Dedication to the Caledonian Hunt ; [V-VI], Table of Contents ; [i]-xxiv, " A Concise Account of the Life and Character of the Author " ; [1]-212, Text ; 1-28 Glossary.

Comment. All the added material, *Jolly Beggars*, etc., that appeared in Oliver's edition of 1801 (§ 54), is here missing.

67. 1802 Edinburgh

POEMS, | CHIEFLY IN THE | SCOTTISH DIALECT | by | ROBERT BURNS. | [*vignette: plough, thistle, etc.*] | Vol. I. | [*diamond rule*] | Edinburgh | printed & sold by James Robertson. | 1802. [*engraved throughout; same plate as § 56 (1801 Edinburgh =Robertson) with change of date*]

Variants

1. . . . . Robertson, & Denham and Dick. 1802.
2. " Robertson and Denham and Dick. 1802."[39]

The rest of the book is identical with § 54 (1801 Edinburgh =Robertson).

68. 1802 Glasgow

LETTERS | ADDRESSED TO | CLARINDA, &c. | [*ornamented rule*] | By | ROBERT BURNS, | the Ayrshire Poet. | [*double rule*] | Never before published. | [*double rule*] | [*ornamented rule*] | Glasgow: | Printed by Niven, Napier and Khull; | for T. Stewart & A. Macgoun, Booksellers. | [*ornamented rule*] | 1802.

---

[39] Chambers, iv.316.

Variant

. . . T. Stewart, Bookseller, Trongate. 1802.[40]

Format. 8vo. 16·3×9·9 cm., untrimmed, unbound.

Signatures. [A]-C8. The first leaf of each sheet is signed.

Contents. Pp. iv+[5]-48. [i], Title-page ; [ii], Registration ; [iii]-iv, " To the Public " ; [5]-48, Text.

Original Material : Twenty-five letters to " Clarinda " [Mrs M'Lehose] :

1.143[41]	1.	" I can say with truth . . ." : Saturday evening	*p.* 5
143	2.	" I had set no small store . . ." : Thursday evening	6
148	3.	" I beg your pardon . . ." : Friday evening	6
163	4.	" Why have I not heard from you . . ." : Monday evening	9
168	5.	" The impertinence of fools . . ." : Sunday night and Monday night	11
176	6.	" I cannot go out today . . ." : Tuesday night	14
184	7.	" I make a numerous dinner party . . ." : n.d.	15
153	8.	" You are right . . ." : n.d. [contains " Talk not of love," by Clarinda]	16
156	9.	" Some days, some nights . . ." : Saturday noon	20
179	10.	" I have just been before the throne . . ." : Sunday morning	21
158	11.	" I am delighted . . ." : Tuesday night	23
172	12.	" I have been tasking . . ." : Thursday morning [" Clarinda, mistress of my soul " appears on p. 26[42]]	25
175	13.	" I was on the way . . ." : n.d.	27
160	14.	" I am certain I saw you . . ." : Thursday noon	27
164	15.	" That you have faults . . ." : Tuesday evening	29
161	16.	" Your thoughts on religion . . ." : Saturday morning	30
166	17.	" There is no time . . ." : Saturday morning and night	31
186	18.	" ' I am distressed ' . . ." : n.d.	33
187	19.	" I have just now received . . ." : n.d.	34
189	20.	"When matters, my love . . ." : n.d.	35
192	21.	" The attraction of love . . ." : Glasgow, Monday evening	36

[40] This is presumably the second issue, after Stewart's partnership with Macgoun had been terminated.

[41] These refs. are to *Letters.*

[42] This had already appeared in § 8·*b* (1788 Edinburgh=Johnson).

Comment. Issued stabbed in French gray paper boards. Not all copies however, are stabbed.

This book was the cause of a lawsuit regarding copyrighted material between Cadell and Davies and Thomas Stewart. As is reported in *Decisions of the Court of Session*:

> A book was published at Glasgow by Thomas Stewart, bookseller, entitled " Letters addressed to Clarinda, by Robert Burns, the Ayrshire poet." This performance consisted of original correspondence, which had never been published, and contained a variety of letters written by Burns to a lady, who, after the death of the poet, put them into the possession of Stewart and consented to their publication.
>
> Soon after their appearance, Cadell and Davies, booksellers in London, and William Creech, bookseller in Edinburgh, having acquired right to all the compositions of Burns, presented a bill of suspension and interdict against the publication. An interdict was granted, and the bill was passed.
>
> The Lords (May 17, 1804) having the information for the parties, continue the interdict, declare the same to be perpetual, and decern. The heirs of Burns were also found entitled to expenses . . .[46]

There are two versions of the story of how Stewart obtained the letters. Sir Walter Scott wrote to Lady Abercorn, on 22 Jan. 1808, that Clarinda had been foolish enough to show the letters

[43] David McWhinnie.
[44] Miss Mabane.
[45] Robert Muir.
[46] *Decisions of the Court of Session from November 1801 to November 1807*, Edinburgh, 1808, pp. 375-8.

around, that a faithless young divine had sat up all night copying them, and had sold them for ten guineas to a Glasgow bookseller.[47]   Scott added that the letters were issued in a six-page pamphlet, whereas it was in fact a book of 48 pages. Clarinda's own later version of the story was somewhat different:

> Mrs. M'Lehose, in a letter dated 16 July 1834, declined Mr. Cunningham's request [to send him the letters], and gave the following account of the original surreptitious appearance of a portion of the letters of Burns:—" Mrs. James Gray, then Miss Peacock, and Mr. Grahame, the author of ' The Sabbath,' (two of my most valued and lamented friends,) applied to me on behalf of a literary gentleman of the name of Findley,[48] who was then engaged in writing a Life of the Poet, for permission to make *a few extracts* from the Letters to enrich his *Life*. This was unfortunately granted; and the Letters lent to Mr. Findley by Mr. Grahame, under this express condition. . . . Besides making use of the Letters, Mr. Findley gave permission to a bookseller to publish all of the Letters which had been intrusted to him, and added, most falsely, in an advertisement prefixed to them, that this was done with my permission (' condescension ' as he termed it,) and that the editor was vested with the sole power to publish these letters. Nothing could be more contrary to the truth."[49]

69. 1802 Glasgow

Stewart's Edition | of | BURNS'S POEMS, | including a Number of | original Pieces | never before published. | [*scrolled rule*] | With his | Life and Character. | [*double rule*] | Embellished with Engravings. | [*double rule*] | To which is added, | an Appendix, | consisting of his Correspondence with | Clarinda, &c. | [*ornamented rule*] | Glasgow: | Printed by Niven, Napier and Khull, | for T. Stewart & A. Macgoun, Booksellers. | [*ornamented rule*] | 1802.

[47] Sir Walter Scott, *Letters*, ed. H. J. C. Grierson, London, 1932, II.5-6.
[48] John Findley (1782-1810) was the author of the life of the Poet which appeared in § 69 (1802 Glasgow=Stewart).
[49] *The Correspondence between Burns and Clarinda*. Edinburgh : Tait . . .1843, p. v.

Variants, etc.

1. . . . T. Stewart, Bookseller, Trongate. 1802.

2. Burns's Poems. Including a Number of original Pieces not hitherto published. Glasgow printed & sold by Thomas Stewart & A. M'Gown, Trongate 1802. [*engraved throughout*]

3. Stewart's Edition of Burns's Poems, including a number of original Pieces. Not hitherto published. Glasgow printed & sold by Thos. Stewart & A. McGown booksellers Trongate. 1802. [*engraved throughout*]

Format. 8vo. 16·2 × 10·3 cm., trimmed, in original boards.

Signatures. [a4] ; b8 ; c6 ; 1-21 (8) ; 22 (6) ;[50] ([A]-C8).

Contents. Pp. xxxvi+348 [+iv+[5]-48] : [i], Title-page ; [ii], blank : [iii]-iv, Dedication to the Caledonian Hunt ; [v]-viii, Table of Contents ; [ix]-xxxvi, Life and Character of Robert Burns ; [1]-348, Text and Glossary.

Comment. Issued, stabbed, with frontispiece ("The Jolly Beggars," engraved by R. Scott), in eight parts from 25 July 1801[51] until early 1802. The parts were gathered, a title-page, Dedication to the Caledonian Hunt, and a Life of Burns (gatherings a4, b8, and c6, as above) were added ; and the whole volume was published during the latter part of February, 1802[52] when it appeared in French gray paper boards with a buff spine.

There may have been a first issue of the edition without the *Letters*, since Stewart had originally planned an edition of the *Poems* in eight parts. Either of the two engraved title-pages (above, Vars. 2, 3) could have been used for such an issue; but I have never seen a copy in this state.

On the other hand, according to Ewing,[53] the eighth

---

[50] N.L.S. copy (in perfect condition) shows the following variants :

    a. Signature, the same, except : 22(2) ; 23(4).

    b. No evidence of stabbing.

    c. Letters to Clarinda, [A]-C8, are bound in at the beginning of the volume between the Life and the Text.

[51] Advertisement in *The Glasgow Courier*, 25 Jul. 1801.

[52] " Stewart's Elegant Pocket Edition " was offered for sale, for 4s. 6d., in *The Glasgow Courier*, 27 Feb. 1802.

[53] J. C. Ewing, *Robert Burns's Letters addressed to Clarinda*, Edinburgh, privately printed 1921 ; also in *Publications of the Edinburgh Bibliographical Society*, xi (1921), 87-112.

H

number, issued (probably) early in 1802, bore the following advertisement:

> Since the Eighth Number of the above Work went to Press, the Publisher has been favoured with a series of letters (about 30 in number), all of which are in Burns's handwriting, with the authority of the Proprietor to publish them. . . . These letters will also be printed as an Appendix to this Edition, making a Ninth Number . . .

The title-page above also suggests that the *Letters* were intended to be part of the edition, and a footnote on p. xxxiii reads: " See his correspondence with Clarinda, to be printed from the original manuscript, as an Appendix to this Edition, . . ." The edition, with the *Letters*, was advertised in the *Glasgow Courier* on 21 Feb. 1802. At the same time the *Letters* were also advertised, " sold separately, price 6d. stitched ": see § 68 (1802 Glasgow).

It seems most probable that Stewart, who knew that his publication of the *Letters* was risky, and that he might be prosecuted (as indeed he was), offered them as an added attraction to this edition of the *Poems*, but at the same time published them separately, so that if they were suppressed, the edition of the *Poems* could still be sold.

A final problem is posed by the advertisement at the end of the *Letters* (p. 48):

> . . . in the Press, and speedily will be published by T. Stewart, The Letters to Clarinda, etc. with other new pieces by R. Burns, Some of which have not yet come to hand: These, when added to the Appendix already published at Glasgow, printed uniformly with *Dr. Currie's* Edition, will form a valuable Supplement to that work.

" The Appendix already published at Glasgow " is most likely to be § 57 (1801 Glasgow=Poems Ascribed to Robert Burns), which was published by Stewart, and was uniform with Currie. It would seem that Stewart had, or knew of, some more Burns material, and intended to exploit the rich vein of the *Letters* to the full by printing them once again with this new material, in the same format as § 57, so that they too could be bound up with § 50 (1800 Liverpool=Currie).

70. 1802 Kirkcaldy

a. VOL. I

Crerar's Edition | of | BURNS' POEMS, | with his | Life and Character. | [*scrolled rule*] | In two Volumes. | [*double rule*] | Embellished with beautiful Engravings. | [*double rule*] | Volume I. | [*ornamented rule*] | Kirkcaldy: | [*double broken rule*] | Printed by J. Crerar. | [*rule*] | 1802.

Format. 18mo, in half-sheets. 13·4 × 8·5 cm., trimmed, in contemporary calf.

Signatures. π1 ; a9 ; b8 ; A-K9. The first five leaves of each half-sheet are signed.

Contents. Pp. xii+[13]-180 : [i-ii], blank ; [iii], Title-page ; [iv], Blank ; [v]-viii, Table of Contents [for both volumes] ; [ix]-xi, Dedication to the Caledonian Hunt ; [xii]-38, Life, including a Monody by " a Gentleman of Kirkaldy " ; [39]-180, Text.

Comment. Issued in boards (?), with frontispiece (" Mark our Jovial Ragged Ring," drawn by A. Carse, engraved by R. Scott).

b. VOL. II

Format. As Vol. I.

Signatures. π1 ; A-M9 ; N2. [G5] is signed " G ".

Contents. [ii]+220 : [i], Title-page ; [ii], blank ; [1]-[220], Text. Pp. 113-[220] contain material lifted from §§ 39-45 (Stewart and Meikle) and § 57, *Poems Ascribed to Robert Burns.*

71. 1802 London

THE WORKS | OF | ROBERT BURNS; | with | an Account of his Life, | and | a Criticism on his Writings. | To which are prefixed, | some Observations on the Character and Condition of | the Scottish Peasantry. | [*diamond rule*] | In four Volumes. | Vol. I. | [*double rule*] | The third Edition. | [*double rule*] | [*vignette: as in § 50a (1800 Liverpool=Currie, Vol. I)*] | London, | Printed for T. Cadell Jun. and W. Davies, Strand; | and W. Creech, at Edinburgh. | [*double rule*] | 1802.

Format.　Octavo.　21·3 × 14 cm., untrimmed, in original boards.

Signatures.　[a2] ; b8 ; B-Bb8 ; Cc6. With the exception of [b3, 4 and E4], signed on the first four leaves of each sheet.

Contents.　Pp. xxiv + 396 : [i], Half-title ; [ii], blank ; [iii], Title-page ; [iv], blank ; [v]-ix, Dedication ; [x], Advertisement ; xi-xv, Table of Contents ; xvi-xxiv, Index to the Poetry ; [1]-342, Text ; [343]-395, Appendixes ; [396], Colophon.

b. VOL. II

Signatures.　[a2] ; b6 ; B-Gg8 ; Hh4.

Contents.　Pp. xx + 470.

Original Material :
　　Letter to the Rev. G[eorge] Lowrie　5 Feb. 1787 [*Letters,*
　　I.171]　　　　　　　　　　　　　　　　　　　　　　　　*p.* 47

c. VOL. III

Signatures.　[a2] ; b4 ; B-Dd8 ; Ee4.

Contents.　Pp. xii + 426.

d. VOL. IV

Signatures.　[A4] ; B-Dd8.

Contents.　Pp. viii + 414 + 2.

72. 1802 Newcastle

THE | POETICAL. | WORKS | of the late | ROBERT BURNS, | with an Account of his Life | [*diamond rule*] | A new Edition | containing many excellent Pieces of the Author's | that never made their appearance | in the Copy Right Edition | [*vignette: beehive, plough, lark, etc.*] | ... *Kidd, Sculpt.* ... *Castle* [? *pinx.*] | Newcastle on Tyne | Printed by M. Angus & Son & sold by them and all the | Booksellers in Town & Country | 1802 [*engraved throughout*]

Format.　12mo, in half-sheets.　16·8 × 10 cm., trimmed, in contemporary calf.

Signatures.　a4 ; b-d6 (-d6) ; A-B6 ; D-Pp6. With the exception of [b2, c2, A2, G2, H2, I2, K2, M2, U2, Y2, Ff2, Nn2, Oo2, Pp2], which are unsigned, the first three leaves of each half-sheet are signed. [A3] is signed " A2 ".

Contents. Pp. xliv+452 : [i], Title-page ; [ii], blank ; [iii]-vi, Dedication to the Caledonian Hunt ; [vii]-xiii, Table of Contents ; [xiv], blank ; [xv]-xliv, " The Life and Character of the Author " ; [1]-451, Text and Glossary ; [452], blank.

Comment. Frontispiece (portrait of R.B. after Nasmyth, by N. Castle).

73. 1803 Belfast

Poems, chiefly in the Scottish Dialect, by Robert Burns. . . . In two volumes. Vol. I. Belfast: printed by Magee. 1803.

Two volumes.

74. 1803 Dublin

Poems, chiefly in the Scottish Dialect, by Robert Burns. Vol. I. [*of two*] Dublin; printed by N. Kelly, 6, Great George's Street, 1803.

75. 1803 Dublin

Poems, chiefly in the Scottish Dialect, By Robert Burns; with an account of his life [by Robert Heron]. In two volumes. Dublin: printed by Gilbert and Hodge's. 1803.

76. 1803 London

Poems, chiefly in the Scottish Dialect. By Robert Burns. A new edition . . . London: published by A. Cleugh, No. 14, Ratcliff High-way. 1803 J. Findlay, Printer, Arbroath.

Variants

1. . . . . A. Cleugh, No. 14, Ratcliff High-way. 1803 . . .
2. . . . . A. Cleugh, No. 14 Ratcliff Highway: and sold by the principal booksellers. 1803.

Re-issued in 1824, § 276 (1824 London=White).

77. 1803 London

Poems, chiefly in the Scottish Dialect. By Robert Burns. In two volumes. . . . Vol. I. London: printed by J. D. Dewick, Aldersgate-street. For R. Thurgood, 39, Newgate-street. 1803.

The copy in Kilmarnock contains the earliest coloured portrait I have seen.

78. 1803 London

The Works of Robert Burns. . . . In four volumes. . . . The
fourth edition . . . London: printed for T. Cadell jun. and W.
Davies, Strand . . . 1803.

Original Material (in Vol. I) :
    Letter to James Smith   30 June. 1787 [*Letters*, 1.98]   *p.* 164

79. 1804 Cork

Poems, chiefly in the Scottish Dialect. By Robert Burns. In
two volumes. Volume I. Cork: printed by A. Edwards,
bookseller and stationer, Castle-street. 1804.

Variant

[*For*] . . . Burns . . . [*some copies have*] . . . Bunrs. . . .

80. 1804 Cupar

«« [Poems by Robert Burns.] Cupar-Fife. 1804 »»

Translated from Angus,[54] who adds : " [12 mo] *Vide* bibliography
in ' Burns Calendar ' (1876) ; also, ditto in Gebbie & Co.'s
Philadelphia edition of the complete works of Robert Burns,
1886." No one, including the Librarian of the Kingdom of Fife,
has heard of a copy since.

81. 1804 Edinburgh

Poems, chiefly in the Scottish Dialect. By Robert Burns. . . .
Edinburgh: printed by John Turnbull, High-street; for Cameron
and Co., booksellers, Trongate, Glasgow. 1804.

82. 1804 Glasgow

Poems, chiefly in the Scottish Dialect. By Robert Burns. . . .
Glasgow, printed by W. Lang, for Cameron & Co., booksellers,
Trongate. 1804.

[54] P. 3 ; his square brackets.

83. 1804 London

The poetical Works of Robert Burns. A new Edition. . . . In three Volumes. . . . Vol. I. London: printed for T. Cadell and W. Davies, Strand. 1804.

The sketch of the life is signed A. C. [=Alexander Chalmers]. Vol. I and II contain the poems in § 25 (1793 Edinburgh). Vol. III the added poems in § 50 (1800 Liverpool).

84. 1804 Philadelphia

The poetical Works of Robert Burns. Vol. I [*of two*]. Philadelphia: Benjamin Johnson, Jacob Johnson, & Robert Johnson. 1804.

85. 1804 Philadelphia

The Works of Robert Burns. . . . In three Volumes. Vol. I. Philadelphia: published by William Fairbairn. 1804.

86. 1804 Wilmington

Poems, chiefly in the Scottish Dialect. By Robert Burns. . . . Wilmington: printed and sold by Bonsal and Niles, in Market Street.—Also sold at their Book-store, Market-Street, Baltimore. 1804.

87. 1805 Belfast

The Works of Robert Burns. . . . In four Volumes. Vol. I. The fifth Edition. Belfast, printed for Archer and Ward, and D. Simms. 1805.

Variants[55]

1. «« . . . Archer & Ward, and D. Simms. 1805.»»
2. «« . . . Archer and Ward, and David Simms. 1805.»»
3. «« . . . Archer & Ward, and David Simms. 1805.»»

A reprint of § 78 (1803 London). It was re-issued in 1806. " Fifth edition " means nothing : the fifth edition of Currie did not appear until 1806 (§ 98).

[55] As reported in *A Tribute to the Memory of Burns from his Countrymen and Admirers in Belfast*, ed. J. Dewar, Belfast 1893, p. 24. I have not seen any such copies.

88. 1805 Edinburgh

Poems, chiefly in the Scottish Dialect. By Robert Burns. Edinburgh: printed for Denham & Dick, 19 College Street, by Thomas Oliver. 1805.

Variant

. . . Denham & Dick, 19 College Street, and J. Scott, 442 Strand, London. 1805.

89. 1805 Edinburgh

Poems, chiefly in the Scottish Dialect. By Robert Burns. With his Life and Character. Edinburgh: printed by Thomas Turnbull, for Denham & Dick, No 19, College-Street. 1805.

Variants

1. . . . College Street, and sold by J. Story, Belfast. 1805.
2. . . . and sold by R. & J. Hodgson, Belfast. 1805.

90. 1805 Edinburgh

Works of the late celebrated Robert Burns. . . . Edinburgh: printed by J. Johnstone, Strichen's Close, and sold at his Book Shop, Blackfriars Wynd. 1805.

91. 1806 Belfast

«« Letters adddressed to Clarinda, &c. By Robert Burns. A new Edition. Belfast: printed by L. Rae. 1806.»»

" This is the only one of five editions bearing his name which claims to have been printed *by* L. Rae; the other four were printed *for* him. . . . Possibly, therefore, the *by* . . . ought to read *for*."[56]

92. 1806 Belfast

Letters addressed to Clarinda, &c. By Robert Burns. A new Edition. Belfast: printed for L. Rae, 1806.

Comment. Mur. copy, in original boards, has on front cover: "London, Printed for the Booksellers."

[56] J. C. Ewing, *Robert Burns's Letters addressed to Clarinda* (Edinburgh : for private circulation, 1921), p. 22.

93. 1806 Belfast

Letters addressed to Clarinda, &c. By Robert Burns. A new edition. Belfast: printed for L. Rae. 1806.

This is not just a variant title-page of § 92; it is a different edition.

94. 1806 Belfast

Letters addressed to Clarinda &c. By Robert Burns, the Ayrshire Poet. A new Edition. Belfast: printed for Archer and Ward & D. Simms. 1806.

Variant

«« . . . Archer and Ward. 1806.»»[57]

95. 1806 Belfast

The Works of Robert Burns. . . . In four Volumes. The fifth Edition. Belfast, printed for Archer and Ward, & D. Simms. 1806.

Re-issue of § 87 (1805 Belfast). The Letters to Clarinda are added at the end of Vol. IV.

96. 1806 Edinburgh

The Poems of Robert Burns. . . . Edinburgh, printed by Oliver & Co., Netherbow. 1806.

Variant

«« . . . Oliver & Co., for Denham and Dick. 1806.»»[58]
Re-issued in 1807 (§ 102), 1809 (§ 117), [1813] (§ 144), 1814 (§ 160), 1816 (§ 186), 1819 (§ 217), and (?) 1820 (§ 236).

97. 1806 London

Poems, chiefly in the Scottish Dialect, by Robert Burns. . . . London: printed by Macpherson and Boyle, Russell-court, Covent-garden. 1806.

[57] Gibson, p. 15.   [58] Angus, p. 19.

98. 1806 London

The Works of Robert Burns. . . . In four Volumes. . . . The fifth Edition. . . . London: printed for T. Cadell and W. Davies, Strand . . . 1806.

99. 1807 Belfast

The Works of Robert Burns. . . . In four Volumes. . . . A new Edition. Belfast: printed by Simms and M'Intyre . . . 1807.

The Letters to Clarinda—§ 94 (1806 Belfast=Archer and Ward) —are bound in at the end of Vol. IV. The whole edition is probably a re-issue of § 86 (1805 Belfast=Archer and Ward, and D. Simms), though I have not been able to examine enough copies to assert this definitely.

100. 1807 Edinburgh

Poems, chiefly in the Scottish Dialect. By Robert Burns. . . . Edinburgh: printed for A. Constable & Co., &c. Printed by F. Ray, Dundee. 1807.

Variant

. . . A. Constable & Co.; W. Anderson, Stirling; T. Donaldson, Dundee; and Vernor, Hood, Sharpe, & Co., London. 1807.

101. 1807 Edinburgh

Poems, chiefly in the Scottish Dialect. By Robert Burns. . . . Edinburgh, printed for W. Anderson, Stirling, by Abernethy & Walker. 1807.

Variants

1. . . . Edinburgh. Printed for Robert Hutcheson, bookseller, Glasgow, by Abernethy & Walker. 1807.

2. . . . Edinburgh: printed for W. Anderson, Stirling. By Abernethy & Walker. 1807.

Re-issued in 1808 (§ 110).

102. 1807 Edinburgh

The poetical Works of Robert Burns. Edinburgh: published
by Oliver & Boyd. 1807. [*engraved throughout*]

A re-issue of § 96 (1806 Edinburgh=Oliver).

103. 1807 Edinburgh

Works of the late celebrated Robert Burns. . . . Edinburgh:
printed by John Johnstone, High Street. 1807.

104. 1807 London

Censura Literaria . . . by Samuel Egerton Brydges, Esq. . . .
Volume III [*of ten*]. . . . London: printed by T. Bensley . . . for
Longman . . . 1807.

Original Material :
    Letter to Francis Grose, June 1790 [*Letters*, II.22]   *p.* 25

105. 1807 London

The poetical Works of Robert Burns. Collated with the best
Editions: by Thomas Park, Esq., F.S.A. In two Volumes. . . .
London: printed at the Stanhope Press . . . for J. Sharpe; and
sold by W. Suttaby . . . 1807.

   The poems in English have been separated from those in Scots,
   and follow them at the end of Vol. II. Re-issued in 1813 (§ 148).

106. 1807 Philadelphia

The poetical Works of Robert Burns. . . . Philadelphia: printed
and sold by Peter Stewart . . . 1807.

107. 1808 Alnwick

The poetical Works of Robert Burns. . . . In Two volumes.
Alnwick: printed by Catnach and Davison . . . 1808. [*woodcuts
by Bewick*].

Publication in parts, to be completed in two numbers, began in 1807 (Parts III and VI are in S.R.) and the whole was gathered and published in 1808.[59] I have, however, found no evidence of stabbing in Vol. II, which would seem to indicate that only Vol. I was issued in parts.

108. 1808 Alnwick

The poetical Works of Robert Burns. . . . In Two volumes. Alnwick: printed by William Davison . . . 1808.

A new edition, published after the partnership between Catnach and Davison had been terminated. Re-issued in 1810 (§ 124).

109. 1808 Belfast

The Works of Robert Burns. . . . In four Volumes A new Edition. Belfast: printed by Simms and M'Intyre, No. 25 High-street. 1808.

According to *M.C.*, § 722, this is a re-issue of § 99 (1807 Belfast). If it was a re-issue, it would probably be a re-issue of § 87 (1805 Belfast). It does not include the Letters to Clarinda, and I am inclined to think it is a new edition. However, I have not examined enough copies to be dogmatic. It uses the frontispiece portrait of § 87, but this proves nothing.

110. 1808 Edinburgh

Poems, chiefly in the Scottish Dialect. By Robert Burns. . . . Printed for the Booksellers, by Abernethy & Walker. 1808.

Re-issue of § 101 (1807 Edinburgh).

111. 1808 Glasgow

Poems, chiefly in the Scottish Dialect. By Robert Burns. Glasgow: printed by D. M'Kenzie, for Robert Smith and Co., Booksellers, Paisley. 1808.

[59] Burman, pp. 47 ff.

112. 1808 London

RELIQUES | of | ROBERT BURNS; | consisting chiefly of |
original Letters, Poems, | and | critical Observations | on |
Scottish Songs. | [*diamond rule*] | Collected and published by |
R. H. CROMEK. | [*diamond rule*] | Ordain'd to fire th'adoring
Sons of Earth | With every charm of wisdom and of worth; | Or,
warm with Fancy's energy to glow, | And rival all but Shakes-
pear's name below. | Pleasures of Hope. | [*double rule*] | London:
| Printed by J. M'Creery, | for T. Cadell, and W. Davies, Strand.
| [*rule*] | 1808.

Format. 8vo, in half-sheets. 23 × 12·3 cm., untrimmed, in original
boards.

Signatures. [a8] ; b4 ; B-M8 ; N4 ; O-Z8 ; AA-GG8 ; HH4 ; II2
(-II2). The first two leaves of each half-sheet are signed.

Contents. Pp. xxiv+454+6 : [i], Title-page ; [ii], blank ; [iii]-xii,
Preface ; [xiii]-xxiii, Table of Contents ; [xxiv], " Corrections " ;
[1]-453, Text ; [454], " J. M'Creery, Printer, Fleet-Street " ;
[1]-5, Advertisement for a print of the Canterbury Pilgrims ; [6],
Advertisement for Blair, *The Grave.*

Original Material :

[60] The entire Ode appeared in *Notes and Queries,* 5th ser., 1 (Mar. 1874), 242.

Original Material :

Also the following letters :

[61] H. & H., II.407. The last stanza of this poem was printed in Cunningham's edition, § 432 (1840), p. 269.

[62] Willie Michie.

[63] H. & H., II.419, imply that this first appeared in Cromek's *Select Scotish Songs*, § 127 (1810 London). This is a somewhat corrupt version.

[64] AA7, *recto.* Cp. below, *Comment.*   [65] These refs. are to *Letters.*

[66] Completed from § 50 (1800 Liverpool = Currie).

Ref.	Addressee	Date	
129	Margaret Chalmers[67]	26 Sep. 1787	p. 37
141	Margaret Chalmers	[c. 1 Dec. 1787]	39
139	Margaret Chalmers	21 Nov. 1787	41
144	Margaret Chalmers	12 Dec. 1787	42
145	Margaret Chalmers	19 Dec. 1787	44
208	Margaret Chalmers	14 Mar. 1788	45
216	Margaret Chalmers	7 Apr. 1788	47
172	Margaret Chalmers	[? 22 Jan. 1788]	47
192	Margaret Chalmers	[17 Feb. 1788]	49
140	Robert Ainslie	23 Nov. 1787	52
137	Margaret Chalmers	[? 6 Nov. 1787]	53
292	Mr Morison	22 Jan. 1788 [1789]	56
218	James Smith	28 Apr. 1788	57
223	Robert Ainslie	26 May 1788	59
228	Robert Ainslie	14 Jun. 1788	61
230	Robert Ainslie	30 Jun. 1788	64
237	George Lockhart	18 Jul. 1788	68
251	Mr Beugo	9 Sep. 1788	70
256	Margaret Chalmers	16 Sep. 1788	72
261	Mrs Dunlop	27 Sep. 1788	79
275	James Johnson	15 Nov. 1788	82
274	Dr Blacklock	15 Nov. 1788	84
286	Robert Ainslie[68]	6 Jan. 1789	87
337	James Hamilton	26 May 1789	89
II.302	William Creech	30 May 1789 [1795]	90
I.339	Robert Ainslie	8 Jun. 1789	92
362	Captain Riddel	16 Oct. 1789	95
334	Captain Riddel	[? 1789]	98
363	Robert Ainslie[69]	1 Nov. 1789	99
II.6	Peter Hill	2 Feb. 1790	101
8	William Nicol	9 Feb. 1790	105
30	Mr [John] Murdoch	16 Jul. 1790	109
46	Crauford Tait	15 Oct. 1790	111
I.349	[Robert Aiken]	[Aug. 1789]	116
II.61	Alexander Dalziel	19 Mar. 1791	118
86	Thomas Sloan	1 Sep. 1791	120
139	Robert Graham	[31] Dec. [1792]	130
115	S. Clarke	16 Jul. 1792	132
140	Mrs Dunlop	31 Dec. 1792	133

[67] Note in original (p. 37) : " The following fragments [pp. 37-50] are all that now exist of twelve or fourteen of the finest letters that Burns ever wrote. In an evil hour, the original were thrown into the fire by the late Mrs Adair of Scarborough ; the *Charlotte* so often mentioned in his correspondence, and the lady to whom ' The Banks of Devon ' is addressed."

[68] First published in *Scots Magazine*, LXIII (1801), 664.

[69] First published in *op. cit.*, p. 665.

Ref.	Addressee	Date	
156	Patrick Miller	Apr. 1793	*p.* 137
169	John Francis Erskine	13 Apr. 1793	138
174	Robert Ainslie	26 Apr. 1793	144
I.21	Miss K———[70]	[Autumn 1785]	147
378	Lady Glencairn[71]	[23 Dec. 1789]	149
II.230	Earl of Buchan	12 Jan. 1794	152
157	Earl of Glencairn	[Mar. or Apr. 1793]	153
47	Dr Anderson	[1 Nov. 1790]	155
246	Mrs Dunlop	25 Jun. 1790	156
233	James Johnson	[Feb. 1794]	158
132	Miss Fontenelle	[*c.* 20 Nov. 1792]	160
239	Peter Miller	Nov. [*c.* 1 May] 1794	161
I.142	Gavin Hamilton	[Dec. 1787]	163
II.249	Samuel Clarke	n.d.	167
232	Alexander Findlater	[Feb. 1794]	169
285	Editors of the *Morning Chronicle*	[Jan. 1795]	170
53	Col. W. Dunbar	[17 Jan. 1791]	173
291	The Heron of Heron	[Mar. 1795]	174
I.303	The Right Hon William Pitt[72]	[*c.* 1 Feb. 1789]	177
II.154	The Magistrates of Dumfries	[Mar. 1793]	182
322	James Johnson[73]	4 Jul. 1796	184

Comment. Issued in gray (or green) paper boards. The gathering AA8 in most copies has the last three leaves removed. These contain the beginning of the *Journal of the Border Tour*, which, if we can judge by this sample, would have been a complete text. However, Ainslie, Burns's *compagnon de voyage*, objected strongly to the inclusion of the *Tour* in Cromek's edition,[74] and Cromek reluctantly had to agree to publish without it. All of the text of the *Tour* had probably been printed,[75] and began on AA6, p. 355, with a title-page, "Journals" (verso blank), and the first four days' account of the trip. It was easy enough for Cromek to destroy the sheets that followed, but what was he to do with AA? His solution, apparently, was to continue the rest of the text, "Fragments, Miscellaneous Remarks, & c.," on BB1 [355], and cut out the offending three leaves AA6-AA8. The cutting-out was to be be done by the binder, and the signal to him for this excision was a vertical tear through the three leaves. A few copies seem to have been overlooked in this operation (I have seen one), and part

---

[70] Miss Margaret Kennedy.　　　　[71] Lady Elizabeth Cunningham.
[72] First published in *Edinburgh Evening Courant*, 9 Feb. 1789.
[73] Completed from § 8.*e* (1787-1803 Edinburgh=Johnson), Vol. V.
[74] The correspondence regarding the matter is in *B. Chr.*, VIII (1899), 42-5.
[75] Catchword "sold" at bottom of p. 360.

of the *Tour* was accidentally included. In most copies, therefore, the collation, after Z, is AA8 (−AA6,7,8) ; BB-GG8, with the pagination remaining as in the original. In some copies the signature B2 is missing ; R2 is a cancel.

One of the most important publications noted in this bibliography. R. H. Cromek, an engraver, spent a great deal of time combing Ayrshire for material, and the result of his labours is highly commendable, as can be seen from the list of original material above.[76]

Reviews

Francis Jeffrey, in *The Edinburgh Review*, XIII (Jan. 1809), p. 249.
Sir Walter Scott, in *The Quarterly Review*, I (Feb. 1809), p. 19.
James Montgomery, in *The Eclectic Review*, V (Pt. 1 : Jan.-Jun. 1809), p. [393].
The Monthly Review, LX (Dec. 1809), p. 399.

113. 1808 London

The Works of the British Poets, collated with the best edition: by Thomas Park, F.S.A. Vol. XL. Containing two volumes of Burns. London: printed for J. Sharpe . . . 1808.

Variant

. . . printed by the Stanhope Press, by Charles Whittingham, 103 Goswell Street: for J. Sharpe . . . 1808.

Vol. XLI, with a similar title-page, was also devoted to Burns. According to the B.M. catalogue, a re-issue of § 105 (1807 London=Sharpe).

114. 1808 Musselburgh

The Poems of Robert Burns. . . . Musselburgh: printed by and for J. Findlay. 1808.

115. 1809 Alnwick

«« Poetical Works. W. Davidson.»»

Burman, p. 51. He had not seen a copy.

---

[76] Cromek's trustworthiness has often been questioned. There is a vindication of his character by Davidson Cook, " Annotations of Scottish Songs," in *B.Chr.*, XXXI (1922), 1-21, and J. De Lancey Ferguson, " In Defense of R. H. Cromek," in *Phil. Q. IX*, No. 3 (Jul. 1930), 239-48.

I

116. 1809 Edinburgh

Amusements of Leisure Hours. . . . By the late Reverend John Skinner. . . . Edinburgh: printed by John Moir . . . 1809.

Original Material : Two letters to the Rev. John Skinner, dated 25 Oct. 1787 (here described as undated), and 14 Feb. 1788.[77]   *Pp.* 28, 33

117. 1809 Edinburgh

The Works of Robert Burns. . . . Edinburgh: printed by and for Oliver & Boyd, Netherbow. 1809.

Variants

1. . . . Edinburgh: printed by and for Oliver & Boyd. 1809.
2. . . . «« London: Oliver & Boyd.»» [Gibson, p. 18.]

Re-issue of § 96 (1806 Edinburgh=Oliver).

118. 1809 London

Poems, Letters, &c. &c. ascribed to Robert Burns. . . . London: printed for J Dick . . . Wm Brown, Deptford. 1809.

According to Gibson, p. 25, the figure of the little urchin at the bottom right-hand corner of the plate is the work of George Cruikshank. His father, Isaac Cruikshank, the engraver, used to let him try his hand on some of his plates in this way and this is the first appearance of George's work in print.

119. 1809 London

«« Poems, Letters, &c. ascribed to Robert Burns. . . . London: Prout. 1809.»»

M'Kie, *Bib. B.*, p. 34. This, if it exists, might well be the same as §118 (1809 London) with a different imprint.

120. 1809 London

The Caledonian Musical Museum. . . containing upwards of two hundred Songs by [Burns]. . . The Whole edited by his Son [Robert]. . . . London: printed for J. Dick . . . 1809.

The frontispiece portrait was recommended by the editor to be an excellent likeness.

[77] *Letters*, 1.133, 188. Ferguson says that both first appeared in § 368 (1834 London=Cunningham).

121. 1809 London

The Works of Robert Burns. . . . In four Volumes. . . . The sixth Edition. . . . London: printed for T. Cadell and W. Davies, Strand . . . 1809.

122. 1809 Philadelphia

Letters addressed to Clarinda, &c. Never before published in America; with a choice Selection of Poems and Songs. By Robert Burns. Philadelphia. . . . John B. Austin . . . 1809.

123. 1809 Philadelphia

Reliques of Robert Burns. . . . Bradford and Inskeep, Philadelphia . . . 1809.

124. 1810 Alnwick

The poetical Works of Robert Burns. In two Volumes. Alnwick: W. Davison. 1810.

Re-issue of § 107 (1808 Alnwick).

125. 1810 London

«« Poetical Works of Robert Burns. . . . W. Lewis & Co.: London, 1810.»»

Mentioned in B.M. catalogue as existing. Lewis printed an edition in 1812 (§ 140) and published another in 1816 (§ 192), which has the same frontispiece and portrait as § 126 (1810 London=Oddy). *Camb. Bib.*, II.975, mentions a *Poetical Works* by W. Lewis, 2 vols., but no place of publication.

126. 1810 London

The poetical Works of Robert Burns. In two Volumes. . . . London: printed for S. A. Oddy, No. 17, Pickett Street, by Joseph Smith, No. 7, King Street, Seven Dials. 1810.

127. 1810 London

Select Scottish Songs, ancient and modern; with critical Observations and biographical Notices, by Robert Burns. Edited by
R. H. Cromek, F.A.S., Ed. Vol. I. [*of two*] London: printed
for T. Cadell and W. Davies, . . . 1810.

Original Material: Letter to the Rev. John Skinner [n.d.: 1.215
  Letters, 1. 133].
  Letter to the same, 14 Feb. 1787 [*Letters*, 1. 188].   221
  Letter to William Tytler, Aug. 1790 [*Letters*, 1. 116].   11.194

Ferguson says that these three Letters all first appeared in § 368
(1834 London=Cunningham), and dates the first 25 Oct. 1787,
and the last [Aug. 1787].

128. [1810 London]

In *Robert Burns' Poems, selected and edited with Notes*, Heidelberg
1906, p. xxxiv, T. F. Henderson suggests that § 78 (1803 London
=Currie) was re-issued in this year with notes and additions by
Gilbert. He must have meant 1820 (§ 242).

129. [1810]

«« Fornicator's Court, . . . One of ten thick-paper copies . . .
1810.»»

Angus, p. 114: " ' The Court of Equity.' published privately in
pamphlet form about 1810. . . ." Cp. also *The Merry Muses*,
Burns Federation, 1911, p. xx. It is possible that these references
might be to § 273 (1823).

130. [1811] Alnwick

The poetical Works of Robert Burns. . . . Alnwick printed by
W. Davison. [*engraved throughout*]

Comment. In 2 vols.; frontispiece is the same as in § 55, " The Holy
  Fair " (1801 Edinburgh=Oliver).

The spine (? original) in the Mur. copy is stamped " Alnwick
1811," and the leaf Pp 6 of Vol. II is an advertisement for

Fergusson's *Poems*, " In the press and speedily will be published
. . . Alnwick: printed by W. Davison. 1811." This same leaf
is bound in at the beginning of Vol. I in the Mitch. Copy,
which, however, has " 1812 " stamped on the original boards.
Burman, p. 51, gives: " Works. W. Davison, 3 vols in 18
numbers. Reference. Advertisement on back of my copy of
Adams' Poems, 1811. . . . D. C. Thomson . . . says ' the project
was abandoned.' " But according to *M.C.*, §355, a copy was
exhibited at Glasgow in 1896.

131. 1811 Edinburgh

Poems by Robert Burns: with an account of his Life, and
miscellaneous Remarks on his Writings. Containing also many
Poems and Letters, not printed in Doctor Currie's Edition. In
two Volumes. Vol. I.... Edinburgh: Printed for the Trustees
of the late James Morison, by John Moir, Royal Bank Close.
1811.

Original Material (Vol. II) :
    Epitaph on a Country Laird [" Bless Jesus Christ, O
    C******** "] [David Maxwell of Cardoness]   *p.* 217

    Six letters, all to Richard Brown :

151[78]	30 Dec. 1787	242
190	15 Feb. 1788	245
195	24 Feb. 1788	246
206	7 Mar. 1788	248
211	20 Mar. 1788	249
336	21 May 1789	251
365	4 Nov. 1789	252

    Inscription to Mrs Graham of Fintry [Apr. 1793] in a 1793
    edn. of the *Poems*.   329

Comment. Also issued large-paper, quarto (*M.C.*, § 87).

James Morison, an Edinburgh bookseller, had planned this
edition, but died before it was completed. As can be seen from
the title-page, the book was published by the trustees of his
estate. Morison apparently knew Captain Richard Brown and
obtained from him the seven letters that Burns had written to
him.
    The " Account of Burns's Life " was written by Josiah
Walker.[79]

[78] These refs. are to *Letters*, I.   [79] *M.C.*, § 86.

132. 1811 London

The poetical Works of Robert Burns, in two Volumes. . . .
London: printed for James Goodwin, Jun. . . . by Joseph
Smith. . . . 1811.

133. 1811 Newcastle

The poetical Works of the late Robert Burns. . . . Newcastle-
on-Tyne . . . M. Angus & Son . . . 1811 [*engraved throughout*]

134. 1811 Philadelphia

Poetical Works of Robert Burns. . . . Philadelphia: printed for
Benjamin Chapman. A. Small, Printer. 1811.
Re-issued in 1815 (§176).

135. [1812] Alnwick

«« Poetical Works [of Robert Burns]. . . . W. Davison.»»[80]

Re-issue of §107 (?). *M.C.*, §356, and Sneddon, p. 16, both give
the date in brackets; Angus, p. 43, and Gibson, p. 20, have no
brackets. Cp. also §130 (1811 Alnwick).

136. 1812 Baltimore

Poems, chiefly in the Scottish Dialect. . . . Baltimore: printed
and sold by A. Miltenberger . . . 1812.

137. 1812 Edinburgh

The poetical Works of Robert Burns. . . . Edinburgh: . . . Oliver
and Boyd. 1812.
Re-issue of § 96 (1806 Edinburgh=Oliver).

138. 1812 London

Letters addressed to Clarinda and Others. . . . London: printed
for the Booksellers, by J. Marshall, Newcastle. 1812.

---

[80] Burman, p. 51. "Advertisement on end leaf of vol. 1 of my copy of
Fergusson's Poems, 1813."

139. 1812 London

«« Poems by Robert Burns. 2 vols. 8vo. London: Hamilton, 1812.»»

Chambers, iv.317.

140. 1812 London

The poetical Works of Robert Burns, in two Volumes. London: printed by W. Lewis . . . for James Goodwin . . . 1812.

141. 1812 Philadelphia

«« Letters addressed to Clarinda. . . . Philadelphia: 1812.»»
Camb.Bib., ii.974.

142. 1813 Alexandria [Virginia]

Poetical Works of Robert Burns. A new Edition. Alexandria: printed by John A. Stewart. 1813.

143. 1813 Alnwick

« Poetical Works. W. Davison, 2 vols.»»

Burman, p. 51. He gives the price as 12s. in boards, and quotes as his reference: " Advertisement on end leaf of Vol. I of my copy of Ferguson's Poems, 1813."

144. [1813] Edinburgh

Poetical Works of Robert Burns. . . . Published by Oliver & Boyd, Edinburgh. [*Engraved throughout*]

M.C., §149 gives the date 1813 in square brackets: Angus, p. 19, gives it without brackets. This may perhaps have been § 160 (1814 Edinburgh) with " 1813 " on the front cover.[81]
Re-issue of § 96 (1806 Edinburgh=Oliver).

145. 1813 Edinburgh

The poetical Works of the late Robert Burns; with an Account of his Life. . . . Edinburgh printed for Don & Grant, Publishers, Crosscauseway. 1813.

[81] Cp. *B. Chr.*, iii (1894), 165.

Variant

. . . Edinburgh: printed for Thomas Neilson, Publisher, West Bow. 1813.

Re-issued in 1814 (§ 158).

146. 1813 Edinburgh

«« Macredie & Co. ed Alex Peterkin.   4 vols.   8vo.»»

Gebbie, vi.337.

147. 1813 London

«« Burns's Poems, 24to.   London: Walker.   1813.»»

Chambers, iv.317; Gebbie, vi.337.

148. 1813 London

The poetical Works of Robert Burns.   Collated with the best Editions: by Thomas Park. . . .   In two Volumes. . . .   London: printed at the Stanhope Press . . . 1813.

Variant

Sharpe's Edition of the British Poets.   Vols. LXI and LXII.

Re-issue of § 105 (1807 London=Sharpe).

149. 1813 London

The poetical Works of Robert Burns, including the Pieces published in his Correspondence. . . .   London: printed for T. Cadell and W. Davies, Strand; and W. Creech, at Edinburgh. 1813.

Issued in one and two volumes with no indication on the title-page.   In *The Publishing Firm of Cadell and Davies*, London 1938, p. xxii, Theodore Besterman says that a one-volume edition of the poems was published in this year, and that Alexander Chambers was commissioned to write the Life.   Re-issued in 1816 (§ 191), 1817 (§ 201), and 1822 (§ 260).

150. 1813 London

The Reliques of Robert Burns. . . . London: printed by J. M'Creery, for T. Cadell . . . 1813.

This is the second edition of § 112 (1808 London).

151. 1813 London

The Works of Robert Burns; with an Account of his Life, and a Criticism on his Writings. . . . In four Volumes. The seventh Edition. London: printed for T. Cadell and W. Davies, Strand. 1813.

152. 1813 Perth

Poems, chiefly Scottish. . . . In two Volumes. Perth: printed by R. Morison and sold by the principal Booksellers . . . 1813.

With the exception of pp. vi and 144 the first volume is identical with pp. [i]-xiv+144 of the following item.

153. 1813 Perth

Poems, chiefly Scottish. . . . Perth: printed by R. Morison, and sold by the principal Booksellers . . . 1813.

154. 1813 Philadelphia

«« Reliques.»»

Camb. Bib., II.974.

155. 1814 Alnwick

«« Poetical Works.»»

Burman, p. 52. He gives as reference: " Bell's Catalogue of Works by Thomas Bewick, page 50, No. 65."

156. 1814 Baltimore

«« Works of Robert Burns. In four volumes. Baltimore: published by F. Lucas, jr., and J. Cushing. 1814.»»

M.C., § 746; Angus, p. 85.

157. 1814 Belfast

Letters addressed to Clarinda, &c.   By Robert Burns.   A new
Edition.   Belfast: printed for L. Rae.   1814.

158. 1814 Edinburgh

Poetical Works. . . .   Edinburgh: printed for Don & Grant,
Publishers, No. 7 Alison's Square.   1814.

Re-issue of § 145 (1813 Edinburgh).

159. 1814 Edinburgh

«« Poetical Works of Robert Burns.   18mo.   Edinburgh, 1814.»»
Chambers, iv.317.   (? Same as next item.)

160. 1814 Edinburgh

The poetical Works of Robert Burns. . . .   Edinburgh: published
by Oliver & Boyd . . . 1814.

Mur. and S.R. copies have " 1813 " on front board.   Cp. § 144.
Re-issue of § 96 (1806 Edinburgh=Oliver).

161. 1814 London

The poetical Works of Robert Burns. . . .   London: printed for
John Bumpus . . . and sold by all Booksellers.   1814.

162. 1814 London

The Works of Robert Burns; with an Account of his Life, and
a Criticism on his Writings . . . The eighth Edition.   To which
are now added the Reliques of Robert Burns.   In five Volumes.
London: printed for T. Cadell and W. Davies, Strand.   1814.

Illustrated throughout with woodcuts by Thomas Bewick.   The
Reliques are in Vol. V.

163. 1814 Newcastle

The poetical Works of Robert Burns. . . .   Newcastle upon
Tyne: printed and sold by J. Marshall, in the Old Flesh Market.
1814.

164. 1814 Philadelphia

««Reliques.»»

Camb. Bib., II.974. Perhaps a re-issue of § 154.

165. 1814 Stirling

Scenes of Gloamin': Original Scottish Songs. By Willison
Glass . . . Stirling: printed for the Author by M. Randall,
Bookseller, 1814.

Original Material:
    Epitaph . . . for . . . Wm. Nichol [" Ye maggots feed on
    Willie's brains . . ."][82]   *p*. 39

166. 1815 Alnwick

««Poetical Works. W. Davison, 2 vols.»»

Burman, p. 52. His reference was his own copy, with copper-
plate frontispiece and title-page: " comparison of this issue and
part No. 10 (1815) proves them to be identical though undated."
    Mitch. has Pts. V (Vol. I pp. 219-78) and IX (Vol. II, pp.
113-60). The wrapper is dated 1815, which probably means a
re-issue, since the parts are identical with those of § 130 (1811
Alnwick). *M.C.*, § 357, gives: " Re-issue. 1815. (No. 8 only).
The last (recorded) Bewick edition with date."

167. 1815 Baltimore

Poems, chiefly in the Scottish dialect. By Robert Burns.

Baltimore: F. Lucas, jr., and J. Cushing. 1815.

168. 1815 Baltimore

The Works of Robert Burns; . . . In four Volumes. . . . Baltimore, published by F. Lucas, jun., and J. Cushing . . . 1815.

[?] Re-issue of § 156.

[82] H. & H., II.453, say that this was first published in § 251 (1821 London=
Richards).

169. 1815 Belfast

The Poems of Robert Burns; . . . Belfast: printed by Thomas Mairs & Co. for David Simms, Donegall Street. 1815.

Dewar mentions two editions in this year, one Mairs and one Simms.[83] Re-issued in 1820 (§ 233).

170. 1815 Edinburgh

The Life and Works of Robert Burns. . . . Edinburgh: printed by Michael Anderson, for Macredie, Skelly, and Muckersy . . . 1815.

Edited by Alexander Peterkin. Contains some original letters to Peterkin from Gilbert Burns, James Gray, Alexander Findlater, and George Thomson. Re-issue, n.d. (§ 1012).

171. 1815 Edinburgh

The poetical Works of Robert Burns. Edinburgh: published by Doig & Stirling. 1815. [*engraved throughout*]

The Mitch. copy has the above engraved title-page, and a printed one dated 1817. Kil. and *M.C.*, § 59, have only the engraved title-page. Re-issued in 1817 (§ 198).

171A. 1815 Edinburgh

The poetical Works of the late Robert Burns; with an Account of his Life. . . . Edinburgh: printed for Don & Grant, Publishers, No. 7 Alison's Square. 1815.

172. 1815 Edinburgh

The poetical Works of Robert Burns; with his Songs and Fragments. . . . printed by W. Aitchison, 187, High Street, for James Sawers. 1815.

[83] *A Tribute to the Memory of Burns from his Countrymen and Admirers in Belfast*, ed. J. Dewar, Belfast [1894], p. 24.

173. 1815 London

The Works of Robert Burns. . . . In four Volumes. . . . London: printed for Gale & Fenner, London; Oliver & Boyd, Edinburgh; W. Turnbull, Glasgow; and John Cumming, Dublin.   1815.

174. 1815 London

«« Works of Robert Burns. . . .   5 vols., 18 mo. . . .   London 1815.»»

Chambers IV.317, which describes it as " a scarce edition." Perhaps it was the same as § 162, with the *Reliques* in Vol. V.

175. [1815 New York]

There is some doubt whether this edition exists.   Cp. John Macintosh, *Life of Robert Burns*, Paisley 1906, p. 301, and Gebbie, VI.337: " J. P. Reynolds, 2 vols. 24mo."

176. 1815 Philadelphia

Poetical Works. . . .   Philadelphia: printed for Benjamin Chapman . . . 1815.

Re-issue of § 134 (1811 Philadelphia).

177. 1815 Salem, N.Y.

The poetical Works of Robert Burns. . . .   In two Volumes. Salem, N.Y. printed by J. P. Reynolds, Sign of the Bible.   1815.

178. 1816 Alnwick

«« Works.»»

Burman, p. 54.   His reference is: " W. Garret's second hand book catalogue for July, 1844."

179. 1816 Baltimore

Works of Robert Burns. . . .   Baltimore: published by F. Lucas, jun and J. Cushing.   G. Palmer, Printer.   1816.

Gibson, p. 24, gives the imprint as: " F. Lucas & J. Cushing."

180. 1816 Belfast

«« Findlay's edition of Burns's poems. Belfast: 1816.»»

Camb. Bib., II.975, which also gives another issue, same date,
" with the Introduction in different type."
A re-issue (?) of § 183 (1816 Dublin).

181. 1816 Belfast

Letters addressed to Clarinda, & c. By Robert Burns. A new
edition. Belfast: printed for L. Rae. 1816.

182. 1816 Belfast

The Poetical Works of Robert Burns. A new Edition. Belfast
printed for Alexander M'Donald . . . by Hu. K. Gordon . . .
1816.

Contains a selection of letters, and the worst portrait of Burns I
have ever seen.

183. 1816 Dublin

Findlay's Edition of Burns's Poems, including a Number of
Pieces never before published. . . . Dublin: printed and sold
by J. Findlay, Army-printer . . . 1816.

Variants

1. ««. . . Belfast: 1816. [§ 180].»»
2. Poems, chiefly in the Scottish dialect. By Robert Burns.
Edinburgh: printed by J. Findlay, and sold by the Booksellers.
[*n.b. Cp. also* §185.]

This edition offers a rather special problem. It may be three
issues, or two editions, one of them with two issues. Findlay[84]
moved from Edinburgh to Dublin during 1816, presumably
because of a Government contract (he describes himself as
" Army Printer "), and the entire edition might have been
printed before he left. Copies vary slightly in so far as some

---

[84] This is the same James Findlay of Arbroath who printed § 76 (1803
London) and § 114 (1808 Musselburgh) ; *Notes and Queries*, 6th Ser., IV
(22 Oct. 1881), 335.

of the ornaments have been re-set, but the text remains consistent, except that in the Mur. copy, which has the Dublin title-page, the Dedication to the Caledonian Hunt has been re-set. I am inclined to think that Findlay had completed the work in Edinburgh before he left, that he issued part of it there (" sold by the booksellers "), and took the remaining sheets with him to be issued in Dublin and Belfast. The re-setting of ornaments is not necessarily evidence of anything more than a change of mind, and a new set-up of the Dedication may merely mean that Findlay had not printed enough sheets of this particular gathering and had to do the work over again in Ireland.

184. 1816 Dublin

Letters addressed to Clarinda, &c. By Robert Burns. A new Edition. Dublin: printed for R. Lindsay. 1816.

There are two editions: both have pp. 48, but the first has A-D6 the second A-B12.

185. [1816] Edinburgh

Poems, chiefly in the Scottish Dialect. By Robert Burns. Edinburgh: printed by J. Findlay, and sold by the principal Booksellers.

Probably the original issue of § 181 (1816 Belfast) and § 183 (1816 Dublin).

186. 1816 Edinburgh

The poetical Works of Robert Burns. Edinburgh: published by Oliver & Boyd, High Street. 1816.

Two editions, with identical printed title-pages but different engraved title-pages.

187. 1816 Edinburgh

The poetical Works of the late Robert Burns. . . . Edinburgh: printed for J. Dick, 142 High Street. 1816.

188. 1816 Edinburgh

«« The poetical works of the late Robert Burns . . . a new edition
. . . Edinburgh: printed for T. Neilson. 1816.»»

B. Chr., III (1894), 166.   (? Same as preceding item.)

189. 1816 Glasgow

«« Letters.   1 vol.   8 vo.»»

Gebbie, VI.337.

190. 1816 Glasgow

The poetical Works of Robert Burns.   Glasgow: printed by
Edward Khull & Co. for W. Somerville, A. Fullarton, J. Blackie,
& Co., 5 Saltmarket.   1816.

Variants

1. . . . J. Blackie, & Co., East Clyde-street.   1816.
2. «« . . . A. Fullarton, & Co., Saltmarket.   1816.»»[85]

Published in thirteen numbers at 6d.   Re-issued in 1819 (§ 223).

191. 1816 London

The poetical Works of Robert Burns, including the Pieces
published in his Correspondence. . . .   London . . . T. Cadell
and W. Davies . . . 1816.

Re-issue of § 149 (1813 London).

192. 1816 London

The poetical Works of Robert Burns, in two Volumes. . . .   London
. . . W. Lewis and Co. . . . 1816.

Variant

[*After*] Burns [*some copies have a point instead of a comma.*]

[85] M'Kie, *Bib. B.*, p. 10.

193. 1816 Montrose

The Works of Robert Burns. . . . In four Volumes. Montrose: printed by Smith & Hill, and sold by the Booksellers of London and Edinburgh. 1816.

194. 1816 Newcastle

The prose Works of Robert Burns. . . . Newcastle upon Tyne: printed and published by J. Marshall, in the Old Flesh-market. 1816.

195. 1817 Belfast

«« The poems of Robert Burns. Belfast. Printed by Joseph Smyth. 1817.»»

A Tribute to the Memory of Burns from his Countrymen and Admirers in Belfast, ed. J. Dewar, Belfast (Marcus Ward) [1894], p. 24.

196. 1817 Darvel

The Fornicators Court, a poem written by Robert Burns. Never before published—printed for Mackenzie and Sandilands . . . Darvel. 1817.

Probably the first appearance of this poem in print, but see § 129.

197. 1817 Edinburgh

A complete Collection of the Songs of Robert Burns, extracted from his Works and various other Publications. Edinburgh: printed by C. Stewart; and sold by Doig and Stirling. 1817.

198. 1817 Edinburgh

The Poetical Works of Robert Burns. . . . In two Volumes. . . . Doig and Stirling. 1817.

Re-issue of § 171 (1815 Edinburgh=Doig and Stirling).

K

199. 1817 Kirkcaldy

Poems, by Robert Burns. Kirkcaldy: published by G. Morison. 1817.

A made-up volume consisting of § 131 (1811 Edinburgh = Morison), Vol. I, pp. 3-214, and Vol. II, pp. 215-316.

200. 1817 London

The Letters and Correspondence of Robert Burns. To which are added some Letters never before published . . . London: printed for the Booksellers. 1817 [*two vols.*]

Original Material. Four letters, all to James Johnson :

1.340[86]	19 Jun. 1789	*p.* 209
II.75	Ellisland [1791]	210
298	[1795]	211
312	[Aug.-Sep. 1795]	213

Despite " London " on the title-page, this may have been printed in Edinburgh, since the MSS. of the four original letters were undoubtedly in Scotland at the time. Vol. I consists of general correspondence, Vol. II of correspondence with Thomson. Re-issued in 1819 (§ 225), " London: for the booksellers," with added vol. of poems, and 1820 (§ 238, Edinburgh = Orphoot).

201. 1817 London

The poetical Works of Robert Burns. . . . London . . . T. Cadell and W. Davies . . . 1817.

Re-issue of § 149 (1813 London). Extra engraved title-page dated 1816.

202. 1817 London

Reliques of Robert Burns. . . . London . . . T. Cadell and W. Davies . . . 1817.

Fourth edition of § 112 (1808 London).

[86] These refs. are to *Letters*. Ferguson ascribes all these to § 238 (1820 Edinburgh = Orphoot).

203. 1817 Philadelphia

«« Reliques.»»

Camb. Bib., II.974. Perhaps a re-issue of § 164 (1814 Philadelphia).

204. 1818 Alnwick

«« Works. W. Davison.»»

Burman, p. 52. His entry reads: " 16 numbers forming four volumes. 12mo. A few copies on superfine demy paper, with proof impressions of cuts. Reference. Advertisement on outside back cover of my copy of the ' Cave of Hoonga ', 1818. . . . This, like the 3 vols., advertised in 1811, has never been traced [but see § 130]. Again, I presume, ' The project was abandoned.' "

205. 1818 Belfast

The Poems of Robert Burns. . . . Belfast: printed by Joseph Smyth, 34, High-street. 1818.

Re-issued in Dublin, 1819 (§ 215).

206. 1818 Dunbar

«« Poetical Works of Robert Burns. Dunbar: printed by and for G. Miller. 1818.»»

Two issues [? editions] have been noted: the one, 12mo, pp. 216, untrimmed; the other 24mo, pp. 220.[87]

207. 1818 Edinburgh

The Works of Robert Burns, with an Account of his Life, Criticism on his Writings, &c., &c. As edited by James Currie, M.D. A new edition. In four Volumes. Edinburgh: printed for Thomas Nelson, West Bow, by W. Blair, Edinburgh. 1818.

Variants

1. . . . Burns. With . . . Life. In four Volumes. Glasgow: printed for A. Leslie by W. Blair, . . .

[87] *Catalogue of the Burns . . . Exhibition . . . Victoria Galleries*, Dundee 1896-7. pp. 11-12.

2. . . . Burns. In four volumes. Glasgow: printed for W. and P. Jenkins by W. Blair, . . .

3. Works of Robert Burns, as edited by James Currie, M.D. In four volumes. Durham: printed for George Walker by W. Blair, . . .

4. . . . Edinburgh: printed for James Robertson, Parliament Square, and Wm. Nivison, North Bridge, Edinburgh. By W. Blair, James' Court. 1818.

5. . . . Edinburgh: printed for William Sawers, College Street, By Wm. Blair, James' Court. 1818.

This edition contains, at the end of Vol. IV, "Holy Willie's Prayer," and other poems, which were not in the early editions of Currie.

208. 1818 London

Illustrations of the Literary History of the Eighteenth Century . . . by John Nichols . . . Volume III [*of eight*]. . . . London . . . 1818.

Original Material :
    Letter to James Sibbald [Jan. 1787 : *Letters*, 1.62]   *p.* 780

209. 1818 Newcastle

The poetical Works of Robert Burns. . . . Newcastle upon Tyne: printed and published by Mackenzie and Dent . . . 1818.

Issued in parts. *M.C.*, § 697, notes pts. 19-20 and 25-26. Ayr Library copy shows stabbings. Re-issued in 1821 (§ 252) and 1826 (§ 378).

210. 1818 Philadelphia

The poetical Works of Robert Burns with an Account of his Life and his Correspondence with Mr. Thomson. Philadelphia: published by Benjamin Warner . . . Printed by Thomas H. Palmer. 1818.

In 2 vols.

211. 1818 Philadelphia

The Scottish Minstrel: being a complete Collection of Burns' Songs. . . . Philadelphia: published by Benjamin Warner, No. 147, Market-Street. Printed by Thomas H. Palmer. 1818.

With The Thomson Correspondence from Currie §50.*d* (Liverpool 1800).

212. 1818 Sunderland

«« Poems by Robert Burns. Sunderland. T. Rae. 1818.»»

Angus, p. 80.

213. 1818 Washington, D.C.

Letters addressed to Clarinda, &c. By Robert Burns. First American Edition. Washington City: printed for J. M'Laughlin. 1818.

Very rare. Perhaps the only Burns edition ever printed in Washington.

214. 1819 Ayr

The Poems & Songs of Robert Burns, with a Life of the Author, containing a Variety of Particulars, drawn from Sources inaccessible by former Biographers. To which is subjoined, an Appendix, consisting of a panegyrical Ode, and a Demonstration of Burns' Superiority to every other Poet as a Writer of Songs, by the Rev Hamilton Paul, Minister of Broughton, Glenholm & Kilbucho. Air: Printed by Wilson, M'Cormick & Carnie. 1819.

Original Material :
     The Farewell [" Farewell old Scotia's bleak domains . . ."] *p.* 197

215. 1819 Dublin

The Poems of Robert Burns. . . . Dublin: printed for William Pickering and Co. 1819.

Re-issue of § 205 (1818 Belfast).

216. 1819 Edinburgh

«« Complete Collection of the Songs of Robert Burns.   Edinburgh: . . . Doig & Stirling.   1819.»»

M.C., § 175.

217. 1819 Edinburgh

«« Poems and songs by Robert Burns.   Edinburgh. . . .   Oliver and Boyd.   1819.»»

Angus, p. 20.   It is not certain that this edition exists.

218. 1819 Edinburgh

«« The Poetical Works of Robert Burns : to which is prefixed a Sketch of his Life.   In two Volumes.   Edinburgh . . . Stirling Slade.   1819.»»

M.C., § 181.   According to Gibson, p. 30, a reprint of § 171 (1815 Edinburgh=Doig and Stirling).

219. 1819 Edinburgh

The poetical Works of Robert Burns.   To which is prefixed, the Author's Life.   Edinburgh: Oliver & Boyd . . . 1819.

Gibson, p. 28, gives : The poems of Robert Burns . . ."   It is not clear how this differs from § 217.

220. 1819 Edinburgh

The poetical Works of Robert Burns: with his Songs and Fragments . . . Edinburgh: printed for Peter Brown, Nicolson Street.   By W. Aitchison.   1819.

Variant

. . . for J. Dick.   High Street, by W. Aitchison.   1819.

221. 1819 Edinburgh

The Works of Robert Burns: with an Account of his Life, and a Criticism on his Writings . . . In two Volumes. Edinburgh: printed for J. Bumpus . . . Smith & Hill, printers, Montrose. 1819.

Variant

. . . Volumes. Montrose: printed by Smith & Hill, for J. Bumpus . . . 1819.

222. 1819 Edinburgh

The Works of Robert Burns, with an Account of his Life, Criticism on his Writings, &c., &c. . . . In four Volumes. Edinburgh: printed for James Robertson, and Stirling & Slade, Parliament Square, Edinburgh; Reid & Henderson, Glasgow; and G. & W. B. Whittaker, London. 1819.

Variant

. . . Volumes. London: printed for William Allason, 31 New Bond Street, and J. Maynard, Panton Street, Haymarket, London; and W. Blair, Edinburgh. 1819.

223. 1819 Glasgow

The poetical Works of Robert Burns. . . . Glasgow . . . Sommer-ville . . . East Clyde-street. 1819.

Re-issue of § 190 (1816 Glasgow = Sommerville).

224. 1819 London

The Letters of Burns. [*2 vols.*] London. Published by John Sharpe, Piccadilly. 1819. [*engraved throughout*]

Variants

1. Sharpe's Select Edition of the British Prose Writers. Burns's Letters. In two volumes. London: John Sharpe. 1819.
2. The British Prose Writers. Vol. XXIII. Burns's Letters. London . . . John Sharpe . . . 1819-21.

225. 1819 London

Poetical Works of Robert Burns. . . . London: printed for J. Offor . . . 1819.

This is the work which furnishes the third volume of § 228 (1819 London) and § 238 (1820 Edinburgh=Orphoot).

226. 1819 London

The poetical Works of Robert Burns. . . . In two Volumes. London: . . . James Thomson . . . 1819.

227. 1819 London

«« Songs of Robert Burns. . . . London: James Thomson. 1819.»»
M.C., § 633.

228. 1819 London

The Works of Robert Burns. . . . In three Volumes. . . . London: printed for the booksellers. 1819.

The first two volumes, *Letters*, are a re-issue of § 200 (1817 London, for the booksellers). The last volume is another issue of § 225 (1819 London=Orphoot). Re-issued in 1840 (§ 430).

229. 1819 London

«« S. Walker. 2 vols. 24mo.»»
Gebbie, vi.338.

230. 1819 Montrose

Poetical Works of Robert Burns. Montrose: printed for J. Smith, Bookseller. Smith & Hill, Printers. MDCCCIX.

231. 1819 Montrose

The Lyric Muse of Robert Burns. Containing all his Songs. . . . Montrose: . . . John Smith, Bookseller. MDCCCXIX.

232. 1819 Newcastle

The prose Works of Robert Burns. . . . Newcastle upon Tyne: printed and published by Mackenzie and Dent . . . 1819.

Original Material :
    Address of Beelzebub[88]   *p.* 591
    Letter to Charles Hay [Dec. 1787][89]   593
    On the Death of the late Lord President[90]   594

Issued in parts, stabbed. *M.C.*, § 701, lists pts. 6 and 25-26.

233. 1820 Belfast

«« The poems of Robert Burns . . . Belfast: printed by Thomas Mairs & Co. for Simms and M'Intyre . . . 1820.»»

M.C., § 723. Re-issue of § 169 (1815 Belfast).

234. 1820 Boston

Letters of Robert Burns. Two Volumes in One. Boston: Wells and Lilly, Court Street. 1820.

235. [1820 Edinburgh]

[? Letters to Clarinda. Edinburgh: Orphoot, 1820.]

Lacks a title-page. " Robert " misspelled " Roebrt " on half-title (not all copies have this error), otherwise the same as the edition of the *Letters*[91] sometimes bound with §238 (1820 Edinburgh=Orphoot).[91]

236. 1820 Edinburgh

«« The Poems of Robert Burns . . . Edinburgh: Printed for Oliver & Boyd. 1820.»»

M.C., § 156. Perhaps a re-issue of § 217 (1819 Edinburgh).

---

[88] *Scots Magazine*, n.s. II (Feb. 1818) 130.
[89] Originally published in *Scots Magazine*, n.s., II (Jun. 1818), p. 527 ; *Letters*, I.147. Ferguson says it first appeared in the Chambers edition of 1839 (§ 417).
[90] Originally published in *Scots Magazine*, n.s., II (Jun. 1818), p. 527.
[91] Cp. James C. Ewing, *Robert Burns's Letters to Clarinda*, (Edinburgh : for private circulation, 1921), p. 24.

237 1820 Edinburgh

The poetical Works of the late Robert Burns. . . . Edinburgh:
printed for Thomas Nelson . . . 1820.

238. 1820 Edinburgh

The Works of Robert Burns. In three Volumes. Edinburgh:
printed and sold by John Orphoot . . . 1820.

Re-issue of § 228 (1819 London).

239. 1820 Edinburgh

The Works of Robert Burns: with an Account of his Life. . . .
In four Volumes. Edinburgh: printed for Ogle, Allardice &
Thomson, and Stirling & Slade, Edinburgh. 1820.

According to *Camb. Bib.*, ii.976, there are two different editions
of the same date.

240. 1820 Edinburgh

Works of Robert Burns. . . . In four Volumes. . . . Edinburgh:
printed for Alex Peat, 59 South Bridge. 1820.

241. 1820 Glasgow

Letters addressed to Clarinda &c. &c. By Robert Burns. . . .
Glasgow: printed by R. Chapman, Trongate. 1820.

242. 1820 London

The Works of Robert Burns with an Account of his Life. . . .
The eighth Edition . . . [ed.] by Gilbert Burns. London: printed
for T. Cadell and W. Davies . . . 1820. [*in four volumes*]

Vol. II

Original Material. Three letters :

Ref.[92]	Addressee	Date	
i.15	James Burness	17 Feb. 1784	*p.* 18
307	James Burness	9 Feb. 1789	215
ii.326	Gilbert Burns	10 Jul. 1796	481

[92] To *Letters.*

VOL. IV

Original Material :
    The Fête Champetre [" O wha will to Saint Stephen's House"] 402

This was to have been an elaborate re-doing of Currie's edition
(§ 50) by the poet's brother in which Gilbert was going to
vindicate Robert's character as it had been limned by Currie,
but the edition is a disappointment. Apart from the original
material there is practically nothing else to commend it.

243. 1820 New York

Burns' select Works, Prose. Vol. 1. New-York: . . . R. & W. A.
Bartow . . . 1820.

One volume of what may have been a projected larger set.
Re-issued in 1821 (§ 253).

244. 1821 Chiswick

The poetical Works of Robert Burns. Vol. I. [*of two*] Chiswick:
from the Press of C. Whittingham . . . 1821.

See also § 250 (1821 London).

245. 1821 Edinburgh

The poetical Works of Robert Burns. . . . Edinburgh: printed
by W. Aitchison. 1821.

Also with engraved title-page.

246. 1821 Glasgow

The poetical Works of Robert Burns. . . . Glasgow: . . . Khull,
Blackie, & Co. . . . 1821.

247. 1821 London

Lives of the Scottish Poets. [By Joseph Robertson] London . . .
T. Boys . . . 1821. [*three volumes*]

Original Material (in Vol. I) :
    Letter to [Peter Stuart] 18 May 1789 [*Letters*, 1.336]   *p.* 195

248. 1821 London

The poetical Works of Robert Burns. With a Life of the Author.
. . . London: printed and sold by Dean and Munday . . . 1821.

249. 1821 London

The poetical Works of Robert Burns: with the Life of the
Author . . . In two Volumes. London: printed and published
by C. Baynes . . . 1821.

Gibson, p. 34, has this and also a variant: " London, C. Baynes.
Front boards dated 1822."

250. 1821 London

«« The poetical works of Robert Burns. 2 vols. [Vols. 32 and 33
of *Whittingham's Cabinet Library*] London: Whittingham. 1821.»»

Chambers, iv.318. Another issue (Chambers's square brackets)
of § 244 (1821 Chiswick).

251. 1821 London

The Works of Robert Burns; including his Letters to Clarinda,
and the Whole of his suppressed Poems: with an Essay on his
Life, Genius, and Character. In four Volumes. Vol. I. London:
Printed for the Editor, by Richards and Co. Grocers' Hall Court,
Poultry. 1821.

This is one of the more important editions of Burns's works, in
that it attempts to be as complete as possible. It reprints everything that had appeared in either Cromek or Currie, and restores
many lines which former editors had omitted. The editor, who
remains anonymous, defends Burns's character passionately and
damns Currie for a cheat and an impostor. This edition may have
been the result of Gilbert Burns's weak-kneed editorial policy
in the edition of 1820 (§ 242).
    Vol. IV, p. 238, has a spurious set of " My Nanie O." Cp.
H. & H., iv.76.

252. 1821 Newcastle

The poetical Works of Robert Burns. . . . Newcastle upon Tyne
. . . Mackenzie and Dent . . . 1821

M.C., § 698, calls this a re-issue of § 209 (1818 Newcastle).

253. 1821 New York

The Works of Robert Burns. . . . New York: published by
R. & W. A. Bartow . . . 1821. [*engraved throughout*]

In two volumes. Vol. I is a re-issue of § 243 (1820 New York),
with the addition of the autobiographical letter to Dr Moore as
a preface.

254. 1822 Boston

The Works of the British Poets. . . . Edited by Robert Walsh, Jr.
Vol. XXVIII. Robert Burns. Boston: published by Charles
Ewer and Timothy Bedlington. William Brown, Printer. 1822.

Variant

. . . Burns. Philadelphia: published by Samuel F. Bradford,
for John Laval. William Brown, . . .
In two volumes. The second contains poems by Hector MacNeill
as well as by Burns.

255. 1822 Chiswick

«« The British Poets. . . . In one hundred volumes. LXXV
[-LXXVI] Burns. Chiswick: printed by C. Whittingham . . .
1822.»»

Variant

««The Poems of Robert Burns. [*In two volumes.*] Chiswick:
from the press of C. Whittingham . . . 1822.»»

M.C., § 678. *M.C.'s* square brackets. (? Re-issue of § 244,
1821 Chiswick.)

256. 1822 Glasgow

Letters addressed to Clarinda &c. By Robert Burns. Glasgow:
printed for A. Leslie . . . 1822.

257. 1822 Liverpool

««Improved Edition.   Songs of Robert Burns.   Liverpool, 1822.»»

Camb. Bib., II.976.

258. 1822 London

The poetical Works of Robert Burns. . . . London: printed for the Booksellers: and for J. Kendrew, York. 1822. Edited by William Roscoe.

The first edition printed in Yorkshire; rare. *Camb. Bib.*, II.976, says that there were two issues.

259. 1822 London

The poetical Works of Robert Burns; including the Pieces published in his Correspondence and Reliques: with his Songs and Fragments. To which are prefixed, a History of the Poems . . . In two Volumes. London: printed for John Bumpus . . . and Galignani, Paris. 1822.

The first edition, perhaps, to have been printed for any publisher outside Britain and the U.S.A.

260. 1822 London

The poetical Works of Robert Burns, including the Pieces published in his Correspondence and Reliques, with his Song and Fragments. To which is prefixed a Sketch of his Life. London: printed for T. Cadell and W. Davies . . . Adam Black . . . Edinburgh . . . and G. Clark, at Aberdeen. 1822.

Re-issue of § 149 (1813 London).

261. 1822 Philadelphia

The poetical Works of Robert Burns. In two Volumes. Philadelphia: published by M'Carty and Davis . . . 1822.

262. 1822

«« Burns' (R.) Poetical Works.   With life.   Two vols.   1822 [12mo with portrait]»»

M'Kie, *Bib. B.*, p. 36 (M'Kie's square brackets).

263. 1823 Edinburgh

The poetical Works of the late Robert Burns. . . . Edinburgh: printed by Thomas Turnbull, Old Assembly Close. 1823.

Variant

. . . Thomas Turnbull for James Scott, Bookseller.   1823. [*engraved throughout*]

264. 1823 London

«« Stothard's Illustrated Edition.»»

Camb. Bib., II.976.   According to Cook, this is " a re-issue of Gilbert B.'s edn. of London: 1820.   Remainder copies with extra plates were issued in 1823."

265. 1823 London

The poetical Works of Robert Burns; including several Pieces not inserted in Dr Currie's Edition. . . .   In two Volumes. London: published by W. T. Sherwin . . . 1823.

266. 1823 London

The poetical Works of Robert Burns, including the Pieces published in his Correspondence and Reliques; with his Songs and Fragments. . . .   In three Volumes.   London: printed for T. Cadell, in the Strand . . . 1823.

Chambers, IV.314, has " Cadell & Davies."

267. 1823 London

The poetical Works of Robert Burns, the Ayrshire bard. . . .
London: published by Jones and Company . . . 1823.

Two volumes in one. Re-issued in 1824 (§ 281), 1825 (§ 295),
1826 (§ 305), 1827 (§ 309), 1828 (§ 320), 1829 (§ 326), 1832
(§ 349), 1833 (§ 355), 1837 (§ 402), and perhaps oftener.

268. 1823 London

The Songs and Ballads of Robert Burns: Including ten never
before published; with a preliminary Discourse, and illustrative
Prefaces. London: printed for William Clark, 52, Paternoster
Row. 1823.

Original Material [?] :

The Patriarchs [" The Boniest lass that ye meet neist . . ." A
note reads : " This song has not hitherto appeared in any
collection of the poetry of Burns. We give it verbatim from
a manuscript in the possession of a friend."]   *p.* 177
Ye hae lien wrang, Lassie [" Your rosy cheeks are . . ." A
note reads : " Now first published."]   180
Supper is na ready [" Roseberry to his lady says . . ."]   227
Wha'll kiss me now ? [" O I hae tint my rosy cheek . . ." A
note reads : " This curious lamentation . . . is given from a
manuscript in the possession of a friend."]   249
The Fornicator [" This leads me on . . ." A note reads :
" This song . . . is printed from a manuscript in the handwriting of Burns."]   261
You jovial Boys   265
The Case of Conscience [" I'll tell you a tale . . ." A note
reads : " This song, with the exception of a few words, is
printed from a manuscript in the Editor's possession.
Where it is mutilated or torn, which is unfortunately the
case in two or three instances, an attempt has been made to
restore it."]   276
Jacob and Rachel [" As honest Jacob on a night " A note
reads : " This singular paraphrase . . . is printed from a
manuscript in the Editor's possession."]   278
Donald Brodie met a Lass. [A note reads : " This song has
not hitherto been printed in any collection of the Poetry of
Burns."]   283

This volume was edited by J. Barwick.[93]   It contains nine new pieces, most of them of a bawdy nature.   Henley and Henderson do not print any of them.   Barwick seems to have found some of the songs in MS., and others in § 51 (1800= *The Merry Muses*).   There is no proof that any of these pieces was written by Burns.

Re-issued in 1825 (§ 296).

269. 1823 London

The Songs of Robert Burns.   A new Edition.   London . . . J. Sudbury . . . 1823.

270. 1823 London

«« The Songs of Robert Burns, with a glossary and biographical notice.   A new edition.   London and Edinburgh.   1823.»»

M'Kie, *Bib. Bur.*, p. 37.   Probably the same as the previous item.

271. 1823 Montrose

The Works of Robert Burns. . . .   In two Volumes.   Montrose: printed by David Hill, and sold by the Booksellers . . . 1823.

Re-issued in 1824 (§ 285).

272. 1823 Philadelphia

The poetical Works of Robert Burns.   Philadelphia: published by B. Chapman.   Abm. Small, Printer.   1823.

This is an American edition of Gilbert Burns's edition of 1820 (§ 242).

273 [1823]

The Fornicator's Court; by Robert Burns.

Variant

[*Instead of*] . . . Fornicator's . . . [*both Mur. copies have*] . . . Fornicators . . .

See also § 129 (1810), and *Court of Equity*, Edinburgh, privately printed, 1910.

[93] Cp. *Gentlemen's Magazine*, xciii, Pt. 2 (Oct. 1823), 346-7.

The copy at Abbotsford is dated 1823 by James Maidment who had the poem printed. He adds: "Thick paper—only ten copies printed [*sc.* on thick paper; there seem to be any number on thin paper]. To Sir Walter Scott, Bart., June, 1823."

274. 1823

«« Poetical Works; exhibited under a new plan of arrangement. 2 vols. 1823.»»

Camb. Bib., II.976.

275. 1824 Edinburgh

The poetical Works of Robert Burns. . . . Edinburgh: printed by Wm. Aitchison. 1824 [*engraved throughout*]

276. 1824 London

Poems, chiefly in the Scottish Dialect. By Robert Burns. Including all the Poems and Songs in that printed at Edinburgh, in 1787. . . . London . . . J. White . . . 1824.

Re-issue of §76 (1803 London=Cleugh). White seems to have purchased Cleugh's stock and sold it off as a second edition.[94] This is on wove paper; the copies of the 1803 edition that I have examined are on laid paper.

277. 1824 London

Poems, chiefly in the Scottish Dialect. By Robert Burns. London: . . . John Sharpe . . . MDCCCXXIV.

278. 1824 London

Songs, chiefly in the Scottish Dialect. By Robert Burns. London: . . . John Sharpe . . . MDCCCXXIV.

279. 1824 London

«« Songs of Robert Burns. London . . . J. White. 1824.»»

M.C., § 676.

[94] *Notes and Queries*, 6th ser., IV (22 Oct. 1881), 335.

280. 1824 London

The poetical Works of Robert Burns; including several Pieces not inserted in Dr Currie's Edition . . . Two Volumes in One. London . . . T. and J. Allman . . . 1824.

Re-issued in 1825 (§ 294), 1828 (§ 319), 1830 (§ 332), 1833 (§ 357), 1834 (§ 367), 1835 (§ 378) and n.d. (§ 1110).

281. 1824 London

The poetical Works of Robert Burns, the Ayrshire Bard. . . . London . . . Jones & Company . . . 1824.

Re-issue of § 267 (1823 London=Jones).

282. 1824-5 London

The poetical Works of Robert Burns; with a Glossary. . . . In two Volumes. London . . . Jones & Company . . . 1824.

Vol. II is dated 1825. Re-issued in 1827 (§ 310) and (1833) (§ 356).

283. 1824 London

The Works of Robert Burns. . . . In two Volumes. London: printed by Thomas Davidson . . . for Thomas Tegg . . . 1824.

Also issued two volumes in one. The title-page is identical, except that the words " In two volumes " are omitted.

284. 1824 London

The Works of Robert Burns. . . . London: published by Jones and Company, 3 Acton Place, Kingsland Road. 1824.

285. 1824 Montrose

The Works of Robert Burns. . . . Montrose: printed by D. Hill, for George Clark, Aberdeen. 1824.

Re-issue of § 271 (1823 Montrose).

286. 1824 New York

The Life and Works of Robert Burns. . . . By Alexander
Peterkin. . . . In four Volumes. New York: . . . S. King . . .
1824.

287. 1824 New York

The Works of Robert Burns. In four Volumes. . . . W. A.
Bartow, New York. 1824.

288. 1825 Edinburgh

The Works of Robert Burns. . . . Edinburgh: published by
George Clark, Aberdeen. W. Aitchison, Printer. MDCCCXXV.

Variants

1. . . . by J. Dick & Co. W. Aitchison, . . .
2. . . . Edinburgh: Fraser & Co. MDCCCXXV.

Re-issued in 1828 (§ 316) and 1830 (§ 329).

289. 1825 Glasgow

Letters addressed to Clarinda, &c. . . . Glasgow: printed by
J. Carmichael, Hutchesontown, for William Falconer, Bookseller,
1825.

Re-issued in 1826 (§ 302).

290. 1825-6 Glasgow

Spirit of British Song, with biographical and illustrative Notes.
By John Goldie. In two Volumes. Vol. I. Glasgow, W. R.
M'Phun, Publisher. London, Knight and Lacey; Edinburgh,
John Sutherland; Dublin, W. Curry, Jun & Co. 1825.

Original Material (in Vol. II) :
    Election ballad for Westerha' [" The laddies by the
    banks . . ."]   *p.* 53

Comment. Each volume issued stabbed, in eight parts. Vol. II is dated
1826.

291. 1825 Glasgow

««The Works of Robert Burns. [*In two volumes.*] Glasgow: published by James Imray, and John Dick, Edinburgh. 1825.»»

M.C., § 247.

292. 1825 Glasgow

««Works. 2 vols. Allman.»»

Camb. Bib., II.976. Probably the same as § 297 (1825 London =Allman).

293. 1825 Glasgow

««Works. 2 vols.»»

Camb. Bib., II.976.

294. 1825 London

The poetical Works of Robert Burns; including several Pieces not inserted in Dr Currie's Edition . . . Two Volumes in One. London . . . T. and J. Allman . . . and John Anderson, jun. Edinburgh.

Re-issue of § 280 (1824 London=Allman).

295. 1825 London

The poetical Works of Robert Burns, the Ayrshire Bard. . . . Jones and Company . . . 1825.

Re-issue of § 267 (1823 London=Jones).

296. 1825 London

The Songs of Robert Burns. . . . London . . . William Clark . . . 1825.

Re-issue of § 268 (1823 London=Clark).

297. 1825 London

The Works of Robert Burns [*In two volumes.*] London . . . T. & J. Allman. 1825. [*engraved throughout*]

298. 1825 London

Works of Robert Burns. . . . London . . . published by Jones and
Company . . . 1825. [*Four volumes in one*]

299. 1825 New York

««Poetical Works of Robert Burns.   In two volumes.   N.Y.
D. Mallon. 1825.»»

Angus, p. 96.   Gibson, p. 39, has " D. Mallory "; Gebbie,
vi.338, " Mallory."

300. 1826 Belfast

«« Letters to Clarinda, by Robert Burns, 12mo. Belfast 1826.»»

Chambers, iv.319.   According to Ewing,[95] " such an edition
appears to be unknown to collectors; probably ' Belfast ' should
read ' Glasgow.' "   Andrew Gibson[96] says flatly that the edition
never existed.

301. 1826 Belfast

««The Poems of Robert Burns . . . Belfast: printed by Joseph
Smyth, 34, High-street. 1826.»»

M.C., § 732. Andrew Gibson[97] maintained that in 1901 there
were only three copies in existence.   It might possibly be a
re-issue of § 195 (1817 Belfast). Re-issued in 1832 (§ 347).

302. 1826 Glasgow

Letters addressed to Clarinda, &c. By Robert Burns. . . . Glasgow: printed by J. Carmichael for William Falconer. 1826.

Re-issue of § 289 (1825 Glasgow).

---

[95] J. C. Ewing, *Robert Burns's Letters to Clarinda* (Edinburgh: for private
circulation, 1921), p. 34.
[96] *Belfast News Letter*, 14 Mar. 1901.
[97] *Ibid.*

303. 1826 London

Dove's English Classics. The poetical Works of Robert Burns. ... London: printed by J. F. Dove; for the Booksellers of England, Scotland, and Ireland. 1826.

304. 1826 London

The Life of Robert Burns. . . . with his Correspondence and Fragments . . . London: printed by J. F. Dove; for the Booksellers of England, Scotland, and Ireland. 1826.

305. 1826 London

The poetical Works of Robert Burns, the Ayrshire Bard. . . . London . . . Jones and Company . . . 1826.

Re-issue of § 267 (1823 London=Jones).

306. 1826 London

«« Works of Robert Burns; containing his poems, letters, &c., with life by Currie. 2 vols., 24to London, 1826.»»

Chambers, 1891, iv.319.

307. 1826 Newcastle

The poetical Works of Robert Burns. . . . Newcastle upon Tyne . . . Mackenzie and Dent . . . 1826.

Re-issue of § 209 (1818 Newcastle).

308. 1826 New York

Works of Robert Burns. From the last London Edition. In two volumes . . . New-York: published by William Borradaile. 1826.

By " the last London edition " apparently is meant § 297 (1825 London=Allman). Gibson, p. 39, is at his best on this one: " The first American edition to acknowledge its indebtedness to English copyright for being able to issue a pirated edition and do penance on the title page as a slight atonement." Re-issued in 1828 (§ 321), 1829 (§ 327), 1831 (§ 345), 1832 (§§ 352, 353), 1833 (§ 358), 1834 (§ 369), and (?) 1839 (§ 423).

309. 1827 London

The poetical Works of Robert Burns, the Ayrshire Bard. . . . London . . . Jones and Company . . . 1827.

Re-issue of § 267 (1823 London=Jones).

310. 1827 London

The poetical Works of Robert Burns; with a Glossary. . . . London. . . . Jones . . . 1827.

Re-issue of § 282 (1824 London=Jones).

311. 1827 [=?1872]

Not for Maids, Ministers, or Striplings. The Merry Muses—a choice Collection of favourite songs gathered from many sources. —By Robert Burns.—To which are added Two of his Letters and a Poem—hitherto suppressed and never before printed . . . Privately printed (not for sale) 1827. (99 copies).

Original Material. Letters :

Ref.[98]	Addressee	Date	
I.199	Robert Ainslie	3 March 1788	*p.* 117
222	James Johnson	25 May 1788	119

This is, perhaps, the place to talk about various other editions of the *Merry Muses* published during the nineteenth and twentieth centuries, because most of the copies that fall into the hands of the reading public are dated 1827. The above title-page is transcribed from one such of these editions, and they are all more or less alike. They vary considerably as to format; some are

[98] To *Letters.*

quartos, some octavos, etc., and their pagination varies from
90 to 162 pp. They are all, needless to say, illegitimate children
of the *Merry Muses* § 51 [? 1800]. The date on the title-pages, as
one can see by a glance at the typography and the paper, is
fraudulent, and they were probably issued in 1872 (Mr G.
Legman, Cagnes-sur-Mer, A.M., who is making a thorough
study of the subject, assures me that the " 1827 " editions were
turned out by a certain firm of London publishers, John
Camden Hotten) or thereafter. The material in these volumes is
basically the same as in § 51 but considerably amplified with verse
and prose. Most of them assure the reader that only ninety-nine
copies were printed. This may or may not be true of any one
issue or edition, but there were many of these, apparently. The
publishers were making heavy capital of the salacious taste
of part of the reading public and the supposed tremendous reputation that Burns had in his own day as a composer of bawdy
compositions. With the exception of two letters, they add nothing
to the Burns canon. I have noted below the copies I have
examined.

The most modern edition of the *Merry Muses* (edd. James
Barke and Sydney Goodsir Smith, for the Auk Society,
Edinburgh, 1959) has a more extended treatment of the whole
subject in a series of prefatory essays. The dates that I have
given below are based on paper and type-face, and are merely
conjectural.

a. [?1820] Glasgow

The Merry Muses; a choice Collection of favourite songs . . .
Glasgow: printed for the Booksellers.

Pp. 108.

b. [?1820] Dublin

[*Same title-page as (a) above, except for the imprint, which reads*] . . .
Dublin: Printed for the Booksellers.

Pp. 108.

c. [?1825-30]

[*Same title-page as (a) above, except that after the imprint there follows*]
. . . Price three shillings.

> Pp. 126. The material in this edition is quite different from that
> in the three previous items : there are additional verses, and a
> rearrangement of the material. The B.M. copy contains 24 pp.
> of MS. material supposedly copied by Allan Cunningham from
> Burns's own MS.

d. 1843 London

The Merry Muses: a choice Collection of favourite songs . . .
London: printed for the Booksellers. 1843.

e. [?]1870-80

Forbidden Fruit. A Collection of popular Tales by popular
Authors . . . Also the expurgated Poems of Robert Burns' Merry
Muses, copied from the authentic M.S.S. The whole forming
the most unique Collection on an all-absorbing Topic ever
issued. Not for sale.

This is a sizeable volume which contains a number of prose pieces
of obviously English origin in the first part and the *Merry Muses* in
the second.

f. 1911

The Merry Muses of Caledonia; (original Edition) . . . printed
and published under the Auspices of the Burns Federation . . .
1911.

750 copies officially were printed and, unofficially, perhaps, a great
many more. The introduction is signed "Vindex," *i.e.* Duncan
M'Naught. Another edition is signed "Editor."

312. 1828 Alnwick

The Poems and Songs of Robert Burns. . . . Alnwick: printed
and published by W. Davison, 1828.

Variant

. . . Davison, and sold by J. Barnes. Keswick. [n.d.]

313. 1828 Dublin

««M. C. Warren. 1 vol. 24mo.»»

Gebbie, vi.338.

314. 1828 Edinburgh

Letters addressed to Clarinda &c. &c. By Robert Burns. . . .
Edinburgh: printed for the Booksellers. [by G. Love and Co.,
Glasgow.] 1828.

315. 1828 Edinburgh

Life of Robert Burns. By J. G. Lockhart, LL.B. . . . Edinburgh: published by Constable and Co., 19 Waterloo-Place; and Hurst, Chance, and Co., London. 1828.

Variant

. . . Constable's Miscellany. Vol. XXIII. . . .

Original Material :
    Letter to James Smith [1 Aug. 1786 : *Letters*, 1.35]   *p.* 108

This *Life* went through numerous editions during the nineteenth and twentieth centuries. I shall note only one more, the third (1830, § 328), which also contains original material.

316. 1828 Edinburgh

Works of Robert Burns. . . . Edinburgh . . . J. Dick & Co. MDCCCXXVIII

Re-issue of § 288 (1) (1825 Edinburgh=Dick).

317. 1828 Glasgow

The Letters of Robert Burns, chronologically arranged. Comprehending the Whole of Dr. Currie's Collection, and the most valuable Portion of Cromek's Reliques. Glasgow: printed for Richard Griffin & Co. 64 Hutcheson-Street. MDCCCXXVIII.

318. 1828 Glasgow

The poetical Works of Robert Burns: with his Songs and Fragments. Glasgow: printed for George Love & Co. 1828. [*two volumes in one*]

319. 1828 London

The poetical Works of Robert Burns; including several Pieces not inserted in Dr. Currie's Edition . . . Two Volumes in One. London: Joseph Smith . . . 1828

Re-issue of § 280 (1824 London=Allman).

320. 1828 London

The poetical Works of Robert Burns the Ayrshire Bard. . . .
London . . . Jones and Company . . . 1828.

Re-issue of § 267 (1823 London).

321. 1828 Philadelphia

Works of Robert Burns. . . . Philadelphia: J. Crissy and J.
Grigg. 1828.

Re-issue of § 308 (1826 New York).

322. 1829 Chiswick

The poetical Works of Robert Burns. Vol. I. [*of two.*] Chiswick: printed by C. Whittingham. Sold by Thomas Tegg . . .
London . . . 1829.

Variant

. . . Burns, Two volumes in one. Chiswick . . . 1829.

323. 1829 Dublin

«« Poetical Works complete, 1829.»»

Camb. Bib., II.976: " The date is from Gibson's Bibliography,
but that authority sometimes gives dates of which the title-page
is innocent, and it is probable that the edition is identical with
that noted in Craibe Angus's Bibliography (p. 85) as without
date." Angus's entry is as follows: " The poetical works of
Robert Burns. Complete . . . Dublin: printed by C. M. Warren.
[12 mo.] [n.d.]."[99] Again, this might be the same as Gebbie's
cryptic entry (VI.337) concerning 1828 Dublin (§ 313).

324. 1829 Edinburgh

The Scottish Songs; collected and illustrated by Robert Chambers
. . . In two Volumes. Vol. I. Edinburgh: printed by Ballantyne
and Company, for William Tait . . . MDCCCXXIX.

[99] Angus, p. 85; his square brackets.

Original Material (in Vol. II) :
   Letter to William Robertson of Lude 5 Dec. 1793 [*Letters,*
      II.220]   *p.* 458

This is the first of a long line of publications supervised by
Robert Chambers, who was to develop into one of the better
nineteenth-century editors of Burns.

325. 1829 London

The poetical Works of Robert Burns. In two Volumes. London:
G. Jones & Co. 1829.

326. 1829 London

The poetical Works of Robert Burns, the Ayrshire Bard. . . .
London . . . Jones and Company . . . 1829.

Re-issue of § 267 (1823 London).

327. 1829 Philadelphia

Works of Robert Burns. . . .   Philadelphia: J. Crissy and J.
Grigg. 1829.

Re-issue of § 308 (1826 New York).

328. 1830 Edinburgh

Life of Robert Burns. By J. G. Lockhart. Of him who walked
in glory and in joy, Behind his plough upon the mountain side.
Wordsworth. Third Edition, corrected. Edinburgh: Printed
for Constable and Co.; and Hurst, Chance, and Co. London.
1830.

Original Material :
   " Wi' braw new branks in mickle pride . . ."   *p.* 159
   " Of lordly acquaintance you boast . . ."   219
   " As cauld a wind as ever blew . . ."   220
   " You're welcome, Willie Stewart . . ."[1]   220

   [1] These four poems had all originally appeared in *The Edinburgh Literary
Journal,* 21 Nov. 1829, pp. 349-52.

Four letters :

Ref.[2]	Addressee	Date	
1.376	Lady Winifred Maxwell Constable [in part] [3]		10
289	Lady Henrietta Don [4]	22 Jan. 1789	199
378	Lady Henrietta Don [part] [5]		207
11.327	James Burness [6]	12 Jul. 1796	295

This is a slightly revised edition of § 315 (1828 Edinburgh). It was advertised for sale in *The Edinburgh Literary Journal*, 12 Dec. 1829.

329. 1830 Edinburgh

The Works of Robert Burns. . . . Edinburgh: published by George Clark, Aberdeen . . . 1830.

Re-issue of § 288 (1825 Edinburgh = Clark).

330. 1830 London

The poetical Works of Robert Burns. [*In two Volumes*]. London: William Pickering. 1830.

The first edition of the distinguished Aldine Series, edited by Sir Harris Nicholas. After Pickering's death in 1854, Bell and Daldy acquired the rights to the Aldine Poets. [7]

331. 1830 London

The poetical Works of Robert Burns: with a Sketch of his Life. . . . In two volumes. . . . London: published by G. Jones & Co. 1830.

Re-issued in 1837 (§ 403).

[2] To *Letters*.
[3] Ferguson says that this appeared in the first edition of this work.
[4] Ferguson says that this first appeared in Wallace's edition of *Life and Works*, 1896 (§ 893), and was addressed to Lady Elizabeth Cunningham.
[5] Ferguson says that this was complete in Cromek's *Reliques* and was addressed to Lady Elizabeth Cunningham.
[6] Ferguson says that this first appeared in *Works*, ed. Cunningham, 1834 (§ 368).
[7] Geoffrey Keynes, *William Pickering, Publisher*, London, 1924, p. 22.

332. 1830 London

The poetical Works of Robert Burns, with his Life. . . . Two Vols. in One. . . . London . . . Joseph Smith . . . 1830.

Re-issue of § 280 (1824 London=Allman).

333. 1830 New York

The Works of Robert Burns. . . . From the last London Edition of 1829. . . . New York: S. and D. A. Forbes, Printers, No. 29 Gold-Street. 1830. [*engraved throughout*]

Four volumes in one. The text is from Jones and Co.'s edition of 1829 (§ 326).

334. 1831 Ansbach.

Choice of Burns' Poems; to which is added a Glossary. Ansbach: Dolfuss. 1831.

Probably the first edition to be printed on the Continent. There were other editions in 1832 and 1834, but these will not be noted further.

335. 1831 Edinburgh

The poetical Works of Robert Burns. . . . In two Volumes. . . . Edinburgh: printed for Stirling & Kenney. 1831.

Re-issued in 1834 (§ 363), 1835 (§ 370), and 1837 (§ 396).

336. 1831 Edinburgh

The Works of Robert Burns. . . . Complete in one Volume. Edinburgh: Thomas Nelson and Peter Brown. MDCCCXXXI

Re-issued in 1835 (§ 371), 1837 (§ 398), and 1838 (§ 409.*a*).

337. 1831 Frome

The Cotter's Saturday Night, by Robert Burns; rendered intelligible to those unacquainted with the Scottish Phrases of

the Original, for the use of the poorer Classes in England.
Crocker, Printer, Frome. 1831.

Probably the first time that Burns was consciously used as the
voice of the lower classes.

338. 1831 Glasgow

«« Prose works. Richard Griffin & Co. 1 vol. 8vo.»»
Gebbie, vi.338.

339. 1831 Glasgow

The Songs of Robert Burns. . . . Glasgow: Richard Griffin &
Co. MDCCCXXXI

340. 1831 London

The Songs of Robert Burns: with a biographical Notice and
critical Remarks. London: printed for William Clark, 60,
Paternoster-row. 1831.

341. 1831 London

The Works of Robert Burns: including his Letters to Clarinda
and the Whole of his suppressed Poems. . . . London: printed
for William Clark . . . 1831.

Re-issued in 1843 (§ 452).

342. 1831 London

Works of Robert Burns. . . . London: Samuel Richards. 1831.

343. 1831 London

«« Jones & Co. Diamond Cabinet. 1 vol. 12mo.»»
Gebbie, vi.338.

344. 1831 New York

The complete Works of Robert Burns. . . . Four Volumes complete in One. New-York: S[olomon] King. 1831.

345. 1831 Philadelphia

The Works of Robert Burns. . . . Philadelphia . . . J. Crissy and J. Grigg. 1831.

Re-issue of § 308 (1826 New York).

346. 1832 Australia

«« The Poetical Works . . . Printed for the booksellers in Australia. 1832. [The 1813 Perth edn with an embellished title-page.] »»

Camb. Bib., II.977. Oddly enough, this is the only edition which can even vaguely be termed an Australian edition.[8]

347. 1832 Belfast

Poems. . . . Belfast . . . Joseph Smyth . . . 1832.

Re-issue of § 301 (1826 Belfast).

348. 1832 Edinburgh

The poetical Works of Robert Burns. . . . Edinburgh: Thomas Nelson and Peter Brown. MDCCCXXXII

Re-issued in 1834 (§ 364), 1836 (§ 383), 1837 (§ 397), and 1838 (§ 408).

349. 1832 London

The poetical Works of Robert Burns, the Ayrshire Bard. . . . London . . . Jones and Company . . . 1832.

Re-issue of § 267 (1823 London).

350. 1832 New York

The Works of Robert Burns; containing his Life by John Lockhart . . . Poetry and Correspondence of Dr. Currie's Edition . . . New-York: printed by William Pearson . . . and sold by all the principal Booksellers in the United States. 1832.

Re-issued in 1835 (§ 380), 1836 (§ 387), 1837 (§ 399), 1849 (§ 525), 1852 (§ 563), 1853 (§ 575), and 1857 (§ 610).

[8] Cp. John Alexander Ferguson, *Bibliography of Australia*, Sydney 1945, p. 39.

M

351. 1832 New York

The Works of Robert Burns: with an Account of his Life . . .
from the latest London Edition, embellished with thirty-three
Engravings on Wood. New-York: printed by J. Booth and Sons.
1832.

352. 1832 Philadelphia

The Works of Robert Burns. . . . Philadelphia: J. Crissy and J.
Grigg. 1832.

Re-issue of § 308 (1826 New York=Borradaile).

353. 1832 Philadelphia

The Works of Robert Burns, from the latest London Edition of
1829 . . . Philadelphia: James Locken. 1832.

A re-issue of § 308 (1826 New York=Borradaile).

354. 1833 Edinburgh

The entire Works of Robert Burns; with an Account of his
Life, and a Criticism on his Writings. To which are prefixed,
some Observations on the Character and Condition of the
Scottish peasantry. By James Currie, M.D. The four Volumes
complete in One, with an enlarged and correct Glossary.
Diamond Edition. Embellished with an original Design from
The Cotter's Saturday Night. Edinburgh: published for the
Proprietor, by James Chambers, Hanover Street; W. S. Orr,
and Simpkin & Marshall, London; W. Curry, Jun & Co.,
Dublin; J. M'Leod, Glasgow; and Bancks & Co., Manchester.
MDCCCXXXIII.

Variant

Diamond Edition. The entire Works of Robert Burns; with his
Life and a Criticism on his Writings, &c., &c. By James Currie,
M.D. . . . Second Edition. Embellished with thirteen engravings
on Steel, from original Designs. London: Allen Bell & Co.,
Warwick Square; and Simpkin & Marshall, Stationer's Court;

W. & R. Chambers, Edinburgh; W. Curry, jun. & Co., Dublin;
J. M'Leod, Glasgow; Wilmer & Smith, Liverpool; and Bancks
& Co., Manchester. MDCCCXXXIII.

This is the first of the truly dreadful Diamond Series. It was
printed in London by W. S. Orr and went through a number
of re-issues and editions. Re-issued in 1835 (§ 377), 1836 (§ 388),
1838 (§ 412), 1841 (§ 436), 1842 (§ 443), 1844 (§ 464), 1847
(§ 508), 1848 (§ 518), and 1850 (§ 538).

355. 1833 London

The poetical Works of Robert Burns; with a Glossary . . . in two
Volumes . . . 1833.

Re-issue of § 267 (1823 London=Jones).

356. 1833 London

«« Poetical Works. 2 vols. (Jones & Co.) Re-issue of London:
1824-5.»»

Camb. Bib., II.976. Undoubtedly a re-issue of § 282 (1824-5 London
=Jones).

357. 1833 London

The poetical Works of Robert Burns. . . . London . . . Smith.
1833.

Re-issue of § 280 (1824 London=Allman).

358. 1833 Philadelphia

«« The works of Robert Burns . . . Philadelphia . . . Crissy and
Grigg. 1833.»»

Angus, p. 98. Probably a re-issue of § 308 (1826 New York=
Borradaile).

359. 1834 Boston

The poetical Works of Robert Burns. . . . In two Volumes. . . .
Boston: James B. Dow. 1834

360. 1834-5 Boston

The Works of Robert Burns; with his Life, by Allan Cunningham. . . . In four Volumes. Boston: Hiliard, Gray, and Company. 1834.

Cunningham's edition (§ 368) was published in London in parts between January and December 1834; thus this pirated edition must have appeared almost on the heels of the original. There is no evidence that it was issued in parts, and the fourth volume is dated 1835. It was printed by Manson and Grant, Cambridge, Mass.

361. 1834 Dunbar

The poetical Works of Robert Burns. . . . Dunbar: published by William Miller, Bookseller. James Allan, Printer, East Lothian Printing Office, Haddington. 1834.

362. 1834 Dundee

The poetical Works of Robert Burns. . . . In two Volumes. Dundee: printed and published by D. Hill, and sold by William Livingstone, Bookseller, Dundee. MDCCCXXXIV.

Variant

. . . Dundee: printed and published for the Booksellers.

363. 1834 Edinburgh

The poetical Works of Robert Burns, to which is prefixed a Sketch of his Life. . . . Edinburgh . . . Stirling & Kenney. 1834.

Re-issue of § 335 (1831 Edinburgh), 2 volumes in one.

364. 1834 Edinburgh

The poetical Works of Robert Burns; with an Account of his Life. . . . Edinburgh: Thomas Nelson and Peter Brown. MDCCCXXXIV.

Re-issue of § 348 (1832 Edinburgh).

365. 1834-6 Glasgow

The Works of Robert Burns. Edited by the Ettrick Shepherd, and William Motherwell, Esq. Vol. I. Glasgow: Archibald Fullarton, and Co. 34, Hutcheson Street; and 31, South Bridge, Edinburgh. 1834.

a. (1834) Vol. I

Comment. Issued in three parts, beginning on 1 April 1834.[9] Part 1 included the first 144 pages of Vol. I ; Part 2, pp. 145-288 ; Part 3, pp. 289-332 and the first 88 pp. of Vol. II. Engraved frontispieces were included with each of the parts.

Original Material : John Bushby's Lamentation   *p.* 312

b. (1834) Vol. II

Original Material :

The Hermit [" Whoe'er thou art . . ."]	*p.* 48
On William Graham[10]	86
Verses addressed to the Landlady at Roslin Inn [" My blessings on you . . ."]	67
To Dr McKenzie [" Friday first's the day . . ."]	69
On Thanksgiving for a naval Victory ["Ye hypocrites . . ."][11]	71
On Andrew Turner	81
On Mr W. Cruickshanks ["Honest Will's to Heaven gane . . ."]	84
On Grizel Grim [" Here lies with death . . ."]	86
Lines on the same [*i.e.*, William Roddick : " Rest gently, turf, upon his breast . . ."][12]	87

Comment. The first 88 pp. were included in Part 3 ; Part 4 consisted of pp. 89-232, and Part 5 of pp. 233-328 and pp. 1-36 of Vol. III. The complete volume was advertised for sale on 18 Nov. 1834.[13]

c. (1835) Vol. III

Original Material :

Letter to John Richmond, 9 Jul. 1786 [*Letters*, 1.32]   *p.* 309

Comment. Pp. 1-36 were included in Part 5 ; Part 6 contained pp. 37-180 ; Part 7 contained pp. 181-324 ; and Part 8 consisted of pp. 325-48 and pp. 1-108 of Vol. IV.

---

[9] See *The Glasgow Courier* for that date. Snyder, p. 490, says of the biography : " Perhaps the worst life of Burns written before the twentieth century."

[10] H. & H., II.457, say that this did not appear till 1840, (§ 432).

[11] This also appears in Cunningham, 1834 (§ 368).

[12] Cp. another version in § 418 (1839 London=Pickering) and H. & H., II.273, 456.

[13] See *The Glasgow Courier* for that date.

d. (1835) Vol IV

Original Material. Eight letters :

Ref.[14]	Addressee	Date	
1.89	James Johnson	4 May 1787	*p.* 7
91	Mr Patison	17 May 1787	9
102	[Robert Ainslie]	23 Jul. 1787	19
217	William Dunbar	7 Apr. 1787	84
86	[William Dunbar]	30 Apr. 1787	86
II.1	William Dunbar	14 Jan. 1790	193
53	William Dunbar	17 Jan. 1791[15]	222
94	Colonel Fullarton	3 Oct. 1791[16]	245
158	Inscription to John McMurdo in a copy of § 25 (1793 Edinburgh)		298

Comment. Part 8 included the first 108 pp. of this volume ; Part 9 consisted of pp. 109-252 ; and Part 10 of pp. 253-383.

e. (1836) Vol. V

Original Material :

Ah, wae is me my mother dear . . .   *p.* 50
On Seeing his favourite Walks despoiled [" As on the banks . . ."]   406

Comment. This volume comprised Parts 11-13.

Single volumes of this edition were re-issued from time to time individually. This makes it impossible to say whether or not the set was really re-issued as a whole. I have seen the following: 1835, 1836-41, 1838, 1840, 1841, 1848, 1851, 1852, and one undated edition. Cp. Davidson Cook in *The Weekly Scotsman*, 10 Nov. 1934.

366. 1834 Liverpool

«Second edition. The songs of Robert Burns . . . Liverpool: T. Kerr. [1834].»»

Gibson, p. 48.

---

[14] To *Letters.*
[15] Completed from § 112 (1808 London=Cromek).
[16] Originally published in *Paisley Magazine*, 1828, p. 203.

367. 1834 London

The poetical Works of Robert Burns. . . . London: Joseph
Smith. 1834.

Re-issue of § 280 (1824 London=Allman).

368. 1834 London

The Works of Robert Burns; with his Life, by Allan Cunningham.
" High Chief of Scottish song! That could'st alternately impart
Wisdom and rapture in thy page, And brand each vice with
satire strong; Whose lines are mottoes of the heart, Whose truths
electrify the sage." Campbell. In six Volumes. Vol. I.
London: Cochrane and M'Crone, 11, Waterloo Place. 1834.

Variants

1. . . . In eight Volumes. Vol. I . . . 1834.
2. . . . In eight Volumes. Vol. I. London: James Cochrane
and Co. 11, Waterloo Place. 1834.

a. Vol. I

Comment. Announced for publication on 15 Jan. 1834.[17]

b. Vol. II

Comment. Announced for publication on 22 Feb. 1834.[18]

c. Vol. III

Original Material :
Epistle to Major Logan [" Hail, thairm-inspirin' . . ."]	*p.* 9
Epistle to Hugh Parker [" In this strange land . . ."]	91
To John M'Murdo, Esq. [" O, could I give thee . . ."]	114
To John Taylor [" With Pegasus upon a day . . ."]	190
The Bookworms [" Through and through th' inspir'd leaves . . ."]	293
On Robert Riddell [" To Riddell ! Much lamented man . . ."]	308
On Gabriel Richardson [" Here brewer Gabriel's . . ."]	312

Comment. Announced for publication on 22 Mar. 1834.[19]

17 *The Glasgow Courier*, 9 Jan. 1834.
18 *The Glasgow Courier* for that date.
19 *The Glasgow Courier* for that date.

d. VOL. IV

Original Material :

Masonic Song [" Ye sons of old Killie . . ."]   *p.* 32

Comment. Announced for publication on 17 Apr. 1834.[20]

e. VOL. V

Comment. Announced for publication on 31 May 1834.[21]

f. VOL. VI

Original Material. Twenty-three letters :

Ref.[22]	*Addressee*	*Date*	
1.18	James Burness	3 Aug. 1784[23]	*p.* 46
23	Robert Muir	20 Mar. 1786	54
24	John Ballantine	n.d.[24]	64
33	David Brice	17 Jul. 1786	65
35	John Richmond	30 Jul. 1786	66
41	Robert Muir	[8 Sep. 1786]	67
52	Robert Muir	18 Nov. 1786	80
60	Robert Muir	20 Dec. 1786	88
1.128	William Nicol	[8 Oct. 1787]	143
129	William Cruickshank	[8 Oct. 1787][25]	149
100	John Richmond	7 Jul. 1787	144
200	Robert Ainslie	Jul. 1787[26]	172
120	Robert Muir	26 Aug. 1787	174
131	James Hoy	20 Oct. 1787[27]	189
136	James Hoy	6 Nov. 1787[27]	194
142	Gavin Hamilton	Dec. 1787[27]	222
190	Mrs Rose	17 Feb. 1788[28]	233
199	Robert Ainslie	3 Mar. 1788	241
229	Robert Ainslie	23 Jun. 1788	273

---

[20] *The Glasgow Courier* for that date.
[21] *The Glasgow Courier* for that date.
[22] To *Letters.*
[23] Here in part. Completed in § 783 (1877=Scott Douglas).
[24] Ferguson dates this letter 15 Apr. 1786 and says it was addressed to Gavin Hamilton.
[25] Originally published in *Gentleman's Magazine*, CII (1832), p. 101.
[26] Ferguson says that this letter was addressed to William Nicol.
[27] Ferguson says that this first appeared in Currie, 1800 (§ 50).
[28] Originally published in *Gentleman's Magazine*, CII (1832), p. 100.

Ref.	Addressee	Date	
281	William Cruickshank	Aug. 1789[29]	p. 284
281	John Tenant, enclosing two sets of "Written in Friar's Carse"	22 Dec. 1788	328

Comment. This volume was announced for publication on 24 June 1834.[30]

g. VOL. VII

Original Material :

On Receiving a Work of Hannah More's [" Thou flattering mark . . ."] p. 336

Nineteen letters :

Ref.[31]	Addressee	Date	
I.32	John Richmond	9 Jul. 1786[32]	p. 1
328	Mrs M'Murdo	2 May 1789	35
221	Samuel Brown	4 May 1789[33]	41
287	John M'Murdo	19 Jun. 1789[34]	51
350	John Logan	7 Aug. 1789	61
II.37	John M'Murdo	2 Aug. 1790[35]	124
II.38	John Mitchell	1790	117
77	Literary Scolding	1791[36]	169
231	Captain Miller	[Jan. 1794][37]	260
245	David McCulloch	21 Jun. 1794	278
282	Mrs Riddel	[Jan. 1795]	289
327	James Burness	12 Jul. 1796	327
329	James Gracie	16 Jul. 1796[38]	332
330	James Armour	18 Jul. 1796	333
I.22	John Kennedy	3 Mar. 1786	334
23	Robert Aiken	3 Apr. 1786	336
25	John Kennedy	20 Apr. 1786	338
30	John Kennedy	17 May 1786	339
36	John Kennedy	Aug. 1786	340
377	Provost Maxwell	20 Dec. 1789	342

Comment. This volume was announced for publication on 9 Oct. 1834.[39]

[29] Ferguson dates this Dec. 1789. Originally published in *Gentleman's Magazine*, CII (1832), p. 99.

[30] *The Glasgow Courier* for that date.

[31] To *Letters*.

[32] Ferguson says that this first appeared in Hogg and Motherwell (§ 365).

[33] Ferguson dates this letter 1788.

[34] Ferguson says that this first appeared in Chamber's edition, 1851 (§ 540), and dates it 9 Jan 1789.

[35] Cunningham does not claim that this is a first appearance.

[36] Originally published in *Gentleman's Magazine*, CII (1832), p. 101.

[37] Cunningham does not claim that this was its first appearance.

[38] Ferguson dates this letter [13 Jul.]

[39] *The Glasgow Courier* for that date.

h. VOL. VIII

Original Material :

Comment. This volume was announced for publication on 6 Dec.
    1834.[42]

Cunningham had originally planned the work to be in six
volumes, but he apparently succeeded in gathering more material
than he had anticipated. In the preface to Vol. VI, published
on 24 June 1834, appeared the following notice:

> When this edition of Burns was first announced, six
> volumes, it was calculated, would contain all that was
> desirable to publish of his writings. . . . To enable the
> Editor to do justice to the genius of Burns, he must give
> him at full length, and extend the work to eight volumes.
> . . . Belgrave Place June, 15 1834.

We can conclude from this statement that only the first five
volumes appeared with the original title-page. After 24 June all
the volumes which were published contained the second issue of
the title-page reproduced above.

There was a so-called second edition in the same year. Vol. I
is definitely a new set-up, with two prefaces and a re-casting of
the Life. Vol. II has a different title-page and Table of Contents;
the rest of the volume is a re-issue. Vols. III-VIII are re-issues.

This edition has so many merits and so many faults that it is
useful only for the student who knows Burns thoroughly. It is
a baffling mixture of truth and fiction; while many of the
statements are certainly true, an equal number probably sprang
from gossip or from Cunningham's own fertile imagination.

[40] See J. de Lancey Ferguson, " Burns Journal of his Border Tour," *P.M.L.A.*,
XLIX (Dec. 1934), 1107-15, for an account of Cunningham's omissions.

[41] The manuscript that Cunningham used seems to have disappeared : see
Scott Douglas, *The Works of Robert Burns*, IV.264. It was an expanded version
of the notebook Burns carried with him on the tour, but we do not know how
much of the expanded material Cunningham used.

[42] *The Glasgow Courier* for that date.

369. 1834 Philadelphia

The Works of Robert Burns. . . . Philadelphia: J. Crissy and J. Grigg. 1834.

Re-issue of § 308 (1826 New York=Borradaile).

370. 1835 Edinburgh

The poetical Works of Robert Burns. . . . Edinburgh . . . Stirling & Kenney. 1835.

Re-issue of § 335 (1831 Edinburgh).

371. 1835 Edinburgh

The Works of Robert Burns. . . . Edinburgh: Nelson and Brown. 1835.

Re-issue of § 336 (1831 Edinburgh).

372. 1835 Edinburgh

«« The Works of Robert Burns. . . . Edinburgh: Fraser & Co. 1835.»»

Angus Sale Catalogue, Cat. M. Edinburgh: 1902.

373. [1835] Glasgow

The complete Works of Robert Burns: containing his Poems, Songs, and Correspondence . . . by Allan Cunningham. In two Volumes. Glasgow: M'Gready, Thomson, & Niven, 38 John Street.

The preface is dated 1835. Davidson Cook, *The Weekly Scotsman*, 1 Dec. 1934, notes a second edition in eight volumes.

374. 1835 Glasgow

The Works of Robert Burns. Edited by the Ettrick Shepherd, and William Motherwell, Esq. . . . Fullarton . . . Glasgow . . . 1835. [*five volumes*]

A half-baked re-issue of § 365. Vol. I is dated 1835; Vol. II, 1834; Vols III and IV, 1835; Vol. V, 1836. In other words, only Vol. I is a re-issue.

375. 1835 Leipzig

The Works of Robert Burns, with selected Notes of Allan Cunningham, a biographical and critical Introduction, and a comparative etymological Glossary to the Poet. By Dr. Adolphus Wagner. Complete in one Volume. Leipsic: printed for Frederick Fleischer. 1835.

This contains an interesting essay of 28 pp., very German, very Romantic. Excellent glossary, in which the editor traces Scots words through O.E., O.H.G., M.H.G., Gr., Lat., and modern European languages.

376. 1835 Liverpool

«« Songs T. Kerr. 1 vol. 32mo.»»

Gebbie, VI.339.

377. 1835 London

The entire Works of Robert Burns. . . . Diamond Edition. . . . London: Allan Bell & Co. . . . MDCCCXXXV.

Re-issue of § 354 (1833 Edinburgh).

378. 1835 London

The poetical Works of Robert Burns. . . . London: Joseph Smith . . . 1835.

Re-issue of § 280 (1824 London=Allman).

379. 1835 London

The Works of Robert Burns. . . . Second Edition. . . . London: James Cochrane & Co. . . . 1835.

This really is a re-issue of the second issue of Cunningham's edition of 1834 (§ 368), *i.e.*, only Vol. I is a new edition.

380. 1835 New York

The Works of Robert Burns. . . . New York . . . Pearson . . . 1835.

Re-issue of § 350 (1832 New York=Pearson).

381. 1835 Philadelphia

The Works of Robert Burns: with an Account of his Life . . . Philadelphia . . . J. Crissy . . . 1835.

Re-issue of § 308 (1826 New York=Borradaile).

382. 1835 Philadelphia

The Works of Robert Burns: with an Account of his Life. . . Philadelphia, published by John Locken. 1835.

383. 1836 Edinburgh

The poetical Works of Robert Burns. . . . Edinburgh: Peter Brown. MDCCCXXXVI.

Variant

. . . P. Brown . . .

Re-issue of § 348 (1832 Edinburgh=Nelson and Brown). *M.C.*, § 96, notes a re-issue " Nelson and Brown."

384. [1836-41] Glasgow

The Works of Robert Burns. Edited by the Ettrick Shepherd, and William Motherwell Esq. . . . Glasgow: Archibald Fullarton. 1836.

Re-issue of § 365 (Glasgow 1834-6).

385. 1836 Glasgow

The Works of Robert Burns, including his Letters to Clarinda. . . . Glasgow: Duncan Mackenzie, 48, Nelson Street. 1836.

Re-issued (?) in 1845 (§ 472).

386. 1836 Halifax

The poetical Works of Robert Burns. . . . Halifax: printed for H. Pohlman. 1836.

Variant

. . . Halifax: printed for William Milner. 1836.

Re-issued in 1837 (§ 401) and 1838 (§ 415).

387. 1836 Hartford (Conn.)

The Works of Robert Burns. . . . Hartford: published by Judd, Loomis and Co. 1836.

Re-issue of § 350 (1832 New York=Pearson).

388. 1836 London

Fifth Diamond Edition. . . . Entire Works. . . . London: Allen Bell . . . MDCCCXXXVI.

Variant

Sixth Diamond Edition. . . . MDCCCXXXVI.

Re-issue of § 354 (1833 Edinburgh), although the " Fifth Edition " is rather difficult to explain. There were two issues of this work in 1833 and another in 1835. There may have been one in 1834, though I have never seen a copy: in that case this would be the so-called fifth " edition." However, since a " Sixth Edition " also appears in this year, and another " Sixth Edition " in 1838 (§ 412), too much faith should not be put in what appears on these title-pages.

389. 1836 London

The poetical Works of Robert Burns: comprising an entire Collection of his Poems. . . . Magnet Edition. London: William Mark Clark . . . and all the booksellers. 1836.

390. 1836 London

The poetical Works of Robert Burns, with a Memoir of the Author's Life and a Glossary. London: printed for T. Allman. 1836.

391. 1836 London

The poetical Works of Robert Burns, with a Memoir of the Author's Life, and a Glossary. London: Renshaw and Kirkman. 1836.

392. 1836 London

The poetical Works of Robert Burns, with his Life, Glossary, &c. London: printed by and for William Jeffery, 7, Mark Lane. MDCCCXXXVI.

393. 1836 New York

«« Poetical Works of Robert Burns. Two volumes in one. New York : C. Wells. 24mo. 1836.»»

Angus, p. 96. Gibson, p. 52, says: " This edition appears to be printed from the same plates as that of E. Kerney of New York. It is also published by Leavitt & Allan in 1852."

394. 1836 Philadelphia

The Works of Robert Burns. . . . Philadelphia: J. Crissy . . . 1836.

Re-issue of § 308 (1826 New York=Borradaile), with 18 pp. of additional poems, apparently lifted from Allan Cunningham's edition, bound in at the back of the volume. Re-issued in 1837 (§ 404), 1838 (§ 416), 1839 (§ 423), 1842 (§ 447), 1845 (§ 480), 1846 (§ 494), 1848 (§ 520), and 1850 (§ 539).

395. 1837 Belfast

The poetical Works of Robert Burns. . . . Belfast: Simms and M'Intyre, Donegall-Street. 1837.

This may also have been issued in the same year with no date on the title-page. An undated copy in Mur. has " 1837 " pencilled on the title-page, and M.C., § 730, lists an undated issue. Re-issued in 1838 (§ 405), and 1851 (§ 545), and n.d. (§ 1115).

396. 1837 Edinburgh

The poetical Works of Robert Burns: to which is prefixed a Sketch of his Life. . . . Edinburgh . . . Stirling & Kenney . . . 1837.

Re-issue of § 335 (1831 Edinburgh).

397. 1837 Edinburgh

The poetical Works of Robert Burns: with an Account of his Life. . . . Edinburgh: Peter Brown. 1837.

Re-issue of § 348 (1832 Edinburgh=Nelson).

398. 1837 Edinburgh

The Works of Robert Burns. . . . Edinburgh: Peter Brown . . . 1837.

Re-issue of § 336 (1831 Edinburgh=Nelson and Brown).

399. 1837 Hartford, Conn.

The Works of Robert Burns. . . . Hartford: published by Judd, Loomis, & Co. And sold by the principal Booksellers of the United States. 1837.

Re-issue of § 350 (1832 New York=Borradaile).

400. 1837 London

The complete poetical Works of Robert Burns. . . . London . . . Scott, Webster and Geary . . . 1837.

Re-issue (?) of § 1058 (Complete Poetical Works, London n.d.). Geary's name is not on the undated title-page. Re-issued in 1840 (§ 429), 1846 (§ 490), and 1853 (§ 572).

401. 1837 London

The poetical Works of Robert Burns, with a Memoir of the Author's Life. . . . London: printed for the Booksellers, by William Milner, Halifax. 1837.

Re-issue of § 386 (1836 Halifax=Pohlman).

402. 1837 London

The poetical Works of Robert Burns; with a Glossary. . . . London. . . . Jones. . . . 1837.

Re-issue of § 267 (1823 London=Jones) Second volume, undated, has imprint, " London: Published by Wm. S. Orr & Co. . . ."

403. 1837 London

The poetical Works of Robert Burns: with a Sketch of his Life. . . . London . . . G. Jones . . . 1837.

Re-issue of § 331 (1830 London=Jones).

404. 1837 Philadelphia

The Works of Robert Burns. . . . Philadelphia: J. Crissy . . . 1837.

Re-issue of § 394 (1836 Philadelphia=Crissy).

405. 1838 Belfast

The poetical Works of Robert Burns. . . . Belfast . . . Simms & M'Intyre . . . 1838.

Re-issue of § 395 (1837 Belfast).

406. 1838 Edinburgh

The Life of Robert Burns, with a Criticism on his Writings; by James Currie, M.D. Originally published in connection with the Works of Burns, in 1800: Here considerably extended by additional Particulars, many of which were never before made public. Edinburgh: Published by William and Robert Chambers; and W. S. Orr and Company, London. 1838.

Original Material :
    Letter to Gavin Hamilton, 7 Jan. 1787 [*Letters*, 1.62]   *p*. 39
    N

Published, with § 407 and § 417, by the scholar-publishers, William and Robert Chambers, in a series called " The People's Edition," sold at two shillings a copy. This volume contains as much new biographical material as Robert Chambers was then able to muster. The new material is in brackets in the Table of Contents.

407. 1838 Edinburgh

The poetical Works of Robert Burns. To which are now added, Notes illustrating historical, personal, and local Allusions. Edinburgh: published by William and Robert Chambers; and W. S. Orr and Company, London. 1838.

Original Material :

Verses written under violent Grief [" Accept the gift . . ."][43] *p.* 63
The Tree of Liberty [" Heard ye o' the tree . . ."]   86
On an illiterate Country Gentleman [" Free through the leaves . . ."][44]   139

408. 1838 Edinburgh

The poetical Works of Robert Burns; with an Account of his Life. . . . Edinburgh: Peter Brown. 1838.

Re-issue of § 348 (1832 Edinburgh=Nelson and Brown).

409. 1838 Edinburgh

The poetical Works of Robert Burns. . . . Edinburgh: Fraser & Co. North Bridge. 1838.

409 A. 1838 Edinburgh

Works . . . Edinburgh: Thomas Nelson MDCCCXXXVIII

Re-issue of § 336 (1831 Edinburgh=Nelson and Brown).

[43] According to a note appended to this poem, it was first published in *The Sun* newspaper, Apr. 1823. It is not included in H. & H.
[44] This is another version of " The Bookworms " (" Through and through th' inspired leaves "), which was originally published in § 368 (1834 London=Cunningham), III. 293.

410. 1838 Glasgow

M.C., § 234, lists a re-issue in this year of § 365 (1834 Glasgow = Fullarton).

411. 1838 London

Poetical Works of Robert Burns. . . . London: Charles Daly. 1838.

Re-issued in 1839 (§ 420) and 1841 (§ 437).

412. 1838 London

Sixth Diamond Edition. The entire Works of Robert Burns. . . . London: Allan Bell & Co. . . . MDCCCXXXVIII.

Re-issue of § 354 (1833 Edinburgh=Chambers).

413. 1838 London

Standard Library Edition. The poetical Works of Robert Burns. . . . London: William Smith, 113, Fleet Street. MDCCCXXXVIII.

414. 1838 London

The poetical Works of Robert Burns, with a Memoir of the Author's Life, and a Glossary. London: printed for the Booksellers, by W. F. Pratt, Howden. MDCCCXXXVIII.

415. 1838 London

The poetical Works of Robert Burns; with a Memoir of the Author's Life, and a Glossary. London: published by the Booksellers. William Milner, Halifax. 1838.

Re-issue of § 386 (1836 Halifax=Pohlman).

416. 1838 Philadelphia

The Works of Robert Burns. . . . Philadelphia: J. Crissy . . . 1838.

Re-issue of § 394 (1836 Philadelphia=Crissy).

417. 1839 Edinburgh

The prose Works of Robert Burns, with the Notes of Currie and Cromek, and many by the present Editor [*Robert Chambers*]. Edinburgh: published by William and Robert Chambers; and W. S. Orr and Company, London. 1839.

Original Material :

Letter to James Burness, 26 Sept. 1786[45]   *p.* 14

Letter to Charles Hay [24 Dec. 1788][46]   29

See note to § 406. This volume contains all the letters previously published, and the two others noted above. In it also are the Commonplace Book, Memoranda of Tours, and Strictures on Scottish Songs and Ballads.

417 A. 1839 Edinburgh

The Scots Musical Museum. . . . [ed.] William Stenhouse. . . . William Blackwood and Sons, Edinburgh: . . . M.DCCC.XXXIX.

Original Material :

Letter to [Robert] Cleghorn, n.d. [*Letters*, I.82], VI.103.

Elaborate notes and illustrations by Stenhouse and a preface by David Laing. Re-issue, in six volumes, of the final form of § 8 (1788-1803 Edinburgh=Johnson).

418. 1839 London

The poetical Works of Robert Burns. London: William Pickering. 1839.

a. VOL. I

Original Material :

Letter to James Smith, 11 Jun. 1787[47]   *p.* xlvii

---

[45] *Letters*, I.43. Ferguson gives the addressee as [John Kennedy]. Originally published in *Scots Magazine*, LXXI (Nov. 1809), 818.

[46] *Letters*, I.147. Originally published in *Scots Magazine*, n.s., II (Jun. 1818), 527. Ferguson dates this [? 24 Dec. 1787].

[47] *Letters*, I.95. Ferguson says that this letter was originally published in Cunningham's edition of 1834 (§ 368).

b. Vol. II

Original Material :

c. Vol. III

Original Material :

This is the second Aldine edition. Textually, it is noteworthy. The editors made a careful search for manuscript material, and printed as much as possible from original sources. The preface is dated 10 Mar. 1839.

The " Epigram to Tam the Chapman " on p. 140 of Vol. II was accompanied by the following note:

> These verses were printed by the late Mr. Cobbett, with this account of them: " It is our fortune to know a Mr. Kennedy, an aged gentleman, a native of Scotland, and the early associate and friend of Robert Burns. Both were born in Ayrshire, near the town of Ayr. . . . Kennedy . . . subsequently became the agent to a mercantile house in a neighbouring town. Hence he is called, in the epitaph which his friend the Poet wrote on him, ' The Chapman '. These lines, omitted in all editions of Burns' works, were composed on Kennedy's recovery from a severe illness . . .' ' Kennedy's occupation,' says Allan Cunningham, ' which gave him a knowledge of the world at that time far beyond that of the humble cotter's son, made him an extremely acceptable companion, while his social, friendly, honest heart,' converted acquaintance into friendship. They maintained a regular correspondence until about the time of Burns' departure for Edinburgh.'

I have searched Cobbett's *Register*, where these lines are supposed to have appeared, but have been unable to find them. This does not necessarily mean that they are not there; for the *Register* numbers well over eighty volumes, some of which are

---

[48] *I.e.*, William Roddick. For another version cp. § 365 (Glasgow=Fullarton) II.87.

indexed, some partially indexed, and a great many not indexed at all. I am, however, inclined to doubt the authenticity of the story, if for no other reason than that I can find no trace of Burns's association with this particular Mr. Kennedy. Taking into account the part of the above quotation which was a gloss by Allan Cunningham, I am even more convinced that this is one of that editor's fabrications.

419. 1839 London

The poetical Works of Robert Burns. London: William Smith, 113, Fleet Street. MDCCCXXXIX.

Re-issued in 1848 (§ 516), 1857 (§ 606), 1859 (§ 632), and 1868 (§ 717).

420. 1839 London

The poetical Works of Robert Burns, with a Life of the Author . . . London . . . C. Daly . . . 1839.

Re-issue of § 411 (1838 London=Daly).

421. 1839 London

The poetical Works of Robert Burns, with a Memoir of the Author's Life. . . . London: published by Jones and Co. Fordyce, Dean-street, Newcastle; and Mytongate, Hull. 1839.

Variant

. . . Hull. MDCCCXXXIX.

422. 1839 New York

The Works of Robert Burns. . . . New-York: Robinson & Franklin. 1839.

423. 1839 Philadelphia

«« Works of Robert Burns. From the London Edition of 1828. Philadelphia: J. Crissy. 1839.»»

Angus, p. 98. Despite the title-page, this is more probably a re-issue of § 394 (1826 New York=Borradaile), as were the other Crissy editions.

424. 1840 Edinburgh

«« The Poetical Works of Robert Burns . . . Edinburgh: published by William and Robert Chambers . . . 1838 . . . Re-issue (' People's Edition ').»»

Chambers, 1851, IV.89 n.

425. 1840 Glasgow

The Land of Burns, a Series of landscape Portraits, illustrative of the Life and Writings of the Scottish Poet. The Landscapes from Paintings made expressly for the Work, by D. O. Hill, Esq., R.S.A. The literary Department, by Professor Wilson . . . and Robert Chambers, Esq. . . . Vol. I. Blackie & Son, Queen Street, Glasgow; South College Street, Edinburgh; and Warwick Square, London. MDCCCXL.

Original Material :
Rusticity's Ungainly Form	*p.* 58
The Night was still	58
Letter to Archibald Laurie, 13 Nov. 1786 [*Letters*, 1.48]	60

Comment. The book contains numerous engraved plates consisting of portraits and illustrations of places, most of them designed by Hill. A few sets were printed in folio. Some editions contain a two-page, one-leaf, preface.

Issued in twenty-three parts at 2*s.* each from Nov. 1837 to Nov. 1840. It was edited by Robert Chambers.[49] Parts 1, 2, and 3 were announced in the *Gentleman's Magazine*, n.s., IX (Apr. 1838), p. 404. *B. Chr.*, I (1892), p. 108, has: " The Land of Burns, a series of Landscapes and Portraits, etc., etc. 2 vols. (4to) Glasgow: Blackie & Son. 1839."

426. 1840 Glasgow

The Works of Robert Burns. Edited by the Ettrick Shepherd, and William Motherwell, Esq. . . . Glasgow . . . Fullarton . . . 1840.

---

[49] W. G. Blackie, *Origin and Progress of the Firm*, Glasgow, for private circulation 1897, pp. 36, 114.

This is one of those maddening re-issues of § 365 (1834 Glasgow). In one set of five volumes I have examined, the dates are as follows: Vol. I, 1840; Vol. II, 1841; Vol. III, 1838; Vols. IV and V, 1839. In another set the dates are: Vol. I, 1840; Vol. II, 1841; Vol. III, 1837; Vol. IV, 1841; Vol. V, 1839.

427. 1840 Glasgow

«« Blackie & Son. Wilson Chambers, editors. Trade edition for the booksellers. 2 vols. 4to.»»

Gebbie, VI.339.

428. 1840 Halifax

The poetical Works of Robert Burns. . . . Halifax: printed and published by William Milner, Cheapside. MDCCCXL.

Re-issued in 1843 (§ 451), 1845 (§ 474), 1846 (§ 489), 1850 (§ 533), 1851 (§ 544), 1852 (§ 558), 1853 (§ 570), 1854 (§ 580), 1856 (§ 597), 1858 (§ 614), 1859 (§ 630), 1860 (§ 638), 1862 (§ 649), 1866 (§ 687), and n.d. (§§ 1047, 1107).

429. 1840 London

The complete poetical Works of Robert Burns. . . . New Edition. London: Scott, Webster, and Geary . . . 1840.

Re-issue of § 400 (1837 London).

430. 1840 London

The complete Works of Robert Burns. . . . Three Volumes. . . . London . . . for the Booksellers. 1840.

Re-issue of § 200 (1817 London=For the Booksellers) and § 228 (1820 Edinburgh=Orphoot).

431. 1840 London

The poetical Works of Robert Burns. . . . London: published by Walker and Co. Fordyce, Dean Street, Newcastle, and Myton-gate, Hull. MDCCCXL.

432. 1840 London

The Works of Robert Burns. With Life by Allan Cunningham, and Notes by Gilbert Burns. ... Wordsworth &c., &c., &c. ... London, T. Tegg, Cheapside; C. Daly, Red Lion Square. MDCCCXL.

Re-issued in 1842 (§ 442), 1844 (§ 463), 1845 (§§ 477, 478), 1847 (§§ 506, 507), 1850 (§ 536), 1854 (§ 581), 1858 (§ 617), 1860 (§ 642), 1862 (§ 650), and perhaps oftener.

Original Material :
  The Dean of Faculty (1st st. only)   *p.* 269

433. [Cancelled]

434. 1840 Montrose

«« Songs. James Watt. 1 vol. 32mo.»»

Gebbie, vi.339.

435. 1841 Glasgow

Works. ... Glasgow. ... Fullarton. ... 1841.

Re-issue of § 365 (1834 Glasgow = Fullarton).

436. [1841] London

The complete Works of Robert Burns. ... London: ... Andrew Moffat. 1841. [*engraved throughout*].

Seventh Diamond Edition. Printed title-page not dated.

Re-issue of § 354 (1833 Edinburgh = Chambers).

437. 1841 London

Poetical Works. ... London. .. C. Daly ... 1841.

Re-issue of § 420 (1838 London = Daly).

438. 1841 London

Remarks on Scottish Songs and Ballads. . . .   Robert Burns.
London: John Chidley, 123, Aldersgate Street.   1841.

Re-issue of § 368*h* (1834 London = Cunningham), vol. viii.

439. 1841 Newcastle

The poetical Works of Robert Burns. . . .   Newcastle: published
by W. & T. Fordyce.   MDCCCXLI.

Variant

Newcastle: printed and published by W. & T. Fordyce.   1841.

Re-issued in 1842 (§ 446).

440. 1842 Glasgow

«« Works of Robert Burns.   Blackie & Co.   21 parts.   2S.»»

Blackie, W. G.   *Sketch of the Origin and Progress of the Firm* (Glasgow: for private circulation.   1897), p. 115.

441. 1842 Halifax

The complete Works of Robert Burns. . . .   Halifax: printed and
published by William Milner, Cheapside.   MDCCCXLII.

At least sixteen re-issues: 1844 (§ 460),   1845 (§ 473),   1846
(§ 488),   1847 (§ 503),   1848 (§ 514),   1850 (§ 532),   1851 (§ 543),
1852 (§ 557),   1854 (§ 579),   1855 (§ 587),   1857 (§ 604),   1859
(§ 629),   1863 (§ 654),   1865 (§ 675),   1867 (§ 704),   1875 (§ 769),
and n.d. (§ 1057).

442. 1842 London

Works. . . .   London: Henry G. Bohn . . . MDCCCXLII.

Re-issue of § 432 (1840 London = Tegg and Daly).

443. 1842 London

Entire Works. . . . Four Volumes complete in One. . . . Seventh
Diamond Edition. . . . London: Andrew Moffat . . . and D. A.
Borrenstein, Glasgow. 1842.

The Mitch. copy has an engraved title-page dated 1841. This is
a re-issue of § 354 (1833 Edinburgh=Chambers).

444. 1842 London

The poetical Works of Robert Burns. . . . London: published by
J. S. Pratt. MDCCCXLII.

445. 1842 London

The poetical Works of Robert Burns. . . . London: William
Smith, 1842.

446. 1842 Newcastle

Poetical Works. . . . Newcastle . . . W. & T. Fordyce. 1842.

Re-issue of § 439 (1841 Newcastle = Fordyce).

447. 1842 Philadelphia

Works . . . Philadelphia: J. Crissy. 1842.

Re-issue of § 394 (1836 Philadelphia = Crissy).

448. 1843 Derby

The poetical Works of Robert Burns. . . . Derby: published by
Richardson and Son; Simpkin, Marshall and Co., London.
1843.

Variants

1. [*The above, with*] (Richardson's Pocket Library)—
2. London: Thomas Richardson and Son. [n.d.]

Re-issued in 1844 (§ 459), 1845 (§ 468), 1847 (§ 500), and n.d.
(§§ 997, 998, 1114).

449. 1843 Edinburgh

The Correspondence between Burns and Clarinda. With a Memoir of Mrs M'Lehose, (Clarinda.) Arranged and edited by her Grandson, W. C. M'Lehose, Edinburgh: William Tait, 107, Prince's Street; Simpkin, Marshall & Co., London; and John Cumming, Dublin. MDCCCXLIII.

Original Material :

    Behold the Hour[50]   *p.* 274
    Twenty-three new letters, all to [Mrs Agnes M'Lehose]:

Ref. [50a]	*Date*	
I.145	[12 Dec. 1787]	*p.* 85
146	[20 ? Dec. 1787]	88
153	[3 Jan. 1788]	108
162	[12 Jan. 1788]	140
173	[25 Jan. 1788]	167
175	[27 Jan. 1788]	171
181	[7 Feb. 1788]	190
170	[21 Jan. 1788]	205
177	[1 Feb. 1788]	210
185	[13 Feb. 1788]	213
193	[22 Feb. 1788]	228
210	[17 Mar. 1788]	252
210	[18 Mar. 1788]	253
211	[19 Mar. 1788]	254
209	[14 Mar. 1788]	256
312	9 Mar. 1789	259
II.7	[Feb. ? 1790]	261
82	[Jul. ? 1791]	263
100	23 Nov. 1791	266
101	11 Dec. [? 1791]	268
101	[Dec. 1791 ?]	271
102	27 Dec. 1791	272
155	[Mar. ? 1793]	279

Comment. Lithograph frontispiece of a variety of subjects concerning Burns and Clarinda. Second title-page, also a lithograph. Issued in brownish-purple cloth boards. Stamped on the spine, in gold, " The Correspondence between Burns and Clarinda Price 8/6."

This is the first authorised edition of the Letters; twenty-five had been published without the permission of Mrs M'Lehose in § 68 (1802 Glasgow = Stewart).

[50] Another version of the song that appeared in § 50*d*. (Liverpool=Currie) IV. 111.   [50a] To *Letters.*

450. 1843 Glasgow

The Works of Robert Burns; with Dr. Currie's Memoir of the Poet, and an Essay on his Genius and Character by Professor Wilson. Also numerous Notes, Annotations, and Appendices. Embellished by eighty-one Portrait, and Landscape Illustrations. In two Volumes. Vol. I. Blackie and Son, Queen Street, Glasgow; South College Street, Edinburgh; and Warwick Square, London. MDCCCXLIII.

Vol. II [1844]

Original Material. Letters :

Ref.[51]	*Addressee*	*Date*	
I.78	Gavin Hamilton	[8 March 1787]	*p.* 173
II.130	William Johnston	[13 Nov. 1792]	275

Comment. The Mitch. copy is the best I have seen. The notice in the catalogue there reads as follows: " The only pictorial edition worthy of the Author's genius. First issue, with brilliant impressions of the delicate engravings; later issues are very inferior."

This is the final shape of the edition which began to be issued in parts about 1840 and to which Blackie may have been referring.[52]

It was re-issued at least as follows: 1846 (§ 487), 1847 (§ 502), 1850 (§ 530), 1853 (§ 569), 1854 (§ 578), 1855 (§ 586), 1859 (§ 626), 1861 (§ 645), 1865 (§ 680), 1866 (§ 695), 1868 (§ 719), 1870 (§ 739), 1874 (§§ 761, 766), 1877 (§ 788), 1878 (§ 796), and n.d. (§ 1044).

451. 1843 Halifax

Poetical Works. Halifax . . . Milner . . . MDCCCXLIII.

Re-issue of § 428 (1840 Halifax = Milner).

452. 1843 London

The complete Works of Robert Burns. . . . London : James Cornish, 1, Middle Row, Holborn ; 37 Lord Street, Liverpool ; and 18 Grafton Street. Dublin. 1843.

Re-issue of § 341 (1831 London = Clark).

---

[51] To *Letters*.
[52] " Works of Robert Burns, 21 parts at 2s." Blackie, W. G. *Origin and Progress of the Firm*, Glasgow, for private circulation, 1897, p. 115.

453. 1843 London

The poetical Works of Robert Burns. . . . London . . . J. S. Pratt. MDCCCXLIII.

454. [1843] New York

The Correspondence between Burns and Clarinda. . . . New York: Robert P. Bixby and Co.

The first American pirated edition of § 449 (1843 Edinburgh = Tait). It must have been issued almost immediately. The date appears on the verso of the title-page.

455. 1843 New York

The complete poetical Works of Robert Burns. . . . The second complete American Edition. New York: D. Appleton & Co., 200 Broadway; Philadelphia: Geo. S. Appleton, 148 Chestnut St. MDCCCXLIII.

Re-issued in 1844 (§ 466), 1846 (§ 492), 1847 (§ 509), 1849 (§ 523) and 1851 (§ 548). Query: Was there a " First Edition " ?

456. 1843 New York

The poetical Works of Robert Burns. . . . In two Volumes. . . . New York: published by Edward Kearney. 1843.

According to Gibson (p. 66), this is to be re-issued in 1852 (§ 562) and may be a re-issue of a slightly earlier edition bearing no date (cp. § 1155).

457. 1843 Nuremberg

The poetical Works of Robert Burns. With a Life of the Author. . . . by E. Cunningham . . . Campe's edition. Nurenberg and New York . . . Frederick Campe and Co. 1843.

Re-issue n.d. (§ 1169).

458. 1843 Philadelphia

The Works of Robert Burns . . . from the last London Edition. . . .
Philadelphia: John Locken, 311 Market Street. 1843.

Re-issued in 1844 (§ 467), 1846 (§ 495), and (?) 1849 (§ 526).

459. 1844 Derby

Poetical Works. . . . Derby . . . Richardson and Son . . . 1844.

Re-issue of § 448 (1843 Derby=Richardson).

460. 1844 Halifax

Complete Works. . . . Halifax . . . William Milner . . . MDCCCXLIV.

Re-issue of § 441 (1842 Halifax = Milner).

461. 1844 London

«« Pocket English classics. The songs of Robert Burns. . . .
London: Sherwood and Bowyer, 137, Strand. Thoms, printer,
Warwick Square. MDCCCXLIV.»»

M.C., § 614.

462. 1844 London

The Works of Robert Burns. . . . London: Henry G. Bohn, York
Street, Covent Gardens. 1844.

Comment. Purports to have (engraved between pp. 466 and 467) an
original facsimile of letter to Capt. Miller of Dalswinton, beginning; "—The following Ode is on a subject which I know you
by no means regard with indifference ' O Liberty——'."

Re-issued in 1845 (§ 477). The letter to Capt. Miller appeared
originally in § 368 (1834 London = Cunningham).

463. 1844 London

Works. . . . London . . . T. Tegg . . . 1844.

Re-issue of § 432 (1840 London = Tegg).

464. 1844 Manchester

The entire Works of Robert Burns . . . Four Volumes complete in One . . . Diamond Edition . . . Manchester: published by S. Johnson and Son, Livesey St., & Church St., Liverpool. 1844.

Re-issue of § 354 (1833 Edinburgh=Chambers).

465. 1844 Montrose

«« James Watt. 1 vol. 32mo.»»

Gebbie, VI. 339.

466. 1844 New York

«« Complete Poetical Works of Robert Burns. . . . The second complete American Edition. New York: D. Appleton & Co. MDCCCXLIV.»»

Angus, p. 90. Re-issue of § 455 (1843 New York = Appleton).

467. 1844 Philadelphia

The Works of Robert Burns. . . . A new Edition . . . Philadelphia: John Locken, 311 Market Street. 1844.

Re-issue of § 458 (1843 Philadelphia=Locken).

468. 1845 Derby

Poetical Works. . . . Derby: Thomas Richardson and Son; and 172, Fleet Street, London. 1845.

Re-issue of § 448 (1843 Derby = Richardson).

469. 1845 Glasgow

The poetical Works of Robert Burns. . . . Complete in one Volume. . . . Glasgow: Francis Orr & Sons. MDCCCXLV.

Re-issued in 1846 (§ 485) and 1848 (§ 513).

470. 1845 Glasgow

The Works of Robert Burns . . . Glasgow: printed for Richard Griffin and Co. 1845.

471. 1845 Glasgow

The Works and Correspondence of Robert Burns. . . . Glasgow: Mackenzie, White & Co., 6 Maxwell Street. 1845.

Variant

William Mackenzie: London, 22 Paternoster Row. Glasgow. 43 & 45 Howard Street. Edinburgh, 59 South Bridge. [n.d.] Re-issued in 1846 (§ 486).

472. 1845 Glasgow

Works. . . . Glasgow: Mackenzie, White & Co. 1845.

According to *M.C.* § 262, a re-issue of § 385 (1836 Glasgow = Mackenzie).

473. 1845 Halifax

Complete Works. . . . Halifax . . . Milner . . . MDCCCXLV.

According to *M.C.*, § 389, a re-issue of § 441 (1842 Halifax = Milner).

474. 1845 Halifax

Poetical Works . . . Halifax . . . William Milner. 1845.

Re-issue of § 428 (1840 Halifax = Milner).

475. 1845 Leipzig

The poetical Works of Robert Burns. . . . Leipzig. Bernhard Tauchnitz. 1845.

Variant

Leipzig Bernh. Tauchnitz Jun. 1845.

This is Vol. 90 of a series called *Collection of British Authors.*

o

476. 1845 London

The poetical Works of Robert Burns. . . . London: . . . J. S.
Pratt. 1845.

477. 1845 London

Works. . . . London . . . Bohn. 1845.
Re-issue of § 462 (1844 London = Bohn).

478. 1845 London

Works . . . London: T. Tegg . . . 1845.
Re-issue of § 432 (1840 London = Tegg).

479. 1845 Manchester

The entire Works of Robert Burns. . . . Tenth Diamond Edition.
. . . Manchester: S. Johnson . . . MDCCCXLV.

Variant

Manchester: S. Johnson, and Son, 3, Oldham-Street. MDCCCXLV.

480. 1845 Philadelphia

Works. . . . Philadelphia: J. Crissy . . . 1845.
Re-issue of § 394 (1836 Philadelphia = Crissy).

481. 1846 Belfast

The poetical Works of Robert Burns. . . . Complete in one
Volume. . . . Belfast: published by John Henderson. MDCCCXLVI.
Re-issued in 1847 (§ 496).

482. 1846 Boston

The poetical Works of Robert Burns, including several Pieces
not inserted in Dr. Currie's Edition: exhibited under a new

Plan of Arrangement. . . . In two Volumes. Vol. I. Boston: Timothy Bedlington 1846.

An American reprint of § 226 (1819 London = Thomson).

Re-issued in 1847 (§ 497), 1848 (§ 511), 1849 (§ 521), and n.d. (§ 989).

483. 1846 Boston

The Works of Robert Burns. Boston: Otis, Broaders, and Company. 1846.

Re-issued in 1847 (§ 498), 1848 (§ 512), and n.d. (§ 988).

484. 1846 Glasgow

The poetical Works of Robert Burns. . . . Glasgow: published by John Morrison, 21 New Bridge Street. MDCCCXLVI.

485. 1846 Glasgow

Poetical Works . . . Glasgow: Francis Orr & Sons, 63 Brunswick Street. MDCCCXLVI.

Re-issue of § 469 (1845 Glasgow = Orr).

486. 1846 Glasgow

Works and Correspondence. . . . Glasgow: Mackenzie, White & Co. . . 1846.

Re-issue of § 471 (1845 Glasgow = Mackenzie, White & Co.).

487. 1846 Glasgow

Works. . . . Glasgow: Blackie and Son, Queen Street, Glasgow: South College Street, Edinburgh: and Warwick Square, London. MDCCCXLVI.

Re-issue of § 450 (1843 Glasgow = Blackie).

488. 1846 Halifax

Complete Works. . . . Halifax . . . Milner . . . MDCCCXLVI.

Re-issue of § 441 (1842 Halifax = Milner).

489. 1846 Halifax

Poetical Works. . . . Halifax . . . Milner . . . MDCCCXLVI.

Re-issue of § 428 (1840 Halifax = Milner).

490. 1846 London

The complete poetical Works of Robert Burns. . . . London: printed for Adam Scott, (late Scott and Webster,) Charterhouse Square. 1846.

Re-issue of § 400 (1837 London= Scott, Webster, and Geary).

491. 1846 London

The poetical Works of Robert Burns. . . . London: C. Daly, 17 Greville Street, Hatton Garden. 1846.

Re-issued in 1850 (§ 534).

492. 1846 New York

The complete Works of Robert Burns. . . . The second complete American Edition. New York: D. Appleton . . . MDCCCXLVI.

Re-issue of § 455 (1843 New York = Appleton).

493. 1846 Philadelphia

«« The Works of Robert Burns. Philadelphia: Henry F. Anners. 1846.»»

M.C., § 789.

494. 1846 Philadelphia

Works. . . . Philadelphia: J. Crissy . . . 1846.

Re-issue of § 394 (1836 Philadelphia = Crissy).

495. 1846 Philadelphia

The poetical Works of Robert Burns. Philadelphia: published by John Locken . . . 1846.

Re-issue of § 458 (1844 Philadelphia = Locken).

496. 1847 Belfast

Poems ... A new Edition. Belfast: ... Henderson. 1847.

Re-issue of § 481 (1846 Belfast = Henderson).

497. 1847 Boston

The poetical Works of Robert Burns. . . . Two Volumes in one. . . . Boston: Phillips and Sampson, 110 Washington Street. 1847.

Re-issue of § 482 (1846 Boston = Bedlington).

498. 1847 Boston

The Works of Robert Burns. Boston: Otis, Broaders & Company. 1847.

Re-issue of § 483 (1846 Boston = Otis, Broaders).

499. 1847 Cincinnati

«« Currie's edition 1 vol. 8vo.»»

Gebbie, vi. 340.

500. 1847 Derby

Poetical Works. . . . Derby . . . Richardson . . . 1847.

Re-issue of § 448 (1843 Derby = Richardson).

501. 1847 Edinburgh

The poetical Works of Robert Burns. . . . Edinburgh: published by Robert Martin, Brown's Lane. MDCCCXLVII.

502. 1847 Glasgow

Works. In two volumes. Glasgow: Blackie & Son. MDCCCXLVII.

Re-issue of § 450 (1843 Glasgow = Blackie).

503. 1847 Halifax

Complete Works. . . . Halifax . . . William Milner . . .
MDCCCXLVII.

Re-issue of § 441 (1842 Halifax = Milner).

504. 1847 London

The poetical Works of Robert Burns . . . London: published by
J. S. Pratt. MDCCCXLVII.

505. 1847 London

Works . . . Edited by the Ettrick Shepherd and William Motherwell, Esq. . . . London, Edinburgh and Dublin. A. Fullarton
and Co. 1847.

Re-issue of § 365 (1834 Glasgow = Fullarton).

506. 1847 London

Works. . . . New Edition. London: Henry G. Bohn . . . 1847.
Re-issue of § 432 (1840 London = Tegg).

507. 1847 London

Works. . . . London: T. Tegg . . . 1847.
Re-issue of § 432 (1840 London = Tegg).

508. 1847 Manchester

Entire Works. . . . Tenth Diamond Edition. . . . Manchester:
printed and published by Thomas Johnson, Livesey Street.
MDCCCXLVII.

Re-issue of § 354 (1833 Edinburgh = Chambers). This, and the
re-issues of 1848 (§ 518) and 1850 (§ 538), are called Tenth
Diamond Edition.

509. 1847 New York

Complete poetical Works. . . . The second complete American
Edition . . . New York: D. Appleton and Co. . . . Philadelphia:
Geo. Appleton . . . MDCCCXLVII.

Re-issue of § 455 (1843 New York = Appleton).

510. 1848 Aberdeen

The complete Works of Robert Burns. . . . Aberdeen: published
by George Clark and Son. Ipswich:—J.M. Burton.
MDCCCXLVIII.

511. 1848 Boston

Poetical Works. . . . Two Volumes in One. . . . Boston: Phillips
and Sampson . . . 1848.

Re-issue of § 482 (1846 Boston = Bedlington).

512. 1848 Boston

Works. . . . Boston: Otis, Broaders & Company. 1848.

Re-issue of § 483 (1846 Boston = Otis, Broaders).

513. 1848 Glasgow

Poetical Works. . . . Glasgow . . . Orr . . . MDCCCXLVIII.

Re-issue of § 469 (1845 Glasgow = Orr).

514. 1848 Halifax

Complete Works. . . . Halifax . . . William Milner . . .
MDCCCXLVIII.

Re-issue of § 441 (1842 Halifax = Milner).

515. 1848 Edinburgh

«« W. P. Nimmo. 1 vol. 18 mo.»»

Gebbie, VI. 340.

516. 1848 London

The poetical Works of Robert Burns. London: Chapman and Hall, 186, Strand. MDCCCXLVIII.

Re-issue of § 419 (1839 London = William Smith).

517. 1848 London

Works. . . . Edited by the Ettrick Shepherd, and William Motherwell, Esq. . . . London . . . Fullarton . . . 1848.

Re-issue of § 365 (1834 Glasgow = Fullarton).

518. 1848 Manchester

Entire Works. . . . Tenth Diamond Edition. . . . Manchester . . . T. Johnson . . . MDCCCXLVIII.

Re-issue of § 354 (1833 Edinburgh = Chambers).

519. 1848 New York

«« New York—Baker & Scribner.»»

From a handwritten catalogue of American editions in Horn.

520. 1848 Philadelphia

Works. . . . Philadelphia: Crissy and Markley, No. 4, Minor Street. 1848.

Re-issue of § 394 (1836 Philadelphia = Crissy).

521. 1849 Boston

Poetical Works. . . . Two Volumes in one. . . . Boston: Phillips and Sampson . . . 1849.

Re-issue of § 482 (1846 Boston = Bedlington).

522. 1849 Cincinnati

The Works of Robert Burns. . . . Cincinnati: Published by J. A. & U. P. James, Walnut St., Bet. Fourth & Fifth. Stereotyped by James & Co. 1849.

Re-issued in 1853 (§ 566) and (?) 1857 (§ 602). Cp. also § 613.

523. 1849 New York

The complete poetical Works of Robert Burns. The only complete American Edition. New York: D. Appleton & Co. Philadelphia: G. S. Appleton & Co. MDCCCXLIX.

Re-issue of § 455 (1843 New York = Appleton).

524. 1849 New York

The poetical Works of Robert Burns. . . . In two Volumes. . . . New-York: Leavitt and Company, 191, Broadway. 1849.

Re-issued in 1852 (§ 562), 1855 (§ 591), and 1858 (§ 620).

525. 1849 New York

The Works of Robert Burns. . . . New-York: Leavitt, Trow & Co., 191 Broadway. 1849.

Re-issue of § 350 (1832 New York = Pearson).

526. 1849 Philadelphia

«« Poetical Works of Robert Burns. Philadelphia: Published by John Locken. 1849.»»

Angus, p. 100. Re-issue (?) of § 458 (1846 Philadelphia = Locken).

527. [1850] Belfast

Poetical Works. . . . Belfast: Simms & M'Intyre.

M.C., § 728, notes a re-issue of § 395 (1837 Belfast = Simms & M'Intyre) with wrapper dated 1850.

528. 1850 Boston

The poetical Works of Robert Burns. . . . Boston: Phillips, Sampson and Company, 110 Washington Street. 1850.

Re-issued in 1852 (§ 551), 1853 (§ 565), 1854 (§ 577), 1855 (§ 583), 1856 (§ 593), 1857 (§ 601), 1859 (§ 622), and 1866 (§ 682).

529. 1850 Dumfries

«« The Songs of Robert Burns. David Halliday.»»

Gebbie, VI. 340.

530. 1850 Glasgow

Works. . . . In two volumes. Glasgow. Blackie & Son. MDCCCL.

Re-issue of § 450 (1843 Glasgow = Blackie).

531. 1850 Glasgow

Works. . . . Glasgow . . . Fullarton . . . 1850[-52].

Re-issue of § 365 (1834 Glasgow = Fullarton).

532. 1850 Halifax

Complete Works. . . . Halifax . . . William Milner . . . MDCCCL.

Re-issue of § 441 (1842 Halifax = Milner).

533. 1850 Halifax

Poetical Works. . . . Halifax . . . William Milner. MDCCCL.

Re-issue of § 428 (1840 Halifax = Milner).

534. 1850 London

Poetical Works . . . London: C. Daly . . . 1850.

Re-issue of § 491 (1846 London = C. Daly). Probably the edition noted by Cook in *Camb. Bib.*, II.977.

535. 1850 London

The poetical Works of Robert Burns. London: published by Newman & Co. Aberdeen: Clark & Son. MDCCCL.

536. 1850 London

The Works of Robert Burns. . . . New Edition. London: Henry G. Bohn . . . 1850.

Re-issue of § 432 (1840 London = Tegg).

537. 1850 London

Works. . . . London . . . Fullarton . . . 1850.

Re-issue of § 365 (1834 Glasgow = Fullarton).

538. 1850 Manchester

Entire Works. . . . Tenth Diamond Edition. . . . Manchester . . . Johnson . . . 1850.

Re-issue of § 354 (1833 Edinburgh = Chambers).

539. 1850 Philadelphia

The Works of Robert Burns . . . Philadelphia: published by Crissy & Markley. 1850.

Re-issue of § 394 (1836 Philadelphia = Crissy).

540. 1851 Edinburgh

The Life and Works of Robert Burns. Edited by Robert Chambers. In four Volumes. Vol. I. Edinburgh: William and Robert Chambers. 1851.

Variant

William and Robert Chambers. London and Edinburgh. [n.d.]

a. VOL. I

Original Material:

    The Tarbolton Lasses [" If ye gae up to yon hill tap . . ."]   *p.* 45
    The Ronalds of the Bennals [" In Tarbolton ye ken . . ."]   46

b. Vol. II

Original Material:

c. Vol. III

Original Material:

[53] To *Letters.*
[54] Originally in *Scots Mag.*, LXV (Nov. 1803), 798.
[55] To *Letters.*
[56] Chambers does not claim this to be a first appearance.

d. VOL. IV

Original Material:
O Lord when Hunger pinches sore   *p.* 50
Dear——, I'll gie you some Advice.   240
How daur ye ca' me howlet-Faced?   242
Four letters:

Ref.[57]	Addressee	Date	
II.231	Peter Hill	? July 1793[58]	*p.* 13
186	[Miss —— Gordon]	[Jul.-Aug. 1793][59]	128
286	[Captain John Hamilton]	[31 Jan. 1795]	135
324	George Thomson	4 Jul. [1796]	201
211	Inscription in a copy of Delolme's *British Constitution*	[Sep. 1793]	45

Comment. Issued in blue paper wrappers and sold for 2s 6d.

Part of a series entitled "Chambers' Instructive and Entertaining Library. A Series of Books for the People."

Robert Chambers had long been accumulating material for a life of Robert Burns, as much as possible from people who had known him. He began work on this edition in 1850: ". . . after minute investigation, the *Life and Works of Robert Burns* was produced in 1851. It was well received, and passed through several editions, to suit different classes of purchasers."[60] Chambers had actually begun his study of Burns as early as 1829 (see § 324), published the *Life and Works* in 1838-39 (§ 406, 407, 417), added a great deal more material in this edition, and culminated his labours with the edition of 1856 (§ 594).

541. 1851 Edinburgh

«« The Entire Works of Robert Burns. . . . The four volumes complete in one. . . . Edinburgh: Alexander Gunn, 37 South Bridge. 1851.»»

M.C. (Lamb), § 135. Dundee Catalogue, Victoria Galleries, 1897, p. 27, describes this as another Diamond edition. It undoubtedly is.

---

[57] To *Letters*.
[58] Completed in § 783 (1877 Edinburgh = Scott Douglas).
[59] Also titled "Love-Letters for a Farmer."
[60] *Memoir of William and Robert Chambers*, (Edinburgh and London 1883), p. 291. There is an edition, n.d. (§ 1010).

542. 1851 Glasgow

Works. . . . Glasgow . . . Fullarton . . . 1851.

Re-issue of § 365 (1834 Glasgow = Fullarton).

543. 1851 Halifax

Complete Works . . . Halifax: printed and published by Milner and Sowerby, Cheapside. MDCCCLI.

Re-issue of § 441 (1842 Halifax = Milner).

544. 1851 Halifax

Poetical Works. . . . Halifax: printed and published by Milner and Sowerby, Cheapside. MDCCCLI.

Re-issue of § 428 (1840 Halifax = Milner).

545. 1851 London

The poetical Works of Robert Burns. . . . London: Simms and M'Intyre, 13 Paternoster Row; and 26 Donegall Street, Belfast. 1851.

Gibson, p. 65, mentions a Belfast edition of this year. He probably means this one. Also issued with a green wrapper with " Knight's Series.—London: Charles Knight & Co. . . ." printed thereon. Re-issue of § 395 (1837 Belfast = Simms & M'Intyre).

546. 1851 London

Cabinet Edition of the British Poets. In four Volumes. Vol. II. Henry Kirk White. Burns . . . London: Henry G. Bohn, York Street, Covent Garden. 1851.

547. 1851 London

Works . . . London, Edinburgh, and Dublin . . . Fullarton . . . 1851.

Re-issue of § 365 (1834 Glasgow = Fullarton).

548. 1851 New York

The Complete Poetical Works of Robert Burns. . . . New York: D. Appleton & Co., 200 Broadway. MDCCCLI.

Re-issue of § 455 (1843 New York = Appleton).

549. 1851 Philadelphia

The Complete Works of Robert Burns . . . Philadelphia & New York. Geo. S. Appleton. 1851.

550. 1851 Philadelphia

The Works of Robert Burns. Philadelphia: published by Crissy & Markley . . . and Thomas, Cowperthwait & Co. . . . 1851.

551. 1852 Boston

Poetical Works. . . . Boston: Phillips, Sampson . . . 1852.

Re-issue of § 528 (1850 Boston = Phillips, Sampson).

552. 1852 Dumfries

The Songs of Robert Burns. Dumfries: . . . David Halliday. MDCCCLII.

See also Gebbie, VI.340, for mention of an edition in 1850.

553. 1852 Edinburgh

«« Hogg & Motherwell. A. Fullarton & Co. 5 vols. 12mo.»»

Gebbie, VI.340. This must refer to the London, Edinburgh, Dublin edition of 1852 (§ 559). I have never seen a Fullarton edition with Edinburgh only in the imprint.

554. 1852 Glasgow

The poetical Works of Robert Burns. . . . Glasgow: G. & J. Cameron, 67 Virginia-street. MDCCCLII.

Re-issued in 1855 (§ 584), with *Songs and Ballads*, " Two volumes in one."

555. 1852 Glasgow

The Songs and Ballads of Robert Burns. . . . Glasgow: G. & J. Cameron, 67 Virginia-street . . . MDCCCLII.

Re-issued in 1853 (§ 568), with the *Poetical Works*, " Two volumes in one." Re-issued as *Songs and Ballads* in 1865 (§ 674).

556. 1852 Glasgow

«« Works of Robert Burns. Blackie & Co. 25 parts at 1s and 8 supplementary parts with engravings.»»

This is undoubtedly a re-issue of § 450 (1843 Glasgow = Blackie). Cp. W. G. Blackie, *Sketch of the Origin and Progress of the Firm* (Glasgow: . . . 1897), p. 117.

557. 1852 Halifax

Complete Works . . . Halifax: printed and published by Milner and Sowerby, Cheapside. 1852.

Re-issue of § 441 (1842 Halifax = Milner).

558. 1852 Halifax

Poetical Works . . . Halifax: printed and published by Milner and Sowerby, Cheapside. 1852.

Re-issue of § 428 (1840 Halifax = Milner).

559. 1852 London

Works . . . London, Edinburgh, and Dublin . . . Fullarton . . . 1852.

Re-issue of § 365 (1834 Glasgow = Fullarton).

560. 1852 New York

The complete poetical Works of Robert Burns. . . . The only complete American Edition. New York: D. Appleton & Co., 200 Broadway, MDCCCLII.

Re-issued in 1853 (§ 574), 1855 (§ 589), 1856 (§ 599), and 1857 (§ 608). The " complete " is misleading, in so far as this is merely a reprint of Currie's edition of 1820 (§ 242).

561. 1852 New York

The Life and Works of Robert Burns. . . . Edited by Robert Chambers. In four Volumes. New-York: Harper & Brothers. 1852.

562. 1852 New York

The poetical Works of Robert Burns . . . In two volumes. New-York: Leavitt & Allen. 1852.

According to Gibson, p. 66, ". . . printed from the identical plates owned by Edward Kerney about 1840." Re-issue of § 524 (1849 New York = Leavitt). Kearney has an edition of n.d. (§ 1155) and one in 1843 (§ 456).

563. 1852 New York

Works . . . New York: Leavitt & Allen. 1852.

Re-issue of § 350 (1832 New York = Pearson).

564. 1853 Boston

The complete Works of Robert Burns. . . . Boston: Phillips, Sampson and Company. 1853.

565. 1853 Boston

Poetical Works . . . Boston: Phillips, Sampson . . . 1853.

Re-issue of § 528 (1850 Boston = Phillips, Sampson).

566. 1853 Cincinnati

Works. . . . Cincinnati . . . James . . . 1853.

Re-issue of § 522 (1849 Cincinnati = James).

P

567. 1853 Edinburgh

Life and Works. . . .   Chambers . . . Edinburgh . . . 1853.

This might be termed a partial re-issue of § 540 (1851 Edinburgh = Chambers). Vol. I is dated 1853, Vol. II 1851, and Vols. III and IV 1852.

567 A. 1853 Edinburgh

The Scott Musical Museum. . . .   [ed.] William Stenhouse. New edition [of § 417 A, 1839 Edinburgh = Blackwood] in four volumes. Edinburgh. . . .   Blackwood. MDCCCLIII.

With a few editorial additions, this is otherwise a re-issue of § 8 (1788-1803 Edinburgh=Johnson).

568. 1853 Glasgow

Songs and Ballads. . . .   Glasgow: G. & J. Cameron, 1853.

Re-issue of § 555 (1852 Glasgow = Cameron).

569. 1853 Glasgow

Works. . . .   Blackie and Son . . . Glasgow . . . MDCCCLIII.

Re-issue of § 450 (1843 Glasgow = Blackie).

570. 1853 Halifax

Poetical Works . . . Halifax . . . Milner and Sowerby . . . 1853.

Re-issue of § 428 (1840 Halifax = Milner).

571. 1853 London

«« W. S. Orr & Co.   2 Vols.   64mo.»»

Gebbie, VI.340.

572. 1853 London

Complete Works. . . .   London . . . Adam Scott . . . 1853.

Re-issue of § 400 (1837 London = Scott).

573. 1853 London

The Works of Robert Burns . . . Edited by the Ettrick Shepherd
and William Motherwell Esq. . . . Vol. I. [*of five*]   London,
Edinburgh, and Dublin: A. Fullarton and Co. . . . 1853.

574. 1853 New York

Complete poetical Works. . . . New York: D. Appleton & Co.
1851.

Re-issue of § 560 (1852 New York = Appleton).

575. 1853 New York

The Works of Robert Burns. . . . New-York, Leavitt & Allen,
(Successors to Leavitt & Co.) No. 27 Dey-Street. 1853.

Re-issue of § 380 (1832 New York = Pearson).

576. 1854 Boston

The complete works of Robert Burns . . . Boston: Phillips,
Sampson, and Company.   1854.

Re-issued in 1858 (§ 612).

577. 1854 Boston

Poetical Works. . . . Boston: Phillips, Sampson . . . 1854.

Re-issue of § 528 (1850 Boston = Phillips, Sampson).

578. 1854 Glasgow

Works . . . Glasgow: Blackie & Son.   MDCCCLIV.

Re-issue of § 450 (1843 Glasgow = Blackie).

579. 1854 Halifax

Complete Works. . . . Halifax . . . Milner and Sowerby . . . 1854.

Re-issue of § 441 (1842 Halifax = Milner).

580. 1854 Halifax

Poetical Works. . . . Halifax . . . Milner and Sowerby . . . 1854.

Re-issue of § 428 (1840 Halifax = Milner).

581. 1854 London

Works. . . . London . . . Bohn. 1854.

Re-issue of § 432 (1840 London = Tegg).

582. 1854 Philadelphia

The Life and Works of Robert Burns. . . . 4 vols. . . . ed. by Robert Chambers. . . . Philadelphia: Lippincott, Grambo & Co. 1854.

583. 1855 Boston

Poetical Works. . . . Boston: Phillips, Sampson . . . 1855.

Re-issue of § 528 (1850 Boston = Phillips, Sampson).

584. 1855 Glasgow

The poetical Works of Robert Burns . . . Glasgow: John Cameron . . . 1855. 2 vols. [*Vol. II, Songs and Ballads*] in one.

Re-issue of § 554 (1852 Glasgow = Cameron) and § 555 (1852 Glasgow = Cameron). In this format it was re-issued in 1856 (§ 596), 1857 (§ 603), 1859 (§ 625), 1865 (§ 673), 1883 (§ 819), and perhaps oftener.

585. 1855 Glasgow

«« R. Griffin & Co. 1 volume. 8vo.»»

Gebbie, VI.340.

586. 1855 Glasgow

Works . . . Blackie and Son . . . Glasgow . . . MDCCCLV.

Re-issue of § 450 (1843 Glasgow = Blackie).

587. 1855 Halifax

Complete Works. . . . Halifax . . . Milner and Sowerby . . . 1855.

Re-issue of § 441 (1842 Halifax = Milner).

588. 1855 Hartford

The poetical and prose Works of Robert Burns. . . . Hartford: William Jas. Hammersley. 1855.

589. 1855 New York

Complete poetical Works. . . . New York . . . Appleton . . . MDCCCLV.

Re-issue of § 560 (1852 New York = Appleton).

590. 1855 New York

«« Poetical Works . . . 2 vols. . . . Edward Kerney, New York.»»

Noted in § 744 (1871 Kilmarnock = M'Kie), II.442, and in Gebbie, VI.340. Is this the same as the next item ? See Gibson's comment on § 562 (1852 New York = Leavitt & Allen).

591. 1855 New York

Poetical Works . . . New York: Leavitt & Allen. 1855.

Re-issue of § 524 (1849 New York = Leavitt & Allen).

592. 1855 New York

The poetical Works of Robert Burns. New York: Wm. H. Murphy. 1855.

593. 1856 Boston

Poetical Works. . . . Boston: Phillips, Sampson and Company . . . 1856.

Re-issue of § 528 (1850 Boston = Phillips, Sampson).

594. 1856 Edinburgh

The Life and Works of Robert Burns edited by Robert Chambers
Library Edition in four Volumes Vol. I W. & R. Chambers
Edinburgh and London MDCCCLVI

b. VOL. II

Original Material. Three letters:

Ref.[61]	Addressee	Date	
1.53	George Reid	29 Nov. 1786[62]	*p.* 2
117	Archibald Lawrie	14 Aug. 1787[63]	107
208	[Gavin Hamilton]	[Mar. 1788]	253

c. VOL. III

Original Material. One letter:

1.361	Alexander Fergusson	[Oct. 1789]	*p.* 72

d. VOL. IV

Original Material:
Extempore on Some Commemoration of Thomson.   *p.* 335
Ten letters:

Ref.[64]	Addressee	Date	
11.295	John Edgar	25 Apr. 1795[65]	*p.* 154
1.252	Graham of Fintry	10 Sept. 1788	326
259	Graham of Fintry	23 Sept. 1788	328
334	Graham of Fintry	13 May 1789	329
346	Graham of Fintry	31 Jul. 1789	330
369	Graham of Fintry	9 Dec. 1789[66]	332
11.40	Graham of Fintry	4 Sept. 1790	333
96	Graham of Fintry	6 Oct. 1790	335
145	Mrs Graham of Fintry	[5 Jan. 1793]	335
143	Graham of Fintry	5 Jan. 1793	336
228	Graham of Fintry	[Jan. 1794]	338

[61] To *Letters*.
[62] According to *Letters* and § 783 (1877 Edinburgh = Scott Douglas) this
first appeared in § 540 (1851 Edinburgh = Chambers).
[63] Originally in the *Glasgow Citizen*, 8 Apr. 1854.
[64] To *Letters*.
[65] Completed from § 50 (Liverpool = Currie).
[66] Both Scott Douglas and Ferguson say that this first appeared in § 540
(1851 Edinburgh = Chambers).

Comment. Frontispiece-portrait engraved by R. C. Bell. Issued in brownish-purple cloth binding with Burns's seal stamped on the front cover and the title on the spine, in gold.

This is an extended version of the Chambers edition of 1851 (§ 540). Re-issued in 1859 (§§ 623, 631), 1860 (§§ 637, 639), and 1891 (§ 869), and n.d. (§ 1011).

595. 1856 Edinburgh

The poetical Works of Robert Burns. With Memoir, critical dissertation, and explanatory Notes, by the Rev. George Gilfillan. [*2 vols.*] Edinburgh: James Nichol . . . London: James Nisbet . . . Dublin: W. Robertson. MDCCCLVI.

Re-issued in 1857 (§ 609).

596. 1856 Glasgow

Poetical Works . . . Glasgow: John Cameron . . . 1856.

Re-issue of § 584 (1855 Glasgow = Cameron).

597. 1856 Halifax

Poetical Works . . . Halifax . . . Milner and Sowerby . . . 1856.

Re-issue of § 428 (1840 Halifax = Milner).

598. 1856 London

The poetical Works of Robert Burns. Edited by the Rev. Robert Aris Willmott, Incumbent of Bear Wood. Illustrated by John Gilbert. London: George Routledge and Co. Faringdon Street. New York: 18 Beekman Street. 1856.

Re-issued in 1856, 1857 (§ 607), 1858 (§ 616), 1859 (§ 633), 1860 (§ 641), 1862 (§ 649), 1863 (§ 656), 1865 (§ 679), 1866 (§ 692), 1867 (§ 765), 1869 (§ 727), and perhaps oftener.

599. 1856 New York

Complete poetical Works. . . . New York . . . Appleton . . . MDCCCLVI.

Re-issue of § 560 (1852 New York = Appleton).

600. 1856 Philadelphia

Poetical Works of Robert Burns. With Life, Notes, and Glossary,
by A. Cunningham, Esq. . . . Philadelphia: Willis P. Hazard.
1856.

(?) Re-issued in 1857 (§ 611).

601. 1857 Boston

Poetical Works . . . Boston: Phillips, Sampson . . . 1857.

Re-issue of § 528 (1850 Boston = Phillips, Sampson).

602. 1857 Cincinnati

Works of Robert Burns . . . edited by Allan Cunningham.
Cincinnati: U. P. James. 1857.

Re-issue (?) of § 522 (1849 Cincinnati = James).

603. 1857 Glasgow

Poetical Works. . . . Glasgow: John Cameron . . . 1857.

Re-issue of § 584 (1855 Glasgow = Cameron). This is two volumes in one. There was, apparently, an issue of the volumes
separately this year, *Poetical Works* (see Angus, p. 26) and *Songs
and Ballads* (see *M.C.*, § 210).

604. 1857 Halifax

Complete Works. . . . Halifax . . . Milner and Sowerby . . . 1857.

Re-issue of § 441 (1842 Halifax = Milner).

605. [1857] London

«« Poetical Works of Robert Burns. London: Thomas Allman.
[circa 1857] »»

Angus, p. 48. Gebbie, vi.340, " 1 vol. 48mo."

606. 1857 London

The poetical Works of Robert Burns. London: Groombridge and Sons, Paternoster Row. 1857.

Re-issue of § 419 (1839 London = Smith).

607. 1857 London

Poetical Works. . . . Edited by the Rev. Robert Aris Wilmott . . . Second Edition. London: George Routledge . . . New York: 18, Beckman Street. 1857.

Re-issue of § 598 (1856 London = Routledge).

608. 1857 New York

Complete poetical Works. . . . New York . . . Appleton . . . MDCCCLVII.

Re-issue of § 560 (1852 New York = Appleton).

609. 1857 New York

The poetical Works of Robert Burns . . . [edited] by the Rev. George Gilfillan. Complete, two Vols. in one. New York: D. Appleton and Co., 346 and 348 Broadway. 1857.

Re-issue. The sheets of § 595 (1856 Edinburgh = Nichol), 2 vols. bound in one with a New York title-page.

610. 1857 New York

Works. . . . New York: Leavitt & Allen, No. 379 Broadway, 1857.

Re-issue of § 350 (1832 New York = Pearson).

611. 1857 Philadelphia

The poetical Works of Robert Burns. . . . Philadelphia: Willis P. Hazard, 190 Chestnut St. 1857.

Probably a re-issue of § 600 (1856 Philadelphia = Hazard).

612. 1858 Boston

Complete Works. . . . Boston: Phillips, Sampson . . . 1858.

Re-issue of § 576 (1854 Boston = Phillips, Sampson).

613. 1858 Cincinnati

«« Works of Robert Burns. Cincinnati: U. P. James. 1858.»»

Angus, p. 89. Undoubtedly a re-issue of § 522 (1849 Cincinnati=
James). Gibson, Scott Douglas, M'Kie, and Gebbie, all have
" W. P. James."

614. 1858 Halifax

Poetical Works. . . . Halifax . . . Milner and Sowerby . . . 1858.

Re-issue of § 428 (1840 Halifax = Milner).

615. 1858 London

Poems and Songs. By Robert Burns. . . . London: Bell & Daldy,
186, Fleet Street; Edinburgh: J. Menzies. 1858.

Re-issued in 1858 (§ 619) and n.d. (§ 1033).

616. 1858 London

Poetical Works. . . . London: G. Routledge . . . New York :
18 Beekman Street. 1858.

Re-issue of § 598 (1856 London = Routledge). Another title-
page has " Routledge's British Poets," and " Third Edition."

617. 1858 London

«« The Works of Robert Burns . . . New Edition. London: H. G.
Bohn. 1858.»»

B. Chr., 1 (1892), 110. Probably a re-issue of § 432 (1840 London = Tegg).

618. [1858] Ayr [misplaced]

The Real " Souter Johnny," & etc. A Poem with explanatory Notes, and an Appendix. By the late M. Porteous, Printer, Maybole. Ayr: printed by Hugh Henry.

Original Material:

    Letter to William Niven, Esq., of Kirkbride 30 Aug. 1786[67] *p.* 23

619. 1858 New York

Poems and Songs of Robert Burns. . . . New York: D. Appleton & Co. 1858.

Re-issue. The sheets of § 615 (1858 London = Bell & Daldy), with a New York title-page.

620. 1858 New York

Poetical Works. . . . New York: Leavitt & Allen . . . 1858.

Re-issue of § 524 (1849 New York = Leavitt & Allen).

621. 1858 Philadelphia

The poetical Works of Robert Burns. . . . Philadelphia: Published by E. H. Butler & Co. 1858.

According to the handwritten catalogue of American editions in the Hornel Collection, " This is the most costly & handsome ed. of Burns that has been published in America."

622. 1859 Boston

Poetical Works. . . . Boston: Phillips, Sampson . . . 1859.

Re-issue of § 528 (1850 Boston = Phillips, Sampson).

623. 1859 Edinburgh

Life and Works. . . . In four volumes. Edinburgh . . . Chambers . . . 1859.

Re-issue of §594 (1856 Edinburgh = Chambers). *M.C.*, § 28, notes a re-issue of § 540 (1851 Edinburgh = Chambers) this year.

---

[67] *Letters*, I.39. This did *not* appear in the first edition (Maybole 1834).

624. 1859 Edinburgh

«« W. P. Nimmo.   1 vol.   12mo.»»

Gebbie, VI.340.

625. 1859 Glasgow

Poetical Works. . . .   Glasgow . . . Cameron . . . 1859.

Re-issue of § 584 (1855 Glasgow = Cameron).

626. 1859 Glasgow

Works. . . .   Glasgow : Blackie . . . MDCCCLIX.

Re-issue of § 450 (1843 Glasgow = Blackie).

627. 1859 Glasgow

Centenary Edition.   The poetical Works of Robert Burns. . . .
Edited by John and Angus Macpherson.   Glasgow : George
Cameron. . . .   Sold by all booksellers.   1859.

Re-issued n.d. (§§ 1099, 1119).

628. 1859 Glasgow

The Songs of Robert Burns. . . .   Glasgow : David Jack . . . 1859.

629. 1859 Halifax

Complete Works . . . Halifax . . . Milner and Sowerby . . . 1859.

Re-issue of § 441 (1842 Halifax = Milner).

630. 1859 Halifax

Poetical Works. . . .   Halifax . . . Milner and Sowerby . . . 1859.

Re-issue of § 428 (1840 Halifax and Milner).

631. 1859[-60] London

Life and Works. . . .   Chambers . . . London.   1859.

Re-issue of § 594 (1856 Edinburgh = Chambers).   Vols. III
and IV dated 1860.

632. 1859 London

Poetical Works. . . . London: Groombridge & Sons. MDCCCLIX.

Re-issue of § 419 (1857 London = Smith).

633. 1859 London

Poetical Works. . . . London: Routledge, Warne and Routledge, Farringdon Street. 1859.

Variant

. . . Farringdon Street. New York, 18 Beekman Street. 1859.

This also came out in " Routledge's British Poets." Re-issue of § 598 (1856 London = Routledge). The *Weekly Scotsman*, 27 Oct. 1934, claims this to be a new edition. I think not.

634. 1859 New York

«« Complete Poetical and Prose Works of Robert Burns. New York: S. A. Rollo & Co. 1859.»»

Angus, p. 96.

635. 1859 Philadelphia

The poetical Works of Robert Burns. . . . Philadelphia: G. G. Evans & Co., 439 Chesnut Street. 1859.

636. 1860 Boston

The complete Works of Robert Burns. . . . Boston: Crosby, Nichols, Lee and Company. 1860.

637. 1860 Edinburgh

Life and Works. . . . Edinburgh . . . Chambers . . . 1860.

Re-issue of § 594 (1856 Edinburgh = Chambers).

638. 1860 Halifax

Poetical Works. . . . Halifax . . . Milner and Sowerby . . . 1860.

Re-issue of § 428 (1840 Halifax = Milner).

639. 1860 London

Life and Works. . . . London . . . Chambers, 1860.

Re-issue of § 594 (1856 Edinburgh = Chambers).

640. 1860 London

Poems & Songs by Robert Burns. . . . London: W. Kent & Co. (late D. Bogue) 86, Fleet Street. 1860.

Re-issued in 1861 (§ 647).

641. 1860 London

Poetical Works. . . . London: Routledge, Warne, and Routledge. 1860.

Re-issue of § 598 (1856 London = Routledge).

642. 1860 London

«« The Works of Robert Burns London: Henry G. Bohn. 1860.»»

N. & Q., 9 Ser. (1896), 43. Probably a re-issue of § 432 (1840 London = Tegg).

643. 1860 Philadelphia

The poetical Works of Robert Burns. . . . Philadelphia: James B. Smith & Co. 1860.

644. 1861 Boston

The poetical Works of Robert Burns. Boston: Crosby, Nichols, Lee & Company. 1861.

Re-issued in 1863 (§ 651), and 1864 (§ 660).

645. 1861 Glasgow

Works. . . . Blackie . . . Glasgow . . . 1861.

Re-issue of § 450 (1843 Glasgow = Blackie).

646. 1861 London

[Bigmore, Edward C.] Descriptive List of a Collection of Original Manuscript Poems by Robert Burns. MDCCCLXI.

Original Material:
   " Praise woman still . . ."   *p.* 14

Comment. " Twenty-five copies printed, not for sale," on verso of title-page.

647. 1861 London

Poems and Songs. . . . London . . . Kent . . . 1861.

Re-issue of § 640 (1860 London = Kent).

648. 1862 Halifax

Poetical Works. . . . Halifax . . . Milner and Sowerby . . . 1862.

Re-issue of § 428 (1840 Halifax = Milner).

649. 1862 London

Poetical Works. . . . New Edition. . . . London: Routledge, Warne and Routledge. 1862.

Re-issue of § 598 (1856 London = Routledge).

650. 1862 London

Works. . . . London . . . Bohn . . . 1862.

Re-issue of § 432 (1840 London = Tegg).

651. 1863 Boston

Poetical Works. . . . Boston: Crosby, Nichols, Lee . . . 1863.

Re-issue of § 644 (1860 Boston = Crosby, Nichols, Lee).

652. 1863 Boston

The poetical Works of Robert Burns. In three Volumes. Boston: Little, Brown and Company. MDCCCLXIII.

653. 1863 Edinburgh

«« Cunningham's edn.   Inglis & Jack.   1 vol.   8vo.»»
Gebbie, VI.340.

654. 1863 Halifax

Complete Works. . . .   Halifax . . . Milner and Sowerby . . . 1863.
Re-issue of § 441 (1842 Halifax = Milner).

655. 1863 London

The Poems of Robert Burns. London: Bell and Daldy . . . and
Sampson Low, Son and Co. . . . 1863.

A new edition of the poems taken from § 418 (1839 London =
Pickering).
Re-issued in 1864 (§ 663), 1865 (§ 677), 1868 (§ 714), 1882 (§ 811),
and perhaps oftener.

656. 1863 London

Poetical Works. . . .   London . . . Routledge, Warne and Routledge . . . 1863.

Re-issue of § 598 (1856 London = Routledge).

657. 1863 London

The Songs of Robert Burns. London: Bell and Daldy . . .
Sampson Low, Son, and Co. . . . 1863.

A new edition of the songs taken from § 418 (1839 London =
Pickering), the Aldine Edition, without the critical apparatus.
Re-issued in 1864 (§ 665), 1866 (§ 694), 1868 (§ 718), and 1882
(§ 812).

658. 1864 Boston

«« The poetical works of Robert Burns . . . Two volumes. Boston:
No publisher's name. 1864.»»
Gibson, p. 76.

659. 1864 Boston

«« Poetical Works of Robert Burns. Two volumes. Boston: published by Little, Brown, and Company. 1864.»»

Angus, p. 88. Probably a re-issue of § 652 (1863 Boston = Little, Brown).

660. 1864 Boston

Poetical Works . . . Boston: Crosby & Nichols. 1864.

Re-issue of § 644 (1861 Boston = Crosby, Nichols, Lee).

661. 1864 Edinburgh

The Works of Robert Burns . . . In two Volumes. Edinburgh: Alex Hutchison & Co., 20 Cockburn Street. 1864.

Variants

1. Edinburgh: James Inglis, 20 Cockburn Street. 1864.

2. Edinburgh: Thomas C. Jack, 59 South Bridge. 1864.

662. 1864 Edinburgh

The poetical Works of Robert Burns . . . Notes, by the Rev. George Gilfillan. The Text edited by Charles Cowden Clarke. In two Volumes. . . . Edinburgh: James Nichol. London . . . Nisbet . . . Dublin . . . Robertson . . . Liverpool . . . Philip. MDCCCLXIV.

Re-issued in 1866 (§ 685), and 1868 (§ 712).

663. 1864 London

Poems. . . . London: Bell and Daldy . . . 1864.

Re-issue of § 655 (1863 London = Bell and Daldy).

664. 1864 London

The Ballads and Songs of Robert Burns. With a Lecture . . . by Thomas Carlyle. . . . London: Charles Griffin and Company, Stationers' Hall Court. 1864.

Q

665. 1864 London

Songs . . . London: Bell and Daldy . . . 1864.

Re-issue of § 657 (1863 London = Bell and Daldy).

666. 1864 Philadelphia

The poetical Works of Robert Burns. . . . Philadelphia . . . E. H. Butler. 1864.

Re-issued in 1868 (§ 721).

667. 1865 Boston

Poetical Works of Robert Burns. . . . In three Volumes. Boston: Little, Brown & Company. 1865.

Re-issued in 1877 (§ 781) and 1878 (§ 790).

668. [? 1865] Edinburgh

The complete poetical Works of Robert Burns. Edited by John S. Roberts. . . . Memoir by William Gunnyon. . . . Seventh thousand. Edinburgh: William P. Nimmo.

The preface is dated "July 1865." Re-issued in 1866 (§ 696), 1873 (§ 759), 1874 (§ 757), 1876 (§ 777), 1877 (§§ 782, 787), 1883 (§ 816), 1884 (§ 822), 1887 (§ 839), 1888 (§§ 850, 854), 1890 (§ 862), 1891 (§ 868), 1892 (§ 873), 1893 (§ 878), 1895 (§ 889), and n.d. (§ 1003).

669. [? 1865] Edinburgh

«« The complete prose works of Robert Burns . . . Edinburgh: William P. Nimmo. [1865].»»

M.C., § 133; M.C.'s square brackets. Re-issued in 1871 (§ 743), 1873 (§ 756), 1876 (§§ 778, 780), 1878 (§ 791), and n.d. (§ 1004).

670. 1865 Edinburgh

The complete Works of Robert Burns . . . With a Memoir by William Gunnyon. . . . Edinburgh: William P. Nimmo. 1865.

Re-issued in 1866 (§ 684), 1867 (§§ 698, 710), 1869 (§ 723), 1874 (§ 760), 1877 (§ 784), 1884 (§ 824), 1885 (§ 830), 1886 (§ 833), 1888 (§ 851), and 1892 (§ 874).

671. 1865 Edinburgh

«« The Poetical Works and letters of Robert Burns (expurgated).
12 mo. Gall & Inglis, 1865.»»

Gibson, p. 79. See also Chambers, IV.323.

672. [1865] Edinburgh

«« Works of Robert Burns. With life and notes by Allan Cunningham. In two volumes. Edinburgh: James Inglis. [1865].»»

Angus, p. 12; Angus's square brackets. Angus, p. 12, has also
" Works . . . With Life and Notes by Allan Cunningham; and
many notes by Gilbert Burns and others. Edinburgh: Thomas
C. Jack. [1865] ", (Angus's square brackets). According to
Bib. B., p. 24, this is a reprint of a one-volume Inglis & Jack
edition (n.d.) and paged for two volumes. Chambers, IV.323,
notes: " The Works of Robert Burns, containing his poems, songs,
and correspondence; with life and notes . . . by Allan
Cunningham. 1 vol. Imp. 8vo. 1875."

673. 1865 Glasgow

Poetical Works. . . . Glasgow: John Cameron . . . 1865.

Re-issue of § 584 (1852 Glasgow = Cameron).

674. 1865 Glasgow

Songs and Ballads. . . . Glasgow: John Cameron . . . 1865.

Re-issue of § 555 (1852 Glasgow = Cameron).

675. 1865 Halifax

«« The complete works of Robert Burns . . . Halifax: Milner and
Sowerby. 1865.»»

M.C., § 401. Re-issue of § 441 (1842 Halifax = Milner).

676. 1865 Liverpool

«« Geo. Philip & Son. 1 vol. 8vo.»»

Gebbie, VI.341. Probably a re-issue of § 662 (1864 Edinburgh =
Nichol).

677. 1865 London

Poems. . . .   London: Bell and Daldy . . . 1865.

Re-issue of § 655 (1863 London = Bell and Daldy).

678. 1865 London

The poetical Works of Robert Burns edited from the best printed
and manuscript Authorities, with glossarial Index and a biographical Memoir by Alexander Smith in two volumes.—Vol. I.
London and Cambridge: Macmillan and Co.   1865.

b. VOL. II

Original Material:

Elegy [" Strait is the spot . . ."]	*p.* 343
Extempore to Mr. Gavin Hamilton [" To you, Sir, . . ."][68]	346
Versicles on Signposts	348

Re-issued in 1879 (§ 800), 1883 (§ 818), and 1887 (§ 845).

679. 1865 London

The poetical Works of Robert Burns.   Edited by the Rev. Robert
Aris Wilmott. . . .   New edition. . . .   London: Routledge, Warne,
and Routledge . . . New York: 129, Grand Street.   1865.

Re-issue of § 598 (1856 London = Routledge).

680. 1865 London

Works. . . .   London: Blackie and Son, Paternoster Row; and
Glasgow and Edinburgh.   MDCCCLXV.

Re-issue of § 450 (1843 Glasgow = Blackie).

681. 1865 New York

«« Complete poetical works of Robert Burns.   New York: D.
Appleton & Company.   1865.»»

Angus, p. 91.

---

[68] According to H. & H., II.362, this piece did not appear until 1868 in
§ 715 (London, Macmillan).

682. 1866 Boston

Poetical Works. . . . Boston: Crosby & Ainsworth New York: Oliver S. Felt. 1866.

Re-issue of § 528 (1850 Boston = Phillips, Sampson).

683. 1866 Boston

The Poems of Robert Burns. . . . Two volumes. Boston: Ticknor & Fields. 1866.

Vol. II, " Songs " only.

684. 1866 Edinburgh

Complete Works. . . . Edinburgh . . . Nimmo. 1866.

Re-issue of § 670 (1865 Edinburgh = Nimmo). The t.p. was issued with " Crown Edition " and with " Nimmo's Library."

685. 1866 Edinburgh

Poetical Works. . . . Edinburgh: James Nichol . . . London: James Nisbet . . . Dublin: George Herbert. Liverpool: G. Philip . . . MDCCCLXVI.

Re-issue, two vols. in one, of § 662 (1864 Edinburgh = Nichol).

686. 1866 Glasgow

The Works and Correspondence of Robert Burns. . . . Glasgow: W. Mackenzie, 1866.

Re-issued, n.d. (§§ 1046, 1133).

687. 1866 Halifax

Poetical Works. . . . Halifax . . . Milner and Sowerby . . . 1866.

Re-issue of § 428 (1840 Halifax = Milner).

688. 1866 London

The complete poetical Works of Robert Burns and Sir Walter
Scott. New Edition. London: Charles Griffin . . . 1866.

Re-issued, n.d. (§ 1056), and, perhaps, in 1867 (§ 703).

689. 1866 London

«« Poetical Works of Robert Burns . . . London: Thomas Allman.
1866.»»

Angus, p. 48. Angus claims this to be a re-issue of Thomas
Allman " Circa 1857 " (§ 605).

690. 1866 London

The poetical Works of Robert Burns. In three Volumes. London: Bell and Daldy, Fleet Street. 1866.

This is the Third Aldine Edition. Re-issued in 1870 (§ 741)
and 1875 (§ 771).

691. 1866 London

The poetical Works of Robert Burns. Edited by the Rev. Robert
Aris Wilmott. New Edition. With numerous Additions.
London: George Routledge and Sons. 1866.

692. 1866 London

Poetical Works. . . . Wilmott. Illustrated by John Gilbert. . . .
London: George Routledge and Sons . . . 1866.

Variant

New York: 416 Broome Street. 1866. [*added to the imprint*]

Re-issue of § 598 (1856 London = Routledge).

693. 1866 London

The poetical Works of Robert Burns. Edited by the Rev. Robert
Aris Wilmott, London, Savill. 1866.

694. 1866 London

Songs. . . . London: Bell and Daldy . . . 1866.

Re-issue of § 657 (1863 London = Bell and Daldy).

695. 1866 London

Works. . . . London: Blackie . . . 1866.

Re-issue of § 450 (1843 Glasgow = Blackie).

696. 1866 New York

The complete poetical Works of Robert Burns. Edited by John S. Roberts. Fifteenth Thousand. New York: The American News Company. 1866.

Re-issue of § 668 ([? 1865] Edinburgh = Nimmo).

697. 1866 New York

The complete Works of Robert Burns. . . . New York: Oliver S. Felt. Boston: Crosby & Ainsworth. 1866.

698. 1867 Edinburgh

Complete Works . . . Edinburgh: William P. Nimmo. 1867.

Re-issue of § 670 (1865 Edinburgh = Nimmo).

699. 1867 Glasgow

The complete poetical Works of Robert Burns. . . . Glasgow: John Cameron, 175 Buchanan St. And sold by all the Booksellers. 1867.

According to Gibson, p. 80, " A cheap reprint [?] of the London edition, Adam Scott, 1846 [§ 490 (1846 London = Scott)]."

700. 1867 Glasgow

The complete Works of Robert Burns, including his Correspondence: and the poetical Works of Sir Walter Scott. . . . In two

Volumes. Glasgow and London: William Collins, Sons & Company. 1867.

Re-issued in 1870 (§ 733).

701. 1867 Glasgow

Life and Works of Robert Burns. By P. Hately Waddell, Minister of the Gospel. Enriched with Portraits, and numerous Illustrations in Colour from original Designs, in the highest Style of the Art. Glasgow: Printed and published by David Wilson, 14 Maxwell Street. 1867.

a. Vol. I

Original Material :

New Psalmody ["" O sing a new song. . . .""]   *p.* 411
Originally in Stuart's *Star* (London) 14 May 1789.

b. Vol. II

Original Material. Thirty letters:

Ref.[69]	Addressee	Date	
II.131	[Maria Riddell?]	[1793?]	*p.* 59
299	Maria Riddell	[Spring 1795]	61
305	Mrs Riddell	[Summer 1795]	61
314	Mrs W.[alter] Riddell	[Oct.-Nov. 1795][70]	61
309	Maria Riddell	[? Aug. 1795]	62
163	Mrs Riddell	[Apr. 1793]	62
138	[Alexander Fraser Tytler]	6 Dec. [1792][71]	118
I.89	The Earl of Glencairn	[4 May 1787]	126
II.212	James Johnson	[Oct. 1793?]	130
I.57	Robert Muir	15 Dec. 1786	143
58	Robert Aiken	16 Dec. 1786	146
101	Robert Aiken	[14 Jul. 1787]	146
37	John Logan	10 Aug. 1786	154
38	Thomas Campbell	[19 Aug. 1786]	155
118	St James's Lodge	23 Aug. 1787	167
II.309	Robert Cleghorn	21 Aug. 1795	170
219	Memorandum for Edward Whigham	n.d.	188

[69] To *Letters.*
[70] One line only; completed in § 783 (1877 Edinburgh = Scott Douglas).
[71] Originally in the *Inverness Courier*, 11 Oct. 1866.

Ref.	Addressee	Date	
252	Capt. [John] Hamilton	[Jul. 1794]	*p.* 194
234	S. Clark jun.	[? 1794]	196
147	[David Staig]	[Jan. 1793 ?]	199
I.293	David Blair	23 Jan. 1789	203
122	William Inglis	[4 Sep. 1787]	205
323	William Burns	15 Apr. 1789[72]	215
331	William Burns	5 May 1789	215
351	William Burns	14 Aug. 1789[73]	215
243	Robert M'Indoe	5 Aug. 1788	217
254	Jean Armour Burns	12 Sept. 1788[74]	217
II.3	Dr Mundell	n.d.	217
326	James Armour	10 Jul. [1796]	218
81	Alexander Findlater	[Jun. 1791] Appendix: xxx

Comment. Issued in green cloth boards gold stamped. I have never seen the volumes separately; all the copies I have examined contain the two volumes bound in one. Although extremely cumbersome, the book is packed with interesting material such as maps of the various tours, numerous facsimiles, etc.

Re-issued in 1870 (§ 734) and 1874 (§ 763).

702. [1867] Kilmarnock

Poems, chiefly in the Scottish Dialect, by Robert Burns. . . . Kilmarnock : printed by John Wilson. MDCCCLXXXVI.

Facsimile of § 1 (1786 Kilmarnock = Wilson); 600 copies. Re-issued in 1870 (§ 738) and n.d. (§ 1048).

703. 1867 London

The complete poetical Works of Robert Burns and Sir Walter Scott. New Edition. . . . London: Collins & Co. 1867.

Re-issue, according to *Camb. Bib.*, II.978, of § 688 (1866 London = Griffin).

704. 1867 London

Complete Works. . . . London: Milner and Sowerby. 44 Paternoster Row and Halifax, Yorkshire. 1867.

Re-issue of § 441 (1842 Halifax = Milner).

[72] Waddell does not claim this to be a first appearance.
[73] Originally in the *Newcastle Daily Journal*, 19 Mar. 1868.
[74] Originally in the *Banffshire Journal* (according to Waddell).

705. 1867 London

Poetical Works. . . . London: George Routledge & Sons . . .
New York . . . MDCCCLXVII.

In " Routledge's British Poets," re-issue of § 598 (1856 London =
Routledge).

706. 1867 London

Poems and Songs. . . . London: George Routledge & Sons . . .
New York . . . MDCCCLXVII.

Re-issue of the poetry section of § 1033 (n.d. Glasgow = Mackenzie).

707. 1867 New York

The poetical Works of Robert Burns. [*Two volumes*] . . . New
York: James Miller, 522 Broadway. 1867.

708. 1867 New York

«« Poetical Works . . . W. I. Pooley, New York.»»

Noted in § 744 (1871 Kilmarnock = M'Kie), II.443.

709. 1867 New York

«« Complete Poetical Works . . . Virtue & Yorston.»»

Noted in § 744 (1871 Kilmarnock = M'Kie), II.443.

710. 1867 Philadelphia

Complete Works. . . . Philadelphia: J. B. Lippincott and
Company. 1867.

Re-issue. The sheets of § 670 ([1865] Edinburgh = Nimmo) with
a Philadelphia t.-p. Re-issued in 1875 (§ 775) and n.d. (§ 1172).

711. 1868 Edinburgh

Poems & Songs by Robert Burns. . . . Edinburgh: William P.
Nimmo. MDCCCLXVIII.

Re-issued in 1875 (§ 770), 1882 (§ 810), 1888 (§ 849), and n.d.
(§ 1072).

712. 1868 Edinburgh

Poetical Works. . . . Edinburgh: William P. Nimmo. 1868.

Re-issue of § 662 (1864 Edinburgh = Nichol).

713. 1868 Halifax

The poetical Works of Robert Burns. . . . Halifax: William Nicholson and Sons. London: S. D. Ewins, Jr. & Co., 22 Paternoster Row. 1868.

714. 1868 London

Poems. . . . London: Bell and Daldy . . . 1868.

Re-issue of § 655 (1863 London = Bell and Daldy).

715. 1868 London

The Globe Edition Poems Songs and Letters being the complete Works of Robert Burns. Edited . . . by Alexander Smith London: Macmillan and Co. 1868.

Re-issued in 1868 (§ 720), 1869 (§ 726), 1870 (§ 740), 1871 (§ 747), 1873 (§ 758), 1875 (§ 772), 1879 (§ 798), 1884 (§ 825), 1891 (§ 870), 1900 (§ 917), and perhaps oftener.

716. 1868 London

The poetical Works of Robert Burns. . . . London: John Dicks, 313 Strand: and all Booksellers. 1868.

Re-issued in 1870 (§ 742), 1871 (§ 745), and n.d. (§ 1091).

717. 1868 London

Poetical Works. . . . London: Groombridge . . . MDCCCLXVIII.

Re-issue of § 419 (1857 London = Smith).

718. 1868 London

Songs. . . . London: Bell and Daldy . . . 1868.

Re-issue of § 657 (1863 London = Bell and Daldy).

719. 1868 London

Works. . . . London: Blackie . . . 1868.

Re-issue of § 450 (1843 Glasgow = Blackie).

720. 1868 Philadelphia

The Globe Edition. . . . Philadelphia: J. B. Lippincott and Co. 1868.

Re-issue. The sheets of § 715 (1868 London = Macmillan).

721. 1868 Philadelphia

Poetical Works. . . . Philadelphia: . . . E. H. Butler & Co. 1868.

Re-issue of § 666 (1864 Philadelphia = Butler).

722. 1869 Edinburgh

«« Family Edition. The poetical works and letters of Robert Burns . . . Edinburgh: Gall & Inglis. 1869. A re-print of the purged edition, by the same publishers, 1865.»»

Gibson, p. 89. There is a Gall and Inglis edition, n.d. (§ 1015). " (In this Edition the more Objectionable Passages and pieces are excluded.) "

723. 1869 Edinburgh

Complete Works. . . . Edinburgh . . . Nimmo . . . 1869.

Re-issue of § 670 (1865 Edinburgh = Nimmo).

724. 1869 Kilmarnock

Poems, chiefly in the Scottish Dialect. By Robert Burns. . . . Kilmarnock: printed by James M'Kie. MDCCCLXIX.

Two items with identical title-pages but different contents:
1. " Poems as they appeared in the Early Edinburgh Editions" ;
and 2. " Posthumous Poems." On pp. 185-219 of the volume,
" Early Edinburgh Editions," is a thorough treatise, " Alterations & Additions made by the Author himself." 30 copies on
large paper signed by M'Kie.

Re-issued in 1877 (§ 786).

725. 1869 Kilmarnock

Songs, chiefly in the Scottish dialect. By Robert Burns. Kilmarnock: printed by James M'Kie. MDCCCLXIX.

Original Material:
　　Preface to the Afton Lodge MSS.　　　　　　　　　　*p*. vi

According to Ferguson (*Letters*, 11.97), the Dedication to " Mrs
General Stewart of Afton," which follows the prefatory note,
was first printed in this title, but I was unable to find it.
In his preface M'Kie claims to have achieved a complete collection of the songs. Also a large paper edition of 30 copies only.

726. 1869 London

Globe Edition. . . . London: Macmillan . . . 1869.

Re-issue of § 715 (1868 London = Macmillan).

727. 1869 London

Poetical Works. . . . London: George Routledge and Sons.
1869.

Re-issue of § 598 (1856 London = Routledge).

728. 1869 New York

The complete poetical Works of Robert Burns. . . . New York:
D. Appleton and Company, 90, 92, 94 Grand St. 1869.

729. 1869 New York

The complete poetical and prose Works of Robert Burns. . . .
New York: Geo. A. Leavitt, publisher, No. 8 Howard Street.
1869.

Re-issued in 1881 (§ 807) and 1882 (§ 813).

730. 1870 Edinburgh

Burns in Dumfriesshire: a Sketch of the last eight Years of the
Poet's Life. By William McDowall, Author of "History of
the Burgh of Dumfries," "The Visitor's Guide to Dumfries,"
Etc. Edinburgh: Adam and Charles Black. 1870.

Original Material:
    Gracie, thou art a Man of Worth   *p.* 59, *n.*

Comment. Issued in a heavy brown paper wrapper with the title-page
    reproduced on the front.

731. 1870 Glasgow

The complete Works of Robert Burns. . . . Glasgow: Robert
Forrester . . . MDCCCLXX.

732. 1870 Glasgow

«« The Poetical works of Robert Burns, Glasgow: Cameron
Ferguson. 1870.»»

Gibson, p. 89.

733. 1870 Glasgow

Complete Works. . . . Glasgow . . . William Collins . . . 1870.

Re-issue of § 700 (1867 Glasgow = Collins).

734. 1870 Glasgow

Life and Works. . . . Glasgow . . . David Wilson . . . 1870.

Re-issue of § 701 (1867 Glasgow = Wilson).

735. 1870 Glasgow

Universal Library. The poetical Works of Robert Burns.
Glasgow: Thomas Murray and Son. 1870.

736. 1870 Glasgow

«« The Works and Correspondence of Robert Burns, including his
letters to Clarinda, &c. 8vo. Glasgow, 1870.»»

Chambers, IV.324.

737. 1870 Glasgow

The Works of Robert Burns, poetical and prose. . . . Arranged and edited by " Gertrude [Jane Cross Simpson] " [*In two volumes*] Glasgow and London: W. R. M'Phun & Son, publishers. 1870.

Re-issued in 1874 (§ 762).

738. [1870] Kilmarnock

Poems. . . . Kilmarnock . . . Wilson. MDCCLXXXVI.

Variants

1. [*On verso of t.-p., preceding the imprint*]   American Edition.
2. [*Also on verso t.-p., but following the imprint*]   American Edition.
3. American Edition.   Printed for J. Campbell, Toronto.
4. American Edition.   Printed for John Brown & Co., Newport Rhode Island, U.S.   W. S. Thorburn, Bookseller, Cincinnati, Agent for the Western States.
5. Kilmarnock, printed by J. M'Kie for R. Worthington, Montreal.

Re-issue of § 702 ([1867] Kilmarnock = Wilson).

739. 1870 London

Works. . . . London: Blackie . . . 1870.

Re-issue of § 450 (1843 Glasgow = Blackie).

740. 1870 London

Globe Edition. . . . London: Macmillan . . . 1870.

Re-issue of § 715 (1868 London = Macmillan).

741. 1870 London

Poetical Works . . . London: Bell and Daldy . . . 1870.

Re-issue of § 690 (1866 London = Bell and Daldy). According to *N. & Q.*, 4 ser., v (1870), 353, ". . . a further installment [Vol. I] of the new and wondrously cheap re-issue of the Aldine Poets (in eighteen-penny volumes)." Only Vol. III is dated.

742. 1870 London

Poetical Works. . . . London: John Dicks . . . 1870.

Re-issue of § 716 (1868 London = Dicks).

743. 1871 Edinburgh

Complete prose Works. . . . Edinburgh: William P. Nimmo. 1871.

According to *M.C.*, § 135, a re-issue of § 669 ([1865] Edinburgh = Nimmo).

744. 1871 Kilmarnock

Kilmarnock popular Edition. The complete poetical Works of Robert Burns. Arranged in the Order of their earliest Publication. . . . new Annotations, introductory Notices, &c. [*in two volumes*] Written expressly for the present Work by William Scott Douglas. . . . Kilmarnock: James M'Kie. 1871.

Scott Douglas turns out eventually to be one of Burns's more considerable editors. This is his first appearance in the field. In *The Burns Calendar* (Kilmarnock: 1874), M'Kie tells us that this was an edition of 2,000 ". . . published towards the end of the year 1871." M'Kie had already done notable work in the field of reprints of early editions (§ 724 and § 725).

745. 1871 London

Poetical Works. . . . London: John Dicks . . . 1871.

Re-issue of § 716 (1868 London = Dicks).

746. 1871 London

The poetical Works of Robert Burns. . . . edited by W. M. Rossetti. . . . London: E. Moxon & Sons. 1871.

Re-issued in [1879] (§ 801), [1881] (§ 806), and n.d. (§§ 1108, 1125.)

747. 1871 London

Globe Edition. . . . London: Macmillan . . . 1871.

Re-issue of § 715 (1868 London = Macmillan).

748. 1871 Philadelphia

The poetical Works of Robert Burns. Edited by the Rev. Robert Aris Willmott. . . . Philadelphia: J. B. Lippincott & Co. 1871.

749. 1871 Philadelphia

«« The Poetical Works of Robert Burns. Philadelphia: Porter & Coates. 1871.»»

Gibson, p. 90; Gebbie, VI.341.

750. 1872 Boston

Poetical Works of Robert Burns. Edited by the Rev. Robert Aris Willmott. . . . Boston: Lee and Shepard . . . New York : Lee, Shepard and Dillingham. 1872.

Re-issued in 1873 (§ 755), 1879 (§ 797), and 1880 (§ 803).

751. 1872 Edinburgh

Robert Burns's Common Place Book. Printed from the original Manuscript in the Possession of John Adam, Esq. Greenock. Edinburgh. Privately printed. 1872.

The First Commonplace Book was published fragmentarily by Currie (§ 50), in a much fuller version by Cromek (§ 112), and by many others. But " here at *last* be referred to the original of all copies: and it will be abundantly plain that no one of the Editors, from Currie, down to the latest, had access to the *genuine original manuscript.*" So says the Preface. All of the manuscript is included, as well as some insertions by other hands.

752. 1872 Glasgow

The complete Works of Robert Burns. . . . In two Volumes. . . . Glasgow and London: William Collins, Sons, & Company. 1872.

753. 1872 London

«« Poems and Songs. 4 vols. 8vo. London, 1872.»»

Chambers, IV.324.

R

754. 1872 London

«« The poetical works of Robert Burns . . . Text edited by C. Cowden Clarke. London, 1872.»»

Chambers, iv.324. Gebbie, vi.341, notes a Jas. Blackwood & Co. 1 vol. 12mo. 1872.

755. 1873 Boston

Diamond Edition. Poetical Works. . . . Boston: Lee & Shepard. 1873.

Re-issue of § 750 (1872 Boston = Lee and Shepard).

756. 1873 Edinburgh

Complete prose Works. . . . Edinburgh: William P. Nimmo. 1873.

M.C., § 136, calls this a re-issue of § 669 ([?1865] Edinburgh = Nimmo).

757. 1873 Edinburgh

Complete poetical works. . . . Edinburgh . . . Nimmo. 1873.

Re-issue of § 668 ([?1865] Edinburgh = Nimmo).

758. 1873 London

Globe Edition. . . . London: Macmillan . . . 1873.

Re-issue of § 715 (1868 London = Macmillan).

759. 1874 Edinburgh

Complete poetical Works. . . . Edinburgh: William P. Nimmo. 1874.

Re-issue of § 668 ([? 1865] Edinburgh = Nimmo).

760. 1874 Edinburgh

Complete Works. . . . Edinburgh: William P. Nimmo. 1874.

Re-issue of § 670 (1865 Edinburgh = Nimmo). In a series called " Nimmo's Standard Library."

761. 1874 Glasgow

Works. . . . Glasgow: Blackie . . . 1874.

Re-issue of § 450 (1843 Glasgow = Blackie).

762. 1874 Glasgow

Works. . . . Glasgow and London: W. R. M'Phun . . . 1874.

Re-issue of § 737 (1870 Glasgow and London = M'Phun).

763. 1874 Glasgow

Life and Works. . . . Glasgow . . . David Wilson . . . 1874.

In spite of " Revised, with additions," on the t.-p., this is a re-issue of § 701 (1867 Glasgow = Wilson).

764. 1874 Liverpool

Some Account of the Glenriddell MSS. of Burns's Poems: with several Poems never before published. Edited by Henry A. Bright. [*Printed for private distribution*] Liverpool: Gilbert G. Walmsley, 50, Lord Street. 1874.

Original Material:

Preface to the Glenriddell MSS. [*Letters*, II.73]	*p.* 7
The last four stanzas of the " Epistle to John Goldie "[75]	36
When dear Clarinda	45
On Glenriddell's Fox [" Thou, Liberty . . ."]	47
On Capt. Lascelles [" When Lascelles thought fit . . ."]	50

This book is primarily a catalogue of the contents of the Glenriddell MSS.

765. 1874 London

«« The Complete Works of Robert Burns. With Memoir by William Gunnyon. London and Edinburgh: William P. Nimmo. 1874.»»

Angus, p. 15. Probably a re-issue of § 670 (1865 Edinburgh = Nimmo).

[75] But cp. H. & H., II.356.

766. 1874 London

Works. . . .   London: Blackie . . . Glasgow and Edinburgh.   1874.

Re-issue of § 450 (1843 Glasgow = Blackie).

767. 1874 New York

Poetical Works of Robert Burns. . . .   Notices by Allan Cunningham . . . New York: Albert Mason . . . 1874.

Variant

Philadelphia . . . Porter & Coates.   1874.   [*engraved throughout*].

768. 1874 New York

Poetical Works of Robert Burns. . . .   New York: James Miller. 1874.

769. 1875 London

Complete Works. . . .   London: Milner & Sowerby.   1875.

Re-issue of § 441 (1842 Halifax = Milner).

770. 1875 London

Poems & Songs. . . .   William P. Nimmo: London, 14 King William Street, Strand, and Edinburgh.   MDCCCLXXV.

Re-issue of § 711 (1868 Edinburgh = Nimmo).   It is called " The Edina Edition," and was printed by R. & R. Clark, Edinburgh.

771. [1875] London

Poetical Works. . . .   London: Bell and Daldy . . . [1875].

Re-issue of § 690 (1866 London = Bell and Daldy).   Only Vol. III is dated.

772. 1875 London

Globe Edition . . . London: Macmillan . . . 1875.

Re-issue of § 715 (1868 London = Macmillan).

773. 1875 London

Poetical Works of Robert Burns. A new Edition. . . . William P. Nimmo: London . . . and Edinburgh. 1875.

Re-issued in 1878 (§ 793) and n.d. (§ 1109).

774. 1875 London

«« The Chandos Poets. The poetical works of Robert Burns, re-printed from the best editions. 8vo. Warne. 1875.»»

Gibson, p. 93; Chambers, IV.324. Is this really dated? The Chandos Poets § 1126 (n.d. London) is cautiously dated [1875] by Angus (p. 75). I have never seen a dated t.-p., and the whole thing looks to me as though Gibson pulled a date out of the air (as he so often seems to have done) and Chambers (as *he* so often seems to have done) copied it.

775. 1875 Philadelphia

Complete Works. . . . Philadelphia . . . Lippincott . . . 1875.

Re-issue of § 710 (1867 Philadelphia = Lippincott).

776. 1876 Boston

The complete Works of Robert Burns. . . . Boston: Lee and Shepard . . . 1876.

777. 1876 Edinburgh

Complete Poetical Works. . . . Edinburgh . . . Nimmo . . . 1876.

Re-issue of § 668 ([? 1865] Edinburgh = Nimmo).

778. 1876 Edinburgh

Complete prose Works. . . . Edinburgh . . . Nimmo . . . 1876.

M.C., § 137, calls this a re-issue of § 669 ([?1865] Edinburgh = Nimmo).

779. 1876 Kilmarnock

The complete poetical Works of Robert Burns. . . . [*In two volumes*]. Kilmarnock: M'Kie & Drennan. MDCCCLXXVI.

Re-issued numerous times but with rather confusing terminology
on the various title-pages: 1886 (§ 835) is called " Centenary
Edition "; 1887 (§ 841), " New Edition "; [1890] (§ 861, 865),
" Seventh Edition "; [1891] (§ 867), " Eighth Edition "; [1893]
(§ 880), " Ninth Edition "; [1896] (§ 897), " Tenth Edition ";
1903 (§ 930), " Eleventh Edition "; and 1923 (§ 961), " Thirteenth Edition ".   There are others.

780. 1876 London

Complete prose Works. . . .   Nimmo: London . . . 1876.

Re-issue of § 669 ([1865] Edinburgh = Nimmo).

781. 1877 Boston

Poetical Works. . . .   Boston: James R. Osgood and Company
(late Ticknor and Fields, and Fields, Osgood and Co.).   1877.

Re-issue of § 667 (1865 Boston = Little, Brown).

782. 1877 Edinburgh

Complete poetical Works. . . .   Edinburgh . . . Nimmo . . . 1877.

Re-issue of § 668 ([? 1865] Edinburgh = Nimmo).

783. 1877 Edinburgh

The Works of Robert Burns Volume First Poetry [ed. *William
Scott Douglas*] Edinburgh: William Paterson MDCCCLXXVII.

a. Vol. I

Original Material:
Epitaph on James Grieve [" Here lies Boghead . . ."]   *p.* 61

b. Vol. II

Original Material:
Epigram on Rough Roads [" I'm now arrived . . ."]   *p.* 15
To Alex Cunningham [" My god-like friend . . ."]   159
Rhyming Reply to a Note from Captain Riddell   199
[" Dear Sir, at ony time . . ."]
Sweet are the Banks   331

c. VOL. III

Original Material:

To the beautiful Miss Eliza J——n [" How, Liberty . . ."] *p.* 204

On being Shewn a Beautiful Country Seat [" We grant   206
they're thine . . ."]

The last three volumes contain Burns's prose works. The entire Burns-Thomson correspondence has been corrected and emended. There are some sixty-eight new letters or parts of letters added. The new material is marked with asterisks in the Index.

d. VOL. IV [Dated 1878]

Original Material. Twenty-two letters:

Ref.[76]	Addressee	Date	
1.5	Alison Begbie	[1781 ?]	*p.* 27
12	[Sir John Whitefoord]	[Nov. 1782?]	38
20	Thomas Orr	11 Nov. 1784	50
26	John Arnot	[Apr. 1786]	115
31	James Burness	5 Jul. 1786	132
41	John Mackenzie	[3 Sep. 1786]	147
41	John Richmond	3 Sep. 1786	147
50	Miss Alexander	[18 Nov. 1786][77]	159
53	John Ballantine	20 Nov. 1786	162
61	[Lord Monboddo]	[? 30 Dec. 1786]	184
66	[John Ballantine]	14 Jan. 1787[78]	189
82	Robert Cleghorn	[1787 ?]	199
84	John Ballantine	18 Apr. 1787	219
84	George Reid	19 Apr. 1787	220
88	William Tytler	[4 May 1787][79]	226
91	Peter Hill	17 May 1787	242
102	Peter Hill	19 Jul. 1787	257
123	James Burness	4 Sep. 1787	275
124	James Burness	[13 Sep. 1787]	280
125	James Burness	19 Sep. 1787	283
135	Mrs Dunlop	4 Nov. 1787	301
142	Mr Beugo	n.d.	309

The Journal of the Highland Tour[80]   264

The Commonplace Book, 1783-85 " *verbatim et literatim* "[81]   53-98

[76] To *Letters.*

[77] Completed from § 50 (1800 Liverpool = Currie).

[78] Completed from § 112 (1808 London = Cromek).

[79] According to *Letters*, (I.89) this first appeared in § 50 (1800 Liverpool = Currie).

[80] This is a reproduction of the notebook that Burns carried.

[81] Complete for the first time.

e. VOL. V [Dated 1879]

Original Material. Twenty-four letters:

Ref.[82]	Addressee	Date	
I.194	Clarinda	[23 Feb. 1788]	p. 94
235	Peter Hill	18 Jul. 1788	139
237	Alex. Cunningham	27 Jul. 1788	141
249	Robert Ainslie	23 Aug. 1788	150
272	Mrs Dunlop	13 Nov. 1788[83]	172
294	James Johnson	23 Jan. [1789]	196
297	Alex. Cunningham	24 Jan. 1789	198
318	Peter Hill	2 Apr. 1789[84]	223
325	James Johnson	24 Apr. 1789	227
349	David Sillar	5 Aug. 1789	251
380	George Sutherland	[31 Dec. 1789]	282
II.8	Clarinda (one paragraph)	[5 Feb. 1790] Received	288
6	Peter Hill	2 Feb. 1790[85]	291
15	Peter Hill	2 Mar. 1790[86]	303
13	Alex. Findlater	[1790]	310
31	Robert Cleghorn	23 Jul. 1790	315
32	Dugald Stewart	[Oct. 1790]	332
64	Alex. Cunningham	11 Mar. 1791[87]	356
74	John Somerville	11 May 1791	374
111	Rev. William Moodie	1792	381
80	Provost of Edinburgh	[Jun. 1791]	382
79	John Mitchell	[16 Jun. 1791]	384
90	Ltr for Mr Clark	[Sep. 1791]	396
108	Mr Corbet	1792	398

f. VOL. VI [Dated 1879]

Original Material. Thirty-four letters:

Ref.[88]	Addressee	Date	
II.112	J. Leven	[Mar. ? 1792]	p. 17
113	William Creech	16 Apr. 1792	18
114	James Johnson	[May 1792 ?]	19
91	Duke of Queensberry	24 Sep 1791	23

---

[82] To Letters.
[83] Completed from § 50 (1800 Liverpool = Currie).
[84] Completed from § 50 (1800 Liverpool = Currie).
[85] Completed from § 112 (1808 London = Cromek).
[86] Completed from § 50 (1800 Liverpool = Currie).
[87] Completed from § 50 (1800 Liverpool = Currie).
[88] To Letters.

Ref.	Addressee	Date	
123	Mr Corbet	[Sep. 1792]	p. 31
139	Robert Cleghorn	12 Dec. 1792	43
150	[William Nicol]	20 Feb. 1793[89]	55
149	[Alexander Cunningham]	20 Feb. 1793	57
151	William Creech	28 Feb. 1793	59
155	Clarinda	[Mar.? 1793][90]	59
169	[John Francis Erskine]	[13 Apr. 1793][91]	70
175	Miss Lesley Baillie	[end of May 1793]	79
185	Jean M'Murdo	[Jul. 1793]	81
183	[Gavin Hamilton ?]	16 Jul. 1793	83
128	James Johnson	[Oct. 1793]	90
212	James Johnson	[Oct. 1793][92]	91
219	Miss Fontenelle	4 Dec. 1793[93]	94
212	Robert Cleghorn	25 Oct. [1793 ?]	99
103	Robert Cleghorn	n.d.	101
231	Peter Hill	[Feb. 1794][94]	120
233	[James Johnson]	Feb. 1794[95]	122
236	[Alexander Cunningham]	3 Mar. 1794[96]	123
249	James Johnson	29 Jun. [1794]	134
285	Captain Hamilton	29 Jan. 1795	147
319	James Johnson	[Mar. ? 1796]	155
308	William Lorimer	[Aug. 1795]	166
314	Mrs. Walter Riddell	[Oct. or Nov. 1795]	172
315	Robert Cleghorn	31 Jan. [1796]	178
318	James Johnson	[24 Feb. 1796 ?]	179
314	Peter Hill	29 Jan. 1796	181
330	John Clark	[16 Jul. 1796]	203
308	Alexander Cunningham	[3 Aug. 1795]	349
I.293	Robert Cleghorn	23 Jan. 1789	401
II.109	Alexander Cunningham	5 Feb. 1792	402

Three inscriptions:

II.158	Mrs Graham	[Mar. 1793]	p. 63
158	Robert Riddell	[Mar. 1793]	63
159 [n.d.]	Mr [Thomas] White	Apr. 1793	68

[89] Completed from § 50 (1800 Liverpool = Currie).
[90] Completed from § 449 (1843 Edinburgh=Tait).
[91] Completed, by addition of the prefatory note, from § 112 (1808 London=Cromek).
[92] Completed from § 701 (1867 Glasgow = Waddell).
[93] Completed in § 892 (1896 Edinburgh=Chambers).
[94] Completed from § 540 (1851 Edinburgh = Chambers).
[95] Completed from § 112 (1808 London = Cromek).
[96] Completed from § 50 (1800 Liverpool = Currie).

Eighteen new letters:

Ref.[97]	Addressee	Date	
II.135	George Thomson	4 Dec. [1792]	*p.* 229
146	George Thomson	Jan. 1793	231
152	George Thomson	20 Mar. [1793]	236
180	George Thomson	[2 Jul.? 1793]	255
187	[George Thomson]	[Aug. 1793]	259
190	George Thomson	[Aug. 1793]	264
191	[George Thomson]	[Aug. 1793]	266
196	[George Thomson]	[Sep. 1793]	284
213	George Thomson	29 Oct. [1793]	292
221	[George Thomson]	[Dec. 1793]	295
243	George Thomson	[? May 1794]	296
279	George Thomson	9 Dec. [1794]	331
287	George Thomson	[6 Feb. 1795]	335
293	George Thomson	[Apr. 1795]	337
303	George Thomson	[3 Jul. 1795]	345
306	George Thomson	3 Aug. [1795]	346
317	[George Thomson]	[Feb. 1796]	351
321	George Thomson	[18 May 1796]	355

Twenty-two letters completed here:

Ref.[98]	Addressee	Date	
II.166	[George Thomson]	7 Apr. 1793	*p.* 239
160	[George Thomson]	[Apr. 1793]	243
172	George Thomson	26 Apr. [1793]	248
179	George Thomson	30 Jun. [1793]	250
178	[George Thomson]	[? 25 Jun. 1793]	252
181	[George Thomson]	[Jul. 1793]	256
188	George Thomson	13 Aug. [1793]	260
189	[George Thomson]	[Aug. 1793]	262
193	George Thomson	[28 Aug. 1793]	268
196	[George Thomson]	[Sep. 1793]	284
206	George Thomson	15 Sep. [1793]	286
207	George Thomson	[Sep. 1793]	288
250	[George Thomson]	[Jul. 1794]	298
255	[George Thomson]	[Sep. 1794]	301
256	[George Thomson]	[Sep. 1794]	303
264	[George Thomson]	14 Oct. [1794]	310
270	[George Thomson]	[Nov. 1794]	318
275	[George Thomson]	[19 Nov. 1794]	325
283	George Thomson	[Jan. 1795]	332

[97] To *Letters.*   [98] To *Letters.*

Ref.	Addressee	Date	
288	[George Thomson]	7 Feb. 1795	*p.* 336
300	George Thomson	[May 1795]	341
320	George Thomson	[May 1796]	358

The *Second* [or Edinburgh] *Commonplace Book*[99]   387

Save for a few more modern editions, this is the best edition of Burns's *Works* we have. True, there are some slips, and it has been the habit of more recent editors to sneer at these. It is, nevertheless, a monumental edition in many ways, and has more than eased the burden for later scholars in the field. Re-issued in 1883 (§ 817), 1891 (§ 872), and 1895 (§ 890) ; first 3 vols. re-issued in 1886 (§ 834), 1892 (§ 876), and n.d. (§ 1023).

784. 1877 Edinburgh

Complete Works. . . . Edinburgh . . . Nimmo . . . 1877.

Re-issue of § 670 (1865 Edinburgh = Nimmo).

785. [1877] Glasgow

The complete poetical Works of Robert Burns. . . . Glasgow: James McGeachy, 1877.

Engraved title-page. Printed title-page undated.

786. 1877 Kilmarnock

The Peoples' Statue Edition. Poems, chiefly in the Scottish Dialect, by Robert Burns. Kilmarnock: M'Kie & Drennan. MDCCCLXXVII.

Re-issue of § 724 (1869 Kilmarnock = M'Kie).

787. 1877 London

Complete poetical Works. . . . Nimmo: Edinburgh . . . 1877.

Re-issue of § 668 ([? 1865] Edinburgh = Nimmo), with notes by W. Scott Douglas.

---

[99] Originally in *Macmillan's Mag.*, xxxix and xl (Mar.-Jul. 1879), 453, 560; 32, 124 and 250.

788. 1877 London

Works. . . . London: Blackie . . . 1877.

Re-issue of § 450 (1843 Glasgow = Blackie).

789. 1877 New York

The Works of Robert Burns. . . . New York: The World Publishing House. 1877.

790. 1878 Boston

Poetical Works. . . . Boston: James R. Osgood and Company. Late Ticknor and Fields . . . 1878.

Re-issue of § 667 (1865 Boston = Little, Brown).

791. 1878 Edinburgh

Complete Prose Works. . . . Edinburgh . . . Nimmo . . . 1878.

Re-issue, " Red Line Edition," of § 669 ([? 1865] Edinburgh = Nimmo).

792. 1878 London

«« Complete Prose Works . . . London and Edinburgh . . . Nimmo . . . 1878.»»

Angus, p. 18. Undoubtedly a re-issue of § 669 ([? 1865] Edinburgh = Nimmo).

793. 1878 London

Poetical Works. . . . London . . . Nimmo . . . 1878.

Re-issue of § 773 (1875 London = Nimmo).

794. [1878] London

«« Poetical Works of Robert Burns. Edited by the Rev. Robert Aris Willmott. London: Griffith and Farran. 1878.»»

Angus, p. 60.

795. 1878 London

The poetical Works of Robert Burns. Notes and Correspondence by Allan Cunningham. Edited . . . by Charles Kent. London: George Routledge and Sons. 1878.

Re-issued in 1883 (§§ 820, 821), 1884 (§ 828), 1885 (§ 831), 1890 (§ 866), 1893 (§ 884), 1895 (§ 891), 1896 (§ 904), and n.d. (§ 1117).

796. 1878 London

Works. . . . London and Glasgow . . . Blackie . . . 1878.

Re-issue of § 450 (1843 Glasgow = Blackie).

797. 1879 Boston

Diamond Edition. Poetical Works of Robert Burns. Boston : Houghton, Osgood and Company. 1879.

Re-issue of § 750 (1872 Boston = Lee, Shepard and Dillingham).

798. 1879 London

Globe Edition . . . London: Macmillan . . .1879.

Re-issue of § 715 (1868 London = Macmillan).

799. 1879 London

National Burns. . . . ed. Gilfillan . . . 2 vols. William Mackenzie London, Glasgow, Edinburgh. 1879. [Vol. II: 1880].

Re-issue, n.d. (§ 1070).

800. 1879 London

Poetical Works. . . . London and Cambridge: Macmillan . . . 1879.

Re-issue of § 678 (1865 London and Cambridge = Macmillan).

801. [1879] London

The poetical Works of Robert Burns. Edited . . . by William Michael Rossetti. . . . London: Ward, Lock & Co. . . .

Re-issue of § 746 (1871 London = Moxon).

802. 1879 London

«« Simpkin & Co.   1 vol.   8vo.»»

Gebbie, VI.342.

803. 1880 Boston

Diamond Edition.   Poetical Works of Robert Burns. . . .   Boston:
Houghton, Osgood and Company.   1880.

Re-issue of § 750 (1872 Boston = Lee, Shepard and Dillingham).

804. 1881 Glasgow

Life and Works of Robert Burns. . . .   By P. Hately Waddell.
. . . In two volumes.   Revised.   New Edition.   Glasgow:
printed and published by David Wilson . . . 1881.

805. 1881 London

Poems of Robert Burns. . . .   In two Volumes. . . .   London:
W. Kent & Co., Paternoster Row.   MDCCCLXXXI.

806. [1881] London

Poetical Works. . . .   London: Ward, Lock. . . .

Re-issue of § 746 ([1879] London = Moxon).

807. 1881 New York

The complete poetical and prose Works of Robert Burns. . . .
With original Pieces from the Collection of Sir Egerton Brydges,
Bart. . . . New York: R. Worthington, 770 Broadway.   1881.

Re-issue of § 729 (1869 New York = Leavitt).

808. 1881 New York

The poetical works of Robert Burns. . . .   New York: John
Wurtele Lovell . . . 1881.

809. 1882 Boston

Poetical Works. . . . Boston: Houghton, Mifflin and Company
. . . 1882.

810. 1882 Edinburgh

Poems & Songs. . . . Edinburgh . . . Nimmo . . . 1882.

The " Edina " Edition. Re-issue of § 711 (1868 Edinburgh =
Nimmo).

811. 1882 London

Poems. . . . George Bell & Sons, York Street, Covent Garden.
1882.

Re-issue of § 655 (1863 London = Bell and Daldy).

812. 1882 London

Songs. . . . London: George Bell & Sons. 1882.

Re-issue of § 657 (1863 London = Bell and Daldy).

813. 1882 New York

Complete poetical and prose Works. . . . New York: R. Worthington, 770 Broadway. 1882.

Re-issue of § 729 (1869 New York = Leavitt).

814. 1882 New York

Complete Works of Robert Burns. New York: D. Appleton &
Company. 1882.

815. 1883 Boston

The poetical Works of Robert Burns. . . . Boston: D. Lothrop
& Co. 1883.

816. 1883 Edinburgh

Complete poetical Works . . . Edinburgh . . . Nimmo . . . 1883.

Re-issue of § 668 ([? 1865] Edinburgh = Nimmo).

817. 1883 Edinburgh

Works. . . . Edinburgh . . . Paterson. MDCCCLXXXIII.

Re-issue of § 783 (1877 Edinburgh = Paterson).

818. 1883 London

Poetical Works. . . . London and Cambridge: Macmillan . . . 1883.

Re-issue of § 678 (1865 London and Cambridge = Macmillan).

819. 1883 London

Poetical Works . . . London: J. S. Marr. 1883.

Re-issue of § 584 (1855 Glasgow = Cameron).

820. 1883 London

Poetical Works. . . . London: George Routledge and Sons . . . New York: 9 Lafayette Place. 1883.

Re-issue of § 795 (1878 London = Routledge).

821. 1883 New York

Poetical Works of Robert Burns. With all the Correspondence and Notes by Allan Cunningham. New York: John B. Alden. 1883.

Re-issue of § 795 (1878 London = Routledge).

822. 1884 Edinburgh

Complete poetical Works. . . . Edinburgh: W. P. Nimmo, Hay & Mitchell. 1884.

Re-issue of § 668 ([? 1865] Edinburgh = Nimmo).

823. 1884 Glasgow

«« The poetical works of Robert Burns. (Pearl Edition.) 6 Vol.»»

Noted in catalogue of N.L.S. Re-issued in 1894 (§ 886), [1907] (§ 940), and n.d. (§ 1035). Cp. also § 826 (1884 London = Simpkin).

824. 1884 London

Complete Works. . . . London . . . Nimmo . . . 1884.

Re-issue of § 670 (1865 Edinburgh = Nimmo). " Red Line Edition."

825. 1884 London

Globe Edition . . . London: Macmillan . . . 1884.

Re-issue of § 715 (1868 London = Macmillan).

826. 1884 London

«« Pearl Ed. Poems. Simpkin & Co. 1 vol. 64mo.»»

Gebbie, VI.342.

827. 1884 London

«« Poems, chronologically arranged.»»

Gebbie, VI.342.

828. 1884 New York

The poetical Works of Robert Burns. Notes and Correspondence by Allan Cunningham. Edited by Charles Kent. . . . New York: John B. Alden. 1884.

Re-issue of § 795 (1878 London = Routledge).

829. 1885 Chicago

The poetical Works of Robert Burns. . . . Chicago and New York: Belford, Clarke & Co. 1885.

830. 1885 Edinburgh

Complete Works. . . . Edinburgh . . . Nimmo . . . 1885.

Re-issue of § 670 (1865 Edinburgh = Nimmo).

s

831. 1885 London

Poetical Works. . . . London: George Routledge. . . . New York: 9 Lafayette Place. 1885.

Re-issue of § 795 (1878 London = Routledge). There was another issue this year with the addition of a red-line border.

832. 1885 London

The poetical Works of Robert Burns [*with prefatory notice*] by Joseph Skipsey. London: Walter Scott . . . 1885.

M.C., § 593, has: " The poetical works of Robert Burns [in two volumes] Poems [Songs] . . . by Joseph Skipsey. London: Walter Scott . . . and Newcastle-on-Tyne." The copy in the Mitchell Library is in one volume, the songs occupying the latter half. Horn. copy: one vol., poems only. Re-issued in 1887 (§ 844) and n.d. (§ 1118).

833. 1886 Edinburgh

Complete Works. . . . Edinburgh . . . Nimmo . . . 1886.

Re-issue of § 670 (1865 Edinburgh = Nimmo).

834. 1886 Edinburgh

Poetical Works. . . . Edited by Wm. Scott Douglas. In three Volumes. Edinburgh: William Paterson. 1886.

Re-issue of Vols. I-III of § 783 (1877 Edinburgh = Paterson).

835. 1886 Kilmarnock

Complete Poetical Works. . . . Kilmarnock : James M'Kie. MDCCCLXXXVI.

Re-issue of § 779 (1876 Kilmarnock = M'Kie & Drennan). This is called " Centenary Edition."

836. 1886 Kilmarnock

Poems, chiefly in the Scottish dialect. . . . Kilmarnock . . . John Wilson. 1886.

This is cited by *M.C.*, § 295, as a re-issue of " Poems, chiefly in the Scottish dialect . . . Kilmarnock . . . John Wilson,"—*i.e.*, § 702 ([1867] Kilmarnock = [M'Kie])—" Centenary reprint and fac-simile of the original Kilmarnock edition. (Limited to 120 Copies.) "

837. 1886 London

«« The Complete Works of Robert Burns, with his life and letters. Illustrated. (People's edition) 4 to. London, 1886.»»

Chambers, IV.325.

838. [1886] Philadelphia

Edition de luxe. The complete Works of Robert Burns. (Self interpreting) [*In six volumes*] Philadelphia: Gebbie & Co., publishers.

Variant

Philadelphia: Gebbie and Hunter.

Original Material:
    Letter to Peter Hill[1] [May 1794]   VI.135

The copyright is dated 1886. This enormous set is really little more than a doctored-up version of Scott Douglas's edition of 1877 (§ 783). Re-issued in 1909 (§ 950).

839. 1887 Edinburgh

Complete poetical Works . . . Edinburgh . . . Nimmo, Hay & Mitchell. 1887.

Re-issue of § 668 ([? 1865] Edinburgh = Nimmo).

840. 1887 Glasgow

The poetical works of Robert Burns. Glasgow : C. L. Wright, 100-102 West George Street, and Stirling Road. 1887.

---

[1] *Letters*, II.241.

841. 1887 London

Kilmarnock Edition. The complete poetical Works of Robert
Burns. Arranged in chronological Order . . . with New Annotations . . . by William Scott Douglas. London: Swan Sonnenschein, Lowrey & Co. 1887. [*In two volumes*]

Re-issue of § 779 (1876 Kilmarnock = M'Kie & Drennan).

842. 1887 London

Complete poetical Works. . . . London . . . Nimmo . . . 1887.

Re-issue of § 688 ([?1865] Edinburgh = Nimmo). This is a
" Red Line Edition."

843. 1887 London

The Letters of Robert Burns, selected and arranged . . . by J.
Logie Robertson. . . . Walter Scott, London, 24 Warwick
Lane, Paternoster Row. 1887.

Issued as " Camelot Series " and " The Scott Library."

844. 1887 London

«« Re-issue (' Poems ' and ' Songs '), 1887.»»

M.C., § 594. Re-issue of § 832 (1885 London = Scott).

845. 1887 London

Poetical Works. . . . London and Cambridge: Macmillan . . .
1887.

Re-issue of § 678 (1865 London and Cambridge = Macmillan).

846. 1887 New York

The poetical Works of Robert Burns. . . . New York: Frederick
A. Stokes successor to White, Stokes, & Allen. 1887.

847. 1887 New York

The poetical Works of Robert Burns . . . New-York: Worthington Co. 1887.

848. 1887 Troy

The complete Works of Robert Burns. Edited by Alexander Smith. Troy, N.Y. Nims and Knight. 1887.

849. 1888 Edinburgh

Poems and Songs. . . . Edinburgh . . . Nimmo 1888.

Re-issue of § 711 (1868 Edinburgh = Nimmo).

850. 1888 Edinburgh

Complete poetical Works. . . . Edinburgh . . . Nimmo, Hay & Mitchell. 1888.

Re-issue of § 668 ([? 1865] Edinburgh = Nimmo).

851. 1888 Edinburgh

Complete Works. . . . Edinburgh . . . Nimmo . . . 1888.

Re-issue of § 670 (1865 Edinburgh = Nimmo). This is called " Nimmo's Standard Library."

852. 1888 Glasgow

The poetical Works of Robert Burns. . . . Maclaren & Sons, 128 Renfield Street, Glasgow. 1888.

853. 1888 London

Complete poetical Works. . . . London . . . Nimmo . . . 1888.

Re-issue of § 668 ([? 1865] Edinburgh = Nimmo).

854. 1888 London

Poems and Songs. . . . London . . . Nimmo . . . 1888.

Re-issue of § 711 (1868 Edinburgh = Nimmo). It is called the " Edina Edition."

855. 1888 London

The poetical Works of Robert Burns. . . . London and New York:
Frederick Warne & Co. 1888.

Re-issued in 1889 (§ 859), 1891 (§ 871), 1892 (§ 877), 1893
(§ 885), 1894 (§ 888), 1895 (§ 892), 1896 (§ 905), and n.d.
(§ 1126). It is called the " Albion Edition."

856. 1888 London

The Works of Robert Burns. . . . Edited by Charles Annandale
[*in five volumes*]. . . . London: Blackie & Sons, 49 and 50 Old
Bailey, E.C., Glasgow, Edinburgh, and Dublin. 1888.

Re-issued in 1890 (§ 864).

857. 1889 Edinburgh

The Book of Robert Burns. Genealogical and historical Memoirs
of the Poet, his Associates and those celebrated in his Writings.
By the Rev. Charles Rogers. In three Volumes. . . . Edinburgh
Printed for the Grampian Club 1889

Original Material:
    On Dr Johnson's Opinion[2]   1.157*n*.
    Letter to Thos. Orr, 7 Sep. 1782[3]: in facsimile   facing 1.vi

Vol. III, by the Rev. J. C. Higgins, was published in 1891.

858. 1889 Kilmarnock

Burns holograph Manuscripts in the Kilmarnock Monument
Museum . . . Compiled and edited by David Sneddon. Kil-
marnock: printed by D. Brown & Co. (Successors to James
M'Kie), 2 & 6 King Street. 1889.

Original Material:
    Letter to Wm Stewart [n.d.]   *p.* 84[4]

---

[2] Originally in *The Scotsman*, 20 Nov. 1882.
[3] *Letters*, I.11.
[4] *Letters*, II.225.

859. 1889 London

Poetical Works. . . . London and New York: Frederick Warne
and Co. 1889.

Re-issue of § 855 (1888 London and New York = Warne).

860. 1889 Newcastle

The poetical Works of Robert Burns. Printed and published by
G. Handyside, Bentinck, Newcastle-on-Tyne. 1889.

861. 1890 Edinburgh

Complete poetical Works. . . . Edinburgh and Glasgow: John
Menzies & Co. Kilmarnock: D. Brown & Co. (Successors to
James M'Kie). 1890.

Re-issue of § 779 (1876 Kilmarnock = M'Kie & Drennan).

862. 1890 Edinburgh

Complete poetical Works. . . . Edinburgh . . . Nimmo, Hay
& Mitchell . . . 1890.

Re-issue of § 668 ([? 1865] Edinburgh = Nimmo).

863. 1890 Halifax

The poetical Works of Robert Burns . . . Halifax: William Milner.
1890.

Variant

The poetical Works of Robert Burns. . . . London: William
Milner, 1890.

864. 1890 London

Works. . . . London: Blackie . . . 1890.

Re-issue of § 856 (1888 London = Blackie).

865. 1890 London

Kilmarnock Edition. . . . [*In two volumes*]. London: Swan Sonnenschein & Co., Paternoster Square. 1890.

Re-issue of §779. (1876 Kilmarnock = M'Kie & Drennan).

866. 1890 London

Poetical Works. . . . London: George Routledge and Sons, Limited . . . Glasgow, Manchester and New York. 1890.

Variant

[*With*] Routledge's Hearth and Home Library [*on title-page*].

Re-issue of § 795 (1878 London = Routledge).

867. 1891 Edinburgh

Complete poetical Works. . . . Edinburgh and Glasgow . . . Menzies . . . 1891.

Re-issue of § 779 (1876 Kilmarnock = M'Kie & Drennan).

868. 1891 Edinburgh

Complete poetical Works. . . . Edinburgh . . . Nimmo . . . 1891.

Re-issue of § 668 ([? 1865] Edinburgh = Nimmo).

869. 1891 Edinburgh

Life and Works. . . . [Library Edition]. In four volumes. W. and R. Chambers, Edinburgh and London. 1891.

Variant

[*With*] Library Edition [*on title-page*].

Re-issue of § 594 (1856 Edinburgh = Chambers). Also issued four vols. in two. Bibliography added.

870. 1891 London

Globe Edition . . . London: Macmillan . . . 1891.

Re-issue of § 715 (1868 London = Macmillan).

871. 1891 London

Poetical Works. . . . London and New York . . . Warne . . . 1891.

Re-issue of § 855 (1888 London and New York = Warne).

872. 1891 London

Works. . . . London: William Paterson . . . MDCCCXCI.

Re-issue of § 783 (1877 Edinburgh = Paterson). Limited to
500 copies.

873. 1892 Edinburgh

Complete poetical Works. . . . Edinburgh . . . Nimmo . . . 1892.

Re-issue of § 668 ([? 1865] Edinburgh = Nimmo).

874. 1892 Edinburgh

Complete Works. . . . Edinburgh . . . Nimmo . . . 1892.

Variant

[*With*] Nimmo's Standard Library [*on title-page*].

Re-issue of § 670 (1865 Edinburgh = Nimmo).

875. 1892 London

The poetical Works of Robert Burns. . . . In three volumes.
London: J. M. Dent & Co., Aldine House, 69 Great Eastern
Street. 1892.

876. 1892 London

Poetical Works. . . . London . . . Paterson . . . MDCCCXCII.

Re-issue of the first three volumes of § 783 (1877 Edinburgh =
Paterson).

877. 1892 London

Poetical Works. . . . London and New York: Frederick Warne
. . . 1892.

Variant

[*With*] The " Lansdowne " Poets [*on title-page*].

Re-issue of § 855 (1888 London and New York = Warne).

878. 1893 Edinburgh

Complete poetical works. . . . Edinburgh . . . Nimmo . . . 1893.

Re-issue of § 668 ([? 1865] Edinburgh = Nimmo).

879. 1893 Edinburgh

Edinburgh Edition. Poetical Works of Robert Burns. [*Three
volumes*] Edinburgh: James Thin. MDCCCXCIII.

Re-issued in 1896 (§ 894).

880. 1893 Edinburgh

Kilmarnock Edition. . . . [*Two volumes in one*] Edinburgh
and Glasgow: John Menzies & Co. . . . 1893.

Re-issue of § 779 (1876 Kilmarnock = M'Kie & Drennan).

881. 1893 London

The poetical Works of Robert Burns edited with a Memoir by
George A. Aitken in three Volumes. . . . London: George Bell &
Sons, York St., Covent Garden New York: 112, Fourth Avenue.
1893.

Original Material:

Epitaph on Robert Muir	II.196
Ode Sacred to . . . Mrs. Oswald [*2 lines*]	II.232
There was an auld Man	III.287

882. 1893 London

«« The poetical Works of Robert Burns.   Ed. by J. R. Tutin.
London: 1893.»»

Sale Catalogue of the Muir Collection (Glasgow: 1899), p. 5.

883. 1893 London

The poetical Works of Robert Burns. London: Henry Frowde,
Oxford University Press Warehouse, Amen Corner. 1893.

884. 1893 London

Poetical Works. . . . London: George Routledge and Sons,
Limited, Broadway, Ludgate Hill.   Manchester and New
York. 1893.

In a series entitled " Sir John Lubbock's Hundred Books."
No. 58. Re-issue of § 795 (1878 London = Routledge).

885. 1893 London

Poetical Works. . . . London: Frederick Warne and Co. and
New York. 1893.

Variants

1. The " Albion " Edition.

2. The " Imperial " Poets.

Re-issue of § 855 (1888 London = Warne).

886. 1894 Glasgow

Pearl Edition.   The poetical works of Robert Burns.   [*In six
volumes*] Glasgow: David Bryce and Son. 1894.

Variant

David Bryce and Son (Stanley edition).

Re-issue of § 823 (1884 Glasgow = ? Bryce).

887. 1894 Glasgow

«« Pearl Edition. The songs of Robert Burns. Glasgow: David Bryce and Son. 1894.»»

M.C., § 204. Another issue, n.d. (§ 1043).

888. 1894 London

Poetical Works. . . . London . . Warne . . . 1894.

Variants

1. The " Albion " Edition.
2. Cabinet Poets.
3. The Chandos Classics.

Re-issue of § 855 (1888 London = Warne).

889. 1895 Edinburgh

Complete poetical Works. . . . Edinburgh . . . Nimmo . . . 1895.

Re-issue of § 668 ([? 1865] Edinburgh = Nimmo).

890. 1895 Edinburgh

Works. . . . Edinburgh: James Thin. 1895.

Re-issue of § 783 (1877 Edinburgh = Paterson).

891. 1895 London

Poetical Works. . . . London . . . Routledge . . . 1895.

Re-issue of § 795 (1878 London = Routledge).

892. 1895 London

Poetical Works. . . . London . . . Warne . . . 1895.

Re-issue of § 855 (1888 London = Warne).

893. 1896 Edinburgh

The Life and Works of Robert Burns edited by Robert Chambers revised by William Wallace in four Volumes   Volume I.   W. & R. Chambers, Limited   Edinburgh and London   1896.

Variant

New York : Longmans, Green, and Co.   1896.

a. VOL. I

Original Material.   Three letters:

Ref.[5]	Addressee	Date	
I.12	[Thomas Orr]	17 Nov. 1782[6]	*p.* 85
17	Gavin Hamilton	18 Oct. 1783	111
45	John Ballantine	[Sep. 1786]	419

b. VOL. II

Original Material.   Ten letters:

Ref.[7]	Addressee	Date	
I.59	Rev. Mr. William Greenfield	Dec. 1786	*p.* 19
92	Peter Hill	24 May 1787[8]	116
92	Robert Ainslie	29 May 1787	117
118	—— Scott	1787?	135
130	Peter Miller	20 Oct. 1787	197
148	James Steuart	[26 Dec. 1787]	236
182	John Tennant	7 Feb. 1788	284
214	William Creech	31 Mar. 1788	328
216	Alexander Blair	3 Apr. 1788[9]	330
274	Archibald Lawrie	15 Nov. 1788[10]	389

[5] To *Letters.*
[6] Originally in *Macmillan's Mag.*, LXVII (Jan. 1893), 202.
[7] To *Letters.*
[8] Originally in *B. Chr.*, II (1893), 147.
[9] Originally in *B. Chr.*, I (1892), 40.
[10] According to *Letters*, this first appeared in § 540 (1851 Edinburgh= Chambers).

c. VOL. III

Original Material.   Fifteen letters:

Ref.[11]	Addressee	Date	
1.289	[Lady Elizabeth Cunningham]	22 Jan. 1789	*p.* 29
333	Editor of the *Star*	7 May 1789	55
332	Editor of the *Star*	7 May 1789	56
336	Lady Betty Cunningham	15 May 1789	73
II.14	David Staig	[1 Mar. 1790]	151
1.321	To the Editor of the *Gazetteer*	10 Apr. 1789	245
322	To the Editor of the *Star*	13 Apr. 1789	246
II.97	Lady Hariot Don	23 Oct. 1791	251
74	Alexander Coutts	28 Apr. 1791	258
69	Thomas Sloan	[Apr. 1791]	259
13	Alexander Findlater	n.d.[12]	261
88	John Ballantine	[Sep. 1791]	285
177	[Deborah Duff Davies]	[Jun.? 1793[13]]	428
1.260	William Dunbar	25 Sep. 1788	441
300	William Dunbar	[Feb. 1789]	442

d. VOL. IV

Original Material.   Fourteen letters:

Ref.[14]	Addressee	Date	
1.74	Archibald Lawrie	[Feb. 1787[15]]	*p.* 13*n.*
82	Archibald Lawrie	n.d.	14*n.*
II.226	John M'Murdo	[Dec. 1793?]	64
244	—— M'Leod	18 Jun. 1794	110
1.296	William Stewart	n.d.	112
II.225	William Stewart	n.d.	113
261	Robert A. Riddell	22 Sep. 1794	144
260	[Alexander Findlater?]	[Sep. 1794]	144
284	William Stewart	15 Jan. 1795	189
290	Patrick Miller, jun.	8 Mar. [1795]	210
327	Alexander Cunningham	[12 Jul. 1796]	278
35	Helen Craik	9 Aug. 1790	518
104	Helen Craik	12 Jan. 1792[16]	519
1.90	M. Fyffe	[5 May 1787]	519

[11] To *Letters.*

[12] The *Verses on Eggs* was sent with this letter. Wallace prints it in part, but says: " The verses (which are unpublishable) are not now with the note, which is in the Monument at Edinburgh."

[13] Originally in the *Western Luminary*, Glasgow, No. 19 (9 May 1824), 151.

[14] To *Letters.*

[15] Originally in the *Athenaeum*, II (25 Jul. 1896), 130.

[16] *Letters* dates this January; Chambers has "Aug."

A complete re-editing and expansion of the Robert Chambers *Life and Works* of 1856 (§ 594). This is the most important edition of the complete works since Scott Douglas (§ 783), ". . . the most important [of any]," (*Camb. Bib.*, II.978).

894. 1896 Edinburgh

Robert Burns Poems and Songs Complete. . . [*In three volumes*] Published by James Thin Edinburgh 1896

Re-issue of § 879 (Edinburgh = Thin 1893). There is an extra volume of biography in this edition.

895. 1896 Edinburgh

The poetical Works of Robert Burns. . . . Edinburgh: John Grant and John Menzies . . . 1896.

896. 1896 Edinburgh

The Poetry of Robert Burns. Edited by William Ernest Henley and Thomas F. Henderson. . . . [*In four volumes*] Edinburgh T. C. and E. C. Jack, Causewayside. 1896.

Variant

London: The Caxton Publishing Co. Clun House, Surrey St., W.C. [n.d.]

b. VOL. II

Original Material:

A Mauchline Wedding	*p.* 42
On the Duchess of Gordon's Reel Dancing[17]	61
To William Stewart[18]	135
A Sonnet upon Sonnets	232
Sketch for an Elegy	236
The Cares o' Love	239
At Whigham's Inn, Sanquhar[19]	245
To the Hon. Wm. R. Maule of Panmure	256
On Marriage	261
As I cam doon the Banks o' Nith	398
Grim Grizzel was a mighty Dame	459

[17] Originally in Stuart's [London] *Star*, 31 Mar 1789.
[18] Originally in *N. & Q.*, v (1881), 86.
[19] Originally in *B. Chr.*, iv (1896), 93.

Surely the best edition of the poems to date. It is thoroughly annotated, and Henderson's meticulous work has resulted in what can truly be called a definitive text. I have not included other issues, *i.e.*, large paper, extra-illustrated, etc., in so far as the text remains standard.

897. 1896 Edinburgh

Kilmarnock Edition. . . . Tenth Edition. . . . Edinburgh and Glasgow: John Menzies . . . 1896.

Re-issue of § 779 (1876 Kilmarnock = M'Kie & Drennan).

898. 1896 Edinburgh

The People's Edition of the poetical Works of Robert Burns. . . . Edinburgh and Glasgow: John Menzies & Co., Kilmarnock: D. Brown & Co., (Successors to James M'Kie) 1896.

899. 1896 Glasgow

The poetical Works of Robert Burns. . . . Glasgow: David Bryce & Son. MDCCCXCVI.

Re-issued in 1899 (§ 915).

900. 1896 London

Complete Edition. Poetical Works of Robert Burns. London: Henry Frowde. 1896.

901. 1896 London

In Memory of Robert Burns. . . By Richard Le Gallienne London Marcus Ward . . . 1896.

Original Material:
Letter to Maria Riddell[20] [Jun. or Jul. 1795]: in facsimile between pp. 10 and 11.

A selection of poems and songs with an introductory essay.

[20] *Letters*, II.304, which says it appeared originally in § 50 (1800 Liverpool = Currie).

902. 1896 London

Poems and Songs of Robert Burns. Edited by Andrew Lang. London: Methuen & Co. 1896.

903. 1896 London

The poetical Works of Robert Burns Edited by John Fawside ... London Bliss, Sands and Foster MDCCCXCVI.

Variants

1. Edinburgh, Sands & Company.
2. New York, Longmans, Green, ...

Re-issued in 1897 (§ 910), 1901 (§ 919), and n.d. (§ 1083).

904. 1896 London

Routledge's Centenary Edition. . . . London: George Routledge . . . 1896.

Re-issue of § 795 (1878 London = Routledge).

905. 1896 London

Robert Burns' poetical Works. National Edition. . . . London: Frederick Warne and Co. And New York. 1896.

Re-issue of § 855 (1888 London = Warne).

906. 1896 London

Robert Burns: The Poems, Epistles, Songs, Epigrams, and Epitaphs. Edited by James Manson ... [*In two volumes*] Clement Wilson London: 29 Paternoster Row, E.C. MDCCCXCVI.

Re-issued in 1901 (§ 920).

907. 1896 New York

«« Poems and Songs of Robert Burns. By Andrew Lang. N.Y.: Dodd, Mead and Company. 1896.»»

(?) Reissue of § 902 (1896 London = Methuen). Angus, p. 93.

T

908. [1897] Boston

Complete poetical Works of Robert Burns   Cambridge Edition
Boston and New York   Houghton Mifflin Company [1897]

American edition of § 896 (1896 Edinburgh = Jack). Re-issued
numerous times as a standard American text. It will not be
noted again.

909. 1897 Kilmarnock

People's Edition . . . Poetical Works . . . Kilmarnock . . . Brown
. . . 1897.

Re-issue of § 779 (1876 Kilmarnock = M'Kie & Drennan).

910. [1897] London

Poetical Works. . . . London: Bliss, Sands & Co. . . . [1897].
Re-issue of § 903 (1896 London = Bliss, Sands and Foster).

911. 1897 New York

Poetical Works of Robert Burns.   Edited by Alexander Smith.
New-York: Frederick A. Stokes & Company. 1897.

912. 1897 New York

Poetical Works . . . New York: Thomas Whittaker. 1897.

913. 1898 London

The Poems of Robert Burns. MDCCCXCVIII. [*In two volumes*]
Published. by. J. M. Dent. and. Co: Aldine. House. London.
E.C.

914. 1898 London

Robert Burns and Mrs. Dunlop Correspondence now published
in full for the first Time with Elucidations by William Wallace
Editor of Robert Chambers's Life and Works of Robert Burns
[*In two volumes*] London Hodder and Stoughton 27 Paternoster
Row 1898

Original Material:

Thirty-three entirely new letters to Mrs Dunlop:

Ref.[21]	Date	
I.103	[Jul. 30 or 31, 1787]	*p*. 27
212	Mar. 26 1788	50
215	Mar. 31, 1788	53
247	Aug. 21, 1788	85
266	Oct. 23, 1788	104
268	Oct. 29, 1788	106
295	[Jan. 1789]	134
301	Feb. 5, 1789	142
309	[Feb. 21, 1789]	150
316	Mar. 25, 1789	156
321	Apr. 3, 1789	162
324	Apr. 21, 1789	165
343	Jul. 7, 1789	187
345	Jul. 17, 1789	190
355	Aug. 19, 1789	197
360	Oct. 2, 1789	212
367	Nov. 8, 1789	221
II.16	[Mar. 1790]	244
21	Jun. 6, 1790	261
25	Jul. 9, 1790	265
34	Jul. 30, 1790	271
45	Oct. 6, 1790	285
50	Dec. 6, 1790	293
98	Oct. 26, [1791]	333
105	Jan. 14, 1792	337
107	Feb. 3, 1792	343
176	[Jun. 1793]	381
221	[1793]	385
192	[Aug. 25, 1793]	389
253	[Mar. 13, 1794]	399
258	[Sep., 1794]	409
269	Oct. 29, 1794	411
311	[Midsummer. 1795]	419

Letters partly new:

I.49	Nov. 15, 1786	2
80	Mar. 22, 1787	14
183	Feb. 12, 1788	44
221	May 4, 1788	59
223	May 27, 1788	61

[21] To *Letters*.

Ref.	*Addressee*	*Date*	
p. 282		Jan. 1, 1789	*p.* 128
341		Jun 21, 1789	177
242	[Miss Rachel Dunlop]	2 Aug. 1788	81
269	[Miss Agnes Dunlop]	[? Nov. 1788]	114
225	[Andrew] Dunlop	[31 May 1788]	62

Another edition, with a somewhat fuller text: New York: Dodd, Mead and Company, 1898.

915. 1899 Glasgow

Poetical Works of Robert Burns. . . . Glasgow . . . Bryce. 1899.

Re-issue of § 899 (Glasgow = Bryce).

916. [1900] Boston

The complete poetical Works of Robert Burns. . . . Boston and New York Houghton Mifflin [1900]

Copyright dated 1900.

917. 1900 London

Globe Edition. . . . London: Macmillan . . . 1900.

Re-issue of § 715 (1868 London = Macmillan).

918. 1901 Edinburgh

Poetry . . . Edited by . . . Henley . . . and Henderson. . . . Edinburgh . . . Jack . . . 1901.

Re-issue, without facsimiles and missing most of the portraits, of § 896 (1896 Edinburgh = Jack).

919. 1901 London

Poetical Works . . . London: Sand and Co., 1901.

Re-issue of § 903 (1896 London = Bliss, Sands and Foster).

920. 1901 London

Robert Burns . . . Poems. . . . London: Adam and Chas. Black.
1901.

Re-issue of § 906 (1896 London = Wilson).

921. 1901 London

Robert Burns   Burns's Poems   " The New Oxford Library "
London E C   The Oxford Library Co   1901

922. 1901 New York

The Poetical Works of Robert Burns. . . New York James
Pott & Co. MCMI.

923. 1902 Edinburgh

Complete Poetical Works   John Grant, and Oliver and Boyd.
1902.

924. 1902 Glasgow

The Poetical Works of Robert Burns. . . . Glasgow: David
Bryce and Son. 1902.

Part of that ghastly little series printed by the University Press,
Glasgow.

925. 1902 London

The complete poetical Works of Robert Burns. . . . Thomas
Nelson . . . London, Edinburgh, and New York 1902

Re-issued in 1904 (§ 934) and 1927 (§ 967), and perhaps oftener.

926. 1902 London

Temple Classics. The Poems of Robert Burns. MDCCCCII. . . .
J. M. Dent . . . London.

927. 1902 London

The Poems and Songs of Robert Burns. . . London George
Newnes Ltd Southampton St. W.C. MCMII.

928. 1902 London

Poetical Works of Robert Burns. . . . London and Edinburgh: W. & R. Chambers, limited 1902

929. 1903 Edinburgh

The People's Edition of the Poetical Works of Robert Burns . . . revised by D. M'Naught. . . . Edinburgh and Glasgow: John Menzies . . . Kilmarnock: D. Brown . . . 1903.

930. 1903 Edinburgh

The Kilmarnock Edition. . . . Edinburgh and Glasgow . . . Menzies . . . Kilmarnock: D. Brown . . . 1903.

Re-issue of § 779 (1876 Kilmarnock = M'Kie & Drennan) and called " Eleventh Edition."

931. 1903 London

The Poetical Works of Robert Burns London Grant Richards 48 Leicester Square 1903

932. 1903 London

The Songs of Robert Burns Now first printed with the Melodies for which they were written A Study in Tone-Poetry with Bibliography, historical Notes, and Glossary by James C. Dick Part I [*of two*] Henry Frowde London, Edinburgh, Glasgow, and New York 1903

Excellent text and annotations.

933. 1904 Edinburgh

The Poetical Works of Robert Burns. . . . The " Edina " Edition Edinburgh: W. P. Nimmo, Hay, & Mitchell 1904

934. 1904 London

Complete Poetical Works. . . . London . . . Nelson . . . 1904.

Re-issue of § 925 (1902 London = Nelson).

935. 1904 London

The poetical Works of Robert Burns with Notes, Glossary, Index of first Lines and chronological List edited by J. Logie Robertson, M.A. Henry Frowde London, Edinburgh, Glasgow, New York and Toronto 1904

This is the Oxford Complete Edition and, through 1950, was re-issued seventeen times. The text is *not* what it should be. It will not be noted again.

936. 1904 London

The Poetical Works of Robert Burns. . . . London Maclaren & Co. . . . 1904.

937. [1906] London

The Poems and Songs of Robert Burns. London: published by J. M. Dent & Co. and in New York by E. P. Dutton & Co.

Introduction, by James Douglas, dated 1906.

938. [1906] London

Poems by Robert Burns with an Introduction by Neil Munro Blackie & Son Ltd London

This is in a series, " Red Letter Library." On the verso of h.t. " First printed November, 1906."

939. [1906] London

The Poems and Songs of Robert Burns Methuen & Co. 36 Essex Street W.C. London

Verso of t.-p., " Methuen's Standard Library," dated 1906. The text, revised by T. F. Henderson; introduction by Andrew

Lang. Some songs were added from Johnson's *Musical Museum,* among them " The Campbells are Coming " and " Sir John Cope," which were ascribed to Burns from internal evidence.

940. [1907] Glasgow

Poems by Robert Burns. . . . Glasgow: David Bryce & Son New York: Frederick A. Stokes Co.

Verso of t.p. dated MCMVII. Re-issue of § 823 (1884 Glasgow = Bryce).

941. [1907] London

Robert Burns Letters to Clarinda   Sisley's Ltd . . . London

Verso of t.p. dated 1907. A reprint of § 68 (1802 Glasgow = *Letters to Clarinda*).

942. 1907 London

The Poems and Songs of Robert Burns. . . . London: Cassell and Company . . . 1907.

" The People's Library." Re-issued in 1908 (§ 946).

943. 1907 London

Songs by Robert Burns   With biographical Introduction by Hannaford Bennett   London   John Long   13 & 14 Norris Street, Haymarket   MCMVII

944. 1908 Boston

The Geddes Burns. Boston: The Bibliophile Society. Printed for members only. (473 copies). 1908.

A reproduction of the interleaved copy of § 2 (1787 Edinburgh) which Burns presented to Bishop Geddes. There are numerous annotations in the text and Burns's long letter to Bishop Geddes[22] is reproduced in facsimile.

Probably a re-issue of § 778 (Kilmarnock = M'Kie & Drennan).

[22] Letters, 1.298.

945. 1908 London

Notes on Scottish Song by Robert Burns written in an interleaved Copy of The Scots Musical Museum, with Additions by Robert Riddell and others. Edited by the late James C. Dick. London, Henry Frowde . . . 1908.

One of the most important pieces of modern Burns scholarship. Besides the meticulous annotation of the text, Dick has also two essays, " Scottish Songs prior to Burns," and " Burns and his Songs."

946. 1908 London

Poems and Songs. . . . Cassell . . . London . . . MCMVIII

Re-issue of § 942 (1907 London = Cassell).

947. 1908 Saint Louis

Poems and Letters in the Handwriting of Robert Burns reproduced in Facsimile. . . . Introduction and explanatory Notes by Walter B. Stevens Saint Louis Printed for the Burns Club 1908

A superbly-produced set of facsimiles.

948. 1909 Kilmarnock

Poems, chiefly in the Scottish Dialect. . . . MDCCLXXXVI. [*Facsimile* : ? *re-issue of* § 702]

949. 1909 London

The Poetical Works of Robert Burns Edited with biographical Introduction by Charles Annandale. . . Music harmonized by Harry Colin Miller. . . Volume One [*of four*] London MCMIX The Gresham Publishing Company.

The biography is a pastiche of earlier works. Rather elaborately annotated text. The music has more or less followed the original melodic line; the harmonies are often modernised.

950. 1909 New York

Complete Works. . . . Bigelow, Brown & Co., Inc. New York.

Re-issue of § 838 ([1886] Philadelphia = Gebbie).

951. [1909] New York

The Poems and Songs of Robert Burns. . . . New York: P. F. Collier and Co.

1909 of verso of t.p. " The Harvard Classics."

952. 1911 London

Poems published in 1786. London: H. Frowde, 1911.

Another facsimile of the Kilmarnock edition. Re-issued in 1913 (§ 955).

953. 1912 London

The Songs and Poems of Robert Burns with Appreciation by the Right Hon. The Earl of Rosebery . . . T. N. Foulis   London & Edinburgh   MCMXII

The appreciation is Lord Rosebery's Glasgow speech, 1896.

954. 1913 Edinburgh

The People's Edition of the Poetical Works of Robert Burns. . . . Edinburgh and Glasgow: John Menzies . . . Kilmarnock: D. Brown . . . 1913.

Probably a re-issue of § 779 (Kilmarnock=M'Kie & Drennan).

955. 1913 Oxford

Poems published in 1786. . . . Introduction and Notes by M. S. Cleghorn. Oxford: The Clarendon Press, 1913.

Re-issue of the facsimile of § 952 (1911 London = Frowde).

956. 1914 Philadelphia

The Glenriddell Manuscripts of Robert Burns   printed not published   John Gribbel   Philadelphia   1914

A facsimile of one of the most important of Burns's manuscripts, the source of some fifty-seven poems and twenty-seven letters. One hundred and fifty copies; plates destroyed.

957. 1919 Glasgow

Robert Burns as a Volunteer. . . . By William Will. . . . Glasgow: John Smith . . . 1919

Original Material:
    Letter to [Colonel De Peyster][23] [18 May 1795]   *p.* 24

This letter *may* be by Burns.

958. [1920] London

The Poems of Robert Burns . . . edited by James L. Hughes. . . . Hodder & Stoughton Limited   London

Printed in the U.S.A. Copyright dated 1919. The only good thing about this edition is some photographs of the Burns country.

959. 1921 Glasgow

The Truth about Burns by D. McNaught . . . Editor of ' Burns Chronicle ' Glasgow Maclehose, Jackson & Co. . . . 1921

Original Material:
    Letter to James Smith[24] 26 Jun. 1788   *p.* 217

Contains a good bibliography of appearances of Burns's poems and notices in contemporary periodicals.

960. 1922 Buffalo

Autograph Poems and Letters of Robert Burns in the Collection of R. B. Adam . . . printed privately Buffalo, N.Y. 1922.

A meticulous transcription of a great many letters and manuscripts. Included are the first draft of Swinburne's *Burns* and an unpublished epigram of D. G. Rossetti.

961. 1923 Edinburgh

Complete poetical Works . . . 2 vols. in 1. Edinburgh Glasgow . . . Menzies . . . 1923.

Re-issue of § 779 (1876 Kilmarnock = M'Kie & Drennan).

---

[23] *Letters*, II.297.   [24] *Letters*, I.230.

962. 1923 London

Robert Burns. The complete poetical Works . . . London: T. Nelson, 1923.

963. 1923 Tokyo

Select Poems of Robert Burns. . . . Tokyo: 1923.

The poems are in English, the notes in Japanese.

964. 1925 London

Scottish Poems of Robert Burns in his Native Dialect By Sir James Wilson . . . Oxford University Press London: Humphrey Milford 1925

A two-way translation from the dialect, as Burns wrote it, into, first, phonetics of the dialect as it is spoken in central Ayrshire today (1925), and, second, into straight modern English. Very valuable for those who would like to know how, approximately, Burns's dialect really sounded.

965. 1926 Boston

The complete Poems of Robert Burns Vol I [*of ten*] with an Essay on Burns's Life, Genius, Achievement by W. E. Henley and an Introduction by John Buchan Boston and New York Houghton Mifflin Company The Riverside Press Cambridge 1926

e. VOL. V

Original Material:

g. VOL. VII

Original Material. Three letters:

Ref.[25]	Addressee	Date	
1.45	[John Ballantine?]	n.d.	*p.* 84
295	[Alexander Dalziel?] (In part)	n.d.	130
87	Patrick Miller (In part)	[1 May *?* 1787]	137

h. VOL. VIII

Original Material. Six letters:

Ref.[26]	Addressee	Date	
1.158	[John Ballantine?]	n.d.	*p.* 4
255	[Robert Riddell]	[16 Sep. 1788]	73
341	[Patrick Miller]	21 Jun. 1789	196
365	Mrs. Miller	2 Nov. 1789	225
II.3	David Sillar	22 Jan. 1790	247
37	Robert Cleghorn	29 Aug. 1790	290

i. VOL. IX

Original Material. Four letters:

Ref.[27]	Addressee	Date	
1.232	William Stewart	[9 Jul. ? 1788]	*p.* 19
II.53	John Gillespie	[? 1791]	68
113	[John M'Murdo]	[1792]	111
261	[Robert Graham]	[1794]	192

1,000 copies printed; 750 for the United States, 250 for Britain. The first six volumes contain the poems, glossary and notes as edited by Henley and Henderson; the last four the prose, edited by Francis H. Allen.

966. 1927 London

Complete Poems. . . . London The Waverley Book Company . . . 1927

British issue of § 965 (1926 Boston = Houghton).

---

[25] To *Letters.*   [26] To *Letters.*

[27] To *Letters.*

967. 1927 London

Complete Poetical Works . . . London . . . Nelson . . . 1927.
Re-issue of § 934 (1902 London = Nelson).

968. 1927 London

Journal of a Tour in the Highlands made in the year 1787, by
Robert Burns. Reproduced in Facsimile from his original
Manuscript . . . J. C. Ewing [*ed.*]. London and Glasgow:
Gowans and Gray, Ltd. 1927.

969. 1927 London

Robert Burns   the Poems, Epistles, Songs, Epigrams & Epitaphs
Edited by Charles S. Dougall   with notes, Index, Glossary, and
biographical Sketch   A. C. Black, Ltd.   4, 5, & 6 Soho Square,
London, W.1   1927.

970. [1928] Glasgow

Masonic Edition.   Robert Burns   The Complete Works and
Letters. . . London and Glasgow.

Dated from the acquisition dates in the B.M. and N.L.S. copies.
Another issue of § 1030 (n.d. Glasgow = Collins).

971. 1929 Oxford

Burns   Poetry & Prose   with Essays by Mackenzie, Jeffrey,
Carlyle and others   with an Introduction and Notes by R.
Dewar   Oxford   at the Clarendon Press   1929

972. 1931 Oxford

The Letters of Robert Burns   Edited from the original Manuscripts by J. De Lancey Ferguson . . . [2 *vols.*] Oxford . . . The
Clarendon Press 1931

This is the best edition of the letters to date. There are sixty-
nine new letters, forty-five of which are printed in a collected

edition for the first time. Contrary to usual practice, I have not listed this new material, in so far as the *Letters* is readily available. The new appearances are marked with asterisks in the table of contents, which is arranged chronologically.

973. [1932] Edinburgh

Burns' Poems. . . . Andersons, Edinburgh, Ltd. Printed in Scotland.

" The Thistle Library." Dated from the acquisition date in the B.M.

974. [1932] Edinburgh

Burns's Songs. . . . Andersons, Edinburgh, Ltd. Printed in Scotland.

" The Thistle Library." Dated from the acquisition date in the B.M.

975. 1933 [New York]

Private Papers of James Boswell from Malahide Castle . . . [*ed.*] by Geoffrey Scott and Frederick A. Pottle . . . [*Privately printed for Ralph H. Isham in the U.S.A.* 18 *vols.* (1928-34)].

Original Material (in the Journal of James Boswell . . . [Vol. 17] MCMXXXIII):

Letter to Bruce Campbell   13 Nov. 1788   *p.* 126

976. 1935 Glasgow

The Kilmarnock Edition of the poetical Works of Robert Burns . . . The Scottish " Daily Express," Glasgow, 1935.

977. [1936] Glasgow

The Complete Works of Robert Burns . . . London & Glasgow Collins's Clear-cut Press

Re-issue of § 970 ([1928] London and Glasgow = Collins). Dated from acquisition date in B.M.

978. [1937] Glasgow

Robert Burns   The poetical Works   Collins   London and Glasgow

Re-issue of the poetry section only of § 970 ([1928] London and Glasgow = Collins).   Dated from the acquisition date in B.M.

979. 1938 Glasgow

Robert Burns's Commonplace Book . . . reproduced in Facsimile [*ed.*] James Cameron Ewing . . . Davidson Cook. . . .   Glasgow Gowans and Gray . . . MDMXXXVIII.

980. [Cancelled]

981. [1942] Glasgow

Burns' poetical Works . . . London and Glasgow . . . Collins.

Re-issue of § 970 ([1928] London and Glasgow = Collins), with an introduction by W. J. Davies.   Dated from acquisition date in B.M.

982. 1943 Chapel Hill

Robert Burns   his associates and contemporaries   the Train, Grierson, Young, and Hope Manuscripts, edited with an Introduction by Robert T. Fitzhugh   with the Journal of the Border Tour edited by DeLancey Ferguson   Chapel Hill   The University of North Carolina Press   1943

983. [Cancelled]

984. 1953 New York

Selected Letters of Robert Burns. Edited . . . by DeLancey
Ferguson. London: Oxford University Press [1953].

Original Material. Seven Letters:[28]

Addressee	Date	
Patrick Miller	[15 Jan. 1787]	*p.* 31
Mrs. Dunlop	28 Apr 1788	117
Mrs. Dunlop	4 May 1788	119
Dr. John Moore	4 Jan. 1789	163
Robert Ainslie	6 Jan 1789	166
Maria Riddell	n.d.	300
John McMurdo	[Dec. 1793]	315

[28] Actually, these letters had been printed, in part, before. They are
completed here.

U

UNDATED EDITIONS

985. n.d. Aberdeen

The poetical Works of Robert Burns. . . . James Wilson.

986. n.d. Alnwick

The Poems and Songs of Robert Burns . . . printed and published by W. Davison, And sold by J. Banks, Keswick.

987. n.d. Alnwick

The poetical Works of Robert Burns. . . . Engravings on Wood by Bewick. . . . Vol. I. [*of two*] . . . Printed by W. Davison. [*eng.* t.p.

Vol. II. has advertisement for Fergusson's *Poems* dated 1811.

988. n.d. Boston

Burns' Works. . . . Otis, Broaders, & Co.

Re-issue of § 483 (1846 Boston = Otis, Broaders).

989. n.d. Boston

Burns's Works. Phillips & Sampson.

Re-issue of § 482 (1846 Boston = Bedlington).

990. n.d. Boston

The poetical Works of Robert Burns. . . . Houghton, Mifflin and Company. The Riverside Press, Cambridge.

991. n.d. Boston

The poetical Works of Robert Burns. Three Volumes in one. . . . Houghton, Mifflin and Company. The Riverside Press, Cambridge.

992. n.d. Boston

Poetical Works of Robert Burns. . . . Boston: Lee & Shephard. . . .
New York: Lee, Shephard & Dillingham.

993. n.d. Boston

The poetical Works of Robert Burns edited by . . . Charles Kent.
. . . Parry Mason & Co.

994. n.d. Brooklyn

Poetical Works of Robert Burns. Brooklyn and New York :
W. W. Swayne.

995. n.d. Chiswick

The poetical Works of Robert Burns. Vol. I. [*of two*] . . . from
the Press of C. Whittingham, College House. . . . .

Date on original boards in D.C.: " 1824."

996. n.d. Cincinnati

«« Life and Works of Burns. In one Vol. J. & J. A. James. . . ." »»
Bib. B., p. 42.

997. n.d. Derby

The poetical Works of Robert Burns. . . . Thomas Richardson
and Son . . . According to *M.C.*, § 366 a re-issue of § 448 (1843
Derby = Richardson).

998. n.d. Dublin

The poetical Works of Robert Burns. . . . Sold by Michael
Walsh, 41, Lower Ormond Quay.

Re-issue of § 448 (1843 Derby = Richardson).

999. n.d. Dublin

" The Poetical Works of Robert Burns . . . printed by M. C.
Warren, 21, Upper Ormond Quay."

Bib. B., p. 13; Sneddon, p. 63, has " [1829]."

1000. n.d. Dumfries

The Songs of Robert Burns. . . . David Halliday.

Gibson, p. 64, has " 1848."

1001. n.d. Dundee

Burns' Poems [" The Thistle Library "] Valentine & Sons, limited. . . .

1002. n.d. Edinburgh

Burns' Poems [" The Thistle Library "] . . . Andersons. . . .

1003. n.d. Edinburgh

The complete poetical Works of Robert Burns. Edited by John S. Roberts. With . . . memoir by William Gunnyon . . . William P. Nimmo. Sneddon, p. 66, " [1865;] " Gibson, p. 96, " 1879."

Re-issue of § 667 (? 1865 Edinburgh = Nimmo).

1004. n.d. Edinburgh

The complete prose Works of Robert Burns. . . . William P. Nimmo. Sneddon, p. 64, " [1848]."

Re-issue of § 669 (? 1865 Edinburgh = Nimmo).

1005. n.d. Edinburgh

The complete Works of Robert Burns . . . in two volumes . . . Thomas C. Jack.

Gibson, p. 81: " reprint of 1840 Edition." Cp. also B. Chr., III (1894), 169.

1006. n.d. Edinburgh

The complete Works of Robert Burns [ed.] Allan Cunningham . . . with numerous Notes by Lord Byron, Thomas Carlyle . . . Volume I [of four]. . . . Thomas C. Jack, Grange Publishing Works London: 45 Ludgate Hill.

1007. n.d. Edinburgh

The complete Works of Robert Burns . . . memoir by William
Gunnyon . . . W. P. Nimmo, Hay, & Mitchell.

Advertisement at back dated " 1878."

1008. n.d. Edinburgh

The entire Works of Robert Burns . . . in four Volumes.   Complete in One . . . Alexander Currie.

B. Chr., 1 (1892), 111: " [1865]."

1009. n.d. Edinburgh

The entire Works of Robert Burns [*four vols. in one*]. . . . Alexander Gunn, 37 South Bridge.

Sneddon, p. 65: " [1865]."

1010. n.d. Edinburgh

The Life and Works of Robert Burns. . . . William and Robert
Chambers.

Re-issue of § 540 (1851 Edinburgh = Chambers).

1011. n.d. Edinburgh

The Life and Works of Robert Burns. . . . William and Robert
Chambers.

Re-issue of § 594 (1856 Edinburgh = Chambers).

1012. n.d. Edinburgh

The Life and Works of Robert Burns. . . . Macredie, Skelly and
Muckersy.

Re-issue of § 170 (1815 Edinburgh = Anderson).

1013. n.d. Edinburgh

Poems and Songs by Robert Burns. . . . Oliver & Boyd.

1014. n.d. Edinburgh

Poems and Songs. . . . Oliver & Boyd, Tweeddale Court; and Simpkin, Marshall, & Co., London.

1015. n.d. Edinburgh

The poetical Works and Letters of Robert Burns [Family Edition]. . . . Gall & Inglis, 6 George Street. London: Houlston & Wright.

Angus, p. 11: " [1865]."

1016. n.d. Edinburgh

The poetical Works and Letters of Robert Burns. . . . Gall & Inglis.

Probably a re-issue of § 722. N.L.S. has " [1881]."

1017. n.d. Edinburgh

The poetical Works and Letters of Robert Burns. . . . (In this Edition the more objectionable Passages and Pieces are excluded). . . . Gall & Inglis, 6 George Street. London: Houlston & Wright.

Mitch. records four re-issues. B.M. " [1859]."

1018. n.d. Edinburgh

Poetical Works of Robert Burns. Unabridged Edition. . . . W. P. Nimmo, Hay, & Mitchell.

Variant: A New Edition.

1019. n.d. Edinburgh

The poetical Works of Robert Burns. . . . W. P. Nimmo.

1020. n.d. Edinburgh

" Poetical Works. . . . W. P. Nimmo."

Mur. Cat., p. 15. Another edn? Another issue (of § 668)? Or is this the same as " Poetical Works of Robert Burns. A new edition . . . William P. Nimmo " in *Bib. B.*, p. 25 ? Cp. also Sneddon, p. 66, and Gibson, p. 74, where the dates are given respectively as " [1865] " and " 1860."

1021. n.d. Edinburgh

The poetical Works of Robert Burns. . . . Oliver & Boyd.

B.M. and Mur. have identical t.-p.s, but they are two different edns. Chambers (IV.317): " N.D., but probably about 1812."

1022. n.d. Edinburgh

The poetical Works of Robert Burns. . . . Oliver & Boyd. [*two vols.*].

Variant: Oliver & Boyd; and Wingrove, London.

Both t.ps. eng. Mur. Cat., p. 11, gives " [1807]."

1023. n.d. Edinburgh

The poetical Works of Robert Burns. Chronologically arranged; . . . In three Volumes. . . . William Paterson.

Angus, p. 21: " Issued about 1884; re-print of Vols. 1-3 of the ' Library Edition.' "

Actually a re-issue of § 783 (1877 Edinburgh = Paterson).

1024. n.d. Edinburgh

The poetical Works of Robert Burns Edited by John Fawside . . . Edward Stephenson.

1025. n.d. Edinburgh

Songs by Burns. . . . Otto Schulze and Company.

Mitch. Cat., p. 8: " [1901]." There is another edn. limited to 500 copies.

1026. n.d. Edinburgh

«« [Songs of Robert Burns. Edinburgh: W. Chambers. *Circa* 1821].»»

Angus, p. 5. Probably non-existent.

1027. n.d. Edinburgh

The Works of Robert Burns. . . . In two Volumes. . . . James Inglis.

Gibson, p. 81: " reprint of the 1840 edition."

1028. n.d. Edinburgh

The Works of Robert Burns. . . . Inglis & Jack.

Sneddon, p. 65: " [1863]."

1029. n.d. Glasgow

The complete poetical Works of Robert Burns. . . . Memoir by William Gunnyon. . . . James M'Geachy.

1030. n.d. Glasgow

The complete Works of Robert Burns. . . . William Collins Sons & Co.

[? 1928], with numerous re-issues.

1031. n.d. Glasgow

The complete Works of Robert Burns. . . . two Volumes. . . . John McGready, Publishers, Glasgow.

Variant: Glasgow and Sydney: John McGready, publisher.

1032. n.d. Glasgow

The complete Works and Correspondence of Robert Burns. Edited . . . Motherwell and . . . Hogg. In four Volumes . . . .

Thomas D. Morison.   London: Simpkin, Marshall, Hamilton, Kent & Co.

B. Chr., VII (1898), 121, describes this as a re-issue (without corrections or additions) of § 365 (1834 Glasgow = Fullarton).

1033. n.d. Glasgow

The illustrated family Burns. . . .   William Mackenzie.

Variant

Glasgow, Edinburgh, and London: W. Mackenzie
National Burns. . . .   London: William Mackenzie
Illustrated family Burns. . . .   New York . . . Collier.

Bib. B., p. 27: " An extended re-print of [§ 615] Bell and Daldy's 1858 edition. . . .   Published in 12 parts."   Cp. also § 799 (1879 London = Mackenzie).

1034. n.d. Glasgow

«« [Letters from Robert Burns. Glasgow. [8vo] 1816]. *Vide* bibliography in " Burns Calendar " (1876); also, ditto in Gebbie & Co.'s Philadelphia edition. . . . 1886."] »»
Angus, p. 34.

1035. n.d. Glasgow

The poetical Works of Robert Burns. In six volumes. . . .   David Bryce & Son. [Pearl Edition].

Variants

New York: Frederick A. Stokes and Brother, successor to White, Stokes, & Allen.

N.L.S. Cat.: " Glasgow [1889]. A re-issue of the edition of 1884 (§ 823), with the addition of a Glossary." Sneddon, p. 69: " [1887]."

1036. n.d. Glasgow

The poetical Works of Robert Burns. . . .   Cameron & Ferguson.

Gibson, p. 87: " 1868; " Sneddon, p. 65: " [1859]."

1037. n.d. Glasgow

The poetical Works of Robert Burns. Edited . . . by W. M.
Rossetti. . . . William Collins, Sons & Co. [The Grosvenor
Poets].

1038. n.d. Glasgow

The poetical Works of Robert Burns. . . . Dunn & Wright.
[Thistle Series].

Sneddon, p. 69: " [1876] "; Gibson, p. 96: " 1878."

1039. n.d. Glasgow

The poetical Works of Robert Burns. . . . J. P. Forrester.

1040. n.d. Glasgow

The poetical Works of Robert Burns. . . . The Grand Colosseum
Warehouse Co.

M.C., § 240, says that this was re-issued.

1041. n.d. Glasgow

The poetical Works of Robert Burns. . . . John S. Marr, Successor to the late George Cameron.

Mitch. Cat., p. 14, has " [1867]," and notes three re-issues:
[*c.* 1870], [*c.* 1875], and [*c.* 1877]. Sneddon, p. 66: " [1864] ";
Gibson, pp. 89, 91, 92, and 94: " 1870," " 1872," " 1874,"
and " 1877." There is a variant with " McKim's Monumental
Edition " on t.p.

1042. n.d. Glasgow

Songs and Ballads of Robert Burns. . . . J. P. Forrester.

1043. n.d. Glasgow

The Songs of Robert Burns. . . . David Bryce and Sons.

Re-issue, with " Pearl Edition " on t.p., of § 887 (1894 Glasgow
= Bryce).

1044. n.d. Glasgow

The Works of Robert Burns. . . . Blackie & Sons.
In 25 parts at 1s.

Re-issue of § 450 (1843 Glasgow = Blackie).

1045. n.d. Glasgow

The Works of Robert Burns. . . . Archibald Fullarton and Co.

Re-issue of § 365 (1834 Glasgow = Fullarton).

1046. n.d. Glasgow

The Works and Correspondence of Robert Burns. . . . William
Mackenzie.

Variants

Glasgow: Mackenzie, White & Co.
. . . Mackenzie: London, Glasgow, Edinburgh.

Published in 17 parts, re-issue of § 686.

1047. n.d. Halifax

The poetical Works of Robert Burns. . . . printed for William
Milner.

Re-issue of § 428 (1840 Halifax = Milner).

1048. n.d. Kilmarnock

Poems, chiefly in the Scottish dialect. Kilmarnock, 1786.
[? 1886].

Centenary reprint by J. M'Kie of § 738.   120 copies only.
(1867 Kilmarnock = [M'Kie]).

1049. n.d. Kilmarnock

Poems, chiefly in the Scottish Dialect. Kilmarnock, 1786.
[? 1909].

Another facsimile of § 948.

1050. n.d. Kilmarnock

People's Edition. . . . The poetical Works of Robert Burns . . . Kilmarnock: D. Brown & Co.

Probably a re-issue of § 779 (1876 Kilmarnock = M'Kie & Drennan).

1051. n.d. Liverpool

Second Edition [of Liverpool: 1822, § 257 ?]. The Songs of Robert Burns . . . Liverpool: Printed for T. Kerr.

Mitch. Cat. (52462) says " [c. 1834]."

1052. n.d. London

The complete Works of Robert Burns . . . London: James Blackwood and Co.

1053. n.d. London

The complete Works of Robert Burns. London: Cassell, Petter, and Galpin.

Mitch. Cat. (52578): " [1872]." Gebbie, vi.341: " 1873."

1054. n.d. London

The complete Works of Robert Burns. . . . In three Volumes. . . . London: printed for the Booksellers.

Mur. Cat.: " c. 1840." Sneddon, p. 38: " 1840."

1055. n.d. London

The complete Works of Robert Burns and Sir Walter Scott. . . . London: Charles Griffin[.]

Sneddon, p. 68: " [1866]."

1056. n.d. London

The complete poetical Works of Robert Burns. . . . London: Charles Griffin.

Re-issue of § 688 (1866 London = Griffin).

1057. n.d. London

The complete Works of Robert Burns. . . . London: Milner and Company.

There are several issues of this title, all of them re-issues of § 441 (1842 Halifax = Milner).

1058. n.d. London

The complete poetical Works of Robert Burns. . . . London . . . Scott and Webster.

1059. n.d. London

The complete poetical Works of Robert Burns . . . London . . . Scott and Webster.

A new edition; *not* the same as the preceding item.

1060. n.d. London

The complete poetical Works of Robert Burns. London: Ward, Lock, and Tyler.

1061. n.d. London

The complete poetical Works of Robert Burns. . . . London: Thomas Yardley.

1062. n.d. London

Masonic Edition Robert Burns The complete Works and Letters . . . London and Glasgow Collins Clear-type Press

1063. n.d. London

The complete Works of Robert Burns. . . . London: H. Virtue and Company.

1064. n.d. London

The complete Works of Robert Burns: containing his Poems, Songs, and Correspondence. Illustrated by W. H. Bartlett. T. Allom, and other Artists. With a new Life of the Poet, and Notices, critical and biographical, by Allan Cunningham. London: George Virtue.

Variants

London: James S. Virtue.
London: J. S. Virtue, City Road and Ivy Lane.
London: J. S. Virtue & Co., Limited, 294, City Road.
London: Virtue & Co.
Virtue & Co., London.

Eng t.p. dated 1839. A re-issue of " Poems, Letters and Land of Burns," London [1838], with a slightly different arrangement of material and the section on the land of Burns (96 pp.) removed.

1065. n.d. London

The complete Works of Robert Burns. . . . J. S. Virtue & Co., London.

A new, and (according to B.M. Acquisition 1886, 87) later edition of the preceding item. Published in parts, extra eng t.p.

1066. n.d. London

The Correspondence of Robert Burns. With his Notes on Scottish Songs and Ballads, the Border and Highland tours, and assignment of his poems. London: George Virtue.

Variants

J. S. Virtue & Co.
Virtue & Co.

According to Davidson Cook (*Weekly Scotsman*, 3 Nov. 1934), " These changes help to establish priority of issue." The remark is interesting but hardly illuminating.

1067. n.d. London

Letters to Clarinda. . . . London, Sisley's Ltd.
B.M. Acquisition 1908. On front cover, " The Panel Books."

1068. n.d. London

Letters of the Poet; . . . London: Collins.

1069. n.d. London

The national Edition of the Works of Robert Burns . . . Biographies of Currie and Lockhart. . . . Edited by William Wallace. . . . In two Volumes. Cassell, Petter, Galpin & Co. London, Paris, and New York.

1070. n.d. London

The national Burns edited by the Rev. George Gilfillan. . . . William Mackenzie London Glasgow Edinburgh.

[? 1879-80]   Re-issue of § 799 (1879 London = Mackenzie).

1071. n.d. London

Poems of Robert Burns. In two Volumes. Cassell & Company, Limited; London, Paris, New York, & Melbourne.

In " Cassell's Miniature Library of the Poets." Angus, p. 56: " 1886." Mitch. Cat., p. 24: [1890]." N.L.S.: " A re-issue of the edition published by W. Kent & Co., in 1881 [§ 805]."

1072. n.d. London

Poems & Songs [" The Edina Edition "]. . . . Nimmo: London. Re-issue of § 711 (1868 Edinburgh = Nimmo).

1073. n.d. London

The Poems and Songs of Robert Burns. . . . London: Simpkin, Marshall, Hamilton, Kent & Co. Ltd. New York Charles Scribner's Sons. [Extra eng. t.p.]

1074. n.d. London

The Poems, Letters, and Land of Robert Burns: illustrated by W. H. Bartlett, T. Allom, and other Artists. With a new memoir of the Poet, and Notices, critical and biographical, of his Works, by Allan Cunningham. Vol. I [of two] London: George Virtue.

Original Material:
    Letter to Dr. Archibald Laurie 13 Nov. 1786 [*Letters* 1.48.]

The eng t.p. is dated 1838; most of the other engravings throughout the work, 1839; t.p. of Vol. II, 1840. " The life differs from Cunningham's other two biographies of the poet " (*Camb. Bib.*, II.977*b*). In the preface Cunningham rejects as spurious: (*a*) " Lines on the Ruins of Lincluden "; (*b*) " Verses on the Destruction of Drumlanrig Wood "; (*c*) " Verses written on a Marble Slab in the Woods of Aberfeldy "; and (*d*) " The Tree of Liberty."

1075. n.d. London

The poetical Works of Geoffrey Chaucer and Robert Burns. . . . London and Glasgow: Richard Griffin & Company.

Gibson, p. 68, " 1855; " Angus, p. 30, " [ca 1855]."

1076. n.d. London

The poetical Works of Robert Burns. London: Gall and Inglis. [Family Edition.]

1077. n.d. London

The poetical and prose Works of Robert Burns: with Life Notes and Correspondence: by A. Cunningham, Esq. London: Charles Daly, 17, Greville Street, Hatton Gardens.

Camb. Bib., II (1940), 978: ". . . from the collection of Sir Egerton Brydges, Bart. In this edn pbd about the middle of the 19th Cent. we find a fourth life of Burns supposed to be written by Allan Cunningham. The ' original pieces ' consist of sixteen ' Letters of Clarinda to Burns '." Cp. *B. Chr.*, 2nd Ser., IX (1934), 72. The letters are a souped-up, highly elegant version of the originals. There is one letter here, by Clarinda, that did not appear in § 449 (1843 London = Tait)—the letter in which it was suggested that classical names be used [? spurious]. Sneddon, p. 37, dates this [1838].

1078. n.d. London

The poetical and prose Writings of Robert Burns; with Life, Notes, and Correspondence by Allan Cunningham. . . . London: Daly.

x

1079. n.d. London

The poetical Works of Robert Burns. . . . London: Hyman A.
Abraham & Sons. [Ed. W. M. Rossetti.]

1080. n.d. London

The poetical Works of Robert Burns. . . . London: Thomas
Allman, 42, Holborn Hill.

Gibson, p. 70: " 1857," Angus, p. 48: " [c. 1857]."

1081. n.d. London

The poetical Works of Robert Burns. London: Bell and Daldy.
Sneddon, p. 68, " [1870.] " [3 vols.]

Another issue of § 741 (1870 London=Bell), also in three vols.,
with imprint " Bell & Daldy," has the last vol. dated 1870.

1082. n.d. London

The poetical Works of Robert Burns. . . . London: James
Blackwood & Co., Paternoster Row.

Gibson, p. 92: " 1872. The Glasgow Edition, ' Marr,' with a
London publisher's title page; " Angus, p. 51: " [1872]."

1083. n.d. London

The poetical Works of Robert Burns. . . . London: Bliss,
Sands and Co. [The Apollo Poets.]

Re-issue of § 903 (London = Bliss, 1896).

1084. n.d. London

The poetical Works of Robert Burns. A new and complete
Edition, including many Poems not extant in any other Collection. London: printed for the booksellers.

Angus, p. 77, and Sneddon, p. 64: " [c. 1840]." In the Mitch.
copy, inner margin of p. 65 has: " J. H. Green . . . and may be
had of all the Booksellers."

1085. n.d. London

The poetical Works of Robert Burns. . . . In two Volumes, London, Paris, and New York: Cassell, Petter, and Galpin.

Edited by Charles Cowden Clarke, and probably published in 1872, as there is an advertisement for the International Exhibition of that year pasted on the inner front cover. Issued in 6 parts at 6d a part. Also issued as " Cassell's Library Edition of the British Poets." Sneddon p. 68, " [1873]." Gibson; p. 92, " 1872." Gibson adds: "The same edition, issued by . . . Nimmo, printed by Schenck & M'Farlane, Edinburgh."

1086. n.d. London

The poetical Works of Robert Burns. London: W. Collins.

1087. n. d. London

The poetical Works of Robert Burns. London and Glasgow: William Collins, Sons & Co. [The Grosvenor Poets.]

1088. n.d. London

The poetical Works of Robert Burns. London: N. Cooke. Universal Library.

1089. n.d. London

The poetical Works of Robert Burns. . . . [Edited] by William Michael Rossetti. London: Croome & Co.

1090. n.d. London

The poetical Works of Robert Burns, [ed. Allan Cunningham] . . . London: Charles Daly, No. 17, Greville-street, Hatton Garden.

1091. n.d. London

The poetical Works of Robert Burns, with numerous Illustrations. London: John Dicks.

Re-issue of § 716 (1868 London = Dicks).

1092. n.d. London

«« The poetical Works of Robert Burns. Edited by the Rev.
Robert Aris Wilmott, Incumbent of Bear Wood. Illustrated by
John Gilbert. London: Richard Griffin and Company, Sta-
tioners' Hall Court; Glasgow, West Nile Street.»»

M.C., § 501

1093. n.d. London

The poetical Works of Robert Burns. London and Glasgow:
Richard Griffin and Company.

M.C., § 243, n.d.   Gibson, p. 67: " 1855."

1094. n.d. London

The poetical Works of Robert Burns. . . . London: Griffin,
Bohn and Company.

Sneddon, p. 66, " [1861]."

1095. n.d. London

«« The poetical Works of Robert Burns. Edited . . . by William
Michael Rossetti. Griffin, Farran, Okeden, & Welsh, at the
sign of the " Bible and Crown," West Corner of St. Paul's
Churchyard, London.»»

M.C., § 503.

1096. n.d. London

The poetical Works of Robert Burns. Edited . . . by J. R. Tutin.
London: Griffith, Farran & Co., Limited, Newbery House, 39
Charing Cross Road.

Angus, p. 60: " [1893]."

1097. n.d. London

««The poetical Works of Robert Burns. Edited by the Rev.
Robert Aris Willmott. Illustrations by Sir John Gilbert, R.A.,

Griffith and Farran, at the Sign of the " Bible and Sun," West Corner of St. Paul's Churchyard, London.»»

M.C., § 520.

1098. n.d. London

The poetical Works of Robert Burns. Griffith, Farran, Okeden & Welsh, London and Sydney. [The Newbery Classics.]

Angus, p. 60: " 1889."

1099. n.d. London

The poetical Works of Robert Burns. . . . Edited by John and Angus Macpherson. . . . London: Hamilton, Adams & Co. Edinburgh: John Grant. And sold by all the Booksellers.

Re-issue of § 626 (1859 Glasgow = Cameron).

1100. n.d. London

«« The poetical Works of Robert Burns. In two Volumes. London: Jones & Co.»»

Angus, p. 61. Gibson, p. 57: " One of a series of Diamond British Poets."

1101. n.d. London

The poetical Works of Robert Burns; with a Glossary and biographical Sketch of the Author. . . . London: Jones & Co. [Diamond Edition.]

Chambers, *Works* (1891), IV.318: " 2 vols. 96to [!]. . . . [N.D. but probably about 1820. Now published with fresh title-pages by W. S. Orr & Co.]."

1102. n.d. London

The poetical Works of Robert Burns; edited by W. M. Rossetti. London: Kilburn Bon Marche (W. Roper and Co.)

Mitch. Cat.: " [1896]."

1103. n.d. London

The poetical Works of Robert Burns. London: Richard Edward King, 88, Curtain, Road E.C.

The B.C. copy has two different imprints: (*a*) " 106, 108, 110 Tabenade Street, E.C."; and (*b*) " R. E. King & Co. Ltd 106 to 110 Tabenade Street." One copy at B.C. has stamped on t.-p. " Published for P. Vincent . . . Clapham."

1104. n.d. London

The poetical Works of Robert Burns. . . . London: Charles Knight & Co., Ludgate St. [Knight's Series.]

1105. n.d. London

«« The poetical works of Robert Burns. . . . London: published by Edward Lacey, St. Paul's Churchyard.»»

M.C., § 524.

1106. n.d. London

The poetical Works of Robert Burns. . . . London Maclaren & Co. N.L.S. Acquisition date, 23 Oct. 1907.

1107. n.d. London

The poetical Works of Robert Burns. . . . London: Milner and Company.

Re-issue of § 428 (1840 Halifax = Milner).

1108. n.d. London

The poetical Works of Robert Burns. Edited . . . by William Michael Rossetti. Illustrated by John Moyr Smith. London: E. Moxon, Son, & Co., Dover Street, and 1 Amen Corner, Paternoster Row.

Angus, p. 64; Sneddon, p. 68, " [1872]." Gibson, p. 91, " [1871]." Another issue has, "(. . . Illustrated by the Society of Decorative Art) . . ." Angus, p. 64, gives still another issue, " [c 1873]."

Re-issue of § 746 (1871 London = Moxon).

1109. n.d. London

The poetical Works of Robert Burns. . . . London: Nimmo.

Re-issue of § 773 (1875 London = Nimmo).

1110. n.d. London

The poetical Works of Robert Burns. In two Volumes . . .
Printed for S. A. Oddy. Pickett Street. London. [*eng. t.-p.*]

Re-issue of § 280 (1824 London = Allman). Sneddon has
" [1830]."

1111. n.d. London

The poetical Works of Robert Burns. . . . London William S.
Orr and Co. [2 vols. Diamond Classics.]

Mitch. Cat., p. 31: " [? 1853]."

1112. n.d. London

The poetical Works of Robert Burns. A new Edition. . . . London: George Philip & Son, 32 Fleet Street; and 51 Castle
Street, Liverpool.

Gibson, p. 74: " 1860." Sneddon, p. 66: [" 1860]."

1113. n.d. London

The poetical Works of Robert Burns. . . . London: G. Philip
and Son. [Jones' Diamond Classics.]

1114. n.d. London

The poetical Works of Robert Burns. . . . Thomas Richardson
and Son. . . . London. . . . Dublin; and Derby.

Re-issue of § 448 (1844 Derby = Richardson). Gibson, p. 85,
" 1867 . . . A reprint of previous [?] edition." Sneddon, p. 64,
" [1843] "; and, p. 69, " [n.d.]." Does this mean two editions
or two issues ?

1115. n.d. London

The poetical Works of Robert Burns. . . . London. Thomas
Richardson & Son.

Re-issue of § 395 (1837 Belfast = Simms).

1116. n.d. London

The poetical Works of Robert Burns.   Edited by Charles Kent.
London: George Routledge and Sons, Limited.

1117. n.d. London

The poetical Works of Robert Burns; edited by the Rev. Robert
Aris Willmot, illustrated by Sir John Gilbert.   London: G.
Routledge and Sons.   [Routledge's Red Line Poets.]

Variants

London: George Routledge and Sons, Broadway, Ludgate Hill.
   Glasgow, Manchester and New York.
London. . . . New York: 416 Broome Street.
The Blackfriars Poets.
. . . People's Edition.
Routledge's Poets for the People.
Sir John Lubbock's Hundred Books.
. . . New York: 9 Lafayette Place.

Re-issue of § 795 (1878 London = Routledge).   Gibson, p. 96,
" 1878."   N.L.S. Cat., " [1856]."

1118. n.d. London

The poetical Works of Robert Burns . . . . [ed.] Joseph Skipsey.
London : Walter Scott.

Re-issue of § 832 (1883 London=Scott).   Also "The Canterbury
Poets."

1119. n.d. London

The poetical Works of Robert Burns. . . .   Edited by John and
Angus Macpherson.   London: Walter Scott, 24, Warwick
Lane.   New York : 3 East 14th Street.

Re-issue of § 627 (1859 Glasgow = Cameron).

1120. n.d. London

The poetical Works of Robert Burns . . . . London : . . . Scott and Webster (Successors to Mr Dove).

Sneddon, p. 64, notes two issues, " [1837?] " ; Mitch. Cat. " [1833]." The later issue has New Edition on t.p.

1121. n.d. London

The poetical Works of Robert Burns. . . . London: Wm. Smith, 113 Fleet Street.

1122. n.d. London

The poetical Works of Robert Burns . . . edited . . . by Charles Kent . . . London: The Standard Library Company.

1123. n.d. London

The poetical Works of Robert Burns. With photographic illustrations, by G. W. Wilson. London: Suttaby and Co.

1124. n.d. London

The poetical Works of Robert Burns. Edited by W. M. Rossetti. London: John Walker & Company.

1125. n.d. London

The poetical Works of Robert Burns. Edited . . . by William Michael Rossetti. . . . London: Ward, Lock, & Co., Warwick House, Dorset Buildings, Salisbury Square, E.C. [Moxon's Popular Poets.]

Variants

Ward, Lock & Bowden, Limited. London: . . . New York, Melbourne, and Sydney.
Moxon's Standard Poets.
The Warwick Classics.
The People's Standard Library.

. . . A new edition. . . . London: Ward and Lock, 158 Fleet
Street.

. . . New York: East Twelfth Street. Melbourne: St. James's
Street, Sydney: York Street.

Angus, p. 74, " 1879." Re-issue of § 746 (1871 London =
Moxon).

1126. n.d. London

The poetical Works of Robert Burns. London: Frederick
Warne and Company.

Variants

New York: Scribner, Welford and Co.
London: Frederick Warne and Co., Bedford Street, Strand.
Albion Edition.
Chandos Classics.
The Lansdowne Poets.
The Popular Poets.

These seem to have been issued anywhere from " [1858]."
(Sneddon, p. 65) to " [1880] " (Angus, p. 75). Re-issue of
§ 855 (1888 London = Warne).

1127. n.d. London

«« The poetical Works of Robert Burns. London: Thomas
Yardley. [The " Albion " Edition.] »»

M.C., § 682.

1128. n.d. London

«« The poetical Works of Robert Burns. London: Yardley and
Hanscomb, 511 and 513 Liverpool Road.»»

M.C., § 683.

1129. n.d. London

The Poems and Songs of Robert Burns London: published by
J. M. Dent. [Everyman's Library. Intro. by James Douglas.]

1130. n.d. London

The Songs of Robert Burns. London: Walter Scott.

1131. n.d. London

Songs by Robert Burns   Siegle, Hill & Co. 2 Langham Place London, W.

1132. n.d. London

The Songs and Ballads of Robert Burns . . . London: T. N. Foulis.

1133. n.d. London

The Works and Correspondence of Robert Burns. William Mackenzie: London: 22 Paternoster Row. Glasgow, 43 & 45 Howard Street. Edinburgh, 59 South Bridge.

Re-issue of § 686 (1866 Glasgow = Mackenzie).

1134. n.d. London

The Works of Robert Burns. . . . Edited by Charles Annandale. Blackie & Son: London.

B.M. Accession: " 1888."

1135. n.d. London

The Works of Robert Burns. Edited by the Ettrick Shepherd, and William Motherwell, Esq. In five Volumes. A. Fullarton & Co., London and Edinburgh. Fullarton, Macnab & Co., New York.

Re-issue of § 365 (1834 Glasgow = Fullarton). There is a variant without N.Y.

1136. n.d. London

The Works of Robert Burns. London: Gall & Inglis, 30 Paternoster Row. Edinburgh: 6 George Street.

1137. n.d. London

The Works of Robert Burns. . . . [*ed. Cunningham*] . . . Virtue &
Co.: London.

B.M. Cat.: " [1879.] "

1138. n.d. Manchester

The entire Works of Robert Burns [*four vols in one*]. . . . Manchester: . . . S. Johnson and Son. . . .

1139. n.d. Mauchline

The Scottish Keepsake, or, the Songs of the Ayrshire Bard.
Mauchline, Ayrshire: published by William and Andrew Smith.
Angus, p. 39: " 1844." *M.C.*, § 328, 329, 330, notes three
states.

1140. n.d. Montrose

The Songs of Robert Burns, the Ayrshire Bard.   Montrose.
Published by James Watt.

1141. n.d. Newcastle-on-Tyne

The poetical Works of Robert Burns. . . . Newcastle-upon-Tyne:
printed by G. Marshall.

1142. n.d. Newcastle-on-Tyne

The poetical Works of Robert Burns.   Newcastle upon Tyne:
printed and published by W. Stewart, No. 40, Riggmarket.

1143. n.d. New York

The complete Works of Robert Burns. . . .   a biographical
Memoir, by Alexander Smith.   New York: Thomas Y. Crowell
and Co.

Variant

Red-line Edition.

Angus, p. 93: " [1891]."

1144. n.d. New York

The complete poetical and prose Works of Robert Burns. . . .
New York: Leavitt & Allen Bros.

1145. n.d. New York

The complete poetical Works of Robert Burns. New York:
Virtue & Yorston.

1146. n.d. New York

The Correspondence between Burns and Clarinda. . . . edited
by . . . W. C. M'Lehose. New York: Robert P. Bixley & Co.

[1843.] Cp. Ewing, James C., *Robert Burns's Letters to Clarinda*.
Edinburgh: 1921, p. 25.

1147. n.d. New York

Illustrated family Burns. . . . New York. P. F. Collier.

Mur. Cat., p. 42: " *c.* 1866." Another issue of § 799 (1879
London = Mackenzie).

1148. n.d. New York

The poetical Works of Robert Burns. New York: The American
News Company, 39 and 41 Chambers Street.

1149. n.d. New York

The poetical Works of Robert Burns. . . . Edited by Allan
Cunningham . . . New York: Arundel Printing and Publishing
Company.

1150. n.d. New York

The poetical Works of Robert Burns. New-York: A. L. Burt.

1151. n.d. New York

The poetical Works of Robert Burns. New York: P. F. Collier.

1152. n.d. New York

The poetical Works of Robert Burns. . . . [ed. Alexander Smith]
. . . New York: Thomas Y. Crowell & Co.

Davison Cook (*Weekly Scotsman*, 22 Dec. 1934, p. 7) notes " T. Y.
Crowell," and seems to think that it might have something to
do with § 551.

1153. n.d. New York

«« The poetical works of Robert Burns. New York: Excelsior
Printing House.»»

Angus, p. 93.

1154. n.d. New York

The poetical Works of Robert Burns. . . . New York: Hurst
and Company.

1155. n.d. New York

The poetical Works of Robert Burns: . . . by James Currie. . . .
In two Volumes. . . . New York: published by Edward Kearny.

Cp. § 456 (1843 New York = Kearny).

1156. n.d. New York

The poetical Works of Robert Burns [*In 2 vols*]   New York
Thomas R. Knox & Co. Successors to James Miller 813 Broadway.

1157. n.d. New York

The poetical Works of Robert Burns. New York: John W.
Lovell Co., Publishers.

1158. n.d. New York

The poetical Works of Robert Burns. . . In two Volumes. . .
Merrill and Baker New York

1159. n.d. New York

«« The poetical Works of Robert Burns. In two volumes. (Aldine Edition) New-York: James Miller.»»

Angus, p. 95.

1160. n.d. New York

The poetical Works of Robert Burns. New York: W. L. Pooley.

1161. n.d. New York

The poetical Works of Robert Burns. Pearl edition. New York: Frederick A. Stokes and Brother.

1162. n.d. New York

«« The poetical Works of Robert Burns. New-York: Syndicate Trading Company.»»

Angus, p. 96.

1163. n.d. New York

The poetical Works of Robert Burns. . . . New York: White and Allen.

1164. n.d. New York

The poetical Works of Robert Burns. (Apollo Poets) New York, Thomas Whitaker.
Variant: Whittaker . . . 2 & 3 Bible House

Angus, p. 97: " J. Whittaker."

1165. n.d. New York

«« Burns' Works. Appleton.»»

Bib. B., p. 42.

1166. n.d. New York

The Works of Robert Burns . . . New York: Leavitt and Allan. Preface dated 1832.

1167. n.d. New York

The Works of Robert Burns. . . . New York: Sheldon & Co.

1168. n.d. New York

The Works of Robert Burns. New York: C. Wells & Co.

1169. n.d. Nuremberg

The poetical Works of Robert Burns. . . . Nurnberg and New-York: printed and published by Frederick Campe and Co.

Another issue of § 457. Sneddon, p. 64: " [1850]." Davidson Cook (*Weekly Scotsman*, 24 Nov. 1934, p. 7) says ". . . before 1838."

1170. n.d. Philadelphia

«« Burns' Poems. H. F. Anners, Philadelphia.»»

Bib. B., p. 42.

1171. n.d. Philadelphia

«« Burns' Works. Crissy & Markley, Philadelphia.»»

Bib. B., p. 42.

1172. n.d. Philadelphia

The complete Works of Robert Burns. . . . Philadelphia: J. B. Lippincott and Company.

Re-issue of § 710 (1867 Philadelphia = Lippincott).

1173. n.d. Philadelphia

The poetical Works of Robert Burns. . . . Three Volumes. . . . David McKay. . . . Philadelphia.

1174. n.d. Philadelphia

The poetical Works of Robert Burns. Philadelphia: Porter and Coates, 822 Chesnut Street.

Angus, p. 100: " [1871]." Sneddon, p. 69: " [1882]."

1175. n.d. Toronto

The Poems of Robert Burns. The Ryerson Press. Toronto.

1176. n.d. Wakefield

The poetical Works of Robert Burns. . . . Wakefield: William Nicholson and Sons, London: S. D. Ewins jr. and Co., Paternoster Row.

Gebbie, vi.341: " 1873." Gibson, p. 92: " 1873 A reprint of previous edn." Sneddon, p. 65: " [1852]."

Y

TRANSLATIONS

Arranged alphabetically by Languages

AFRIKAANS

1177. Vijfitig uitgesogte Afrikaanse Gedigte, versameld de ur
F. W. Reitz, . . . [1888.]

BOHEMIAN

1178. Robert Burns: výbor z písní a ballad. Prelozil Jos. V.
Slàdek. Nakladatestvi, J. Otto . . . Praze [1892.]

DANISH

1179. Digte og Sange. Ved Caralis. Kjoebenhavn: Chr. Steen
and Sons. 1867.

M.C., § 832.

1180. Hundrede Digte. Ved Caralis. Kjoebenhavn: Chr.
Steen and Sons. 1867.

M.C., § 833.

1181. Nogle Digte af Robert Burns; gendigtet på folkemål med
et rids af hans liv af Martin N. Hansen. Odense. Nyt
Bogforlag. 1951.

ENGLISH

1182. Burns in English. Select Poems of Robert Burns. Translated from the Scottish Dialect by Alexander Corbett.
Boston: Alexander Corbett. 1892.

Variant

. . . Published by subscription. Glasgow: William
Corbett. . . . 1892.

DUTCH

1183. Zaterdagvond op het Land. Vrij Bewerkt naar Robert Burns, door Pol de Mont. S. Warendorg, jr. Amsterdam. [*n.d.*]

FAROESE

1184. Robert Burns[.] Yrkingar[.] Týtt hevur Chr. Matra. Keypmannahavn[:] Bókadeild Føroyingafelags 1945 [.] [Contains 25 songs]

FLEMISH

1185. De schoonste Liedern van Robert Burns. Uit het Schotsch vertaald door Frans de Cort. Brussel: Drukkery van L. Truyts. 1862.

FRENCH

1186. Morceaux choisis de Burns, poète écossais. Traduit par MM. James Aytoun et J. B. Mesnard. Paris: Ferra Jeune. . . . 1826.

B. Chr., 1 (1892), 107, notes an edition in 1825.

1187. Poésies complètes de Robert Burns, traduit de l'écossais par M. Léon de Wailly, avec une introduction du même. Paris: Adolphe Delays, librairie, Rue Voltaire, 4 et 6. 1843.

Variant

. . . . Paris: Charpentier, libraire-éditeur, 29, Rue de Seine.

Another issue in 1853.

1188. Burns traduit de l'écossais, avec préface; par Richard de la Madelaine. [Imprimé à Rouen par E. Cagniardy] 1874.

GAELIC

1189. Dàin, is Luinneagan, Robert Burns, eadartheangaichte do'n Ghaidlig Albannach: Songs and Poems translated into Scottish Gaelic by Charles MacPhater. . . . Glasgow, 1911.

Variant

.... poems of Robert Burns translated.... [*n.d.*]

1190. Dain eadar-theangaichte. Le T. D. Mac Dhomhnuill.
Air an Clo-bhualadh le Aonghnas Macaoidh, Striudhla.
[Eaneas Mackay. Stirling]. 1903.
9 songs done into Gaelic.

1191. Tomas Seannsair [*Tam O' Shanter*], Maile ri naoidh dain
eile le Roibeart Burns . . . [*tr.*] Rob MacDhughaill, . . .
Glascho, 1840.

GERMAN

1192. Lieder und Balladen von Robert Burns. Aus dem
Englischen schottischer Mundart, von A. v. Winterfeld . . .
Berlin. Verlag von A. Hofman und Comp. 1860.

Variant

[With] Classiker des In- und Auslandes [on t.-p.]

1193. Lieder und Balladen von Robert Burns. Deutsch von
Adolf Laun. Berlin. Verlag von Robert Oppenheim.
1869

Re-issues: (1) " Berlin, 1877 " [" Zweite Auflage "];
(2) " Berlin," n.d.; (3) ". . . Dritte Auflage. Oldenburg,"
n.d.

1194. Lieder und Balladen des Schotten Robert Burns. Uebertragen von Heinrich Julius Heintze. . . . Braunschweig.
Verlag von George Westermann. 1840.

1195. Gedichte von Robert Burns. Uebersetzt von Edmund
Ruete. Bremen. . . . M. Heinsius Nachfolger. 1890.

1196. Lieder un Balladen von Robert Burns. . . . Herausgegeben
von Wilhelmine Prinzhorn. Halle a.d. S. . . . Otto
Hendel. 1896.

1197. Robert Burns Niederdeutsch Eingerichtet von Friedrich
Schult Verlag Heinrich Ellerman Hamburg [1937.]
Twelve songs in Low German.

1198. Robert Burns' Lieder und Balladen. Deutsch von Carl Bartsch. . . . Hildburghausen. Verlagdes Bibliographischen Instituts. 1865.

Re-issues: (1) " Leipsig (Meyers Klassiker-Ausgaben)," n.d. [? 1886]; (2) Leipsig und Wien. (Meyers Volksbuecher)," [1895]; (3) " Leipsig. Bibliographischen Institut." [1896].

1199. Robert Burns Gedichte. Deutsch von W. Gerhard. . . . Leipsig: Verlag, Joh. Ambr. Barth. 1840[.]

1200. Robert Burns' Gedichte. Uebertragen von H. Julius Heintze. . . . Leipsig. Verlag von Carl Fr. Fleischer. 1859.

1201. Lieder von Robert Burns. Uebertragen von Georg Perta, mit einer biographischen Skizze von Albert Traeger. . . . Leipzig und Heidelberg: T. F. Winter'sche. . . . 1859.

1202. Robert Burns Lieder und Balladen. . . . Von L. G. Silbergleit, Leipzig. . . . Phillipp Reclam, jun. 1875.

Re-issues: (1) [1878]; (2) [1887]; (3) [1889]. Many more cheap editions from this one.

1203. Burns Album. Hundert Lieder und Balladen von Robert Burns, herausgegeben von C. und A. Kissner. Leipzig: 1887.

1204. Mikrokosmos. Plattdeutsche Lieder nach Burns. . . . von Johannes Ehlers. Leipzig. 1887. C. A. Koch.

Includes 25 of R.B.'s songs done into Low German.

1205. Robert Burns' Gedichte in Auswahl. Deutsch von Gustav Legerlotz. Leipzig . . . . Otto Spamer. 1889.

Re-issue: ". . . Zweite Auflage. Leipzig. 1893."

1206. Gedichte von Robert Burns. Uebersetzt von Phillipp Kaufmann. Stuttgart und Tuebingen. . . . J. G. Cotta'-schen Buchhandlung. 1839.

" This translation was by Goethe's young friend, and as Carlyle anticipated, it was not a successful effort." W. Macintosh, *Burns in Germany*, Aberdeen 1928, p. 28

1207. Ferdinand Freiligrath. Gedichte von Robert Burns . . . J. G. Cotta'schen Buchhandlung. Stuttgart, 1890.

1208. Robert Burns' Werke. . . . Lieder und Balladen. . . . von Otto Baisch. Stuttgart: . . . W. Speeman. [? 1896] Re-issue: n.d.

1209. Lieder von Robert Burns. In das Schweitzerdeutsche, uebertragen von August Corrodi. Winterthur: Bleuler Hausheer & Co. 1870. Translations into Swiss dialect.

GREEK

1210. " Scots wha hae." In Greek and Latin Verse, by Robert Yelverton Tyrrell . . . and William Wallace . . . Dublin University Press. 1896.

1211. " To Mary in Heaven," in *The Glasgow University Album for 1858-59*, Glasgow: 1859.

1212. " A page of Greek." *Auld Lang Syne* translated into Greek by the Rev. Ronald Knox. Single sheet. n.d.

HEBREW

1213. Hebrew Anthology of English Verse; ed. Reuben Avinoam. Tel-Aviv. Massadah Publishing Co. 1956. Contains 9 poems by R.B.

HUNGARIAN

1214. Burns Róbert Költéményei. Forditotta Lévay József. . . . Budapest. Franklin-Társulat. . . . 1892.

1215. Burns Robert Válogatott versei Szérkesztette Kéry László és Kormos István. Budapest. Szépidoralmi Könyvkiadó. 1952.

ICELANDIC

1216. S. Thorsteinsson. Ljödatydingar. Reykjavik. Axel Thorsteinson. 1924. Includes 6 poems by R.B.

ITALIAN

1217. Poemetti e canzoni di Robert Burns; introduzione di Adele Biagi. Firenze. G. C. Sansoni. 1953.

Text in Scots and Italian.

1218. Poesie di Roberto Burns. Prima versione Italiana di Ulisse Ortensi. . . . Parte prima. Modena: E. Sarasino. . . . 1893. . . . Robert M'Clure. . . . Glasgow.

Preface by John Muir.

JAPANESE

1219. Robert Burns [poetical Works in English and Japanese]; by Tameji Nakamura. Tokyo. Kenkyusha. 1934.

1220. Select Poems of Robert Burns; with introduction and notes by Yoshisaburo Okakura. Tokyo. Kenkyusha. [1935]

1221. Banzu shishu, Nakamura Tamejiyaku. [Collected Poems of R.B.] Tokyo. Kishinami Bookshop. [n.d.]

1222. Uemura Shokyu Bunshu, Saite Isamuhen. [" The Cotter's Saturday Night " is here translated by Uemura] Tokyo. Kishinami Bookshop. [n.d.]

LATIN

1223. Cantica Scotica e vulgari sermone in Latinum. Interprete Alexandro Whamond. Hamiltoni: excudebat Gulielmus Naismith. MDCCCXCII.

1224. Florilegium latinum, Translations into Latin Verse. . . . 1899 John Lane, The Bodley Head, London and New York.

4 selections from R.B.

1225. The principal Songs of Robert Burns translated into . . . medieval Latin Verse. . . . By Alexander Leighton. Edinburgh: William P. Nimmo. . . . London: Houlston & Wright. MDCCCLXII.

1226. Sabrinae corolla, 4th edn., London: 1890.
Ten poems by R. B. translated by different hands.

NORWEGIAN

1227. Dikt av Robert Burns. . . . [tr.] Olav Nygard[.] Oslo.
. . . Norske Samlaget. 1923.

POLISH

1228. Robert Burns, z wierszy szkokich. [ed.] A. Krynski
[Warsaw] Panstwowy Instytut Wydawniczy. [1956]

PORTUGUESE

1229. Luiz Cardim. Horas de fuga. Porto. 1952.
Contains 3 songs of R.B.

ROMANIAN

1230. Robert Burns, poetul taranimei. . . . Petre Grimm [tr.]
Cluj: Tipographia " Viata." 1925.

RUSSIAN

1231. Robert Burns v perevodakh, [tr.] S. Marshaka. Moscow:
Khudogestvenni Litteraturi. 1936.

Other edns 1950, 1954.

1232. Marshaka. Steehee, Skaekee, Perevodi. Moscow: Khudogestvenni Litteraturi. 1952.

2 vols. Vol. 2 contains a selection of R.B.'s poems,
pp. 159-241.

1233. English Poets in Biographies and Examples; collected
by Nk. V. Gerbel. [In Russian] St. Petersburg. 1875.

M.C., § 871. Contains eleven poems by R.B. and a notice
of his life.

SPANISH

1234. Burns; Poesias; tradduccion y prologo de Ramon San-
genis. Barcelona: Editorial Fama. 1954.

SWEDISH

1235. Sånger och Ballader af Robert Burns . . . Helsingfors, J. C. Frenckell & Son, 1854.

1236. Några Dikter af Robert Burns. . . . Stockholm: Klemmings Antiquariat. 1872.

1237. Engelska Dikter . . . Erik Blomberg [tr.] Stockholm Albert Bonniers [1942.]

Contains 7 poems by R.B.

1238. Nytt och gammalt Grälstank. . . . Gustav Fröding. Stockholm. Albert Bonniers. 1954.

Contains 2 poems by R.B.

1239. Vin och kvinnor . . . Erik Kruuse [tr.] Stockholm Albert Bonniers [1933]

Contains 26 of R.B.'s poems, including " Tam o' Shanter."

WELSH

1240. Gems of English Verse with Translations into Welsh. Tlysau barddionaeth Seisnig wedi eu cyfieithu i'r Gymraeg. Carmarthen: William Spurrell, 1853.

Contains translations of 5 of R.B.'s poems (including one of " Tam o' Shanter," entitled " Sôn am Ysbridion . . .").

1240 A. Gwaith Talhaiarn, the works of Talhaiarn [John Jones], in Welsh and English. London, 1855.

Vol. I contains adaptations of 3 of R.B.'s poems, and same translation of " Tam o' Shanter " as § 1240.

CHINESE

1240B.

彭斯诗選

王佐良 譯

人民文学出版社

一九五九年·北京

ORIGINAL MATERIAL FIRST PUBLISHED
IN PERIODICALS

1241. " Address to a Haggis "

The " Address to a Haggice " first appeared in *The Caledonian Mercury*. 19 Dec. 1786. It may have been submitted to the paper by William Creech, Burns's Edinburgh publisher.

1242. " Prologue spoken by Mr Woods "

These verses first appeared simultaneously in *The Edinburgh Evening Courant* and in *The Caledonian Mercury* on 19 Apr. 1787.* They had been spoken by the actor, Mr Woods, on his benefit night, which was on 16 April. It is not possible to say whether Burns knew Woods personally or whether he simply sent him the poem because he admired his acting. The explanation given by Henley and Henderson is that the poet's interest in the actor was quickened by Woods's friendship with Robert Fergusson, whom Burns admired.[30] At all events, there is no correspondence between the two men extant. Such a piece as this " Prologue " would be printed in the newspapers because of its public character, and it can also be taken for granted that this sort of thing would not necessarily be published by Burns. We know from his letters that he objected to having his name appear in the papers,[31] and, although he delighted in sending copies of his poems to friends, he practically never submitted them to the public prints.

1243. " Verses . . . at Taymouth "

The " Verses written with a Pencil at Taymouth " were composed by Burns during his tour of the Highlands in the summer of

---

* According to M.C., p. 462, " The Lamb Collection," Item 24, first appeared in *The Edinburgh Advertiser* for 17 Apr. 1778.
[30] H.&H., II.381-2.
[31] Whenever Burns did submit poems to the newspapers he always assumed a *nom de plume*, and he wrote his friend Alexander Cunningham, " I would scorn to put my name to a Newspaper Poem." *Letters*, 1.331.

1787. The poem was written on 29 August[32] and was printed in the Edinburgh *Courant* on 6 September, with the following heading: "For the E.E.C. Sir, a few days ago, being on a visit to Taymouth, I found the following verses (by the celebrated Ayrshire bard) written on the walls of the Hermitage there; and send you a copy of them, which will doubtless be acceptable. O. B. Kenmore. Sept. 1, 1787." The poem is signed "R. B. August 29. 1787." Burns did not return to Edinburgh until 17 September.[33] The verses were written over the chimney-piece of an inn,[34] and there is no record of any other manuscript than the copy in the Glenriddell MS., which was written several years later.

1244. Letter to the Editor of the *Edinburgh Evening Courant*

This appeared in the *E.E.C.* on 22 Nov. 1788.

1245. " Elegy on the departed Year 1788 "

The " Elegy on the Departed Year 1788 " was sent by Burns to The *Courant*, in which publication it appeared on 10 Jan. 1789 over the name Thomas A. Linn[35]. Burns was, at that time, living at Ellisland. This poem was probably written around the first part of January 1789 and may well have been one of the pieces which Burns had composed for Mrs Dunlop, for on 1 January he writes her:

> I have sketched two or three verses to you, but as a private opportunity offers immediately I must defer transcribing them.[36]

He did not correspond with her again for several weeks and, in the meantime, he probably transcribed the poem and sent it off to The *Courant*.

---

[32] Burns has written the following in his *Journal* under the date 29 Aug: " Taymouth—described in Rhyme." Burns, Robert. *Journal of a Tour of the Highlands.* ed. J. C. Ewing. London and Glasgow: Gowans and Gray. (1927), 13.

[33] *Letters*, I.124.

[34] Under the transcription of the poem in the Glenriddell MS. Burns has written, " I wrote this with my pencil over the chimney piece in the parlour of the Inn at Kenmore, at the outlet of Loch Ray." *The Glenriddell Manuscripts*, printed not published, Philadelphia (John Gribbel) 1914, I.78.

[35] H. & H., II.348.

[36] *Letters*, I.284.

1246. " On the Duchess of Gordon's Reel Dancing "

This poem offers some very peculiar problems, the greatest of which is whether or not Burns wrote the piece. According to Henley and Henderson,[37] it was first (?) printed in Stuart's *Star* (a London newspaper) on 31 Mar. 1788. However, if Burns wrote the lines, they could not have been sent until sometime in April, for Burns did not know Stuart's address until after 2 April. On that date he wrote his friend Peter Hill:

> Write me by the first post, & send me the Address to Stuart, Publisher of the Star newspaper: this I beg particularly but do not speak of it.[38]

Burns did not tell Hill why he wanted the address, but the next we hear of anything concerning the Duchess of Gordon is in a letter which the poet sent to the editor of *The Gazetteer* (London). This letter is dated 10 April and reads:

> Sir,
>   By accident I met with your Paper of March the 28th, in which there are four disrespectful lines on the Duchess of Gordon, that you tell us are the composition of " Mr. Burns, the ploughing poet; " who, as you at the same time remind the world, " owes much of his good fortune to her Grace's patronage." I am that Burns, Sir; and I affirm that the wretched Stanza in question is not mine, nor do I know anything of the Author. . . .[39]

This letter was reprinted in *The Gazetteer* on 17 Apr. 1789, with the following comment:

> Mr. Burns will do right in directing his petulance to the proper delinquent, the Printer of *The Star*, from which Paper the Stanza was literally copied into the *Gazetteer*. We can assure him, however, for his comfort, that the Duchess of Gordon acquits him both of the ingratitude and the dullness. She has, with much difficulty, discovered that the *Jeu d'Esprit* was written by the Right honourable the Treasurer of the Navy. . . .[40]

---

[37] H. & H., II.350.
[38] *Letters*, 1.320.
[39] *Letters*, 1.321.
[40] *Letters*, 1.321-2.

This letter, written on 10 April, had doubtless been, for three or four days, in the hands of the editor of *The Gazetteer*. He probably would never have printed it at all had he not been provoked by the fact that the " Printer " of *The Star* inserted the following in his newspaper on 16 April:

> The Printer feels himself exceedingly proud of the receipt of the following Letter; and as it comes from the pen of a *very ingenious Poet*, whose productions are now the delight and admiration of every Reader of Taste, the Printer believes, that the best mode of answering the Author's intentions is by a publication of his sentiments on a subject which appears interesting to his literary reputation.

> Mr. Printer,
>   I was much surprised last night on being told that some silly verses on the Duchess of Gordon, which had appeared in a late Paper of yours, were said to be my composition.—As I am not a Reader of any *London Newspaper*, I have not yet been able to procure a sight of that paper. . . . A Conductor of another London paper was not so candid when he lately inserted a disrespectful stanza on the same highly respectable personage, which he, with unqualified assurance, asserted to be mine; though in fact, I never composed a line on the Duchess of Gordon in my life. . . .[41]

This letter is dated " April 13 "—that is, three days after the communication to the editor of *The Gazetteer* ; and, if we are to believe what Burns says in it, it is clear that he did not write the poem which Henley and Henderson say was published in *The Star* on 31 March. If he did send a poem to this newspaper, it was not until after he had received Stuart's address from Hill, which, as has been shown, was requested on 2 April. Burns did, however, send a poem to *The Star*, for on 4 May he wrote to Mr Alexander Cunningham:

> Thank you, my dearest Sir, for your concern for me in my contest with the London news-men.—Depend on it that I will never deign to reply to *their* Petulance.— The Publisher of the Star has been polite.—He may find his account in it; though I would scorn to put my

name to a Newspaper Poem.—One instance, indeed, excepted, I mean your two Stanzas.—Had the Lady kept her character, she should have kept my verses; but as she prostituted the one, I no longer made anything of the other; so sent them to Stuart as a bribe, in my earnestness to be cleared from the foul aspersions respecting the D[uchess] of G[ordon].—[42]

The " two Stanzas " which Burns mentions in the above letter refer to the little poem called " Anna," written about a lady who was, apparently, a sweetheart of Cunningham's and who had offended Burns in some way or other.[43] Burns sent this " bribe " to Stuart in the letter dated 13 April, for it was printed in *The Star* on 18 April.[44] I am convinced, therefore, that the lines " On the Duchess of Gordon's Reel Dancing " were a forgery, although I have included them here, with a reference to Henley and Henderson's note. These editors probably never saw the letters to the London newspapers because they were not published until after the Henley and Henderson edition of Burns appeared.

1247. Letter to the Right Honourable W[illiam] P[itt] Esq.

This appeared in *the Edinburgh Evening Courant* for 9 Feb. 1789.

1248. " Ode to the Departed Regency Bill "

This poem was published in Stuart's *Star* on 17 Apr. 1789. After the quarrel over the Duchess of Gordon incident, it seems strange that Burns would want to publish such a piece in the newspaper. However, Stuart had " treated him politely," as he wrote to Cunningham, and it was probably this politeness which touched him and flattered him into submitting the poem. He had been contemplating publishing the piece as early as 3 April; on that date he wrote to Mrs Dunlop:

I have this moment finished the following political Squib, and I cannot resist the temptation of sending

---

[42] *Letters*, 1.331.
[43] Burns was probably upset over the fact that the lady married someone other than Cunningham. On 24 January 1789 he had written him: " When I saw in my last Newspaper that a Surgeon in Edin^r was married to a certain amiable and accomplished young lady whose name begins with Ann, . . . I sincerely felt for a worthy much-esteemed friend of mine." Cp. *Letters*, 1.297.
[44] H. & H., 1.448. (Cp. also *Letters*, 1.331.)

you a copy of it—the only copy indeed that I will send
to anybody except perhaps anonymously to some
London Newspaper.—Politics is dangerous ground for
me to tread on, and yet I cannot for the soul of me
resist an impulse of anything like Wit.[45]

He had, apparently, not yet sent it to a " London Newspaper,"
when he wrote to Stuart on 13 April, and so it may be presumed
that he enclosed it in that letter. Stuart's note to the letter
indicates that he already had, or was expecting, other things of
Burns, for he says:

> The Printer has the happiness of flattering himself
> with an assurance of future correspondence of Mr.
> Burns, the sublime flights and inspiration of whose
> Muse, must raise the reputation of the first print.[46]

1249. Delia: An Ode

This first appeared in the Belfast News Letter for 2-5 June 1789.
H. & H. (IV.107) claim its first appearance in Stewart (§ 69).

1250. " Ode sacred to the Memory of Mrs Oswald "

On 7 May 1789, Stuart's *Star* again published one of Burns's
poems: the " Ode sacred to the Memory of Mrs Oswald."
The circumstances surrounding its publication are rather strange
in so far as Stuart was shortsighted enough to disclose Burns as
the author of this biting piece of satire in a very clumsy way.
Burns had sent him two letters at the same time; the first was to
be published with the poem and begins:

> I know not who is the author of the following poem,
> but I think it contains some equally well-told and just
> compliments to the memory of a Matron, who, a few
> months ago, much against her private inclinations, left
> this good world. . . .[47]

This letter is signed " Tim Nettle." The second letter was highly
personal, and revealed Burns to be the author of the " Ode,"[48]
and it is amazing that Stuart should have published it also.

---

[45] *Letters*, I.321.
[46] *Letters*, I.323. *The Star* preserved Burns's anonymity for the poem was
published above the name " Agricola." Cp. H. & H., II.389.
[47] *Letters*, I.332.
[48] *Letters*, I.333-4.

Whether or not Burns took offence at this revelation is not known, but it may be noted that this is the last poem which *The Star* published for him. The "Ode" was composed as early as January 1789, and Burns had intended to send it to the *Courant* in Edinburgh.[49] This he neglected to do, and, in May, he sent it to Stuart.

1251. "On Robert Fergusson"

The epitaph, "On Robert Fergusson," was first printed in *The Edinburgh Advertiser* on 11 Aug. 1789. This epitaph was planned and written more than two years before this date, as Burns petitioned the Bailies of the Canongate for permission to erect a stone over Fergusson's grave as early as 6 Feb. 1787.[50] Burns, apparently receiving a favourable answer from the Bailies, commissioned an architect, by name Robert Burn, to erect the stone. Burn proceeded in such a dilatory manner that the monument was not erected until midsummer 1789.[51] The *Advertiser* seems to have copied its version of the poem directly from the headstone in Canongate Churchyard.

1252. "On the late Captain Grose's Peregrinations"

The poem entitled "On the late Captain Grose's Perigrinations" appeared first in *The Edinburgh Evening Courant* on 27 Aug. 1789. Burns had met Captain Grose, the antiquarian, during the preceding July, and had given him a letter of introduction to his good friend Mrs Dunlop.[52] There is no record of the poet's having sent the verses to the newspaper, although they were published above the name "Thomas A. Linn,"[53] which might indicate that he was following his policy of not using his own name in the public prints. The poem was probably composed sometime during the latter part of July or the first part of August. It is dated 11 August. However, the first time that one hears of a manuscript of it is in a letter to Mrs Miller, written on 2 November:

> Inclosed I send you the verses on Cap[n] Grose which you were pleased to honour so much with your approbation.[54]

---

[49] *Letters*, 1.296.
[50] *Letters*, 1.72.
[51] The poet did not pay the architect for two years either. Cp. *Letters*, II. 109.
[52] *Letters*, 1.346.   [53] H. & H., 1.446. Cp. also § 1245.
[54] *Letters*, 1.365.

Z

1253. "At Carron Ironworks"

"At Carron Ironworks" was published under much the same conditions as "Verses written with a Pencil at Taymouth," that is to say that someone copied the poem and sent it to the newspaper. Burns reached Carron on Sunday, 26 Aug. 1787, during his tour of the Highlands;[55] and, according to The Edinburgh *Courant* for 5 Oct. 1789 (the newspaper in which "At Carron Ironworks" was first published), the poem was "Written on the Window of the Inn at Carron," and signed "R.B., Ayrshire."[56] I should judge by this that two years after they were written these verses were seen on the window, copied, and submitted to the *Courant*.

1254. "The Humble Petition of Bruar Water"

"The Humble Petition of Bruar Water" was composed by Burns during his tour of the Highlands in 1787.[57] It appeared in *The Edinburgh Magazine* for November 1789,[58] and was unsigned. Burns sent a copy of the poem to Mr Josiah Walker on 7 Sep. 1787. This gentleman may have contributed the poem to the magazine two years later.

1255. "The Lament of Mary Queen of Scots"

This poem was finished on 6 Jun. 1790, on which day Burns wrote to Mrs Dunlop:

> It is now near midnight, but I cannot resist the temptation my vanity, or, with respect to *you*, something perhaps more amiable than Vanity yet not quite so disinterested as Friendship, puts in my way to make me transcribe the following Ballad for you—it was finished only this day—You know &, with me, pity the amiable but unfortunate Mary Queen of Scots:
> . . .[59]

---

[55] "Crossed the grand Canal to Carron—breakfast . . ." written under the date 26 August. Robert Burns, *Journal of a Tour of the Highlands*, ed. J.C. Ewing, London and Glasgow (Gowans and Gray) 1927, p. 12.

[56] H. & H., II.434.

[57] *Letters*, I.123.

[58] X.357-8.

[59] *Letters*, II.21.

Burns, a few days later, sent a copy to Mrs Graham of Fintry.[60] The poem was published in *The Gazetteer and New Daily Advertiser*, a London newspaper, on 30 Sep. 1790. It was signed " R. Burns," which leads me to believe that the poet, who objected strongly to having his name signed to poems which appeared in newspapers, did not himself submit " The Lament." Therefore it was probably Mrs Dunlop or Mrs Graham who was responsible for its appearance.[61]

1256. " Prologue for Dumfries Theatre "

" The Prologue for Dumfries Theatre " was recited on New Year's Night, 1790. Burns wrote his brother Gilbert concerning the occasion:

> We have gotten a set of very decent Players here just now.—I have seen them an evening or two.—David Campbell in Ayr wrote me by the Manager of the Company, a Mr Sutherland, who is indeed a man of genius & apparent worth.—On New-yearday evening I gave him the following Prologue which he spouted to his Audience with great applause.[62]

The piece was first printed, as far as we know, in *The St James's Chronicle* for 14 Jan. 1790. Henley and Henderson are of the opinion that Sutherland probably sent it to this newspaper,[63] but it is quite likely that there was an earlier printing, probably in Dumfries or Edinburgh, and the English newspaper copied it from this. It was customary to print these prologues within a very few days after they were given and such was undoubtedly the case with this one. A search of Scottish newspapers for the first week in January 1790, might reveal the first printing of this " Prologue."

1257. " Elegy on Captain Matthew Henderson "

Captain Matthew Henderson, the subject of an " Elegy " by Burns, died on 21 Nov. 1788.[64] The poet probably began work on some elegiac verse as soon as news of his friend's death

---

[60] *Letters*, II.25.
[61] H. & H. (I.425-6) record the first printing of this poem in the Edinburgh edition of 1793.
[62] *Letters*, II.1.
[63] H. & H., II.384.
[64] H. & H., I.423.

reached him, for he writes to Robert Cleghorn, almost two years later when he had finally finished the poem:

> You knew Matthew Henderson. At the time of his death I composed an elegiac Stanza or two, as he was a man I much regarded; but something came in my way so that the design of an Elegy to his memory gave up. ... Meeting with the fragment the other day among some old waste papers, I tried to finish the Piece, & have this moment put the last hand to it.—This I am going to write you is the first fair Copy of it.[65]

This letter was written on 23 Jul. 1790, and the poem was published in the August issue of *The Edinburgh Magazine*.[66] Burns also sent copies of the " Elegy " to Dugald Stewart, on 30 July,[67] and to John McMurdo.[68] That either of these men sent the verses to the magazine is impossible to prove, but there is an even likelihood that Burns submitted them himself, since the poem is printed anonymously.

1258. " Tam O' Shanter "

The composition and publication of " Tam O' Shanter " is best described by Gilbert Burns, the poet's brother:

> Robert requested of Captain Grose, when he should come to Ayrshire, that he should make a drawing of Alloway-Kirk . . . and added, by way of encouragement that it was the scene of many a good story. . . . The Captain agreed to the request, provided the poet should furnish a witch-story, to be printed along with it. *Tam o' Shanter* was produced on this occasion, and was first published in *Grose's Antiquities of Scotland*.[69]

Gilbert, apparently, did not see the first publication of the poem, which was in *The Edinburgh Herald* for 18 Mar. 1791. Grose's *Antiquities* was published in the same year, but not

[65] *Letters*, II.31.
[66] XII.143-4.
[67] *Letters*, II.33.
[68] *Letters*, II.37. Henley and Henderson give the date of this letter as 2 Aug. (H. & H., I.424), but Ferguson assigns it no date.
[69] Burns, Robert, *Works*, ed. Dr James Currie. London: Cadell and Davies, (2nd ed.) (1801), 4 Vols. III.387.

until later than this date.[70] Burns had probably begun to compose the poem shortly after he met the Captain in July 1789, and by the first week in November, 1790, Mrs Dunlop was reading parts of it from a manuscript.[71] Burns had sent her the whole poem by the end of the month, for on 6 December he writes to her:

> After tasking you with the perusal of so long a Poem, it would be Egyptian bondage to burthen you with an additional long letter.[72]

It is impossible to determine who sent the poem to the *Herald*, but, as there were a dozen proof-sheets of it in existence by the end of February 1791,[73] one of these probably found its way into the hands of the printer of that paper.

1259. " The Kiss "

The Kiss

Humid seat of soft affection,
Magic ointment, virgin kiss !
Tenderest tye of young connexion,
Surest pledge of future bliss !

Speaking silence ! Dumb confession,
That each secret wish imparts:
Yielding softness ! Sweet concession,
Balm that heals our wounded hearts.

Friendship's height, and last enjoyment:
Passion's birth, and infant's play;
Love's first snowdrops, young enjoyment,
Earliest dawn of brightest day.

Sorrowing joy, adieu's last action,
O ! What language can express
The thrilling pain, the soft affliction,
Of a tender, parting kiss.

---

[70] H. & H., 1.438.
[71] *Robert Burns and Mrs Dunlop*, ed. William Wallace. New York: Dodd, Mead & Co. (1898), 2 Vols., II.110-11.
[72] *Letters*, II.50.
[73] *Letters*, II.57.

This drivel has masqueraded as a production of Robert Burns since the publication of § 409 (1838 Edinburgh = Chambers). Henley and Henderson have the following note:

> Published in a Liverpool paper called *The Kaleidoscope*, and there attributed to Burns. However, it appeared originally (and anonymously) in *The Oracle*, January 29, 1796, long the favored organ of the wretched Della Cruscan Shoal, and it has the right Anna Matilda smack throughout. After all, too, that a thing is bad enough to be written by Burns for Thomson is no proof that it is Burns's work.[74]

As can readily be seen, this poem, although not agreeing wholly with the version in Henley and Henderson, appeared some six years before its appearance in *The Oracle*, in *The Belfast News Letter*, 25 Nov. 1791. It was signed with the one word, " Anonymous." This, I think, is sufficient proof to throw it out of even the doubtful category of the corpus of Burns's work. In her *Metrical Miscellany* (London 1802, p. 102), Maria Riddell attributes it to R. B. Sheridan. I think that we can drop it permanently from the Burns canon.

1260. " Written in Friars Carse Hermitage "

According to Henley and Henderson, the poem entitled " Written in Friars Carse Hermitage " was first published in *The Weekly Miscellany* (Glasgow) on 31 Nov. 1791,[75] but there was probably an earlier printing of it in some other publication. Burns had, apparently, composed the piece sometime during the last few months of 1788, for in early December of that year he sent two versions of it to Mrs Dunlop.[76] He had also sent copies to several other of his friends, one of whom sent the poem to a publisher of some magazine, which is shown by the letter that Burns wrote to David Blair on 27 Aug. 1789:

> I am much oblidged to you for the magazine you sent me; of which, though the most elegant of that specimen of Publication that I have ever seen, I had never so much as heard the name.—Never mind the bagatelle of a Poem. . . . I know nothing how the Publishers could get it, but as I had given several copies to my friends, it had found its way, I suppose, thro' the well-meant though blameable officiousness of some of them.[77]

[74] H. & H., IV.107.
[76] *Letters*, 1.280.

[75] H. & H., 1.419.
[77] *Letters*, 1.357.

As this " magazine " has as yet remained undiscovered, we must accept the earliest printed version of the poem as that which appeared in *The Weekly Miscellany*, although there is no doubt that it was printed over two years before.

1261. " The Whistle "

This poem was probably composed during the latter part of 1789, as the event it describes took place on 16 October of that year.[78] We hear nothing of the manuscript of it until two years later, when Burns sent a copy of it to the Duke of Queensbery.[79] The letter to the Duke is dated " 24th Septr 1791," and since it was published over Burns's signature, it may well have been the Duke, or his secretary, who submitted it to *The London Star* for 2 November of that year.

1262. " The Devil once Heard that old Grose was a-Dying "

This was first published in *The Belfast News Letter*, 18 May 1792, with " O Willie Brew'd a Peck o' Maut," and " I Gaed a waefu' Gate yestreen," which had both already appeared in § 8 (1787-1803 Edinburgh = Johnson), III (1790). According to Henley and Henderson,[80] " The Devil once Heard . . ." was first published in *The Scots Magazine* for June 1797. I have, however, discovered two appearances before that date, one here, and one in § 26 (1793 Belfast).

The person who sent in the three poems which appeared in *The Belfast News Letter* signed himself " A.K.," and claimed to be a personal friend of the poet, and to have had the MSS. of the poems in his possession. This may have been the first appearance of the lines on Captain Grose.

1263. " A Highland Welcome "

" A Highland Welcome " was published in *The Edinburgh Courant* on 2 Jul. 1792 above the initials " R.B." There is no manuscript of the poem extant. According to Currie,[81] it was

---

[78] *Letters*, I.362-3.
[79] *Letters*, II.91-2.
[80] H. & H., II.437.
[81] Cp. § 50 *d*, IV.405.

" composed and repeated by Burns to the master of the house, on taking leave at a place in the Highlands where he had been hospitably entertained." It was " written at Dalnacardoch in the Highlands."[82]

1264. " The Rights of Woman "

Burns sent a copy of " The Rights of Woman " to two different people, one to the actress Miss Fontenelle,[83] and the other to Mrs Dunlop.[84] Henley and Henderson give no actual date for its publication in the Edinburgh *Gazetteer*, but as Miss Fontenelle's benefit-night was on 26 Nov. 1792 (the piece was apparently written for this occasion), it was probably published within a few days of that date[85] as was the case of " The Prologue spoken by Mr Woods," (§ 1242).

1265. " On . . . Rodney's Victory "

As there is no manuscript version of the verses " On the Commemoration of Rodney's Victory," which appeared in *The Edinburgh Advertiser*[86] on 19 Apr. 1793, or any other proof that they were written by Burns, their authenticity may be doubted. This appearance in the newspaper is the only testimony which has come down to us that Burns wrote this miserable piece of doggerel, and one is permitted, perhaps, to be sceptical about its authorship.

1266. " Sonnet on the Death of Robert Riddell "

The " Sonnet on the Death of Robert Riddell " was first published in *The Dumfries Journal* on 22 Apr. 1794. We know that the poet himself gave it to the newspaper, since, on the previous day, he wrote to John Clarke:

> This morning's loss I have severely felt.—Inclosed is a small heart-felt tribute to the memory of the *man I loved*.—I shall send it to some Newspaper with my name.[87]

1267. " Does Haughty Gaul . . ."

The song, " Does Haughty Gaul Invasion Threat," was first published in The Edinburgh *Courant* on 4 May 1795.

---

[82] *The Edinburgh Courant*, 2 Jul. 1792, p. [3].
[84] *Letters*, II.137.
[86] LIX.254.
[83] *Letters*, II.132-3.
[85] H. & H., II.386.
[87] *Letters*, II.239.

1268. " Scots wha hae . . ."

Burns, fearing that his appearances in periodicals would jeopardise his career in the Excise, sent this poem and the following to *The Morning Chronicle* [London], where it appeared on 8 May 1794, through the good offices of Peter Patrick Millar, Yr.[88]

1269. " Wilt Thou be my Dearie ? "

First published in Perry's *Morning Chronicle*, 10 May 1794.

1270. " Once fondly Loved "

" Once fondly Loved and still Remembered Dear " appeared in *The Belfast News Letter* on 7 Aug. 1797. Henley and Henderson[89] state that this poem did not appear until Currie's edition of 1800.

The short introduction to the poem in this newspaper reads as follows: " The following lines were written by Mr Burns on the blank leaf of a copy of the First Edition of his Poems, which he presented to an old sweetheart, then married." This note is signed " Alexis." It is certainly plausible that " Alexis," whoever he was, had in his possession the lines, for the poem was prefaced in the *Glenriddell Book*:

> Written on the blank leaf of a copy of the First Edition of My Poems which was presented to an old sweetheart, then married. 'Twas the girl I mentioned in my letter to Dr. Moore, where I speak of taking the sun's altitude. Poor Peggy ! Her husband is my old acquaintance, and a most worthy fellow. When I was taking leave of my Carrick relations, intending to go to the West Indies, when I took farewell of her, neither she nor I could speak a syllable. Her husband escorted me three miles on my road and we both parted with tears.[90]

1271. " Address to the Toothache "

" Address to the Toothache " was published in *The Belfast News Letter* on 11 Sep. 1797. Henley and Henderson[91] claim that

---

[88] Cp. *Letters*, ii.240.
[90] H. & H., ii.361.
[89] H. & H., ii.361-2.
[91] H. & H., ii.342.

this poem was first published in *The Scots Magazine* for October 1797. This particular appearance is prefaced by the following note:

> Mr. Editor. The following poem is the production of the late Robert Burns; it is dedicated to me by himself and I believe never published. . . . Yours, etc. Albert.

If we can believe the note, this is probably the source from which *The Scots Magazine* obtained the " Address."

1272. " Ye Banks and Braes "

This song appeared first in *The Scots Magazine* for May 1798.[92] Henley and Henderson date its first appearance § 28.*d* (1793-1818 London = Thomson), III (1793).[93]

1273. " The Thorn "

This piece, beginning " From the white-blossom'd sloe," appeared first in *The Edinburgh Advertiser* on 8 Aug. 1800.[94]

1274. " O Robin Shure in Hairst "

This song was sent by Burns to Robert Ainslie in a letter dated 6 Jan. 1789 from Ellisland. The letter and poem were published in *The Scots Magazine* for October 1801.[95]

1275. Letter to Robert Ainslie 1 Nov. 1789

The Scots Magazine, LXIII (Oct. 1801), 665.

1276. " Verses on Fergusson "

These verses, " Written under the Portrait of Fergusson," were first published in *The Scots Magazine* for November 1803.[96] The poem begins, " Curse on ungrateful man. . . ."

1277. " A Tragic Fragment "

This poem, beginning " All villain as I am . . .," was first published in *The Scots Magazine* for November 1803.[97]

---

[92] LX.349.
[93] H. & H., III.480.
[94] LXXIV.95.
[95] LXIII.664-5.
[96] LXV.798.
[97] LXV.798-9.

1278. "Adam A[rmour]'s Prayer"

This poem, beginning "Guid pity me, because I'm little," was first published in *The Scots Magazine* for June 1803.[98]

1279. "As I Gaed up . . ."

This song was first published in *The Scots Magazine* for June 1808.[99] According to Henley and Henderson[1] the last three stanzas of the poem are not by Burns, and the correct version was published in *The Edinburgh Magazine* ten years later.[2]

1280. Fragment—"Damon and Sylvia"

This poem, beginning "Yon wandering rill . . .," was first published in *The Scots Magazine* for January 1818.[3] Henley and Henderson do not include it in their edition, yet Scott Douglas says that he had seen the manuscript, which was in the possession of Lord Dalhousie.[4]

1281. "Address to Beelzebub"

This poem, beginning "Long life, my Lord, . . ." was first published in *The Scots Magazine* for February 1818.[5] The person who submitted the poem, "R.W.," claims to have obtained it from John Rankine.

1282. "On the Death of the late Lord President"

This poem was first printed in *The Scots Magazine*, for June 1818.[6] It was included in a letter, to Charles Hay, Esq., dated 24 (?) Dec. 1787,[7] which was also printed with the poem.

[98] LXX.48.
[99] LXX.48.
[1] H. & H., IV.98.
[2] January 1818.
[3] II (New Series).70.
[4] *The Works of Robert Burns*, ed. Wm. Scott Douglas. Edinburgh, 1877-9, 6 Vols., III.17.
[5] II (New Series).130-1.
[6] II (New Series).527-8.
[7] Cp. *Letters*, I.147.

1283. Letter to Deborah Duff Davies June 1793

In the *Western Luminary*, No. 19 (9 May 1824), p. 151.

1284.

" Wi' braw new banks "; " Of Lordly Acquaintance you Boast ";
" As Cauld a Wind as ever Blew "; " You're Welcome,
Willie Stewart "; and " There's Death in the Cup."

On Saturday 21 Nov. 1829, *the Edinburgh Literary Journal* [8]
carried an article which had been written as a preview of the
third edition of Lockhart's *Life of Burns*.[9] This article contained
four poems ("Wi' braw new banks," " Of lordly Acquaintance
you Boast,"[10] " As cauld a Wind as ever Blew,"[10] and " You're
Welcome, Willie Stewart ") which Lockhart was about to
publish for the first time.

Two weeks later the same magazine[11] also published for the
first time " There's Death in the Cup." Henley and Henderson[12]
say this did not appear until Cunningham's edition of 1834.

1285. Letter to Mr. Robert P——n, Alnwick
(14 Nov. 1787)

This first appeared in *The Literary Magnet of Belles Lettres, Science
and the Fine Arts*, II (1824), p. 359.

1286. Letter to Archibald Lawrie 14 Aug. 1787

In *The Glasgow Citizen*, 8 Apr. 1854.

1287. Letter to Peter Hill [Oct. 1794]

". . . *Knickerbocker Magazine*, New York, Sept. 1848, vol. 32,
p. 212." Cp. *Letters*, II.264.

1288. Letter to Anthony Dunlop [? Winter 1787-8]

First appeared in David Lester Richardson, *Literary Chitchat*,
Calcutta, 1848, p. 310.

---

[8] No. 54, pp. 349-52.
[9] Cp. § 328.
[10] Henley and Henderson, (II.439), mistakenly say that this poem appeared
in Lockhart's first edition of the *Life* (1828).
[11] No. 54, p. 385.
[12] H. & H., II.447.

1289. Letter to [Alexander Fraser Tytler] 6 Dec. [1792]

In *The Inverness Courier*, 11 Oct. 1866.

1290. Letter to William Burns, 14 Aug. 1789

In *The Newcastle Daily Journal*, 19 Mar. 1868.

1291. The First Commonplace Book

In *Macmillan's Magazine*, xxxix (Mar. 1879), 453, 560 and xl (Jul. 1879), 32, 124, 250.

1292. To William Stewart, " In honest Bacon's
Ingle-nook . . ."

In *N. & Q.*, Sixth Ser. iv (1881), 86.

1293. To ———————— 29 Sep. 1788

First appeared in the Catalogue of Sotheby, Wilkinson & Hodge, London 2-3 Jun. 1881, Lot 328.

1294. " On Doctor Johnson's Opinion "

This dubious piece first appeared in *The Scotsman*, 18 Nov. 1882.

1295. Letter to [Maria Riddell] [Feb. 1792]

First appeared in *N. & Q.*, 20 Jan 1883.

1296. Letter to Professor [Dugald] Stewart
30 Jul. 1790

First appeared in *N. & Q.*, 9 Jul. 1887.

1297. Letter to Alexander Blair 3 Apr. 1788

In *B. Chr.*, i (1892) 40.

1298. Letter to Messrs. Cr[om]bies & Co. 8 Oct. 1790
First appeared in *B. Chr.*, ii (1893), 147.

1299. Letter to [Robert Moore] 26 Oct. 1789
First appeared in *B. Chr.*, ii (1893), 148.

1300. Letter to Thomas Orr 17 Nov. 1782

In *Macmillan's Magazine*, LXVII (Jan. 1893), 202.

1301. Letter to Peter Hill 24 May 1787

First appeared in *B. Chr.*, II (1893), 147.

1302. Letter to Alex[ander] Coutts 29 Apr. 1791

First appeared in *B. Chr.*, III (1894), 55.

1303. Letter to Alexander Findlater n.d.

First appeared in *B. Chr.*, III (1894), 57.

1304. Letter to Will[iam] Stewart n.d.

First appeared in *B. Chr.*, III (1894), 143.

1305. " At Whigham's Inn, Sanquhar "

In *B. Chr.*, IV (1896), 130.

1306. Letter to Archibald Lawrie n.d.

In *The Athanaeum*, II (1896), 130.

1307. Letter to Miss Janet Miller 9 Sep. 1793

Appeared in *B. Chr.*, XIX (1910), 158, ". . . reprinted from a Sotheby catalogue."

1308. Letter to the Rev. Mr. J[oseph] Kirkpatrick
[? 22 Oct. 1791]

First appeared in *The Glasgow Herald*, 12 May 1917.

1309. Letter to [Dr. James Anderson] 1 Nov. 1790

About half the letter was published in *B. Chr.*, XXVII (1918), 134, reprinted from a Sotheby Catalogue of July 1917. Completed in *Letters*, II.47.

1310. Letter to [Thomas Boyd] [8 Feb. 1789]

First completed in *The Weekly Scotsman*, 31 Oct. 1925. An incomplete version appeared in *B. Chr.* xxx (1921).

1311. Letter to [Thomas] Boyd [1 Mar. 1789]

First appeared in *The Weekly Scotsman*, 31 Oct. 1925.

1312. Letter to John Richmond [27 Sep. 1786]

Appeared in *B. Chr.*, xxxiv (1925), 59 " reprinted from a newspaper some years ago."

1313. Letter to Tho[ma]s Boyd 16 Jun. 1791

First appeared in *B. Chr.*, 2nd Ser., i (1926), 105.

1314. Letter to James Hamilton 27 [? 17] Apr. 1789

First appeared in *The Glasgow Herald*, 6 Aug. 1926.

1315. Letter to James Johnson Aug. 1788

First appeared in *B. Chr.*, 2nd Ser., i (1926), 64.

1316. Letter to Mrs. Miller of Dalswinton 2 Nov. 1789

First appeared in *B. Chr.*, 2nd Ser., i (1926), 67.

1317. Letter to Mrs [Jean Armour] Burns 14 Oct. 1788

First appeared in *B. Chr.*, 2nd Ser., ii (1927), 5.

1318. Letter to John Clarke [21 Apr. 1794]

First appeared in *B. Chr.*, 2nd Ser., ii (1927), 7.

1319. Letter to [William Creech] 24 Jun. 1787

First appeared in *B. Chr.*, 2nd Ser., ii (1927), 11.

1320. Letter to [Alexander Cunningham] [Autumn 1794]

First appeared complete in *B. Chr.*, 2nd Ser., iii (1928), 6. The last two pages appeared in *The Illustrated London News* for 24 Dec. 1927, in facsimile.

1321. Letter to [Robert] Riddell [27 Sep. 1791]
First appeared in *B. Chr.*, 2nd Ser., II (1927), 6.

1322. Letter to [?] William Stewart 31 Mar. 1788
First appeared in *B. Chr.*, 2nd Ser., II (1927), 11.

1323. Letter to [John Wilson] 11 Sep. 1790
First appeared in the London *Times*, 16 Oct. 1928.

1324. Letter to William Nicol 29 Jul. 1787
First appeared in *B. Chr.*, 2nd Ser., IV (1929), 12.

1325. Letter to [William Niven] 29 Jul. 1780
Latter portion first appeared in *The Glasgow Herald*, 25 Jul. 1929; completed in *Letters*, 1.1.

1326. Letter to William Niven 12 June 1781
First appeared in *The Glasgow Herald*, 25 Jul. 1929.

1327. Letter to David Blair 27 Aug. 1789.
First appeared in *B. Chr.*, 2nd Ser., V (1930), 1.

1328. Letter to [William Burns] 16 Jul. 1790
First appeared in *B. Chr.*, 2nd Ser., V (1930), 5.

1329. Letter to [? Lady Elizabeth Heron] 3 Apr. 1794
First appeared in Sotheby's catalogue for 19 Mar. 1930.

1330. Letter to David Sillar [Summer 1791]
First appeared in Sotheby's catalogue for 19 Mar. 1930.

1331. Letter to —— Whyter [? Nov. 1788]
First appeared in Sotheby's catalogue for 15-17 Dec. 1930.

1332. Letter to John McMurdo [? 1792]
First appeared in *B. Chr.*, 2nd Ser., VI (1931), 8.

1333. Letter to David Newal 7 Nov. 1789
First appeared in *B. Chr.*, 2nd Ser., VI (1931), 8.

1334. Letter to David Sillar n.d.
First appeared in *B. Chr.*, 2nd Ser., VI (1931), 11.

1335. Letter to Mrs Dunlop n.d.
First appeared in Sotheby's Catalogue, 8-10 Jun. 1931, Lot 619.

1336. Letter to [? Alexander Dalziel Aug. 1791]
First appeared in *B. Chr.*, 2nd Ser., VII (1932), 3.

1337. Letter to ―――― 24 Apr. 1795
First appeared in *B. Chr.*, 2nd Ser., VII (1932), 4.

1338. Letter to Robert Ainslie 6 Jan. 1789
First appeared in *Modern Language Notes*, XLVIII (1933), 168.

1339. Letter to John Ballantine 27 Sep. 1786
First appeared in *B. Chr.*, 2nd Ser., X (1935), 6.

1340. Letter to Mr. Aiken [extract] n.d.
First appeared in *B. Chr.*, 2nd Ser., X (1935), 7.

1341. Letter to Captain Grose 1 Dec. 1790
First appeared in *B. Chr.*, 2nd Ser., X (1935) 9.

1342. Letter to Captain Hamilton 24 Mar. 1794
First appeared in *B. Chr.*, 2nd Ser., XI (1936), 4.

1343. Letter to William Scot 25 May 1787
First appeared in *PMLA*, LI (1936), 978.

1344. Letter to [Robert Ainslie] 29 Jul. 1787
First appeared in *PMLA*, LI (1936), 978.

2A

1345. Letter to Provost Staig n.d.

First appeared in *PMLA*, LI (1936), 980.

1346. Letter to Maria Riddell [restoration of text] n.d.

First appeared in *PMLA*, LI (1936), 982.

1347. Letter [fragment] to ——— n.d.

First appeared in *B. Chr.*, 2nd Ser., XIV (1939), 8.

1348. Letter to Mr. [?] Thomson [Dec. 1787-Jan. 1788]

First appeared in *B. Chr.*, 2nd Ser., XIV (1939), 9.

1348*a*. 1941 New York

Public Sale [*of the library of the late John Gribbel*] Parke-Bernet Galleries Inc . . . [*Jan.* 22] 1941.

Original Material: One sentence from a letter to [?] dated 16 Jul. 1780

1349. Letter to Dr John Mackenzie [*c.* 6 Dec. 1786]

First appeared in *B. Chr.*, 2nd Ser., XVII (1942), 4.

1350. Letter to Patrick Miller [? 1788]

First appeared in *B. Chr.*, 2nd Ser., XX (1945), 4.

1350*a*. 1945 New York

Autograph Letters Manuscripts and rare Books   the entire Collection of the late John Gribbel . . . Public Auction Sale May 7 and 8 . . . Parke-Bernet Galleries Inc . . . 1945

Original Material:

> First paragraph and part of a poem [*To Robt Graham of Fintry*, " When Nature her great Masterpiece designed "] in a letter to Mrs Dunlop, 5 Sep. 1788, pp. 12-13,   Lot 66.

1351. Letter to Patrick Miller [? 1788]

First appeared in *B. Chr.*, 3rd Ser., V (1956), 6: ". . . has already appeared in the *Kilmarnock Standard*."

1352. " On an Innkeeper in Tarbolton "

First appeared in *Fine Books and MSS* [Sale 2148] Parke-Bernet Galleries, New York, 1962, *p.* 14.

BURNS AND THE *SCOTS MUSICAL MUSEUM*[1]

Many of the problems presented by the *Museum* do not differ much from those presented by similar volumes issued in numbers over a period of years. If successful, the early numbers were quickly exhausted and had to be reprinted to supply subscribers who came in late (after cautiously waiting to see if it would be worth subscribing to); new distributors came along whose names had to be added to the title-page; others were deleted; and so on.

To these usual vexations, the *Museum* adds another. Burns was not an especially "selling" name when the *Museum* began in 1787. As the years passed, though, Burns's fame grew, and as earlier numbers of the *Museum* were reprinted (without any notice), it was deemed wise to add his name to those songs which in earlier issues had remained anonymous.

It is going to take the simultaneous examination of numerous copies of the *Museum*, both early and late printings, to arrive at anything like a competent description of its first edition. The following notes, therefore, do not pretend to be definitive, and are, in fact, an appeal for thorough bibliographical analysis.

Variant Title-pages and Prefaces

Volume I. The earliest form of the title-page [A] *does not* have a border around the vignette. The imprint reads: Edinburgh; Sold and Subscriptions taken in by and for the publisher, N. Stewart, R. Bremner, Corri and Sutherland, R. Ross, Edinb. and all the music sellers in London.

A later title-page (probably 1792) [B] has a border around the vignette, with a thistle design at the top and bottom. The imprint reads: Edinr. Printed & Sold by Johnson & Co., Music Sellers head of Lady Stair's Close, Lawn Market; where may be

[1] Extracted from David A. Randall, " Robert Burns and the Scots Musical Museum," in the New Colophon, VOL. I, PT. 2 (Apr. 1948), pp. 191-3.

had a variety of Music, & Musical Instruments, Instruments Lent out, Tun'd & Repaired.

The final title-page (1803 or later) [C] has no vignette, the words " In Six Volumes " first appear, and the imprint is: Printed & Sold by James Johnson Music Seller Edinburgh to be had at T. Preston No. 97 Strand London, McFadyen Glasgow, & at all the principal Music Sellers. (And the price is raised from six to seven shillings.)

The preface in all copies is dated May 22, 1787.

Volume II. In the earliest form of title-page, the vignette has no border. The imprint reads: Edinburgh: Printed and sold by James Johnson, Engraver, Bells Wynd. Sold also by N. Stewart, R. Bremner, Corri and Sutherland, R. Ross, C. Elliot, W. Creech, J. Sibbald, Edinr.; A. McGowan and W. Gould, Glasgow; Boyd, Dumfries; More, Dundee; Sherriffs, Aberdeen; Fisher and Atkinson, Newcastle; Massey, Manchester; C. Elliot, T. Kay & Co., No. 332 Strand; Longman and Broadup, No. 26, Cheapside, London.

The final title-page is as Volume I, [C] above. The intermediate title-page, with the bordered vignette (as Volume I, [B]) may exist, though we have not seen it.

The preface in all copies is dated March 1, 1788, but in the earliest issue ends with the words: " Materials for the third volume are in great forwardness; and as far as can be guessed that will conclude the Collection." The last twelve words are scratched out in the re-issues. Apparently the success of the *Museum* was unexpected, most of all by its publisher.

Volume III. In the earliest form of the title-page the vignette *has* a border with thistle like Vol. I [B]; the imprint is enlarged from that of Vol. II and ends with: J. Preston, No. 97, Strand, London. The only other form in which this title-page has been noted is the late 1803 reprint [C].

The preface in all copies is dated Feb. 2^d 1790. The earliest text ends with " Materials for the 4th and in all probability the last volume are in great forwardness." This line is scratched out in the reprint.

Volume IV. The title-page vignette has the ornamental border with thistle in the earliest state; the imprint reads: Edinr. Printed & Sold by Johnson & Co. Music Sellers head of Lady Stair's Close, Lawn Market, where may be had a variety of Music and Musical Instruments, Instruments Lent out. Tun'd & Repaired. The only other form in which this title-page has been noted is the late 1803 reprint [C].

The preface in each is dated Aug. 13, 1792.

Volume V.   Noted only in the same forms as Vol. IV, above.

The preface in each case is undated (though the volume was issued Dec. 1793).

Volume VI.   The title-page occurs in only one form, without vignette, as [C] in Vol. I.

The preface is dated June 4, 1803.   As will be noted later under a discussion of the Index, however, this volume comes in two issues.

Variant Indexes, and Attributions of Authorship in the Text

As has been noted above, the *Scots Musical Museum* was lax, in its earliest issues, about identifying the songs contributed by Burns.   In the re-issues his name was put on them in the index, and the text often added the boastful line: " Written for this Work by Robert Burns."   It may be taken as an axiom that the fewer ascriptions of songs to Burns, the earlier is the issue.   Of the six hundred songs in the *Museum*, one hundred and four were eventually ascribed to him.

The following record merely notes differences found between early copies, designated [A], and late copies (i.e., the 1803 re-issue), designated [C].   There may be, and probably are, many variants in between.   One difficulty too common with bibliographers is the necessity of working with rebound (and sometimes made-up) copies.   The *Museum* was originally issued in plain boards, unlettered, totally uncut.   Only one untouched set in this state has been available to us and although that was a very fine one, it was not the earliest state of all volumes.   But it was of inestimable value in helping to unravel problems presented by rebound sets whose binders had, apparently, grafted late title-pages to early indexes and middle texts in hopeless confusion.

Volume I.   The index of [A] lists only one song by Burns— " Green Grow the Rashes."   We may remark parenthetically that, though we would love to print Burns's original version of this song, written when he learned that Jean Armour " has just now brought me a fine boy and girl at one throw—God bless them, poor little dears," we simply can't, postal laws being what they are.   The following song, " Young Peggy Blooms Our Bonniest Lass," is anonymous in [A]; [C] credits it to Burns.

Volume II.   The index in [A] lists but one contribution by

Burns; in [C] sixteen are credited to him. In the [A] text a number of songs are signed " B." For example: " Musing on the Roaring Ocean "; " O Whistle an' I'll Come to You, My Lad "; " Tibbie, I Hae Seen the Day," etc., are either unsigned or simply initialed. In the reprint [C], these are signed: "Written for this Work by R. (or Robert) Burns."

Volume III. The index on [A] lists Burns as the author of six songs; in [C] of eleven. Oddly, in each case, one of Burns's most famous songs, " My Heart's in the Highlands." is anonymous and signed " Z."

Volume IV. The index in [A] lists six songs by Burns; [C] lists twenty-seven.

Volume V. The [A] index lists fifteen songs by Burns; [C] lists twenty. Here again it is curious to note that one of Burns's beloved songs, " Comin' through the Rye," is anonymous in [A] and signed only " B " in [C].

Volume VI. This has been noted in the late state only of the title-page. Burns is credited in both the index and the text with the authorship of twenty-six poems. Still this volume appears in two states. In the earlier, the songs, " Gently Blaw Ye Eastern Breezes," " Go Plaintive Sound," " O Gin I were Fairly Shot o' Her," and " You Ask Me Charming Fair," are anonymous in the index, In a later issue, otherwise undistinguishable, these are attributed to Anderson and W. Hamilton, Esq.

A CHECK-LIST OF THE VARIOUS ISSUES AND EDITIONS OF THOMSON'S *ORIGINAL SCOTTISH AIRS*[1]

Year	Vols.	Details
1793	I*a*	First edition. 25 settings by Pleyel. Preface dated May 1793.
? 1794	I*a*	Re-issue, but called " Second Edition." Preface January 1794.
1798	I*b*	First edition. 25 settings by Kozeluch. Preface August 1798.
1799	II*a*	First edition. 25 settings by Kozeluch. Preface undated.
1799	II*b*	First edition. 18 settings by Kozeluch and 7 settings by Pleyel. Preface undated.
1801	I & II	Re-issue of the above. Vignette titles. 32 settings by Pleyel and 68 by Kozeluch, 8 of Kozeluch's being revised versions. Printed title also, dated 1801. Prefaces dated September 1801; colophons 1800.
1802	III	First edition. 50 settings by Haydn. Vignette title with Haydn's, Pleyel's and Kozeluch's names. Printed title also, dated December 1801; colophon 1802.
1804	I-III	Second edition. Vol. I and II have Haydn, Pleyel and Kozeluch titles, and

[1] Reprinted by kind permission of Cecil Hopkinson and C. B. Oldman from the *Edinburgh Bibliographical Society Transactions*, VOL. II, PT. I (Session 1938-9). Edinburgh (R. & R. Clark). 1940.

Vol. III has only a Haydn title now. Prefaces in each volume dated September 1803; colophons 1803.

Vol. I . Haydn 13. Pleyel 18. Kozeluch 19.

Vol. II. Haydn 8. Pleyel 4. Kozeluch 38.

Vol. III. Haydn 50, as in first edition.

1805 IV   First edition. 51 settings by Haydn. Preface undated; colophon 1805.

? 1809 I-IV   Third edition. No alterations in music.

? 1811 I-IV   Fourth edition. No alterations in music.

1815 II & IV   New edition. No alterations in music.

1817 I-IV   Fifth edition.

Vol. I. Preface October 1817; colophon 1817.

Vol. II. Preface July 1815; colophon 1815. One new setting by Haydn, dated 1817.

Vol. III. Preface October 1817; colophon 1817.

Vol. IV. Preface July 1815; colophon 1815. One new setting by Haydn, dated 1817.

1818 V   First edition. 25 settings by Beethoven and 5 by Haydn, with the "Jolly Beggars" by Bishop. Preface dated June 1818; "J.B." Preface May 1818; colophon 1818.

1822-3 I-V   First octavo edition. Preface to Vol. I dated May 1822. General preface ("Dissertation") undated.

Vol. I. Haydn 17. Pleyel 18. Kozeluch 13. Beethoven 1. Anon. 1. New settings are Haydn 2, Kozeluch 1, and Anon. 1. Colophon dated 1822.

Vol. II. Haydn 12. Pleyel 2. Kozeluch 32. Beethoven 3. Smith 1. New settings are Haydn 1, Kozeluch 1,

Beethoven 2, and Smith 1. Colophon
dated 1822.

Vol. III. Haydn 37. Kozeluch 6.
Beethoven 3. Anon 5. New settings
are Kozeluch 1, Anon 5. Colophon
dated 1822.

Vol. IV. Haydn 25. Kozeluch 9.
Beethoven 6. Anon 2. Smith 4. Gow
1. Thomson 1. New settings are
Kozeluch 3, Thomson 1, Gow 1, Smith
4, Anon 2. No colophon date.

Vol. V. Haydn 18. Kozeluch 1.
Beethoven 21. Smith 1. Shield 1.
Bishop 1. Anon 3. Graham 3. New
settings are Kozeluch, Graham, Anon,
Smith, Haydn.

1825	I-VI	Second octavo edition but First edition of Vol. VI. General preface undated.

Vol. I-V exactly the same except for
title, as first octavo edition.

Vol. VI. Haydn 12. Pleyel 1. Koze-
luch 1. Beethoven 20. Anon 3.
Ferrari 4. George Thomson 2. D.
Thomson 1. Preface dated 2 May
1825. Colophon 1824. New settings
are Haydn 2, Beethoven 7, Anon 3,
Ferrari 4, George Thomson 2, D.
Thomson 1.

1826	I-IV	Sixth edition. All volumes have prefaces dated 1826. Only Vol. III has a colophon date, 1826.

Vol. I has 2 new Haydn settings, and
Vol. IV has 1.

	V*a*	Second edition. Preface dated 1826, no colophon date. No new Haydn or Beethoven.

	V*b*	Title dated 1826. No preface. No colophon date. 1 new Haydn setting.

? 1826	Appendix	Re-issue of 12 settings from the 1826 edition, 10 being by Weber.

1828	I-VI	}
1831	I-VI	} { Re-issues of the octavo edition.
1831	I-V	} Seventh edition. Dedication dated 1831. Preface dated March 1831; colophon 1831. Vol. II-V have no prefaces and are undated. 19 new settings, 10 being by Hummel.

Vol. IV contains 1 new Haydn setting.

1838　I-V　　　　Eighth edition.

1839　Appendix　　21 songs supplementary to the 1838 edition. New settings are Beethoven 3 and Haydn 3.

1841　VI　　　　First edition. Preface dated September 1841. Haydn 12. Kozeluch 1. Beethoven 13. Bishop 5. Hogarth 21. New settings are Beethoven 4 and Haydn 1.

1845　VI　　　　Lithographed re-issue, 2 songs by Bishop being added at the end.

INDEX OF PROPER NAMES

INDEX OF TITLES AND FIRST LINES

2 C

PRINTED IN GREAT BRITAIN BY
OLIVER AND BOYD LTD.,
EDINBURGH